STRATUM SERIES

Pre-Reformation Germany

*the text of this book is printed
on 100% recycled paper*

STRATUM SERIES

A series of fundamental reprints from
scholarly journals and specialised works
in European history

GENERAL EDITOR: J. R. HALE

Pre-Reformation Germany

EDITED BY

Gerald Strauss

Harper & Row, Publishers
New York, Evanston, San Francisco, London

This book was originally published in hardcover by The Macmillan
Press Ltd., *London and Basingstoke in 1972.*

First HARPER & ROW edition published 1972.

STANDARD BOOK NUMBER: 06–1394874

Contents

Acknowledgments

B. MOELLER, "Religious Life in Germany on the Eve of the Reformation," translated from "Frömmigkeit in Deutschland um 1500," *Archiv für Reformationsgeschichte*, 56 (1965), Heft 1, Reprinted by permission of Gütersloher Verlagshaus Gerd Mohn.

H. HEIMPEL, "Characteristics of the Late Middle Ages in Germany," translated from "Das Wesen des deutschen Spätmittelalters," *Archiv für Kulturgeschichte*, 35 (1953), Heft 1, 29–51. Also in *Der Mensch in seiner Gegenwart: Sieben Historische Essais* (Göttingen, 1954), 109–35. Reprinted by permission of Böhlau Verlag, Köln.

F. HARTUNG, "Imperial Reform, 1485–1495: Its Course and Its Character," translated from "Die Reichsreform von 1485–1495. Ihr Verlauf und ihr Wesen," *Historische Vierteljahrschrift*, 16 (1913), 24–53, 181–209.

K. S. BADER, "Approaches to Imperial Reform at the End of the Fifteenth Century." Translated from "Kaiserliche und ständische Reformgedanken in der Reichsreform des endenden 15. Jahrhundert," *Historisches Jahrbuch*, 73 (1954), 74–94. Reprinted by permission of the author.

P. JOACHIMSEN, "Humanism and the Development of the German Mind," translated from "Der Humanismus und die Entwicklung des deutschen Geistes," *Deutsche Vierteljahrsschrift für Literaturwissenschaft und Geistesgeschichte*, 8 (1930), 419–80. Reprinted by permission of Max Niemeyer Verlag, Tübingen.

H.-S. BRATHER, "Administrative Reforms in Electoral Saxony at the End of the Fifteenth Century." Translated from "Die Verwaltungsreformen am kursächsischen Hofe im ausgehenden

15. Jahrhundert," *Archivar und Historiker: Studien zur Archiv- und Geschichtswissenschaft zum 65. Geburtstag von Heinrich Otto Meisner* (Berlin, 1956), 254–87. Reprinted by permission of the VEB Deutscher Verlag Der Wissenschaften.

W. KUNKEL, "The Reception of Roman Law in Germany: An Interpretation." Translated from "Das Wesen der Rezeption des römischen Rechts," *Heidelberger Jahrbücher*, 1 (1957), 1–12. Reprinted by permission of Springer–Verlag.

G. DAHM, "On the Reception of Roman and Italian Law in Germany." Translated from "Zur Rezeption des Römisch-italienischen Rechts," *Historische Zeitschrift*, 167 (1943), 229–58. Reprinted by permission of R. Oldenbourg Verlag.

F. LÜTGE, "The Fourteenth and Fifteenth Centuries in Social and Economic History." Translated from "Das 14./15. Jahrhundert in der Sozial- und Wirtschaftsgesschichte," *Jahrbücher für Nationalökonomie und Statistik*, 162 (1950), 161–213. Reprinted by permission of Gustav Fischer Verlag.

H. RUPPRICH, "Willibald Pirckheimer: A Study of His Personality as a Scholar." Translated from "Willibald Pirckheimer: Beiträge zu einer Wesenserfassung," *Schweizer Beiträge zur Allgemeinen Geschichte*, 15 (1957), 64–110. Reprinted by permission of Verlag Herbert Lang & Cie AG, Bern.

Introduction

THE lack of a satisfactory history of Germany at the close of the Middle Ages has often been noted. The brief bibliography at the end of this book is not, of course, complete, but it lists the most important of the available titles, German as well as English, and there are not many. Considering the significance of events in the Holy Roman Empire during the fifteenth and early sixteenth centuries, this paucity is astonishing. Widespread social and economic stresses created a groundswell of discontent throughout the country; political and legal changes put nearly every center of national and regional administration under strain; a serious, intense religious revival was under way; self-conscious intellectuals, aware of their country's anomalous place in a world of emerging nation-states, undertook a searching investigation of German history and society. In some way the Reformation relates to each of these developments. It cuts into the continuity of German history, a true epoch. Only the French Revolution made as profound an impact upon a society as the Luteran Reformation on Germany.

There are many books on the Reformation and innumerable studies of single aspects of the late fifteenth and early sixteenth centuries in Germany. But few scholars have attempted a synthesis of national history. The reason, in all likelihood, is the absence from the German scene of a dominating center. The empire had no vantage ground from which such a survey could be written; the very focus of national history was lacking. Ferdinand and Isabella in Spain, the young Tudor dynasty in England, the Valois in France—these in their respective countries established a fulcrum on which all of national history came to rest. The Holy Roman

Empire had a dynasty, the Habsburgs, but none of the sovereigns of that distinguished family held the legal and administrative reins that controlled the country. Habsburg emperors built no capital and fashioned no court from which the entire land could have drawn an identifying culture. Absence of national unity and lack of centralization were not necessarily disadvantages, though contemporary patriots thought this state of affairs a disgrace, and German historians have not ceased to deplore it down to our own day. However that may be, lack of unity did tend to discourage synoptic history. The fifteenth and sixteenth centuries in Germany are a diffuse period. Its sources are widely scattered; there is no centre of action for the historian to concentrate upon, no high point. The history of Germany at the close of the Middle Ages is the history of its regions and cities: a polycentric country with a disjointed past.

Under the circumstances, students must depend on monographs and journal articles for information on many of the most interesting facets of the history of Germany before the Reformation. The present anthology brings together ten such articles in English translation. Some of them represent older, traditional scholarship (Hartung, Joachimsen); others are revisionist (Bader, Moeller). Several give close examination to specialized topics; a few advance general interpretations. I have tried to select articles that throw light on problems not adequately discussed in the general books. I have also tried to suggest something of the variety of subject and approach to be found in the journal literature.

Firstly, Bernd Moeller, in an article on the German religious temper, analyzes religious motives and their manifestations in many segments of German society on the eve of the Reformation. Hermann Heimpel seeks to define the specifically German element and the explicitly "late" quality of the late Middle Ages in Germany; a venerable medievalist, Heimpel here undertakes to construct a grand synthesis. Two papers by constitutional and legal historians address themselves to the imperial reform movement of the 1480's and 1490's. Fritz Hartung gives a comprehensive and detailed account of issues, procedures, and personalities in the endeavor to reform the constitution of the Holy Roman Empire. His interpretation was, for many years, accepted as standard. Karl Siegfried Bader, on the other hand, takes issue with older views of the reform movement and presents the policies of the imperial Estates as less reactionary than they have often been held to be. Germany's intellectual and cultural milieu is surveyed by Paul Joachimsen, whose influential essay on humanism, first published in 1930, seeks to define this phenomenon with respect to Italian Renaissance thought on the one hand, and to German mysticism, academic scholarship, and the *Devotio moderna* on the other.

Hans–Stephan Brather's paper on administrative reform in Saxony is a meticulously detailed investigation of bureaucratic innovations in that territory from 1450 to 1500. Brather describes the process which made electoral Saxony into a centralized state with a reliable corps of civil servants and orderly procedures. Two articles deal with the important subject of Roman law in Germany. Wolfgang Kunkel presents the introduction of Roman jurisprudence as a special case of a general trend in European society, the rationalization of thought and action; while Georg Dahm views the "reception" as an aspect of the bureaucratization of territorial states. A long and highly provocative esssay by Friedrich Lütge investigates the economic and social effects of recurring epidemics and the consequent population losses. Lütge argues that the year 1350 must be seen as the opening of a new phase in German history, not just in economic history, but in political, cultural, and religious affairs as well. Finally, Hans Rupprich's biographical study of the Nuremberg patrician Willibald Pirckheimer may be taken as evidence that Germany, like Italy, had her "Renaissance man."

It has been thought wise to retain the documentation furnished by each author, and in several cases this has been brought up to date, additions being inserted in square brackets. As for the translation: academic German may not be the most impenetrable of languages, but if there is one more difficult to turn into idiomatic English I do not know it. The translators' objective has been comprehensibility. I hope that in their English dress these essays and articles will tell the student something about the character of German scholarship, and will stimulate his interest in the history of Germany in a crucial, but still only partially understood, period.

I Religious Life in Germany on the Eve of the Reformation

BERND MOELLER

Born in 1931, Bernd Moeller has gained distinction among younger church historians as a shrewd and imaginative investigator of the interpenetration of religious and secular life at the close of the Middle Ages. In addition to articles for learned journals, of which the selection translated below is an example, and contributions to collaborative works, Moeller has published a number of monographs, the most widely read of which is *Reichsstadt und Reformation*, 1962. He teaches at the University of Heidelberg.

IT is remarkable, though by no means an accident, that the century or so before the Reformation has always stimulated German historians to investigate the social and intellectual circumstances of the time, particularly historians of the last generation with their intense interest in the history of ideas. While earlier generations were prompted by confessional disputes, recent scholars have above all shown interest (and it is an interest conditioned at least in part by our attitude toward our own age) in the "enigmatic complexity"[1] and the subtle contrasts of these

Originally a paper entitled *La vie religieuse dans les pays de langue germanique à la fin du XVe siècle*, given in Lyons on October 3, 1963, at the *Colloque d'histoire religieuse* held by the *Commission internationale d'histoire ecclésiastique comparée* and its *Sous commission française*. It has since been partly revised and provided with notes. The preliminary version of the paper was printed in a preparatory volume published by the Commission (Grenoble, 1963, pp. 35–48). The volume brought out to mark the conclusion of the conference (*Cahiers d'histoire*, 9/1, Grenoble, 1964) gives, on pp. 72–74, a highly compressed and rather unsatisfactory account of the discussion aroused by my paper. I found the critical remarks, especially the contributions of G. Ritter, H. Heimpel, H. Bornkamm, O. Vasella, and M. Pacaut, stimulating and I have tried to make use of them in the following pages.

decades during which the end of the "Middle Ages" and the beginning of the "modern era" were taking shape.

It may therefore be inevitable that our historical view of the period tends to be dominated by our attempts to provide a comprehensive picture. This urge to achieve a synopsis has prevented the exact investigation of particular aspects from keeping in step. At the same time, the period has so often been approached in the light of our interest in subsequent developments that its actual features have not always been brought out with sufficient clarity. And, finally, we have often failed to recognize or to allow for the methodological difficulties inherent in any attempt to grasp an entire historical period, especially when its inner spiritual life is to be set in the center of our understanding. For instance, which elements should be considered "typical" and given emphasis—normal and, often enough, banal phenomena, or unusual but possibly significant ones? Traditional commonplaces or words uttered in some obscure corner, yet full of implications for the future?

Despite all my questions and hesitations, this present essay depends on older studies[2] and is in many respects indebted to them. It will try to come to grips with a historical phenomenon of particular elusiveness to the historian: that of piety and religious sentiment. It cannot claim to be "more accurate" than earlier works or to exceed them in the broadness of its approach or the validity of its judgments. It is simply and above all a conscious attempt to appreciate the pre-Reformation era as a period in its own right. It may succeed in making it possible to place our emphases a little more appropriately and to throw some new light on the significance of the late fifteenth century for the ecclesiastical revolution of the sixteenth.

One decisive feature, in particular, of the religious spirit of this era has not yet been grasped with sufficient clarity: its containment within the ecclesiastical organization (*Kirchlichkeit*). A look at the religious life in Germany in the second half of the fifteenth century makes it impossible to speak of dissolution of the medieval world. On the contrary, it would be nearer the truth to say that there was hardly a period in the second millennium of ecclesiastical history which accepted with less resistance the Catholic Church's absolutist claims in matters of dogma.

It will be necessary in the course of this study to make this assertion somewhat more concrete and precise. Nonetheless, it is quite simple to show that its opposite is most certainly not true, since it was during these decades that heresy—meaning the fundamental rejection of the medieval church—lost its impetus and became as good as extinct. It is true that a few scattered groups of Waldensians appear to have held out in remote mountain areas of central Germany down to the sixteenth century,[3] but these remained underground. As far as we know, the last heresy trials of Waldensians or Hussites on German territory took place—with one isolated exception[4]—before 1470.[5] After that date the only cases that came before the Inquisition were more or less harmless agitators,[6] blasphemers and the like,[7] or else religious zealots like those Augsburg sectarians who caused a stir in 1480 for wanting to receive the sacrament daily, or several times a day.[8] The principal business of the Inquisition courts was now with witchcraft.[9] The disappearance of the heretics was, moreover, not brought about by violent suppression. There is a good deal of symbolical significance in the resigned confession of the German Hussite, Friedrich Reiser, who said in 1456: "Our cause is like a fire going out."[10] The great heretical movement which had, ever since the twelfth century, caused the church such lasting anxiety even in Germany petered out in the latter half of the fifteenth century. All its energy and missionary zeal had collapsed; heretical ideas no longer inflamed men's minds.[11]

But this most certainly does not mean that religious fervor and emotion had declined. On the contrary, there is a great deal to suggest that piety in fact increased considerably in intensity during these years. Perhaps the most impressive piece of evidence of this is Karl Eder's demonstration that in the region investigated by him, Upper Austria, the number of Mass-endowments continually grew between 1450 and 1480 to an extent hitherto

unknown, and reached its peak in 1517, only to start falling drasti-
cally from 1518 on and soon to cease altogether: this area remained
Protestant for a long time.[12] The same tendency emerges from
Arnold Oskar Meyer's—admittedly incomplete—list of Silesian
endowments in honor of St. Anne during the Middle Ages,[13]
while for north Germany it has been shown that the city of
Hamburg boasted no fewer than ninety-nine confraternities at
the beginning of the Reformation, of which the majority had
been set up after 1450.[14] It might be added that no other period
saw so many feast days[15] and processions,[16] and, even more
interesting, that from Alsace and Upper Austria right up to
Holland and the Baltic there occurred a "new spring" in church
building,[17] which resulted in the last, most fragile, blossoming
of "late Gothic." These facts would seem to suggest that the picture was essentially the same throughout the German-speaking
territories.[18]

It should not, of course, be overlooked that these phenomena
can be partly explained by external factors. The growth of the
veneration of St. Anne, for instance, was very much a matter of
fashion and was not restricted to Germany.[19] Enthusiasm for
endowments was doubtless prompted to a large extent by the
desire of the burgher class for maintaining its visible status, a wish
that was able to find new forms of expression in the age of early
capitalism, of great merchant companies and the accumulation of
new wealth.[20] One endowment tended to prepare the way for
the next, and it is surely significant that altars came increasingly
to be named after the family that had presented one rather than
after the saint.[21] It is, of course, obvious that external factors such
as these do not account for the phenomena as such. For confirma-
tion we need only turn to the charters of endowment which time
and time again speak of the motives of donors: Endowments are
made for the "obtaining of external salvation";[22] membership in
a confraternity is to ensure "all good things and the salvation of
body and soul."[23] Ecclesiastical and religious life was intimately
and inseparably fused with secular life, and the willingness, indeed
the longing, to sanctify one's secular existence within the frame-

work of ecclesiastical discipline and with the aid of the treasury of grace made available by the church were at no time more widespread than in the late fifteenth century. In no other age did they receive such tangible expression.[24]

When examined more closely, however, expressions of piety and ecclesiastical religion during this period turn out to be varied and differentiated. We must recognize above all two fundamental moods and trends which were in many ways mutually opposed. There prevailed on the one hand an inclination to mass movements; that is to say, a tendency toward hysteria ending often enough in violence, and a habit of oversimplifying and vulgarizing sacred things. On the other hand, the age witnessed a tender individualism and a bent for tranquil spirituality and religious modesty.

The former tendency was certainly not peculiar to this period. It had been characteristic of the later Middle Ages ever since the mid-fourteenth century. We may account for it in part by shifts in the social structure of Western Europe—the rise of urbanism and burgherdom; in part by such shattering collective experiences as the plague epidemics. It was an age in which "people" were not just passive participants in religious and ecclesiastical life, but instead played an active part in shaping this life.

Mass pilgrimages, for example, could flare up like a psychosis from one day to the next, and they could cease again just as suddenly.[25] In some cases the occasion was a notable miracle—a host miracle generally[26]—in others, as for instance in Sternberg (Mecklenburg) in 1492, where a priest was burned for selling a consecrated host to a Jew,[27] the motive seems inappropriate and entirely without sense. In still other cases—for example, the strange children's pilgrimage of 1457 to Mont St. Michel in Normandy, which drew its pilgrims mainly from south Germany—the occasion cannot even be discerned now.[28] But in addition to such religious mass movements, the period produced ugly mass excesses such as the systematic witch-hunting which first appeared in south Germany in the 1480's as a result of the agitation of the Dominican Inquisitor Heinrich Institoris. Although these excesses

met at first with opposition from the authorities and did not yet
enjoy much popular support,[29] they form as much a part of the
general picture of the period as the local persecutions of Jews
which became increasingly frequent in this age of rising capitalism.[30]

The supernatural world was still very real and very close to the
men and women of this age, and the panic aroused by the terrors
and calamities of the time (though these were, comparatively
speaking, not particularly serious) increased their sense of dependence on, and their longing for harmony with, the powers of
heaven. Miracle sites multiplied rapidly and were to be found in
every corner of the empire. Often enough these miracles were
manifest frauds;[31] occasionally they culminated in dreadful scan-
dals, like the notorious Jetzer case in Bern in 1509, where four
Dominicans were burned at the stake because, maliciously or
because they had been duped, they had used the novice Johann
Jetzer to perpetrate a spurious miracle of the virgin directed
against Franciscan doctrines concerning the immaculate conception of Our Lady, and had come to grief with it.[32]

It was probably about this time, too, that the veneration of
saints reached its peak and at the same time took on new outward
manifestations. Saints tended to be brought more and more
closely into the everyday life of average people. In paintings they
emerged from their gilt background, became individualized, and
were brought up to date in both dress and facial expression.[33]
In the cults associated with them, especially in the intimate
atmosphere of confraternities, saints were treated with confidence
and, one might even say, intimacy—an attitude productive of
such quaint and touching practices as the action of the Confraternity of Our Lady at Den Bosch in Holland in 1456 in giving a
dead brother a letter to St. Peter containing a pledge of the
brethren's good works to help him speed through the Gate of
Heaven.[34] Another aspect of this trend is the full development of
the system of patronage, which established certain saints for
particular sections of the population or for particular emergencies,
dividing up the heavenly court to correspond exactly to the struc-

ture of human society and human lives.[35] It was at this time, finally, that it became a general practice to name children after saints, with the result that the old Germanic names pretty well vanished altogether.[36]

Behind all this longing for salvation doubtless there lay an insecurity concerning salvation, an endeavor to bring the mediators between God and man to one's own side as it were, and to procure a guarantee of salvation. At no other time[37] was death conceived with such realism,[38] or feared with quite such anguish.[39] We may see examples of this in the strenuous exertions, very moving in their way, of the well-to-do to utilize every possible advantage offered by the late medieval church in return for good works. We think in this connection of those monster collections of relics made especially at the beginning of the sixteenth century, the decisive motive for which was in each case to receive a correspondingly immense period of indulgence. Cardinal Albrecht of Brandenburg managed to reach 39,245,120 years[40] according to his own estimate. At all events, the general boom in indulgences from the time of Sixtus IV's pontificate on is sure to have been motivated to a considerable extent by the wishes and needs of the faithful and not merely as earlier critics of the papacy used to maintain, by the financial interests of the church. No less grotesque and no less revealing appear some of the testaments drawn up at this time. Count Werner von Zimmern had a thousand Requiem Masses said for his soul in 1483,[41] and Duke Adolf von Geldern, on the death of his wife in 1569, ordered the bells of all the churches in Arnheim to be rung for three days and caused the Office of the Dead to be celebrated and private Masses to be said by all the priests in his lands.[42]

These were the anxious gestures of people in distress and in need of help. Earlier times had not known their like in such cumulative intensity. They form a strange, though by no means fortuitous, contrast with the many expressions of vigorous, even "earthy" worldliness to be found at all levels of society.[43] And yet they show that people took the church's competence and effectiveness in matters of salvation just as much for granted as they did the efficacy of good works. And their reliance on the quantity rather than the quality of such works was thoroughly characteristic of the Middle Ages. Moreover, the greatest hopes of strength and consolation continued to be the Mass and the eucharist, the central mystery of the church. A timid sense of reverential distance from the sacrament, tended to develop, as revealed by the fact that, although people thrust forward enthusiastically to catch sight of the host,[44] there was no increase in the number of communions,[45] despite many efforts on the part of the church.[46]

The zealous resort to force was, however, not the only, nor, in all probability even the dominant characteristic of religious life in the late fifteenth century. Another, essentially different, kind of religious experience existed in Germany.

We may identify two broad religious traditions in the second half of the fifteenth century, both of which originated in the monastic world of the preceding epoch. On the one hand were the offshoots of fourteenth-century German Dominican mysticism; on the other the energetic monastic reform movement, affecting all orders and scoring its most brilliant achievements in the first half of the fifteenth century, notably in its renewal of the Benedictine Order.[47] By 1450 both trends had long since moved beyond the narrow confines of monastic society. As the spiritual life in the monasteries deepened and reordered itself, it produced a great number of edifying devotional ascetic treatises which were disseminated extensively in lay circles. The church's preaching and pastoral work doubtless caught many a new impulse from this source. The most important development, however, took place toward the end of the fourteenth century in Holland in the form of the *Devotio moderna*, a spiritual movement which had made it its virtual object to bridge the distance between secular and monastic life and realize the ideals of monasticism in a way of life which, though set free from the cares of the world, was not confined and set apart by fixed rules and obligations.[48] In the *Devotio moderna* the influences of mysticism and the impulses of the reform movement joined forces.[49]

Religious life in these monasteries and in the lay circles that came under their influence bore no trace of superficial and neurotic violence. But even here there can be no doubting the determination to abide within the established church; if anything, this determination had been on the increase since the fourteenth century. And that profound and anguished longing for salvation which we have already observed would not appear to have been any less acute here. Yet it was precisely this longing which led in the *Devotio moderna* to the rejection of all superficial externals, of all mechanical and rote repetition.[50] As in the heyday of mysticism, the church's means of grace tended to be pushed somewhat aside in favor of an inner feeling of oneness with Christ.[51] There also existed a certain reserve toward theological speculation.[52]

By 1450, it is true, mysticism and monastic reform, as well as the *Devotio moderna*, had on the whole already lost some of their vigor; their power seemed broken. The increasing number of observantists and reformed congregations was perhaps no longer representative of religious ardor so much as of intrigues and partisan quarrels.[53] Ideals had become unbending formalism; the production of devotional literature ceased.[54] And yet it was precisely at this time—a time of exhaustion, superficiality, and conformity—that this religious tendency began to be a moving force in history. It was in this form that mysticism achieved its greatest influence.

The fifteenth century has been called "the inflation period of German mystic literature,"[55] and this expression sums up very well the mystic and ascetic religious attitude of the period. For one thing this particular form of religious expression achieved an extraordinarily widespread influence. We can see this most clearly in the literary sphere, where the printing press (the invention of which had to no small extent been actually motivated by a newly awakened need for books) had multiplied opportunities of disseminating ideas and had made people more enthusiastic for reading and education.[56] The result was that an abundance of religious literature of all kinds was now made generally accessible—from prayer-books and words of consolation[57] to preaching manuals[58] and missals,[59] from the scholastic Summa[60] to the Dance of Death.[61] No comprehensive list has yet been made of religious works printed during the age of *incunabula* in Germany.[62] But there is no mistaking the fact that in the first decades of the age of printing[63] such literature formed by far the greatest part of the enormous book production.[64]

A closer look at this literature will show that it is to a surprising extent lacking in originality and even in profundity. Most of the titles were works written at an earlier time, and if not they were usually compilations or revisions of such, carried out with varying degrees of skill.[65] Titles actually originating in the fifteenth century tended to adhere slavishly to earlier models.[66] Even such renowned churchmen and authors as the Dominican Johann Nider (d. 1438) and the Strassburg cathedral preacher Johann Geiler von Kaisersberg (1445–1510), were original only in that they simplified, diluted, and popularized the ideas and systems they had taken over.[67]

A lack of great men is a fundamental and universal characteristic of this age. [68] But what happened in the literary sphere shows that this must not be attributed merely to intellectual impotence. The astonishing traditionalism of the age was intentional. Originality and profundity were rejected. The famous Viennese preacher, Nikolaus von Dinkelsbühl, a theologian who lived in the first half of the century, boasted of this: "*Nihil locuturus sum de proprio ingenio . . . , sed omnia, que locuturus sum, sunt omnipotentis dei dona et sanctorum doctorum catholicorum virorum doctrinae; solum enim laborem habui in colligendo.*"[69] Geiler remarked: "Those are most to be praised who know best what the virtues are."[70] And the scarcely less renowned Johannes Meyer, a Dominican of Basel, turned against mysticism with the assertion that the reader would draw less profit from visions than from virtues.[71] It is possible to detect here a certain relationship to the *Devotio moderna*, however crudely misrepresented; and also the influence of Gerson, who might almost be described as the church Father of fifteenth-century German religious writers. There was great apprehension about exploring the hidden depths of life and thought. Nothing like the tempestuous profundity of the *Ackermann aus Böhmen* appeared during the second half of the fifteenth century—Nicholas of Cusa's passion for knowledge and wide-ranging theological speculation remained an isolated exception. Just as heresies had largely disappeared and conciliarism and the reforming zeal had petered out,[72] mysticism and religiosity had shed their adventurous audacity.[73] In the printed works of the fifteenth century, heresy or even fundamental criticism of the church are as rare as original works from the heyday of German mysticism.

Even in the early days of printing, the supply of books and titles was governed by demand.[74] It can therefore be assumed that it was precisely *these* books that people wanted to read. The preference for austerity, for adherence to long-established tradition and the avoidance of all extremes were not imposed on the age from without; they were fundamental tendencies of contemporary German religious desires. It was precisely in its late-fifteenth-century guise—popularized, its wings clipped, and its teeth drawn—that mysticism became a potent spiritual and religious force.

In the age of *incunabula* printed Bibles were everywhere of significance, but in no other land did so many of them appear in the vernacular as in Germany.[75] The greatest popular publishing successes were not complete editions of the Bible, of which there were in all only twenty-two up to 1522, but more practical partial editions. At least sixty-two complete or partial editions of the Psalms and 131 Plenaries (Sunday gospels and epistles) had appeared in print before the Reformation.[76]

There is no lack of evidence that this new reading matter had a deepening effect on religious attitudes. Bible reading may occasionally have been carried out as an ascetic exercise. "In 1476 I, Madalena Krefftin, have in honor of the Blessed Trinity read this book right through between mid-Lent and Holy Saturday": such is one case in point.[77] But there is also much to suggest that biblical history and Christ, and especially the suffering Christ, began now to gain prominence over and above the saints. The disturbingly realistic crucifixes and pictures of the Man of Sorrows produced during the late Gothic period in Germany are well known.[78] The depiction of the Passion also occupied the great German artists at the turn of the century:[79] Cranach, Grünewald, Dürer, Tilman Riemenschneider, for instance; and in this case, too, the relation of supply to demand ought to be noted. There was a close connection between the zeal for endowments and the blossoming of the arts. Occasionally the new devotion to Christ proved capable of purifying and deepening traditional forms of religious experience, as can be seen, for example, from the fact that during the second half of the fifteenth century the representation of the Dance of Death in north Germany tended to take a Christocentric turn. In the so-called Berlin Dance of Death of 1484 the dancing was no longer led by, or centered on, the figure of Death; Death did not have the final word, but rather the crucified Christ.[80] And a few years after the turn of the century Grünewald painted the Isenheim altar.

Thus the zeal for simplicity, security, and proven worth was combined with depth of sentiment and spiritual commitment. Marian devotion, too, produced expressions of touching spirituality[81] and the later fifteenth century showed that religious drama[82] and music,[83] as well as the visual arts,[84] abandoned the dominance of the symbolic and the ornamental in favor of a greater individualism. These manifestations, taken as a whole, certainly do not convey the impression that the dominant religious characteristic of this age was indifference, formalism,[85] or worldliness;[86] but rather—and here Lucien Fèbvre's remark on France seems to apply equally to Germany—"*un immense appétit du divin*."[87] Among readers of manuals of spiritual consolation, of the Paradise of the Soul and the *Ars moriendi*, as among those who paid for and came to look at representations of the Passion, there was a yearning for salvation and a fear of death no less intense than among ecstatic pilgrims. They, too, were caught up in the conviction that humility, resignation, and all the other virtues commended to them would open up for them the way to bliss.

If the basic outlines sketched here are correct (and in a general survey of this kind it is impossible to do justice to all the differentiations and nuances), then a coherent and, in some sense, self-contained picture emerges. The religious agitation, in many instances convulsion, to be found throughout society, that "*mobilitas seu mutabilitas animarum et inconstantia mentis nunc in hominibus*" discerned by an Erfurt theologian in 1466,[88] sought peace and certitude in what was traditional, time-proven, and holy; it found rest and composure in the laws of the church. One may, it seems to me, say that the late fifteenth century in Germany was marked by greater fidelity to the church than in any other medieval epoch.

The search was, of course, not for the church as such, but rather for its treasury of salvation. In their intense and subjective preoccupation with eternal bliss, men seized upon the church's conventions and prescribed rituals and, in performing them with a new zeal and entirely of their own accord, they filled them with new content. And this was not merely a matter of exaggeration or excess. In fact, the laity came increasingly to consider itself responsible for the church's constitution and performance. This was an impulse which had long been at work, principally in the cities.[89] Territorial princes and city magistrates, even individual citizens, took energetic action in matters of monastic reform, and toward the turn of the century it became customary to endow preaching benefices for the purpose of guaranteeing regular sermons of high quality (as is proved by the frequent stipulation that incumbents should hold a university degree), as a result of which many regions, especially in southwest Germany, had at least one endowed preacher in almost every city.[90]

There can be no mistaking the fact that these and similar measures occasionally had an element of self-help about them. The widespread ecclesiastical devotion of the later years of the fifteenth century did not necessarily imply an uncritical acceptance of the claims to superiority and leadership put forward by the dignitaries of the church.[91] It is true that, on the whole (and in comparison with the preceding age of reform), explicit criticism of the church was only sporadic and relatively modest in nature. Earlier historians, it seems to me, gave excessive importance to these criticisms, both as to their substance and their significance.

We have, for example, the Grievances of the German Nation,[92] directed against particular abuses, mainly financial; also a few pamphlets demanding extensive church reform, such as the *Reformatio Sigismundi*,[93] which had originated as early as 1439 in connection with the Council of Basel and gained some currency later on in the century, or the rabid pamphlet of the so-called "Upper Rhenish Revolutionary," though this remained as good as unknown.[94]

The most important fifteenth-century critics of the church in the territories of the Holy Roman Empire were three theologians more or less closely connected with the *Devotio moderna*: the two Dutchmen, Johann Pupper von Goch (d. 1475), and Wessel Gansfort (d. 1489), and the Rhinelander Johann Ruchrath von Oberwesel (d. after 1479).[95] They are conspicuous principally for the fact that they were the first to give some evidence of independent religious thinking and reforming tendencies in the world of German scholasticism, which was otherwise "completely colorless, both in matters of theology and in ecclesiastical politics," to quote Gerhard Ritter,[96] and moved firmly along the traditional lines of the schools. Nevertheless, both the influence and the reforming zeal of these theologians remained limited and faint. Though they resolutely emphasized the scriptural principle, even using it to contradict conventional exegesis, and raised repeated objections to such institutions of the church as indulgences and the meritoriousness of religious vows, and even, as in the case of Gansfort, championed Occam's view of the church as the invisible community of the righteous, very few people learned of these opinions, and fewer still took any interest or were carried along by them.

Only the humanists gave such ideas a certain echo.[97] Though at this time still few in number and membership, humanist circles provided for the first and, in effect, only time in the fifteenth century, a forum for a general transformation in matters of religion and philosophy.[98] In the case of some humanists—Celtis, for one—we can sense an alienation resting on fundamental principles, the emergence of a feeling for life akin to (and to some extent influenced by) that of the Italian Renaissance, and also a new optimism in regard to human existence. But even in this instance one must guard against the danger of making false assessments.

Though the German humanists were to play a significant role in the triumph of the Reformation,[99] around 1500 they showed scarcely any signs of a deliberate rejection of traditional religion within the church. Rudolf Agricola wished to be buried in a monk's cowl in 1485,[100] not a few of the humanists contributed their talents as poets and authors to the service of popular religiosity, and a number of them, such as the Basel preacher Surgant, used their new ideals in an attempt to make the influence of the church more effective,[101] just as Reuchlin and Erasmus were to do later. Inasmuch as humanism was to exercise considerable historical influence in later years, and its advocates were always inclined to draw more attention to themselves than was their due, historians are inclined to attach too much importance to the movement at this early stage. Humanists were not representative of German religious life in the latter years of the fifteenth century.

Criticism of the church in humanist and popular literature, and the movement to extend lay influence in the church, may have been limited in scope and significance, but they provide a component which it would be a mistake to leave out of our picture. Along with the subjectivism of religious attitudes, the emancipation from religious tutelage implied in a man's choice of his own means of salvation, we witness a sense of disillusionment with the clergy's failure to live up to the demands and expectations of the devout. Criticism of the ignorance and immorality of the secular and regular clergy, and the efforts on the part of the laity to counteract abuses with the means at their disposal, might well be described as acts of self-defense. The fact that these things were done suggests that men were seeking salvation and wished to find it with the help of the church.

To what extent were disillusionment, criticism, and self-help justified? An attempt will be made here to sum up the conclusions reached by historians in regard to that old and still controversial problem of the moral and intellectual condition of the hierarchy on the eve of the Reformation.

As regards intellectual standards[102] it has been shown that, in south Germany at least, between a third and half of all clerics had attended a university where they had at least studied the liberal arts.[103] In north Germany the percentage of university-educated priests is sure to have been lower,[104] and in any case it should be remembered that only a very small proportion of these men had actually studied theology.[105] Not until after the Reformation did it become accepted as a principle that the study of theology should be an indispensable qualification for the clerical calling. Furthermore, the diocesan examinations for which prospective clergymen had to present themselves were extremely modest in their requirements.[106]

In matters of clerical morality the situation in 1500 was not completely catastrophic either. Exact and reliable figures are unobtainable in this regard, although Oskar Vasella, the expert on these problems, is undoubtedly near the truth with the dark picture he has recently drawn of conditions in Switzerland.[107] It is certain that the number of clerics living in concubinage was extraordinarily high; though these relationships were often marital in character,[108] and there are signs of attempts to legalize these unions and thus bring them to some extent within the sphere of morality.[109]

Concerning pastoral activity and care of the soul, finally, we may observe that the majority of clerics confined themselves to the reading of Masses. In the many parishes served only by a vicar on behalf of a nonresident parish priest,[110] preaching and spiritual guidance were often neglected altogether, and there is evidence that even the activities of responsible and conscientious priests were largely confined to a perfunctory administration of the sacraments and devotions to the saints.[111] All the same, a great deal of preaching went on, done by mendicant friars and by appointed preachers and even by parish priests; in fact, there is possibly a good deal to be said for the view that there was too much rather than too little preaching, especially since the standard of these sermons, so far as can be judged from extant drafts and copies[112] (which would obviously be of particularly highly prized examples) was in keeping with the temper of the age and was often astonishingly, occasionally unbelievably, low.[113]

The abuses among the late medieval clergy and the affront which these abuses presented to religious attitudes around 1500 make a complex set of phenomena. One contributory factor was the steep rise in the number of clerics, the product of that same pious zeal which endowed all those Masses and benefices, which introduced an element of assembly-line production into their ministrations and diminished their quality.[114] In pre-Reformation Worms about 10 per cent of the population consisted of secular or religious clerics.[115] The church had reached the point where it was unable to do anything more than react to stimuli given by others.[116] Its theology and its spiritual life lacked the genuine inner impulse[117] to find its way out of the maze into which its own historical development had brought it. It produced no relevant, helpful response to the yearnings and explosive passions of men who submitted themselves to the church for guidance. The most characteristic symptom of this lack of response is the fatal importance given in this age to indulgence preaching, with its vulgar materialism and its preaching which was of its very nature so open to misunderstandings.[118]

It would appear, therefore, that the revitalization and deepening of religious life in the second half of the fifteenth century aroused virtually no echo within the clergy.[119] There are, in fact, indications that the condition of the clergy simply went on deteriorating right up to the brink of the Reformation.[120] The role of leadership which had been accorded to the clergy ever since the early Middle Ages was still being claimed and was scarcely disputed anywhere; but the clergy were hardly capable of fulfilling this role. With their benefice-oriented mentality they remained essentially feudal. They were, moreover, long accustomed to forming a caste set apart from the laity, a state of affairs justified on the grounds of their sacramental functions, the *opus operatum*. Confronted now for the first time in the Middle Ages with intellectual and religious demands of an exacting and subtle nature, they had their power taken away, while the deterioration of their intellectual and moral standards would inevitably be found more and more intolerable as the level of the laity rose, particularly in Germany, for at the beginning of the sixteenth century the center of European spiritual and religious life began for the first time in history to shift north of the Alps.

There can be no doubt that the points discussed here, if not actually "causes" of the Reformation, were at least "prerequisites" of the great change.[121] There is no room to go any further into the problems touched on—a brief indication must suffice. Nikolaus Glassberger, a Franciscan chronicler of Franconia during the later fifteenth century, once raised a troubled lament at the sorry condition of the church in contemporary France, the collapse of worship and the godlessness of the people, contrasting this with the flourishing religious life of Germany, where the divine service was celebrated with all solemnity and the people were devout and faithful to the church.[122] What he saw may well have been true. In the late Middle Ages Germany was "a particularly medieval country,"[123] and this was evidently true right up to the Reformation. Luther's triumph in Germany— in other words, his power to carry men along with him—will clearly be misunderstood if we do not realize that one of its prerequisites was the extreme acceleration of medieval ecclesiastical religiosity.[124] That the Reformation broke out, not in France, but in traditional, slow-moving medieval Germany, a land noted for its respectful attitude toward the powers that be, is a fact which should be carefully considered; it was certainly not a matter of chance.

NOTES TO CHAPTER I

1. Joseph Lortz, *Die Reformation in Deutschland*, Vol. 1 (3rd ed., 1949), p. 96
2. Various aspects of the present theme have been discussed in a number of general histories. In addition to the largely superseded work of G. von Below, *Die Ursachen der Reformation* (1917), the most valuable works would seem to be W. Andreas, *Deutschland vor der Reformation* (6th rev.

ed., 1959); Lortz, *op. cit.*, along with Lortz's more thoroughgoing treatment of certain points in "Zur Problematik der kirchlichen Misstände im Spät-Mittelalter," *Trierer Theologische Zeitschrift*, 58 (1949), pp. 1–26, 212–27, 257–79, 347–57; R. R. Post, *Kerkelijke verhoudingen in Nederland voor de Reformatie* (Utrecht and Antwerp, 1954). Cf. also *idem, Kerkgeschiedenis van Nederland in de middeleeuwen*, esp. Vol. II (1957), p. 268 ff. Informative also are G. Schnürer, *Kirche und Kultur im Mittelalter*, Vol. III (1929), p. 206 ff., and the general survey of the problem by O. Clemen, "Die Volksfrömmigkeit des ausgehenden Mittelalters," *Studien zur religiösen Volkskunde*, 3 (1937); and the following two important, though somewhat one-sided books: R. Stadelmann, *Vom Geist des ausgehenden Mittelalters (Deutsche Vierteljahrsschrift für Literaturwissenschaft und Geistesgeschichte*, 15, 1929), and W.-E. Peuckert, *Die grosse Wende* (1948). Less satisfactory is the bibliographical essay by P. Wunderlich, "Die Beurteilung der Vorreformation in der deutschen Geschichtsschreibung seit Ranke" (*Erlanger Abhandlungen zur mittleren und neueren Geschichte*, 5, 1930), and the lectures of K. Eder, *Deutsche Geisteswende zwischen Mittelalter und Neuzeit* (1937). My own view has been most profoundly influenced by H. Heimpel's essay, "Das Wesen des deutschen Spätmittelalters." [See chapter 2 of this book.]

3. H. Haupt, *Die religiösen Sekten in Franken vor der Reformation* (1882), p. 48 ff.; H. C. Lea, *Geschichte der Inquisition im Mittelalter* [*History of the Inquisition of the Middle Ages*, New York, 1888–90] (1909), p. 473 f.

4. For persecutions of Waldenses in the Brandenburg Marches from 1478 to 1483 cf. W. Wattenback, "Über die Inquisition gegen die Waldenser in Pommern und der Mark Brandenburg," *Abhandlungen der königlichen Akademie der Wissenschaften zu Berlin* (1886), *Phil.-Hist. Klasse* 3), 87 ff.; G. Brunner, *Ketzer und Inquisition in der Mark Brandenburg im ausgehenden Mittelalter* (diss., Berlin, 1904), p. 26 ff.

5. The last heresy trials—against Hussites, Strassburg, 1458, cf. H. Köpstein, "Über den deutschen Hussiten Friedrich Reiser," *Zeitschrift für Geschichtswissenschaft*, 7 (1959), 1068–82. The importance of this man is, however, much overrated—Köpstein depicts him as though he were a Communist-party functionary in a capitalist society. Cf. *idem, Aus 500 Jahren deutschtschechoslowakischer Geschichte* (1958), p. 22 ff. Also in 1458, trials of Waldenses with Taborite leanings in the Brandenburg Marches: cf. Wattenback, *loc. cit.*, p. 71 ff.; Brunner, *op. cit.*, p. 18 ff.; in 1461 against Waldenses in the diocese of Eichstätt: cf. Haupt, *op. cit.*, p. 47; in 1462 against Taborite Waldenses in Saxony and Thuringia: H. Boehmer, "Die Waldenser von Zwickau," *Neues Archiv für sächsische Geschichte und Altertumskunde*, 36 (1915), 1–38; in 1467 against the "Wirsberger," an apocalyptic sect probably connected with Hussitism: cf. G. Ritter, *Zeitschrift für Kirchengeschichte*, 43 (1924), 158 f.; O. Schiff, "Die Wirsberger," *Historische Vierteljahrsschrift*, 26 (1931), 776–86; R. Kestenberg-Gladstein, "The 'Third Reich,'" *Journal of the Warburg and Courtauld Institutes* 18 (1955), pp. 245–95 (the author tends to overrate the importance of this group; heresies are *not* "characteristic of this epoch in general"). For other

individual heretics, cf. I. Döllinger, *Beiträge zur Sektengeschichte des Mittelalters*, Vol. II (1890), 626 ff., G. Ritter, *loc. cit.*, pp. 150–58 (concerning a spiritualist who said, "*Ecclesia tota inferior est dampnata et haeretica*"); K. Schornbaum, *Zeitschrift für bayerische Kirchengeschichte*, 8 (1933), 203 f.

6. For instance, the so-called Piper of Niklashausen, Hans Beheim, executed in 1476, and the movement that gathered round him with songs directed against the clergy but which collapsed soon after the death of its leader: Haupt, *op. cit.*, p. 57 ff.; Peuckert, *op. cit.*, p. 263 ff.; G. Franz, *Der deutsche Bauernkrieg* 4th ed. (1956), p. 45 ff. It emerges clearly that this movement, which originated with a vision of Our Lady, took on its revolutionary character in consequence of the reactions of the church authorities. For executions of Flagellants in Quedlinburg and Halberstadt in 1461 and 1481, cf. G. Zschäbitz, "Zur mitteldeutschen Wiedertäuferbewegung nach dem grossen Bauernkrieg," *Leipziger Übersetzungen und Abhandlungen zum Mittelalter*, Vol. I (1958), p. 123.

7. See Post, *Kerkgeschiedenis*, Vol. II, 338 ff.

8. A. M. Koeniger, *Ein Inquisitionsprozess in Sachen der täglichen Kommunion* (1923); A. Schröder, "Die tägliche Laienkommunion in spätmittelalterlicher Auffassung," *Archiv für die Geschichte des Hochstifts Augsburg*, 6 (1929), 609–29. The ecclesiastical authorities probably suspected these sectarians of Hussitism: cf. P. Browe, *Die häufige Kommunion im Mittelalter* (1938), p. 32 ff.

9. See itemization in H. C. Lea and A. C. Howland, *Materials Toward a History of Witchcraft*, Vol. I (New York and London, 2nd ed., 1957), pp. 237, 241, 251, 253.

10. A. Jung, *Timotheus*, Vol. II (Strassburg, 1822), p. 256. Reiser compounded a mixture of Waldensian and Hussite ideas, as has been shown by Köpstein and, after him, by V. Vinay, "Friedrich Reiser e la diaspora valdese di lingua tedesca nel XV secolo," *Bollettino della Società di Studi Valdesi*, 109 (1961), 35–56.

11. This to me is a significant fact that has hitherto very largely escaped notice, even in the informative recent study by C. P. Clasen, "Medieval Heresies in the Reformation," *Church History*, 32 (1963), pp. 392–414. The conclusion reached there, as in many earlier works, is that the kinship of Reformation sects in matters of theology and ecclesiastical discipline with their medieval equivalents implies historical continuity. While it is certainly impossible simply to deny the hidden survival and influence of medieval sects, the assumption of historical continuity is not convincing. It takes, for example, no account of the fact that the range of variation of sectarian ideas within the Christian religion is comparatively restricted.

12. K. Eder, "Das Land ob der Enns vor der Glaubensspaltung," *Studien zur Reformationsgeschichte Oberösterreichs*, I (1933), 105 ff., 421 ff. For Styria, K. Amon, *Die Steiermark vor der Glaubensspaltung*, Vol. I (*Geschichte der Diözese Seckau*, Vol. 3/1, 1960), 85 f. Comparable, though less precise and comprehensive figures for the Netherlands in Post, *Kerkelijke verhoudingen*, p. 402. A. Schüller, "Messe und Kommunion in einer stadttrierischen Pfarrei vor und nach der Reformation," *Trierisches Archiv*, 21 (1913),

65–98, arrives at similar results for the parish of St. Gangolf in Trier. Compared with these, the endowments for the Charterhouse of Marienkron in Pomerania maintained a fairly steady level during both halves of the fifteenth century (a total of 2,570 titles between 1406 and 1528): cf. H. Lemcke (ed.), "*Liber beneficiorum* des Karthäuserklosters Marienkron bei Rügenwalde," *Quellen zur pommerschen Geschichte*, 5 (1919–22). Similar results in the list of benefice endowments in Lüneburg drawn up by G. Matthaei, *Die Vikariestiftungen der Lüneburger Stadtkirchen im Mittelalter und im Zeitalter der Reformation* (1928), p. 151 ff.

13. A. O. Meyer, "Studien zur Vorgeschichte der Reformation aus schlesischen Quellen," *Historische Bibliothek*, 14 (1903), 42 ff. For a general view, see B. Kleinschmidt, "Die heilige Anna," *Forschungen zur Volkskunde*, 1–3 (1930), 138.

14. G. Brandes, "Die geistlichen Brüderschaften in Hamburg während des Mittelalters," *Zeitschrift des Vereins für hamburgische Geschichte*, 34 (1934), 75–176; 35 (1936), 57–98; 36 (1937), 65–110. According to T. Kolde, *Friedrich der Weise und die Anfänge der Reformation* (1881), pp. 15, 74 f., Pfeffinger, a councillor of the electorate of Saxony who died in 1519, was simultaneously a member of no less than thirty-five fraternities, to which he bequeathed legacies in his will.

15. See Amon, *op. cit.*, p. 211 ff.

16. There were twenty-two in Bruges alone in 1475: Post, *Kerkelijke verhoudingen*, p. 398. In Breisach in 1502 one was held each week in honor of the city patrons; W. Müller, "Der Wandel des kirchlichen Lebens vom Mittelalter in die Neuzeit, erörtert am Beispiel Breisach," *Freiburger Diözesan-Archiv*, 82–83 (1962–63), 231.

17. Cf. A. Barthelmé, "La réforme dominicaine au XVᵉ siècle en Alsace," *Collection d'études sur l'histoire . . . de l'Alsace*, 7, (Strassburg, 1931), 151; Eder, "Das Land ob der Enns," in *op. cit.*, 123 ff.; Post, *Kerkgeschiedenis*, Vol. II, p. 266 f.; E. Schnitzler, "Das geistige und religiöse Leben Rostocks am Ausgang des Mittelalters," *Historische Studien*, 360 (1940), 63.

18. Among the monographs by local historians the following are still important: E. von Lehe, "Die kirchlichen Verhältnisse in den Marschländern Hadeln und Wursten vor der Reformation," *Jahrbuch der Männer vom Morgenstern*, 24 (1928–30), 136–215; G. Rücklin, "Religiöses Volksleben des ausgehenden Mittelalters in den Reichsstädten Hall und Heilbronn," *Historische Studien*, 226 (1933); W. Jannasch, *Reformationsgeschichte Lübecks . . . 1515–1530* (1958), pp. 7–79.

19. P. V. Charland, *Madame sainte Anne et son culte au moyen age*, Vols. I–III (Québec, 1911–21); Kleinschmidt, *loc. cit.*

20. The basic monograph on Augsburg is J. Strieder, *Zur Genesis des modernen Kapitalismus* (2nd ed., 1935). The attempt of H. Bechtel, *Wirtschaftsstil des deutschen Spätmittelalters* (1930) to see these economic processes in the context of the history of ideas is only partly successful.

21. This was observed by H. Witte, *Archiv für Kulturgeschichte*, 29 (1939), 276.

22. For Württemberg, cf. J. Rauscher, *Württembergische Jahrbücher für Statistik und Landeskunde* (1908–12), p. 156.

23. Rücklin, *loc. cit.*, p. 134.
24. The contemporary efforts to lift commercial life into the realm of religion are brought out clearly in the essay of A. Schulte, "Die grosse Ravensburger Handelsgesellschaft und die Pflege der kirchlichen Kunst in ihrer Gesellschaftskapelle," *Archiv für Kulturgeschichte*, 26 (1936), 73–88. Corresponding material is provided in abundance by N. Lieb, *Die Fugger und die Kunst*, Vol. 1 (1952). A comprehensive study of piety among medieval merchants has been announced by E. Maschke; in the meantime see his essay, "Das Berufsbewusstsein des mittelalterlichen Fernkaufmanns," *Miscellanea Mediaevalia*, 3 (1964), 323 ff.
25. G. Schreiber, "Wallfahrt und Volkstum," *Forschungen zur Volkskunde*, 16/17 (1934); L. A. Veit, *Volksfrommes Brauchtum und Kirche im deutschen Mittelalter* (1936), p. 54 ff.; J. Staber, *Volksfrömmigkeit und Wallfahrtswesen des Spätmittelalters im Bistum Freising* (1955).
26. P. Browe, *Die eucharistischen Verwandlungswunder im Mittelalter* (1938), *passim*.
27. Schnitzler, *loc. cit.*, p. 56. Bauerreiss (cf. note 78 below), p. 62, appears to be mistaken.
28. On this see Veit, *op. cit.*, p. 54; and his references on p. 221, note 76.
29. Cf. Lea and Howland, *op. cit.*; the study of F. Byloff, "Hexenglaube und Hexenverfolgung in den österreichischen Alpenländern," *Quellen zur deutschen Volkskunde*, 6 (1934), 30 ff. Further literature in *Lexikon für Theologie und Kirche*, Vol. v (2nd ed., 1960), col. 319.
30. Cf. R. Straus, *Die Judengemeinde Regensburg im ausgehenden Mittelalter*, 1.2 (1932–60). For general discussion, cf. S. Dubnow, *Weltgeschichte des jüdischen Volkes*, 5 (1927), 322 ff.
31. See F. Roth, "Die geistliche Betrügerin Anna Laminit von Augsburg," *Zeitschrift für Kirchengeschichte*, 43 (1924), 355–417.
32. Most recently K. Guggisberg, *Bernische Kirchengeschichte* (1958), p. 38 ff., with literature cited on p. 742.
33. J. Braun, *Tracht und Attribute der Heiligen in der deutschen Kunst* (1934), *passim*; W. Messerer, "Verkündigungsdarstellungen des 15. und 16. Jahrhundert als Zeugnisse des Frömmigkeitswandels," *Archiv für Liturgiewissenschaft*, 5/2 (1958), 362–69.
34. Post, *Kerkgeschiedenis*, vol. II, p. 246, note 1.
35. In the case of the Fuggers, the city patron of Augsburg, St. Ulrich, is even portrayed as a partner in 1515—though this was the adoption of a practice already established in Italy (cf. Lieb, *op. cit.*, p. 131).
36. Summary in A. Back, *Die deutschen Personennamen*, Vol. II (2nd ed., 1953), p. 22 ff. Still useful: J. Trier, "Der heilige Jodocus," *Germanistische Abhandlungen*, 56 (1924), 138 ff. The specialized study by J. Scheidl, "Der Kampf zwischen deutschen und christlichen Vornamen im ausgehenden Mittelalter, nach altbaierischen Quellen für das dachauer Land dargestellt," *Zeitschrift für Namensforschung*, 16 (1940), 193–214, is valuable only for its compilation of material.
37. For some general observations on this, cf. W. Rehm, "Der Todesgedanke in der deutschen Dichtung vom Mittelalter bis zur Romantik," *Deutsche*

Vierteljahrsschrift für Literaturwissenschaft und Geistesgeschichte, Buchreihe, 14 (1928), 73 ff.

38. An instance of this would be the contemporary tombstones in Marburg (Lahn), Lorch, in Upper Austria and other places, which depict the corpse of the deceased consumed by worms.

39. For this, see note 61 below.

40. N. Paulus, *Geschichte des Ablasses im Mittelalter,* Vol. III (1923), p. 292. P. M. Halm and R. Berliner, *Das Hallesche Heiltum* (1931). Lesser sovereignties, too, like the city of Heilbronn, were zealously concerned about increasing their stocks of relics: Rücklin, *loc. cit.,* p. 118 f. For the monastery of St. Peter in Erfurt: O. Scheel, *Martin Luther,* Vol. I (3rd ed., 1921), p. 130.

41. H. Tüchle, *Kirchengeschichte Schwabens,* Vol. II (1954), p. 385.

42. Post, *Kerkgeschiedenis,* Vol. II, 293. Similar examples in Eder, "Das Land ob der Enns," p. 259; Schnitzler, *loc. cit.,* p. 59; R. Wackernagel, *Geschichte der Stadt Basel,* Vol. 2/2 (1916), p. 869 f.

43. These expressions are, to some extent, found in direct connection with religious acts and institutions. Thus in 1504 there was a *Kalandsgelage* [a ceremonial meal by a group of *Kalandsbrüder,* or *fratres calendarii,* a fraternity that met originally on the first day of each month (*Kalendae*)] in Lüneburg, a carouse lasting three days, and involving 124 persons and twenty barrels of beer: *Die Altertümer der Stadt Lüneburg,* Vol. V (1862), p. 2.

44. Cf. the vexed comment aroused by, and the remarkable penalties imposed on, the people at Mass who congregated in the choirs of churches after the consecration "in order to see the unveiled Sacrament." They are cited in H. B. Meyer, "Die Elevation im deutschen Mittelalter und bei Luther," *Zeitschrift für katholische Theologie,* 85 (1963), 162–217.

45. Communion once a year was usual. Cf. Schüller, *loc. cit.;* also Post, *Kerkelijke verhoudingen,* p. 407.

46. In addition to the confraternities of the Blessed Sacrament who strove for more frequent communion, there were also movements in the opposite direction—whether from spiritual motives, as an aftereffect of the idea, advocated by German mysticism and the *Devotio moderna,* that spiritual delight was superior to carnal (see below, note 51), or as a defensive reaction against Hussitism, with its demand for more frequent communion. (See above, note 8; also, in addition to Browe, mentioned there, the account given by Post, *Kerkelijke verhoudingen,* p. 405 ff., and S. Tromp, "S. congregatio concilii de communione frequenti," *Divinitas,* I [1957], 550–7; 4 [1960], 61–80.)

47. The complex history and motivation of monastic reform in the fifteenth century are well brought out by Lortz, "Zur Problematik," *loc. cit.,* p. 212 ff.

48. *Non sumus religiosi, sed in seculo religiose vivere nitimur et volumus,* was the motto of the members of the confraternity in Hildesheim: E. Barnikol, "Studien zur Geschichte der Brüder vom gemeinsamen Leben," *Zeitschrift für Theologie und Kirche, Ergänzungsheft,* 27 (1917), 109.

49. The best summary of the ideas of the *Devotio moderna* is still Paul Mestwerdt, "Die anfänge des Erasmus—Humanismus und Devotio moderna," *Studien zur Kultur und Geschichte der Reformation*, 2 (Leipzig, 1917), 78 ff. In addition to this, the most important works are R. R. Post, "Studien over de Broeders van het Gemene Leven," *Nederlands Historiebladen*, 1 (1938), 304–35; 2 (1939), 136–62; *idem, De Moderne Devotie* (Amsterdam, 2nd ed., 1950). Post has shown that the spread and the immediate influence of the *Devotio moderna* were more limited than previously supposed. For its dissemination in Germany, there is a fundamental monograph: B. Windeck, *Die Anfänge der Brüder vom gemeinsamen Leben in Deutschland* (diss., Bonn, 1951). For its influence on France: G. G. Coulton, *Five Centuries of Religion*, Vol. IV (Cambridge, 1950), 365 ff.

50. S. Axters, *Geschiedenis van de vroomheid in de Nederlanden*, Vol. III (1956), p. 76.

51. Thomas à Kempis, *Imitatio Christi*, IV/10 (ed. M. J. Pohl, *Opera omnia*, Vol. II [1904], 22 ff.). Cf. Axters, *op. cit.*, p. 402; W. Brüggeboes, *Die Fraterherren ... im Lüchtenhofe zu Hildesheim* (diss., Münster, 1939), p. 87 ff.

52. In the *Devotio moderna* this aversion was occasionally even extended to Thomas Aquinas. Cf. Godest van Toarn in C. van der Wansem, "Het ontstaan en de geschiedenis der Broederschap van het Gemene Leven tot 1400," *Recueil de Travaux d'histoire et de philologie de Louvain*, 4/12 (1958), 104 f.

53. Cf. G. M. Löhr, *Die Teutonia im 15. Jh.* (1924), *passim*; Erich Molitor, *Aus der Rechtsgeschichte benediktinischer Verbände*, Vol. II (1932), 1 ff.; G. Spahr, "Die Reform im Kloster St. Gallen 1442–1457," *Schriften des Vereins für Geschichte des Bodensees*, 76 (1958), 1–62.

54. For the Brethren of the Common Life, cf. Windeck, *op. cit.*, p. 63 ff. Strange examples of formalism in monastic piety are given by F. Rapp, "La prière dans les monastères des Dominicaines observantes en Alsace au XVᵉ siècle," *La Mystique Rhénane* (Paris, 1963), pp. 207–18.

55. G. Pickering, *Bulletin of the John Rylands Library*, 22 (1938), 458.

56. This reciprocality has been brought out impressively by C. Wehmer in his informative synopsis, "Inkunabelkunde," *Zentralblatt für Bibliothekswesen*, 57 (1940), 214–32, though he perhaps places excessive emphasis on Gutenberg's work as an "invention."

57. F. Falk, *Die deutschen Sterbebüchlein von der ältesten Zeit des Buchdruckes bis zum Jahre 1520* (1890); H. Bohatta, *Bibliographie der Livres d'Heures, Officia, Hortuli Animae ... des XV und XVI Jahrhundert* (2nd ed., 1924); A. Auer, "Johannes von Dambach und die Trostbücher vom 11. bis zum 16. Jahrhundert," *Beiträge zur Geschichte der Philosophie und Theologie des Mittelalters*, 27/1, 2 (1928), 367 ff. For the spirituality and piety expressed in this genre of litereature, cf. especially H. Appel, "Anfechtung und Trost im Spätmittelalter und bei Luther," *Schriften des Vereins für Reformationsgeschichte*, 165 (1938); F. X. Haimerl, "Mittelalterliche Frömmigkeit im Spiegel der Gebetbuchliteratur Süddeutschlands," *Münchener Theologische Studien*, 1/4 (1952), 34 ff.; R. Rudolf, "Ars moriendi," *Forschungen zur Volkskunde*, 39 (1957).

58. Cf. below, note 101.
59. H. Bohatta, *Liturgische Bibliographie des XV, Jahrhundert* (1911; reprinted 1961).
60. There is no comprehensive bibliography or investigation covering the early printed editions of theological works.
61. P. S. Kozaky, *Geschichte der Totentänze*, 2 vols. (Budapest, 1935–1944); H. Rosenfeld, "Der mittelalterliche Totentanz," *Beiheft zum Archiv für Kulturgeschichte*, 3 (1954), containing a good bibliography.
62. Cf. provisionally F. Falk, *Die Druckkunst im Dienste der Kirche* (1879). Informative also: *Bibliotheca Catholica Neerlandica impressa 1500–1727* (The Hague, 1954), which lists, for the period immediately following that under consideration here (1500–1520) and for the Netherlands alone no less than 784 printed editions of ecclesiastical and theological writings.
63. According to Wehmer, *loc. cit.*, a total of about 40,000 printed works appeared between 1450 and 1500, and roughly 43 per cent of these in the territories of the Holy Roman Empire.
64. The literature on the early history of printing (cf. now L. Fèbvre and H. J. Martin, *L'apparition du livre* [Paris, 1958], with extensive bibliography) tends to concentrate on curiosities or works indicating future developments and thus overlooks the basically conservative character of early book production. This is not the case with Wehmer's essay, mentioned above in note 56.
65. In addition to the literature already mentioned, cf. A. Spamer, *Über die Zersetzung und Vererbung in den deutschen Mystikertexten* (diss., Giessen, 1910); F. P. Schmidt, *Beiträge zur thüringischen Kirchengeschichte*, 4 (1939), 155–76; and the essays of W. Stammler and W. Schmidt in K. Ruh's anthology, *Altdeutsche und altniederländische Mystik* (1964), pp. 386 ff., 437 ff., with a comprehensive bibliography.
66. Despite the arguments put forward by J. Kalverkamp, *Die Vollkommenheitslehre des Franziskaners Heinrich Herp* (diss., Freiburg, 1940) this assertion applies, for example, to the "Spieghel der Volcomenheit," ed. L. Verschueren, 2 vols. (Antwerp, 1931) of the most audacious of contemporary mystics, the Dutchman Hendrik Herp. Also instructive is J. Werlin, "Mystikerzitate aus einer Nürnberger Predigthandschrift," *Archiv für Kulturgeschichte*, 43 (1961), 140–59.
67. Cf. G. Gieraths, "Johann Nider und die 'deutsche Mystik' des 14. Jahrhunderts," *Divus Thomas*, 30 (1952), 321–46; *idem*, *Johann Tauler und die Frömmigkeitshaltung des 15. Jahrhunderts* (*Johann-Tauler-Gedenkschrift*, 1961) pp. 422–34; A. Volanthen, "Geilers Seelenparadies im Verhältnis zur Vorlage," *Archiv für elsässische Kirchengeschichte*, 6 (1931), 229–324; E. Breitenstein, "Die Quellen der Geiler von Kaysersberg zugeschriebenen Emeis," *ibid.*, 13 (1938), 149–202.
68. The assertion of K. Eder (*Deutsche Geisteswende*, p. 181), that "it would be difficult to think of an age with a greater number of unusual men than the period from 1450 to 1530" cannot be accepted as it stands.
69. Quoted in F. Schäffauer, *Theologische Quartalschrift*, cxv (1934), 539 f
70. Quoted in Volanthen, *loc. cit.*, p. 285, note 1.

71. Quoted in W. Muschg, *Die Mystik in der Schweiz 1200–1500* (1935), p. 350. This book is valuable for an understanding of the whole trend discussed in my essay.
72. A. Stoecklin, "Das Ende der mittelalterlichen Konzilsbewegung," *Zeitschrift für schweizerische Kirchengeschichte*, 37 (1943), 8–30; H. Jedin, *Geschichte des Konzils von Trient*, Vol. 1 (1949), 24 ff.
73. Cf. Stadelmann, *op. cit.*, p. 98 ff., although his views are spoilt by his biased assumption of the "morbidity" of this age.
74. Nonetheless, it is necessary to keep in mind the many bankruptcies among the earlier printers; cf. Wehmer, *loc. cit.*, p. 227.
75. The oldest German Bible, printed in 1466 (*Gesamtkatalog der Wiegendrucke*, 4 [1930], No. 4295 ff.), has been critically edited by W. Kurrelmeyer in ten volumes of the *Bibliothek des litterarischen Vereins in Stuttgart* (1904–1915). In accounting for this phenomenon, attention should be paid to the observation of H. Volz (*Bibel und Bibeldruck in Deutschland im 15. und 16. Jahrhundert* [1960]), that the frequency of Bible printings fluctuated considerably in the various decades prior to the Reformation.
76. H. Rost, *Die Bibel im Mittelalter* (1939), p. 363 ff. Rost's list is incomplete.
77. Quoted in F. K. Ingelfinger, *Die religiös-kirchlichen Verhältnisse im heutigen Württemberg am Vorabend der Reformation* (diss., Tübingen, 1939), p. 141.
78. R. Bauerreiss, *Pie Jesu—Das Schmerzensmann-Bild und sein Einfluss auf die mittelalterliche Frömmigkeit* (1931), *passim*; G. Wagner, "Volksfromme Kreuzverehrung in Westfalen," *Schriften der volkskundlichen Kommission des Landschafts-verbandes Westfalen-Lippe*, 11 (1960), 77 ff.
79. G. Dehio, *Geschichte der deutschen Kunst*, Vol. 2 (4th ed., 1930), p. 182: "The visual arts tell us more clearly than any theological and literary sources that in the century preceding the Reformation the Christ of the people was not the Christ of Glory, but the Christ of Sorrows."
80. Rosenfeld, *loc. cit.*, p. 212 f.
81. For the Marian lament of the monk Reborch von Bordesholm, see W. Stammler, "Die mittelniederdeutsche geistliche Literatur," *Neue Jahrbücher für das klassische Altertum*, 23 (1920), 134. For the pious exercises known as the *Marientiden*, which were emerging in the cities of northwest Germany toward the end of the fifteenth century, cf. Jannasch, *op. cit.*, pp. 43 ff., 356 f., and the literature given there.
82. H. H. Borcherdt, *Das europäische Theater im Mittelalter und in der Renaissance* (1935), p. 147 ff.
83. *New Oxford History of Music*, Vol. III (London, 1960), p. 239 ff. Also W. Wiora, "Der religiöse Grundzug im neuen Stil und Weg Josquins des Prez," *Musikforschung*, 6 (1953), 23–37.
84. See the essay by Messerer, cited above, note 33.
85. Notwithstanding the drastic and occasionally grotesque instances of formalism, such as counting the drops of Christ's blood (between 36,500 and 54,000) in order to determine the best number of Paternosters; cf. Post, *Kerkelijke verhoudingen*, p. 459 f.
86. A different conclusion is reached by E. Döring-Hirsch, "Tod und Jenseits

RELIGIOUS LIFE IN GERMANY ON EVE OF REFORMATION 39

im Spätmittelalter," *Studien zur Geschichte der Wirtschafts-und Geistes-kultur*, 2 (1927), though this study does not go into very much detail. Cf. also Bechtel, *op. cit.*
87. L. Fèbvre in *Revue historique*, CLXI (1929), 39.
88. The Augustinian Johannes Dorsten, see Kestenberg-Gladstein, *loc. cit.*, 259.
89. Cf. A. Schultze, "Stadtgemeinde und Kirche im Mittelalter," *Festgabe R. Sohm* (1914), pp. 103–42; B. Moeller, "Reichsstadt und Reformation," *Schriften des Vereins für Reformationsgeschichte*, 180 (1962), 10 ff.
90. On this point see J. Rauscher, "Die Prädikaturen in Württemberg vor der Reformation," *Württembergische Jahrbücher für Statistik und Landeskunde* (1908–12), pp. 152–211; E. Lengwiler, *Die vorreformatorischen Praedika-turen der deutschen Schweiz* (diss. Freiburg, 1955). For lay intervention in sermons, cf. Amon, *op. cit.*, p. 276.
91. Cf. A. Störmann, *Die städtischen Gravamina gegen den Klerus am Ausgange des Mittelalters und in der Reformationszeit* (1916).
92. The fundamental work on the *gravamina* is B. Gebhardt, *Die gravamina der deutschen Nation gegen den römischen Hof* (2nd ed., 1895). For the origins of the question: W. Michel, *Das Wiener Konkordat vom Jahr 1448 und die nach-folgenden Gravamina des Primarklerus der Mainzer Kirchenprovinz* (diss., Heidelberg, 1929). Also H. Cellarius, "Die Reichsstadt Frankfurt und die Gravamina der deutschen Nation," *Schriften des Vereins für Reformations-geschichte*, 163 (1938).
93. Ed. by H. Koller, *Monumenta Germaniae Historica, Staatsschriften*, 6 (1964). The *Reformatio Sigismundi* has recently been interpreted as strikingly medieval and conservative in character, especially by L. Graf zu Dohna, "Reformatio Sigismundi," *Veröffentlichungen des Max-Planck-Instituts für Geschichte*, 4 (1960). Typical of the widespread overestimation of these reform writings among historians is the completely misleading observa-tion of M. Straube (*Die frühbürgerliche Revolution in Deutschland* [1961], p. 111), that the fact of there having been five printed editions of this writing between 1476 and 1520 proves "that the demands of the *Reformatio Sigismundi* really corresponded with the views of broadest(!) circles of the population in Germany and that they remained influential for may years." Cf. note 62 above.
94. Partial edition by H. Haupt, *Westdeutsche Zeitschrift für Geschichte und Kunst*, Ergänzungsheft, 8 (1893). More recently, though highly unsatis-factorily, O. Eckstein, *Die Reformschrift des sog. oberrheinischen Revolu-tionärs* (diss., Leipzig, 1939). [A complete edition is now available: Gerhard Zschäbitz and Annelore Franke, eds., *Das Buch der Hundert Kapitel und der vierzig Statuten des sogenannten oberrheinischen Revolu-tionärs* (Berlin, 1967).] Even the peasant risings in southwest Germany, which may have been incited by this pamphlet, had many striking feat-ures of medieval church devotion; thus Joss Fritz, after the failure of the rising at Lehen in 1513, went off to Einsiedeln dressed as a pilgrim in order to consecrate the banner of the *Bund* to the Mother of God. Franz, *op. cit.*, p. 74.

95. The best account of the ideas of these men is given by G. Ritter, "Romantische und revolutionäre Elemente in der deutschen Theologie am Vorabend der Reformation," *Deutsche Vierteljahrsschrift für Literaturwissenschaft und Geistesgeschichte*, 5 (1927), 342–80. On Wessel Gansfort, see also Stadelmann, *op. cit.*, *passim*. For the reform writings of the Erfurt Carthusian Johannes Hagen, who was much more restrained in his criticisms, cf. the monograph by J. Klapper, *Der erfurter Kartäuser Johannes Hagen. Ein Reformtheologe des 15. Jahrhunderts*, 2 vols. (Leipzig, 1960–61).

96. Ritter, *op. cit.*, p. 355.

97. Cf. N. Paulus, "Wimpfeling als Verfasser eines Berichts über den Prozess gegen Johann von Wesel," *Zeitschrift für die Geschichte des Oberrheins*, N.F. 42 (1929), 296–300.

98. For fifteenth-century German humanism, see especially G. Ritter, "Die geschichtliche Bedeutung des deutschen Humanismus," *Historische Zeitschrift*, 127 (1923), 393–453; P. Joachimsen, "Loci communes," *Lutherjahrbuch*, 3 (1926), 27–97; O. Herding, "Probleme des frühen Humanismus in Deutschland," *Archiv für Kulturgeschichte*, 38 (1956), 344–89; more recently the valuable and penetrating general account by L. W. Spitz, *The Religious Renaissance of the German Humanists* (Cambridge, Mass., 1963), and my own review of this in *Zeitschrift für Kirchengeschichte*, 76 (1965). Also R. Newald, *Probleme und Gestalten des deutschen Humanismus* (1963), *passim*.

99. B. Moeller, "Die deutschen Humanisten und die Anfänge der Reformation," *Zeitschrift für Kirchengeschichte*, 70 (1959), 46–61.

100. H. E. I. M. van der Velden, *Rudolphus Agricola* (diss., Leiden, 1911), p. 254.

101. D. Roth, *Die mittelalterliche Predigttheorie und das Manuale Curatorum des Johann Ulrich Surgant* (diss., Basel, 1956), p. 179 ff.; D. Meinhardt, *Predigt, Recht und Liturgie* (diss., Göttingen, 1957). Less fruitful: F. Schmidt-Clausing, "Johann Ulrich Surgant," *Zwingliana*, Vol. II, No. 5 (1961), 287–320. Cf. also the assertion of Dehio in *op. cit.*, p. 155, on architecture: "What is traditionally known as Renaissance is nothing but a new cloak beneath which Late Gothic continues to live on unperturbed."

102. For the following cf. esp. O. Vasella, "Untersuchungen über die Bildungsverhältnisse im Bistum Chur," *62. Jahresbericht der Historisch-Antiquarischen Gesellschaft von Graubünden* (1932); *idem*, "Über das Problem der Klerusbildung im 16. Jahrhundert," *Mitteilungen des Instituts für österreichische Geschichtsforschung*, 58 (1950), 441–56; *idem*, "Reform und Reformation in der Schweiz," *Katholisches Leben und Kämpfen im Zeitalter der Glaubensspaltung*, 16 (1958); P. Staerkle, *Beiträge zur spätmittelalterlichen Bildungsgeschichte St. Gallens* (1939); A. Braun, "Der Klerus des Bistums Konstanz im Ausgang des Mittelalters," *Vorreformatorische Forschungen*, 14 (1938); F. W. Oediger, "Über die Bildung der Geistlichen im späten Mittelalter," *Studien und Texte zur Geistesgeschichte des Mittelalters*, 2 (1953); Post, *Kerkelijke verhoudingen*, p. 50 ff. Less informative on this point and what follows is J. Vincke, "Der Klerus des Bistums Osnabrück im späten Mittelalter," *Vorreformatorische Forschungen*, 11 (1928).

103. Oediger, *loc. cit.*, p. 66.

104. *Ibid.* In Holland, according to Post, *op. cit.*, 53, about 20 per cent of candidates for ordination between 1505 and 1518 held an academic degree generally that of *Magister artium.*

105. During the whole of the late Middle Ages there was only one doctor of theology among the parochial clergy of the diocese of Chur: Cf. Vasella, "Untersuchungen," p. 99.

106. Oediger, *loc. cit.*, p. 80 ff.

107. Vasella, "Reform und Reformation," which gives additional literature. Important also is the earlier work of the same author, "Über das Konkubinat des Klerus im Spätmittelalter," *Mélanges Ch. Gilliard* (Lausanne, 1944), pp. 269–83.

108. According to Enea Silvio Piccolomini's *Historia de Europa* (*Opera omnia,* Basel, 1571, p. 429), celibates were tolerated *non facile* in Friesland in order that nuptial beds might not be defiled; a curious piece of information which need not be taken literally.

109. Cf. Rücklin, *loc. cit.*, p. 56 f.; also the fundamental account of F. Flaskamp in *Jahrbuch der Gesellschaft für niedersächsische Kirchengeschichte,* 53 (1960), 128 ff. The same suggestion is made by Vasella, "Über das Konkubinat," p. 275 ff., where reference is made to several generations of clerics living in concubinage. All the same, one must not carry this too far; priestly marriages remained punishable and offspring were deprived of all rights!

110. On the lower Rhine around 1500 these amounted to almost half of all parishes: Oediger, "Niederrheinische Pfarrkirchen um 1500," *Annalen des historischen Vereins für den Niederrhein,* 135 (1939), 32. Similarly in parts of the Netherlands: Post, *loc. cit.*, p. 44. Exact figures for the diocese of Liège in J. Absil, "L'absentéisme du clergé paroissial au diocèse de Liège au XVe siècle et dans la première moitié du XVIe siècle," *Revue d'histoire ecclésiastique,* 57 (1962), 5–44, though this work is not very helpful in connection with the period under consideration here.

111. Cf. F. Falk, *Die pfarramtlichen Aufzeichnungen des Florentius Diel zu St. Christoph in Mainz (1491–1518)* (1904). Also J. B. Götz, *Das Pfarrbuch des Stephan May in Hilpoltstein vom Jahre 1511* (1928), esp. p. 87 ff.

112. There are numerous publications and outlines of fifteenth-century sermons. Cf. (from the last few decades): F. Schäffauer, *loc. cit.*, pp. 516–547; A. Murith, *Jean et Conrad Grütsch de Bâle* (diss., Freiburg, 1940), p. 60 ff.; F. Landmann, *Archiv für elsässische Kirchengeschichte,* NS 2 (1947–48), 205–34; NS 3 (1949–50), 71–98; P. Renner, *Archiv für Kulturgeschichte,* 41 (1959), 201–17; Amon, *op. cit.*, p. 261 ff.; Werlin, *loc. cit.*

113. In 1469 an Augsburg preacher, in a funeral sermon for Cardinal Peter von Schaumberg, quoted the *Corpus iuris* no less than sixty times, with exact references (A. Schröder, *Archiv für die Geschichte des Hochstifts Augsburg,* 6 [1929], 704), though this is a rather extreme example.

114. In the records of Mainz there appears for 1506 a vicarage in Thuringia which appears to have had no fixed income at all and whose incumbent *propter paupertatem aufugit*: *Zeitschrift des Vereins für thüringische Geschichte,* N.F. 2 (1882), 58.

115. H. Eberhardt, *Die Diözese Worms am Ende des 15. Jahrhunderts* (1919), p. 51 f.

116. Marxist historians see the situation the other way round. See M. Steinmetz, *Die frühbürgerliche Revolution*, p. 43, note 73, who states that the religious commotion prior to the Reformation was deliberately provoked by the church for the purpose of "binding the masses to the church and diverting social unrest in a tried and proven way without any danger to the continued existence of the feudal social order."

117. The information given by L. Meier, "Wilsnack als Spiegel deutscher Vorreformation," *Zeitschrift für Religions-und Geistesgeschichte*, 3 (1951), 53–69, about the impotence of the theologians to do anything about the Wilsnack Precious Blood pilgrimage is highly instructive in the present context.

118. The standard work here is that of Paulus, cited in note 40 above. The best specialized study: E. Laslowski, *Beiträge zur Geschichte des spätmittelalterlichen Ablasswesens nach schlesischen Quellen* (1929).

119. Only a very few examples suggest anything else, Surgant (see note 101, above), or the *Epistola de miseria curatorum seu plebanorum* of 1489, printed by A. Werminghoff in *Archiv für Reformationsgeschichte*, 13 (1916), 200–27; or, again, the pastoral concern revealed in the writings investigated by F. Falk, *Die deutschen Mess-Auslegungen von der Mitte des 15. Jahrhunderts bis zum Jahre 1525* (1889).

120. This fact would seem to emerge from J. Löhr's otherwise rather unsatisfactory study, "Methodisch-kritische Beiträge zur Geschichte der Sittlichkeit des Klerus besonders der Erzdiözese Köln am Ausgang des Mittelalters," *Reformationsgeschichtliche Studien und Texte*, 17 (1910).

121. Cf. H. Heimpel, *Archiv für Kulturgeschichte*, 35 (1953), 50.

122. *Analecta Franciscana* 2, Quaracchi (1887), p. 439 f. Cf. also the similar judgment of an Italian after a comparison of divine service in Germany and in his native land, G. Vale, "Itinerario di Paolo Santonino," *Studi e Testi*, 103 (Città del Vaticano, 1943), 195 f. Agrippa of Nettesheim wrote, prior to Luter's emergence: "*Insignes sunt litteratura Itali, navigatione Hispanes, civilitate Galli, religione et mechanicis artificiis Germani.*" Quoted in Stadelmann, *op. cit.*, p. 10, note 3.

123. Heimpel, *loc. cit.*, p. 38.

124. This is not the view of E. W. Zeeden, *Die Entstehung der Konfessionen* (1965), p. 7, who asserts that "no one disputed the necessity of a thoroughgoing reform around 1500" and, "for that very reason Luther found an overwhelming echo."

2 Characteristics of the Late Middle Ages in Germany

HERMANN HEIMPEL

Hermann Heimpel, one of Germany's most distinguished medievalists, was born in 1901. He has taught in the Universities of Freiburg, Leipzig, Strassburg, and—from 1946—Göttingen. He has served as director of the Max Planck Institute for History at Göttingen, and as one of the directors of the Monumenta Germaniae Historica.

THE problem of the late Middle Ages in Germany has formed the subject of a number of studies since Johan Huizinga's well-known book, first published in 1919, appeared in German translation in 1924 under a title which has done much to influence our interpretation of the period: *Herbst des Mittelalters* (*The Waning of the Middle Ages*). A few years later, in 1929, Rudolf Stadelmann wrote his highly original *Vom Geist des ausgehenden Mittelalters* (*The Spirit of the Waning Middle Ages*). The intent of both these works was to sum up the character, mood, and life of an age. Stadelmann examined the signs of decadence he found in fifteenth-century German literature and art, while Huizinga turned to an analysis of the life and ideas of the nobility in France and the Low Countries. In 1932 a descriptive synthesis of the fifteenth and sixteenth centuries in Germany was provided by Willy Andreas in his *Deutschland vor der Reformation*. Andreas included political life, neglected by earlier writers, in his synthesis, and worked it into an impressionistic and finely shaded portrait of a "turning point" that lived in anticipation of its ultimate "reformation." The *Weltgeschichte Europas*, published by Hans Freyer in 1948, contained

Paper read before the Kant-Gesellschaft of Munich, September 1949. The present altered version appeared in the *Mainzer Akademie der Wissenschaften und der Literatur* (July 1952).

a chapter on the "Gothic world" which embraced the whole of European and trans-European life. Freyer took in a more extensive span of time than his predecessors. He named the period stretching from high scholasticism to the great geographical discoveries "the realm of reason"; during this period the earth "became round" and the final blow was dealt to the classical-medieval system to which, in Freyer's opinion, the Gothic world from the thirteenth century to the sixteenth still adhered. My own interest will, in the present essay, be confined to the late Middle Ages and in one country only: Germany.

I shall try to discover the terminal dates of the "late Middle Ages," and to define their distinguishing features. In presenting my argument, I shall take it for granted that history can be divided into specific periods, that each of these periods possesses a historical identity, and that the problems of particular periods form a legitimate object of historical investigation.[1] I shall assume, moreover, that the so-called Middle Ages constitute a real historical period,[2] stretching from the Germanic tribal migrations to the Protestant Reformation, a genuine civilization, a world, composed of the remains of classical antiquity and of such new elements as a hierarchically organized Christianity, and a politically active nobility. These are, of course, historical contentions which my essay will have to prove. In any case, the publication of W.-E. Peuckert's book *Die grosse Wende* (*The Great Turning Point*) in 1948 made a renewed analysis of the entire problem of the late Middle Ages in Germany almost mandatory.[3] Peuckert's book may therefore serve as the point of departure for my own effort.

The late Middle Ages in Germany have often been seen as a general period of transition and the years around 1500, in particular, as a great and crucial turning point of medieval society. This view is also found in Willy Andreas's volume, as its very title makes clear. Peuckert, however, replaces the descriptive approach taken by Andreas with an attempt to prove the argument concerning the *grosse Wende* with the aid of evidence taken from folklore, sociology, and comparative religion. Peuckert adopts the synoptic view of the universal historian, setting the period in the line of present and future development; and describing cultures in terms of those groups and classes that manifest them. He thus distinguishes between a pre-peasant culture, a peasant culture proper, and, finally, a culture of urban burgher classes—the latter now approaching its end and being replaced by a proletarian culture still in the process of formation. He characterizes the peasant and burgher cultures according to their religious germs as being, respectively, mythological and rational. For our present purpose it is significant that Peuckert synchronizes these two mythological and rational cultures with the traditional epochs that have been customary with historians. He, too, speaks of a "modern age" and of the "Middle Ages," and to this extent at least he admits the validity of epochal divisions in history. But this equation of sociological categories and historical periods forces him, in this instance, to take the "Middle Ages" as the era of peasant culture, "peasant" meaning here "old" or "medieval"; while the "modern world" is seen to represent all that is "new," urban, and "bourgeois." The great changeover from Middle Ages to modern world in other words, all the events of the late Middle Ages and their final culmination in the Reformation—is tantamount to the death of the rural, medieval world and the birth of the burgher class, the modern world.

At first glance, historians would seem to have excellent reason to accept Peuckert's analysis. They are encouraged to do so by the great skill and tact with which Peuckert associates the two cultures, allowing the later gradually to grow out of the earlier instead of making them follow abruptly one upon the other. The new culture, urban, middle-class, rational, had been "co-existing for years and even for centuries with the old one;" it "was there from the very beginning, but had had to take second place to the dominant culture." We read with approval that "the burgher had once been a peasant himself: age-old ideas, institutions, and beliefs taken from the pre-urban age, came, once within city-walls, to be transformed into bourgeois values, which means that the rural heritage continued to live on among the burghers." Another reason for agreeing with Peuckert's train of thought is the new dimension of historical depth imparted by his folkloristic approach. Historians, after all, have every reason to entertain doubts and suspicions about their own methods. Their source material is largely taken from the special little world of chronicles, documents and official records. There is no reason to doubt that, while historians scale the peaks of church and governments and contemplate constitutional developments and economic trends, they fail to reach down to the everday life of ordinary people.

On Peuckert's terms we are therefore very much inclined to approve when medieval kings are called "peasant kings" (even though this is not more than half the story), whether the "peasant king" be Frederick III in the fifteenth century, or the Merovingians in the fifth, moving cross-country on their oxcarts, bestowing the *Ernteheil*, the harvest-blessing, according to the countryman's belief. And, to the extent that we can still, in our own time, observe the peasant world in its death throes, we may agree also when Peuckert identifies the folk religion of the Middle Ages, with its relic worship, its consecrations and blessings, its efficacious signs, its amulets and its *Längen Christi* as a peasant religion. And we note with approval that Peuckert sees the fifteenth century as a time of preparation for the Reformation when the religion of the faithful in city and country alike was not (as so many history books are fond of repeating) an "externalized" rite and nothing more, and when he affirms that, despite the many signs of decadence in the life and constitution of the church it is possible to trace the religious sentiment of the fifteenth century back to the Merovingian world of the first millennium.

This impression of the Middle Ages as a rural world is corroborated by the events leading up to the Peasants' War. It was the peasant who gave ear and voice to the age-old hope in a savior emperor, an eschatological Frederick, a Messiah-ruler who would one day establish peace and justice upon earth, riding out of the Black Forest on his white horse. Peasants were prepolitical and nonpolitical, they were alien and hostile to the pragmatic mentality of city and state. Conservative revolutionaries, they fought for the old law, and held fast to the imperial idea, to the empire in its timeless, politically obsolete form, inseparable from the person of the emperor. Opposed to all this were the objective, calculating, rational attempts of the Estates during the fifteenth century to achieve imperial reform in a direction opposed to the emperor, in the style of Nicholas of Cusa. It is possible to grant Peuckert the contention that these attempts were dominated by a cast of thought foreign to the peasant mind, by a pragmatic mentality which one might label middle class, as exemplified in the declaration of the burghers of Strassburg in August 1473 that, though they belonged to the empire, they would not pay homage to the emperor. Equally objective, modern, and therefore opposed to peasant ideas are the policies of Frederick III for promoting his territorial state and his dynastic interests.

If we turn our attention from the old world of the countryside to the new world of the cities we can be in no doubt that the later Middle Ages in Germany witnessed a time when life took on an extremely urban character. The bourgeoisie and burgher ideas made a good deal of progress, and the pace of this development increased during the course of the fourteenth century. We need only cast our mind's eye to the statue of Emperor Charles IV by the Brückentorturm in Old Prague, stripping it of crown and orb, and what do we have left but a cobbler sitting at his bench, putting a shoe over the last! Is it not obvious that the great German hall churches are structures erected by and for prosperous middle-class burghers,[4] buildings in which the citizenry was the congregation, heard the sermons, endowed the multitude of chantries and donated altar benefices? Peuckert rightly points out that even the political enterprises of the princes during the fifteenth century came to a very large extent into the hands of burgher politicians, as exemplified by their bourgeois pragmatism and their middle-class eye for profit. Under Rudolf of Habsburg high offices had been held by tradesmen's sons only in very exceptional cases: Heinrich Knoderer of Isny, for example, or Konrad, Bishop of Toul, a smith's son from Mainz. But a century and a half later we have Kaspar Schlick, the chancellor of Emperor Sigismund, King Albert, and King Frederick; Martin Mair, a politician in imperial, Bohemian, and Bavarian service; Gregor

Heimburg, a specialist in antipapal policies; and Peter Knorr, counsellor to Albert of Hohenzollern, and these men signify the character of their age. Meanwhile the world had moved from the Minnesinger to the Mastersinger, from symbolism to realism, from a vertical society to a horizontal one—a move very largely in the direction of an urban middle-class society. The old hierarchical order of Estates and values was enriched rather than destroyed by the rise of the burgher class; all the same, it was exposed to disquieting new disturbances. And one more point: the bourgeoisie in the German cities was undoubtedly of the greatest importance for the development of humanism.

After so much agreement it is time to ask whether Peuckert's sociological categories of peasant cultures and burgher cultures, together with their respective religious associations as "mythological" and "rational," really get to the heart of the late medieval period in Germany as a distinct, individual period of history, and, especially, can we say that the outcome of the fifteenth century and the Reformation really was a burgher culture? When Peuckert speaks of the bourgeoisie as the cause and harbinger of the new culture of later centuries he seems to be referring only to the artisan class, to guild members, with the result that he depends for his evidence on a broad discussion of the journeyman literature of Shrovetide plays and farces with their boorish mockery of peasant life. It seems to me that this is casting the social net rather too low on the ground. Rowdy journeymen—most of them nothing more than vulgar yokels ready to abuse the villages from which they had only just escaped—were not identical with the civic bourgoisie of the late medieval German municipality. Nor had they much in common with master artisans, who were, by and large, refined, dignified and peaceful men. The builders of Ulm Cathedral and the middle-class prebends of Strassburg Minster were not the gravediggers of what we call the German Middle Ages, but count among their most typical representatives.

Up to a point Peuckert is right in distinguishing the patriciate from the artisan class and in considering the former as belonging, to some extent, to the peasant-noble culture. The members of the

Konstaffeln, that is, the patricians, of Strassburg and Zürich were connected with the nobility by ties of family and intellectual interests; the patricians of Nuremberg aspired no less to the knightly tournament than did their opposite numbers in Florence; and Jakob Fugger received his patent of nobility with eager appreciation. But despite all its connections with the nobility, the urban patriciate was essentially a commercial, moneyed, and success-oriented class of councillors and officeholders, a civic estate capable of providing a city like Nuremberg with generations of political leaders, closely bound up with a wholly medieval ecclesiastical life of endowments, hospital administration, admissions to monasteries and convents, and pious bequests.

Arnold Reimann has given us a description of such an urban patrician tradition from the fourteenth century to the sixteenth in his history of the ancestors of the humanist Willibald Pirckheimer.[5] On the other hand, the patriciate was a status which could be gained or lost in the most burgherly way possible. For Regensburg—to give just one instance—it can be shown that if a man's fortune sank below a certain level or he had sustained severe business reverses, he lost his seat on the council and was forced to step down into the common citizenry.[6] The immediate implication of this is that the bourgeoisie did not overcome the Middle Ages but was itself an element of the Middle Ages, whether in its capacity as guild members, or as a patriciate. In other words the late medieval period remained genuinely medieval.

Before drawing the conclusions from my counterthesis it would be well to make a few more critical observations. Quite apart from its more general assumptions, the view that the civic bourgeoisie burst through the framework of the Middle Ages suffers from a tacit identification of bourgeoisie and reason. Now, this identification is correct and evident insofar as the burgher class did incline toward an objective, sober, calculating, pragmatic realism, and hence toward rationality. In its later history it was, indeed, to become the class of the Enlightenment. Historically speaking, however, it is a mistake to identify the bourgeoisie with rationality. The medieval world had a rationality all its own, which had nothing to do with the middle class as a social factor. Thus Freyer is perfectly right when he declares that the old prerational era of the "kingdom of God" was followed by an "age of reason" in the Gothic era; and when saying this, he is not merely referring to the bourgeoisie and its way of life. It might perhaps be said that this simply puts Peuckert two hundred years out in his reckoning, since—to go back to our former example—the early medieval idea of kingship, drawing partly on its own powers and partly on magical sources, was precisely what Peuckert would have described as an archetype of peasant life. Its real antagonist was the urban burgher class, at least from the twelfth century in Italy. But that was in Italy. Taking European medieval society as a whole, it seems clear that the great check to the old kingly principle was not the bourgeoisie, but the internal development of the church. Medieval rationality originated in the bosom of the church; in fact, it had been implicit in the church's very nature from the beginning. Canon law itself was a product of *ratio*, as was the church's concept of *idoneitas*, or appropriateness. This idea of passing rational judgment upon a ruler's suitability had long (certainly since the eleventh century) been wearing down the old principle of kingship based on a belief in the power of blood. In other words, here we have the real opponent of what Peuckert calls the mythologically oriented peasant culture. Rationality did not dissolve the Middle Ages any more than the middle classes dissolved the Middle Ages. Rationality was, in fact, part and parcel of the Middle Ages. The rationality of antiquity, the Greek *logos* that is to say, was preserved in the church and in some of the political institutions of the early Middle Ages as well, as Theodor Mayer has recently pointed out.[7] There are such things as transmissions of continuity in spiritual and intellectual matters from one age to another, and this process imposes limits to the folkloristic and sociological view of history. The medieval edifice certainly had rural foundations; but one should not just look at the cellar and ignore the upper stories.

An even more serious flaw in Peuckert's theory of a peasant Middle Ages and a bourgeois modernity is the following: The theory fails in the realm of politics which is, of course, precisely the realm of hard facts and of the germs of development. If Peuckert is to be believed, the new bourgeois phase in fifteenth-century German history brought to an end not only the empire, but the state as well. Peuckert sees no difference between empire and state. We read in his book that both empire and state were falling to pieces—on p. 350, in fact, we learn that "man, now the creature of bourgeois culture, attempted to throw off the old patriarchal political order of the medieval monarchy, since the sovereignty of the prince had no longer a logical place in his civic bourgeois world." Unfortunately, not a single word of all this will stand up to examination. Peuckert is here identifying factors which might, and often do, coincide, but which do not neces-sarily belong together and in historical fact did not go together at all, namely, empire and state, patriarchal system and the political order, monarchy and sovereignty.

I am aware that the power aggregates of the fourteenth and fifteenth centuries, which might at a pinch be called "states," had certain patriarchal features—I mean the paternal feudalism of the manor, the liege lord, and the *Landesvater*.[8] I also know that Albert of Brandenburg, a working prince if ever there was one, was still very much an exception compared with such leisure-time rulers as Ludwig of Landshut. Bourgeois contemporaries of such princely playboys may well have looked on them as relics of a bygone era upon whom middle-class counsellors and forward-looking legal advisers were trying to impress a modicum of reason and discipline. But such subjective reactions of contemporaries should not be accorded unlimited trust, especially when it is also possible to find opinions on the other side. It is simply not true that, as Peuckert claims on p. 309, contemporaries were "in a better position to understand the real condition of the empire than the modern historian." Quite the contrary is true. "Mommsen knows Roman history better than Livy." Frederick the Victorious of the Palatinate, Archbishop Dieter of Mainz, Albert of Branden-burg and even, despite his penchant for tournaments, Louis the Rich of Bavaria, would have been surprised and rightly indignant if they had heard themselves described by us as representatives of a bygone era. It was, after all, they who gave employment to Martin Mair and his colleagues. They were the ones who subjected cities like Mainz and Donauwörth to their territorial authority in order to round off, and thus rationalize, their territories. In fact, they came within an ace of finishing off for good and all the so-called "new" middle class, which is to say that they nearly put an end to the old-established freedom of the cities.

From the political viewpoint the modern world in Germany began just as it did in the rest of Europe—whether in the Italy of the Medici and the Sforza, the Burgundy of Philip and Charles or the France of Louis XI—under the auspices not of the bourgeoisie and of urban independence, but of prince and territorial state, and it is absolutely fatal for Peuckert's arguments that the cultural historian's approach which he adopts finds no place for the crucial factor of the territorial state. One might even venture to suggest the formulation that the fourteenth century was more bourgeois than the fifteenth. Sovereignty, after all, and the entire concept of "state," have nothing to do with the old age insofar as this was "peasant-oriented." In the fifteenth century this sover-eignty was a thing neither of the past nor of the present. It was a princely daydream of a desirable and tempting future. Charles the Bold of Burgundy dreamed of this, and so did his ally Frederick of the Palatinate. If the cities stood in the way of this vision of princely sovereignty, it was not because they represented the power of the future, but because they were formidable citadels of the past, every bit as tenacious in their attachment to long-cherished rights as any peasant community clinging to its ancient usages. The laws and customs of cities were among the most ancient of medieval privileges. They were relics of the feudal order, pieces of the purest medievalism. City freedoms were old rights struggling against the new politics. The empire of Frederick III may have grown "weak, old, and imbecile," but the emperor himself belonged to the new type of princely politician. He was slow, he was passive, but while he passed his time playing with his collection of precious stones he also gained the Burgundian inheritance for his son and laid the foundations for the imperial power ultimately assumed by Charles V. With all his weaknesses and shortcomings Frederick was a politician of the new state occupying the throne of the old empire. Politically, then, it was the ruling princes of the empire, and not the civic bourgeoisie, who put an end to the Middle Ages and brought on the modern era.

Moreover, what I have been saying about politics applies equally to the great turning point in the realm of ideas. The bourgeoisie's final triumph over princes and nobility did not come until the great revolution of 1789; Leibniz, Haydn, Mozart, and Goethe all had to serve in the households or governments of princes. In his chapter on Luther, Peuckert himself furnishes abundant proof that nothing came of the bourgeoisie in the sixteenth century. It goes without saying that the cities adopted the new doctrine more readily than the countryside—they were on the move, they had schools, they were open to new ideas. But the Protestant doctrine itself—though it would be stretching things a bit to describe it in extreme sociological terms as peasant-oriented and anti-urban— was most certainly not "bourgeois." Luther was not a tolerant man, as Nicholas of Cusa, for example, had been. He anathematized free will which, for Erasmus of Rotterdam, the patron-scholar of the Western European middle classes, was the highest good. Reason, the burgher's goddess, he called a whore. Unlike the urban bourgeois, Luther was no moralist. And did the "great turning point" usher in an age of reason and tolerance? It did not. Instead, it brought in an era of denominations and of religious wars conducted by political rulers. If a concrete example is needed, there is one readily to be found in the history of humanistic education in Germany. Franz Schnabel[9] has shown that, while in England a determined middle-class utilitarianism set itself in opposition to the humanistic aristocratic colleges, the German humanist schools of Melanchthon created intellectual and scholarly disciplines that rose *pari passu* with the middle class. "Between the so-called optimates, on the one hand, men whose only pride was in their privileges and who had no need of real merits, and the untaught masses on the other hand, a new class of the 'middle' was to arise, a class of men who would attain success only as a result of their own abilities and efforts." But Schnabel also showed how short-lived this association of middle class and learning was to be. At Johann Sturm's gymnasium in Strassburg the connection began to break down even during Melanchthon's lifetime, and "with the abandonment of the strict principle of humanistic pedagogy during the seventeenth century . . . the privileges of birth became once again decisive." Just as the European middle classes needed the great Revolution to triumph over nobility and clergy, civic burgherdom in Germany needed a "second human-ism" in the style of Wilhelm von Humboldt.

Before turning now from criticism to a positive description of what we have called the late Middle Ages in Germany, we should remind ourselves of the debt we owe to Peuckert for his many concrete observations. His thesis of the bourgeoisie's triumph over tural medieval civilization, is wrong only if it is taken as literal historical truth. Medieval burgherdom was indeed a new force; its unassuming beginnings go back to the thirteenth century; but its hour of real triumph did not come until the eighteenth. It did not come until then because, quite apart from the tenacity of the nobility as such, the monarchical state and Luther's own distinc-tive character impeded and, in part, absorbed a powerful burgher movement in late medieval Germany. Historical epochs and categories of folklore cannot be so easily synchronized.

A number of concrete facts gives the late medieval period in Germany its distinctive consistency, as well as a certain degree of unity. These facts make Germany appear to be an especially "medieval" country, and make the late Middle Ages a character-istically German period. The principal fact which brought the German late Middle Ages into being was the collapse of the empire of the Hohenstaufens. To say this is, of course, to invite immediate argument. A "political" fact, it will be said, is being used to mark the beginning of a period whose unity was surely cultural. But let me explain. When I refer to the end of the Hohenstaufens

I mean an event that led to the formation of a system of states and brought about the fragmentation of Germany into small power structures. I mean the period during which the king of the Romans, as ruler over his dynastic domains, became nothing more than one sovereign among many. It is true that both these developments, European and German alike, were well under way long before the death of Frederick II. For centuries there had been nations and states whose history was in all senses remote from the empire. Moreover, recent constitutional studies will serve us as a reminder that the constitutional history of Germany at that time cannot be summed up simply as the progressive decline of an imperial power which under the Hohenstaufen emperors had been at its zenith. The roots of territorial sovereignty are not to be found in the late Hohenstaufen period, nor in political measures taken by Emperor Frederick II; they reach back far into the early Middle Ages. From the very outset there had been indigenous forces at work against the principle of monarchical rule. The feudal character of the Holy Roman Empire was not a *late* medieval phenomenon; it was a medieval one. Furthermore, the restorative character of the Hohenstaufen empire might mislead us into thinking that the end of the time of the Hohenstaufens marked the beginning of the late Middle Ages in Germany. "Imperial reform," after all, was an overriding issue under the Hohenstaufens; its object: the re-establishment of an empire that had experienced the catastrophe of Canossa. In that experience the king had lost his battle against the princes, as well as against the pope, and the dominion of sovereign and nobles over the church—the fundamental principle of the older empire—had been fatally damaged. It was restoration and it was reform when Frederick Barbarossa and his successors resumed the struggle with the Roman Church. It was reform when Henry VI planned to put the imperial succession on a hereditary basis, and thus keep it in line with the hereditary succession at work in secular principalities. With its restorative and reformative character the era of the Hohenstaufens was, therefore, despite the blossoming of its literature, itself a late period; and when it is remembered that the new

era marked by the personality of Innocent III succeeded immediately upon the death of Henry VI it will be realized all the more
clearly how the history of Frederick II was simply an epilogue to
the golden age of the medieval empire.

Ultimately, however, none of these considerations can keep us
from seeing the middle of the thirteenth century as the opening of
the late Middle Ages in Germany. Other nations and rulers may
have lived altogether independently of the Holy Roman Empire,
but the altercations between pope and emperor had been a
struggle of universal historical significance, and the antagonists
themselves had laid down the rules of the game. But it is here that
the decisive change came in the thirteenth century. The duality of
pope and emperor persisted, unity and dichotomy continued to
define the traditional powers; in fact, under Louis the Bavarian
the dispute flared up once more in the fourteenth century. But
quite apart from the fact that *imperium* and *sacerdotium* had both
undergone internal changes, the rules of the game were no longer
dictated by pope and emperor. They had been very largely taken
over by France. A French era definitely opened for Europe in 1268,
when Charles of Anjou ended the Hohenstaufen cause with the
execution of Konradin. This Charles of Anjou, the French ruler
of Sicily, dominated European politics to the moment of his death
and overshadowed the beginnings, and even the climax, of the
reign of Rudolf of Habsburg. In 1285, the very year in which the
French tyrant of Sicily died, Philip the Fair began his reign as king
of France, and in the years to come the center of France's European
hegemony shifted from Naples to Paris. The assault on Boniface
VIII in Anagni in 1303, the removal of the curia from Rome to
Avignon in 1305, and the moves, beginning in 1307, to besmirch
the late Bonifice VIII and the Templars—all these were stages in
the development of the French preponderance, the era of Avignon.

Avignon allowed no part of the contemporary Western world
to escape its authority. Aragon, the most modern state of the
century, took up the struggle against the Angevins in lower Italy
and won it in Sicily. The history of Hungary was dominated by
the mutual opposition of indigenous forces and the foreign hege-

mony of Germany and France. Italy and its early Renaissance—one thinks of Dante, Rienzo, Petrarch, and Catherine of Sienna— were drawn by Avignon into the struggle against foreign domination, which was no longer German but French. The moment German hegemony in Europe was transformed into French domination, French diplomatic and political hostilities began to determine Europe's affairs, and for Germany this was a fatal turn of events. Under Philip the Fair, France's struggle against her English vassal broke out anew. Just as, in 1214, the dispute between Hohenstaufen and Guelph had been settled on the Anglo-French battlefield of Bouvines, so now Anglo-French antagonisms were to govern the decisions of German kings from Rudolf of Habsburg onward. In fact, I think it is possible to distinguish among German monarchs according to whether they took the French or the English option: Adolf of Nassau opted for England, Albrecht of Habsburg for France, and, in later years, Louis of Bavaria for England and Charles IV once again for France. The only ruler to try to assert the old imperial freedom of decision was Henry VII; but he came to grief against Avignon, against France, and against the house of Anjou. His lawsuits against Robert of Naples were manifestoes in the style of the old imperial concept. Robert's manifestoes, on the other hand, were revisionary proceedings against Henry VII's attempt to revive the old alliance of the imperial tradition of ancient Rome with the German monarchical principle and old Germanic law. The Angevin case was conducted with all the refinements of ecclesiastical natural and rational law combined with Guelphism, Avignonese papalism and French nationalism.

France did not cease to impose its law upon Europe or upon Germany; though it was not really necessary for France to be anxious about her choice of actions, considering the traditions which had established themselves in Europe. All these traditions— Guelphism, the growth of learning, the development of the state—represented the revolution against the Holy Roman Empire, against the Roman *imperium* exercised by the Germans. Given this context, it is possible to describe the particular position of Germany, that is to say of the late Middle Ages in Germany, in terms of the German response to this new era. The response I refer to is characterized by conservatism and historicism (*Historismus*) as these developed in Germany during the thirteenth, fourteenth, and fifteenth centuries. Another way of summarizing this medieval German conservatism and historicism is to describe it as a reflection of the peculiar indetermination (*Unentschiedenheit*) which plagued German affairs and German thought in the late Middle Ages. It was precisely this indetermination, this vacillation between the old and the new, which distinguished the late Middle Ages in Germany. This is true not only in the realm of politics; it is true also of the more general cultural structure of Germany between the end of the Hohenstaufen period and the onset of the Reformation. Other nations, remote from the empire and free from the liability of its legacy, were able to construct a theoretical basis for their government and institutions, and to work out an inner legality for them, availing themselves in the process of all the advantages of religious and juridical legitimation, for example, the *Gesta Dei per Francos* and the "Mirror of Princes" with their political ideas drawn from Aristotelianism and natural law.[10]

Germany, on the contrary, made her entrance into the era of the national state fatally inhibited by her need to legitimize her national existence as an empire—in other words, according to the tradition of her past. This meant that, even where she was seeking new solutions, Germany remained bogged down in her own internal controversy with her imperial past. This it was that gave the history of the late medieval empire its half-real, dreamlike character and its air of illusoriness. Germany's increasingly rarefied imperial ideology was identical with the prepolitical idea of empire to be found in the peasant world, though it was present also, and to a very large extent, among the city folk. We have already referred to this; it is the late medieval image of the emperor described by Peuckert. All that is needed to put these generalizations into clearer focus is to have a look at certain works on the political theory of the empire written during the late Middle Ages. Needless to say, even in Germany there existed a body of literature suggested by the *Politics* of Aristotle—a literature, in other words, whose arguments were directed toward the self-sufficient state and its rational justification. But in comparison with other countries, particularly the Mediterranean countries, German Aristotelians are of very minor importance. Even Marsiglio of Padua— whose revolutionary, antipapal *Defensor Pacis* was based in theory on the *Politics* of Aristotle, and in practice on its author's experiences in the Italian city-state—exercised strikingly little influence in Germany,[11] and this though Marsiglio was one of the literary champions of Emperor Louis of Bavaria in the struggle against Avignon, and even though the years around 1400 (the time of the Western schism and the conciliar movement) resuscitated many of the writings produced by members of Louis's circle. It is true that there are a number of German manuscripts of the *Defensor Pacis*. Two of these, commissioned by the Neithart family, a patrician dynasty of Ulm, seem to show that the German middle classes did have some interest in such tracts which, although antipapal, were altogether alien to the ancient emperor idea. But quotations from Marsiglio's work, though they should have been brought forth in abundance during the conciliar period, were, in fact, a rarity; and even the few passages we do have largely left the real substance of his political theory—his doctrine of the state—untouched. Again, a true Aristotelian such as the eclectic and conservative abbot of Admont, Engelbert of Vokersdorf, was not really representative of German political thought in the late Middle Ages.[12] On the other hand, there is no disputing the permanent influence of Alexander of Roes in the thirteenth century, of Lupold of Bebenburg in the fourteenth, and of Nicholas of Cusa in the fifteenth; and these three political thinkers of late medieval Germany were conservative historians rather than Aristotelian philosophers.

It was the mission of Alexander of Roes to assert the claims of the old against the new (and to him the "new" was identical with France), or at least to preserve as much of the old as possible within the new. Alexander, canon of Cologne in the time of Rudolf of Habsburg, still moved completely in the old monarchical idea. Emotionally he lived in the Ottonian and Franconian era; even the Hohenstaufen emperors were nothing more to this imperial patriot than Swabian kings preoccupied with their dynastic affairs and hence distasteful. Alexander was active in the time of the practical-minded Rudolf of Habsburg, the friend of the urban classes, but he was totally unwilling to make his peace with the emerging political order based on the equality of nation-states, which to his mind were monstrosities paving the way for the coming of Antichrist. To him the Germans were still the true knights of Christendom, holders of a universal office, the *imperium*. It was only out of a sense of justice that he accorded to the other grat European peoples, the Italians and the French, the offices of *Sacerdotium* and of the *Studium*, the papacy and learning.[13]

In Alexander there lived on a surviving remnant of that old, pre-political—and ultimately pre-Christian—spirit which had led the Emperor Frederick to write, when causing the relics of Elizabeth of Thuringia to be deposited in a precious shrine in the year 1236, "that none but the hands of nobles are to touch the ark of the covenant." But—and this is the important point in my present context—the reasons given by Alexander for Germany's universal vocation were purely historical ones. For Alexander, the German right to the *imperium* had to be deduced from Roman, Frankish, Germanic, and French history.[14] It might seem rather bold to suggest that the Germans, unlike other nations, tend to base their arguments not on Aristotelian, scholastic deductive processes, but on history; but Alexander of Roes is not the only example that can be cited as evidence for this contention. His conservative approach was of the greatest significance for the character of the late Middle Ages in Germany; manuscripts and translations of his works, and excerpts taken from them, can be found in plenty throughout the whole of the fourteenth century and during the early part of the fifteenth. In 1433, Nicholas of Cusa devoted the third book of his *Concordantia Catholica* to the subject of imperial reform. Nicholas, too, begins by asserting that help for the ailing empire could come only from a return to the old, traditional, "well-trodden" ways.

It is revealing for our interpretation of the late Middle Ages in Germany that this same Nicholas of Cusa, whose writings on mathematics, astronomy, and the philosophy of religion were so independent of preconceived ideas, came, when he turned to politics, to depend on history and the evocation of the traditional past. His proposals for the imperial courts, the electoral council, the diet, and the imperial cities; even his antagonism to the princes—these were all motivated by his attachment to German history as he understood it. The picture of Germany before his mind's eye was basically the empire as he imagined it to have been at the time of the Saxon emperors. In this discovery of Otto the Great and the Ottonians he had been preceded at the beginning of the fifteenth century by a lesser intellect, the Westphalian Dietrich of Niem, whose writings and, in particular, whose historical knowledge, have come to be seen in a new light as a result of recent investigations.[15] Dietrich's deep ties to the historical developments that took place during the Middle Ages make him for us a newly discovered witness to the continuity of early and late Middle Ages. But the discovery of the Ottonians was tantamount to the discovery of German history, for it replaced the founder myth of Charlemagne with a real ancestral history; and this history provided the model for the hoped-for reform of empire and church. The discovery of German history as a formative idea is an achievement of the late Middle Ages.

The most unmistakable example, however, of history-minded conservatism, as well as of the indeterminateness in Germany during this period, is a political thinker who stood halfway between Alexander of Roes and Nicholas of Cusa: Lupold of Bebenburg, Bishop of Bamberg.[16] Lupold's treatise on kingdom and empire of 1340 defended the freedom of the electors to choose the emperor and the right of the king of the Romans, Louis of Bavaria, to the imperial crown. Since the pope based his claim to the right of approval over the election of the king of the Romans on the theoretical subordination of *imperium* to *sacerdotium*, simultaneously associating this subordination with his right to crown the emperor, every proponent of an autonomous empire independent from the papacy had to define the relationship between *regnum* (that is, the German Empire as pertaining to the rights of the German electors) and *imperium* (the empire as pertaining to Rome and the papacy in the imperial coronation). Lupold argued for the restriction of the papal rights by citing a body of proof that really amounted to a whole history of Germany. German history was for him a variation of the history of Charlemagne, and it led him to understand the concept of empire in three distinct senses. *Regnum* meant the German Empire (*Reich*), Charlemagne's legacy. In the *regnum*, in Aachen, the electors chose the German king without asking leave of the pope. In the *imperium*, too, the king of the Romans reigned independently of the pope. In Burgundy and Italy, in Arles, Milan, and Rome he presided over the *administratio imperii*, the maintenance of those imperial rights which Louis the Bavarian had stated in 1323 and which had aroused the opposition of Avignon. On the other hand, the rights of the king of the Romans in the *imperium* extended only as far as the area of Charlemagne's conquests; these rights were, therefore, "irrational," as there was no question of any rational legitimization in the sense of a *translatio imperii*. It was a matter of rights by conquest and history. The third sphere, for Lupold, lay beyond this historically attained *imperium*. It was the *imperium* in the widest sense, which the pope had taken from the Greeks and conferred upon Charlemagne, the legitimate and eternally valid *translatio imperii*. This alone was the *imperium* as the universal office bestowed by the pope at the time of the imperial coronation.

Before concluding this account of the late Middle Ages in Germany as a period of indeterminateness between the old and the new, it would be well to have a look at the life of the German people taken as the whole populace. The history of the German people, like the history of the empire itself, remained rooted in the twilight world between the past and the present. But if we go in search of the basic factors of popular history which characterized the late Middle Ages in Germany, we shall find in them the close combination of two phenomena: the so-called colonization of eastern Germany, that is to say German expansion into the lands east of the Elbe and Saale, and, secondly, the development of cities and burgher Estates. Both created new achievements, and, at the same time, preserved old traditions. Both played a part in generating the characteristic indeterminateness of the late Middle Ages. And both phenomena helped to mark off the period from the thirteenth to the beginning of the sixteenth century as an historical unity in Germany.

To begin with, let us realize that a colonizing movement could hardly fail to create new forms of existence. Men and families who migrated east were drawn by the freedom that the new lands seemed to offer them. They went to shake off old ties and outworn obligations. They received charters containing new liberties. Insofar as these new liberties expunged the old inequality of rights that existed under feudalism they brought modern features to the areas of colonial settlement. Freedom gradually coalesced into political unity; it was easier, by and large, for the territorial principality, the unitary state, to develop in the east than in the west. Historians have always regarded the territorial state of the Teutonic Order in Prussia as the great symbol of this new system. The *Kulmer Handfeste*—the grand privileges of the city of Kulm— the rights granted by the Teutonic Order to the cities of Kulm and Thorn in 1233, and later on widely extended, contained a paragraph in which the order voluntarily, and in perpetuity, renounced all rights and intentions of buying member houses in those cities. We can take it as an act of self-imposed political renunciation, and as a sign of realistic pragmatism characteristic of the growing modern state, that the order also proposed to create in its territories a uniform system of urban law in order to establish and protect civic communities which were to offer no room to those clerical immunities, which generally served as the last refuge for relics of feudalism in the cities of medieval Germany. In the event that, by means of a donation, a house in one of the named cities should come to the order, the privilege determined that the house must continue to fulfill all its due obligations to the city.

The voluntary contractor of obligations in this case was the new state, the east German colonial state.

Without question this new political entity in the trans-Elbian flatlands makes a less colorful picture than the system of immunities parceled out in old Germany among sovereigns, knights, cities, and the church, with their motley array of special privileges, rights, freedoms, and prerogatives. Owners of village hides in the order's territories had a standardized service to render to their sovereigns, based on the fact of possession—in other words, a service exacted by provincial law; and this again was a "modern" step away from the feudal system. Another example of this trend in the Kulm privilege is its standardization of coins and the official adoption of the Flemish hide measure.

Ever since Heinrich von Treitschke, therefore, historians have not wearied of extolling the government of the Teutonic Order as that of a modern administrative state and of comparing it with Sicily under Frederick II and with modern Prussia. Erich Caspar, however, has shown another side of the picture, namely, the medieval and obsolescent qualities still in evidence in the lands of the order.[17] The state of the Teutonic knights was run by an ecclesiastical order, and was therefore an anachronism. It flourished at a time when the crusading ideal—on which it had been founded—had elsewhere long ceased to express itself in political organization. The Teutonic Order, the last of all the knightly foundations, remained longer than any other an order dedicated to doing battle against the heathen; long after Acre had fallen a medieval crusader state continued to function in the new German territories on the Baltic. But this state had been more "modern" in the thirteenth century than it was in the fifteenth. In its fight for its very existence against Lithuanians and Poles, it had had to take into account the fact that the land had become filled with a nobility engaged in agriculture and military service, as well as with powerful burgher communities. Thus, it was ultimately forced to give way to a political system of divergent constituted interests of the sort characteristic of the late medieval state in Germany. But if we look at the picture as a whole we should remember the caveat of Hermann Aubin, that it is one-sided and inadequate to call the settlement of the eastern regions of Germany a movement of "colonization."[18] For this new territory received not only elements of medieval German economic forces, but also the medieval German culture. The feudal structure of state and church, territorial sovereignty, provincial diets and unions of Estate—none of these was missing in the east. This is equally true of the cities of the east. They sheltered the houses of old and new orders, and they went through all the controversies over clerical immunity and jurisdiction. They felt the same pull of interests between merchant patriciate and craft guilds as did the cities of the older west. Market law and municipal law were distributed equally in west and east; and despite local variations they brought to the whole of Germany its uniform, late medieval, characteristically *German* flavor. As far as peasant life and rights are concerned there is basically little to distinguish a Saxon village ordinance from older German traditions and precedents, or, for that matter, from Flemish laws.[19]

But the life of old Germany, in being transplanted to the east, widened its influence and slowed its effects, thus protracting and prolonging the German Middle Ages. The more the roots of German life spread out, the harder it became for new forces to attack the stem. And of all the influences making for inflexibility and perseverance, the most effective was probably the law. One need only think of the spread of the *Sachsenspiegel* throughout eastern Germany and non-German eastern Europe: every manuscript of the *Sachsenspiegel* and its glosses which found its way east took with it its Hohenstaufen ideas on politics and the state, together with its historical legends and the symbolism of its terms. One is tempted to make this generalization: in areas of relatively immature civilization, though new elements of culture made their appearance, the old ways and traditions persevered all the more stubbornly. The municipal laws of the German colony in Ofen, laid down in 1421, might just as well have been framed in Munich in the fourteenth century. Dietrich von Tiefenau, a knight who migrated to the order's territory around 1236 in order to escape the authority of the bishop of Hildesheim, was evading a new and—to him—hateful development in the old country, namely the growth of territorial sovereignty. In the new country in the east he sought and found something very old: the aristocrat's traditional independence, the freedom of the nobility.[20]

Of the second basic factor of German national history in the late Middle Ages, the urbanization and burgherization of Germany, we have already spoken. But it is important in the present context to counteract the widespread idea that the emergence and final establishment of the burgher classes in German life took place only during the last phase of the medieval era, the fifteenth century. The formation of German city culture extended over all three centuries of the late Middle Ages, and different factors at different times produced periods of great achievement, high population figures, and major building projects. Taken all in all, medieval urban civilization reached its peak in the 1370's, the time of the Peace of Stralsund after Lübeck had led the Hanse to victory over Denmark, and when textile industries and commerce boosted the wealth and the political weight of the Swabian and Rhenish cities. Both suffered a setback in the victory of the princes in the great city war at the end of the century. The fortunes of Nuremberg, a city that profited from the colonization of the east, enjoyed a more steady and unbroken rise, though she, too, was drawn into the political decline of the imperial cities around 1450. Yet it was about that time that Danzig, the city of grain exports, entered its heyday.

But the urban burgher classes did not win a total victory. Germany never became a land of cities to the extent that Italy did. Even in the time of Luther there was still some truth in the old dictum of Alexander of Roes that the Italians were burghers while the Germans were knights. Relations between burghers and feudal landowners led to bloody struggles, to alliances and prorogations, to tensions and settlements—but never to a decisive resolution. The Estates were divided by animosities, and while most cities had occasion to train their arms on aristocratic foes and bring them to justice as "robber knights," there were still opportunities for mutual *rapprochement* and moments of understanding between burghers and the nobility.[21]

All this, of course, served to put off impending crises. The crisis in political affairs was repressed for a time because the empire remained the necessary setting for the controversies among the territorial principalities, while the crisis in national life was left suspended between the evenly balanced cultural influences of old Germany and the new colonial territories on the one hand, and in the unresolved dualism of urban burgherdom and ancient feudal institutions on the other. The decisive feature of the latter half of the fifteenth century, however, was the sharpening and precipitation of the crisis in national life as a whole. We now note the emergence of what Stadelmann has called the "mood of the fifteenth century," the "emotional twilight" between the extremes of horror and delight in the Dance of Death. It was then that Hans Multscher carved his St. George for the altar in Sterzing, in whose face Stadelmann has read a "passive smile" and the "bitter taste of life." Then, also, Tilman Riemenschneider created those impressive figures of weary old men with their "features of sorrowful brooding," as Hubert Schrade described them. It was the time when the recently completed great churches in German cities (1482 the towers of St. Sebald in Nuremberg, 1488 the Frauenkirche in Munich, 1494 the Gate of St. Lawrence in Strassburg, 1513 the choir of Freiburg Minster) were filled with paintings portraying pain and suffering as a personal human experience: the body of Christ covered with beads of blood, the sorrow-filled eyes of Mary emptied of tears. Soon Mathis Neidthart, called Grünewald, was to paint Christ crucified: the sufferer's divinity shines through the utter humanity expressed through a physical torment pursued in detail to the very depths of corporal debasement, to the thorns stuck in the bleeding flesh. On the other hand, Grünewald still wrapped his Madonna at Stuppack in clouds of brocade! In east Germany as well as in west Germany, in city and country alike, the tone of national life still retained for the great mass of ecclesiastical art an accustomed, homely, comfortable form of expression. And yet the people of the fifteenth century were stirring; there can be no mistaking the signs of nervous impatience and, in particular, of religious agitation. This excitement can be observed in certain forms of religious practice in which explosive revolutionary forces were latent: Geiler von Kaisersberg preaching to huge audiences, the literature of the *Ars moriendi*, or the *Devotio moderna* with its emphasis on an evangelical and internalized religion. In 1470 Stefan Scheu, a canon of Ansback, set up a preaching office at the chief church in Rothenburg[22] instead of the usual altar-benefice—a decision inspired at once by humanist learning and by religious zeal.

It should, of course, not be forgotten that the intensified piety of the fifteenth century, the frenzied fear of sin and, one might almost say, the utter despair of that period, led men and women to seek relief in the old familiar ways: Erasmus may have moved from the *Devotio moderna* to an anti-ceremonial and intellectual Christianity, but this way was not, and could not be, the common way. Anyone who has read the *Imitation of Christ* will know how much importance Thomas à Kempis attached to the sacramental principle; the whole of his fourth book is devoted to the sacrament of the altar. The fifteenth century was not only the great age of the rosary but also that of pilgrimages and new pilgrimage shrines, of bleeding hosts, and the full development of the Feast of Corpus Christi—in short, it was the age of the eucharist. These were features characteristic of a medieval spirit which was to persevere tenaciously into the time of Luther, and also—a point worth making in view of the usual oversimplifications—of an ecclesiastical life which had remained very largely intact both inside and outside the monasteries. This medieval piety found expression in the abundance of altar-benefices and in the plenitude of endowments which, true to medieval form, combined religious motives with purposes of status representation for nobility and middle class alike. The altar of the Holy Cross in the Frauenkirche in Munich was painted during Luther's early years in the monastery, and Luther's patron, Frederick the Wise, never ceased to add to his prize collection of relics. To my mind, the last word on the problem of the late medieval civilization in Germany is not the gradual self-dissolution of the Middle Ages during the fifteenth century, but the suddenness of Luther's onslaught. The iconoclasts who destroyed the images were the very men who had donated them.

Although the problem of the causes of the Reformation is inevitably implicit in any consideration of the late Middle Ages in Germany, I have no intention of posing it expressly here. Joseph Lortz has recently dealt thoroughly with the problem. Ultimately there never will be a satisfactory answer, because Martin Luther, acting with the radicalism of his religious genius, destroyed everything that is usually called the origin of the Reformation, though it ought really to be called its prerequisite. The Wittenberg tempest blew away all those features that had made the medieval church "medieval," features which, in the late Middle Ages, had become intensified, exaggerated, and often stretched to a point of sheer intolerability which makes the Reformation understandable, but does not explain it. "Medieval" about the church was its aristocratic and juridical character. In the fifteenth century an increasing number of ecclesiastical offices in chapters and bishoprics became aristocratic. Many came to be reserved for princely families alone. The gap between higher and lower clergy come to yawn ever wider, as did the intolerable discrepancy between the religious needs of the people and the quality of a clergy which to a large extent—though by no means everywhere—was a proletariat in its lower strata, and a princely power prerogative in its higher reaches. An equally dangerous incongruity toward the religious needs of the people was created by the progressively legalistic spirit of the church: popular misinterpretations of the doctrine of indulgences are the clearest among the many signs of the genuinely medieval character of the church during the fifteenth century.

The reasons for the crisis-character of the late Middle Ages in Germany as a whole might, therefore, be summed up as indeterminateness. But the explanation for the crisis of the fifteenth century in particular might be better formulated as a "disappointment." Disappointment seems to me, ultimately, the word for all those elements we know as the popular movements of the late

Middle Ages: peasant uprisings, the revolutionary mood in the cities. It was the disappointment of a nation which had so long put its faith in the stars under which it lived. At the Council of Constance, even at the Council of Basel, this faith had still found expression in the hope that church and empire might be reformed —it was a faith in written law, a confidence in the viability of time-honored institutions and the possibility of their institutional reform. By about 1450 this expectation had collapsed, and what hope still remained in the old order was stamped into the dust by the troopers of the victorious sovereign state. The people demanded their rights of empire and state; but the empire was no longer able to grant them, while the new state was not yet ready to do so. And both empire and state denied the people what it needed (though, still rooted in its pre-political past, it did not make such a demand): a political structure. "We are sheep without a shepherd, shorn but never fed:" this was the answer to the failure of the old order. The answer was rendered in the peasants' revolt, in which Riemenschneider the woodcarver participated. The bishop of Würzburg's instruments of torture put an end to his art.

Luther, however, caught the agitation of the many in his own religious experience. Only for a brief time, around 1520 when his *Address to the Christian Nobility of the German Nation* echoed the chorus of demands that had been building up during the fifteenth century, was he in harmony with the past. His new doctrines destroyed the aristocratic church. He burned the Decretals, and with them he burned the Middle Ages. There is a deep significance in the fact that the German revolution was a religious reformation. The political and social situation remained in suspension, in a state of indeterminateness. When the final decision was taken, it came in a realm where a nation which for nearly three centuries had been estranged from higher politics, had been forced to find itself: in the depths of the heart where men long for justification before God. But this fact, too, only goes to demonstrate what I have been trying to bring out in these pages: the distinctive German character of the late Middle Ages and the relative unity of the period reaching from the thirteenth century to the Reformation.

NOTES TO CHAPTER 2

1. I say this in order to distinguish my own view of history from the—perfectly legitimate—question on the "origins" of "modern" phenomena, such as underlies the investigations of W. Näf, "Frühformen des 'Modernen Staates,'" *Historische Zeitschrift*, 171 (1951), or the recent book of F. A. von der Heydte, *Die Geburtsstunde des souveränen Staates* (1952). Insofar as these and similar studies touch directly on the problem of periodization in history, I shall deal with them in a separate context.

2. H. Heimpel, "Über die Epochen der mittelalterlichen Geschichte," *Die Sammlung*, 2 (1947).

3. Will-Erich Peuckert, *Die grosse Wende. Das apokalyptische Saeculum und Luther. Geistesgeschichte und Volkskunde* (Hamburg, 1948). If I, as a historian, take a different view of the late Middle Ages in Germany from Peuckert, this should not be allowed to conceal the gratitude and, indeed, admiration which Peuckert deserves for his productive familiarity with the sources. Cf. my review in *Das Deutsche Archiv*, 8 (1950), p. 338 f. It is also worthwhile to read the objections raised by E. Benz, *Zeitschrift für Religions- und Geistesgeschichte*, 3 (1951).

4. This idea has been explored in detail by H. Bechtel, *Wirtschaftsstil des deutschen Spätmittelalters* (1930).

5. A. Reimann, *Die älteren Pirckheimer* (1944).

6. An abundant source for the history of the patriciate is provided by the index of names in the third volume of F. Bastian's "Das Runtingerbunch," 1383–1407 (1943). Cf. H. Planitz, "Studien zur Rechtsgeschichte des städtischen Patriziats," *Mitteilungen des Instituts für österreichische Geschichtsforschung*, 58 (1950).

7. Cf. T. Mayer, "Staatsauffassung in der Karolingerzeit," *Historische Zeitschrift*, 173 (1952), p. 467 ff., as well as his earlier works.

8. These, then, would be the "retarding factors" which von der Heydte excluded from his account, the intention of which—in contrast to Peuckert—was to show the period from about 1250 to 1300 as the "hour of birth" of the sovereign state. Cf. note 1, above.

9. *Bericht über die 21. Versammlung deutscher Historiker in Marburg*, supplement to *Geschichte in Wissenschaft und Unterricht* (1951), p. 41 ff.

10. See especially W. Berges, *Die Fürstenspiegel des hohen und späten Mittelalters* (1938).

11. I was able, however, at an earlier time, to show that the *Defensor Pacis* had been used by Dietrich of Niem. As regards the authorship of the most important German reform treatise of the early conciliar period (the so-called *De Modis*, 1410), this fact definitely pointed to Dietrich, despite the arguments of J. Haller. Cf. H. Heimpel, *Dietrich von Niem* (1932), p. 103 ff. That Dietrich used Marsiglio more extensively than I realized at the time has been established by the recent discovery of the *Viridarium* of 1411; cf. K. Pivec in *Mitteilungen des Instituts für österreichische Geschichte*, 58 (1950), p. 386 ff.

12. For Engelbert, cf. the comparatively recent work of G. B. Fowler, *Intellectual Interests of Engelbert of Admont*, Oxford University Press, 79 (1947). Fowler is preparing an edition of Engelbert's writings. His political works are due to appear in the *Monumenta Germaniae*.

13. The tradition behind this trinity of *studium*, papacy, learning, has now been elucidated by H. Grundmann, "Sacerdotium, Regnum, Studium," *Archiv für Kulturgeschichte*, 34 (1951), p. 5 ff.

14. For the evidence, see H. Grundmann, "Über die Schriften des Alexander von Roes," *Deutsches Archiv*, 8 (1951).

15. Most recently, K. Pivec and H. Heimpel, "Neue Forschungen zu Dietrich von Niem," *Nachrichten der Göttinger Akademie* (1951).

16. The barest appreciation must suffice here. New elements have been brought to light by the critical edition provided for the *Monumenta* (based on the posthumous papers of H. Meyer-Rodehüser) and the studies accompanying the edition of Sabin Krüger in Göttingen.

17. E. Caspar, *Vom Wesen des Deutschordensstaates* (1928). For a recent summary, see H. Heimpel, "Hermann von Salza," *Wir Ostpreussen* (1950).

18. Considerable new ground has been broken by H. Aubin, "Wirtschaftsgeschichtliche Bemerkungen zur ostdeutschen Kolonisation," *Aus Sozial- und Wirtschaftsgeschichte: Gedächtnisschrift für G. von Below* (1928).

19. H. Quirin, *Herrschaft und Gemeinde nach mitteldeutschen Quellen des 12. bis 18. Jahrhunderts.* (*Göttinger Bausteine zur Geschichtswissenschaft*, 2, 1952.)

20. H. Aubin, *op. cit.*, p. 186.

21. While Hendrik de Man, in his *Jacques Cœur* (Berne, 1950), sees the courtly style of life and activity of the "regal merchant" as a deviation from the early capitalist middle class, O. Brunner, "Jacques Cœur, ein Beitrag zum Problem 'Bürgertum und Adel,'" *Anzeiger der Osterreichischen Akademie der Wissenschaften* (1951), p. 127 ff., is able, by pointing to many parallel instances, to show that the combination of middle-class financial enterprises with a feudal style of life was very much a feature of the age. He also quite rightly observes (p. 138) that: "Although the feudal structure was gradually transformed by the monarchical principle and the monarchical state, it maintained itself until the end of the eighteenth century. And with it survived the particular form of the old city middle classes. It was only gradually that the modern state arose, and with it the economically based society known as the bourgeoisie. "Early commercial and financial capitalism . . . presupposed the continued existence of the feudal structure with its combination of business with the tenure of high office." Some telling examples are offered by G. von Pölnitz, *Jakob Fugger* (1949). For the association of commercial wealth and landed property, see also the list of names described in note 6 (F. Bastian)—e.g., under "Graner."

22. This piece of information was kindly provided by H. Weigel of Erlangen.

3 Imperial Reform, 1485-1495: Its Course and its Character

FRITZ HARTUNG

Fritz Hartung, whose detailed account of the negotiations leading up to and culminating in the imperial Diet of Worms of 1495 follows here, is a political and constitutional historian, author of a number of important works on late medieval and modern German history. He was born in 1883 and was, from 1923 to 1949, professor at the University of Berlin.

The Imperial Reform Movement During the Last Years of the Reign of Frederick III, 1485-1493

I INTEND in the following essay to trace the development of the idea of imperial reform and thus throw some light on the reform statutes of 1495, the significance of which has recently been disputed by Rudolf Smend.[1] It is not difficult to decide at what point to begin our survey of the events leading up to the imperial diet of 1495. Although the demand for peace, law, and order dominated all the meetings of the German Estates during the fifteenth century, and an especially serious attempt at reorganization was made in the years 1436 and 1438, it was not until the 1480's that the Estates themselves began to contend with the emperor for a fundamental reform of the empire. The specific impetus was given at that time by the increased demands which Frederick III was compelled to make on the Estates as a result of the rapid advances of the Magyars. At first, it is true, the emperor had tried to avoid summoning a diet and contented himself with voluntary contributions by those Estates who were either obliged or disposed to render him aid. But this arrangement was not only thoroughly inadequate, as can be seen from the emperor's continual losses, but gradually became impracticable. Even those among the Estates who were prepared to give help and make sacrifices began to object to the constant burdens; and they found it necessary to band together in order to protect themselves against the ominous new demand to—as they put it—"serve year after year and be under compulsory obligations without any authorization from the whole college of electors."[2]

This uneasy mood must have been widespread. We cannot follow it here in detail; nor do we know whether the emerging leader of the reform party, Berthold von Henneberg, whose election as archbishop of Mainz in May 1484 had placed him at the head of the Estates, had then begun to play an important part. But we do know what the outcome was. When, late in 1484, Count Haug von Werdenberg approached electors and princes on behalf of the emperor to try to enlist their support against the Hungarians, the answer he got in all quarters was that the emperor would first have to convoke a diet. Special negotiations having come to nothing, a proclamation was issued on 13 November, 1484, summoning a diet to meet in Frankfurt early in 1485.

This Frankfurt diet was in a sense the prelude to imperial reform.[3] It produced no results because the emperor had not departed from his custom of summoning only part of the Estates, and because not even all those invited actually came. Hence princes and delegates present confined themselves to a declaration that, while they could not but acknowledge the need for a subsidy, their limited number did not permit them to raise a levy. With its poor attendance the diet was not in any position to set about the long-awaited institution of reforms; but it could at least reformulate the old demands. Although the only subject for discussion mentioned in the convocation had been the imperial subsidy, preliminary negotiations among the Estates concentrated on the questions of "justice, coinage, and dissension in the empire," while during the deliberation at Frankfurt the Bavarian delegates directed attention to a gaping wound in the body of the German Empire, a wound that revealed most clearly the grave flaws in the imperial constitution, namely, the lack of a united front against the outside world. The structure of the empire had become so slack that even attacks by foreign powers did not bring emperor and Estates to any sense of obligation toward mutual defense; indeed, each of the Estates was left with the fear that, just as the emperor had to wage his battle against Matthias of Hungary almost unaided, so the single Estate would look in vain for support if ever it were attacked by a foreign power. Indeed, none could count on imperial support even if such an attack were precipitated as a result of fulfilling an obligation to the empire or of rendering assistance to it. For that reason the Bavarian delegates insisted as a precondition for any support on the part of the Estates that emperor and Estates should form and sign a special alliance for mutual help and protection.

None of these proposals contained new ideas or even any advances beyond earlier drafts. At all previous diets the Estates had discussed questions of public peace and order and the administration of justice; and the union against "alien powers" had been described as the indispensable basis of any general imperial subsidy not only at the Diet of Nuremberg in 1481 (as the Bavarian delegates observed), but as early as 1467. It is not likely that any of the princes present at the Diet of Frankfurt in 1485 thought of the possibility of a fundamental reorganization of the empire. It is known, for example, how preoccupied Albrecht Achilles was at the time with questions of government in his own Franconian lands. It was not much different with the other territorial rulers. The impulse for the reform movement was given not by general constitutional or legal questions, or by theoretical considerations such as the relations between king and Estates, but simply by the practical desire of individual territories to remove those particular defects in the imperial constitution which had been troublesome at one time or another to each of them.

This fact explains why the election of Maximilian as king of the Romans in February 1486 was not used by the electors as a means of binding him to a definite program of reform to ensure that the demands of the Estates would be met, as was to happen in the Electoral Capitulations later on. Even Berthold of Mainz stipulated nothing more than a number of special privileges.

Berthold's restatement of the claims of Mainz to the direction of the royal chancery suggests that he may have been influenced by reform ideas, but even this may have been due more to financial than to political considerations. At all events, Maximilian's election remained at first without any effect upon the history of imperial reform.

Negotiations about peace and justice in the empire were therefore not set in motion by the election of Maximilian. It was the emperor's renewed demand for a subsidy against Hungary that transformed the electoral assembly at Frankfurt into a reform diet. As Frederick III submitted his request for aid immediately after the election on February 16, 1486, the Diet of Frankfurt in the spring of 1486 has been taken as the continuation of the meeting of the previous year.[4] The one sign of progress was that the Estates now came much more closely to grips with specific tasks of reform. They no longer contented themselves with general demands for peace and justice, but submitted comprehensive projects for ensuring the public peace and the administration of justice. Remarkably enough, the leadership of the Estates rested at this time with the princes. They began by declaring that they would approve no subsidy until matters concerning peace, justice, and the system of coinage had been settled.[5] They also drafted a judicial organization which transferred the whole of the emperor's judicial sovereignty to a special court.[6] This court was, to be sure, to remain imperial, and the judges were to be appointed by the emperor; but it was to have a definite fixed location within the empire, separate from the emperor's establishment, and the emperor was to relinquish the "fullness of imperial authority" in favor of the "ordinary authority," namely that of the court.

The electors, for their part, realized that the emperor could not approve such a draft, that they should "not go so far at the outset," and should avoid any suggestion that the Estates intended to "curtail and remove the fullness of sovereignty" of his imperial majesty. Furthermore, though they agreed with the princes that the subsidy should not be granted without imperial reform, they also considered the subsidy to be the principal item at the diet.

For these reasons they agreed to talk about both subsidy and internal reform simultaneously.

On February 25 and 26 the emperor and King Maximilian attempted to cut short the proceedings by demanding a general imperial tax and an emergency subsidy to be paid in cash, and to achieve their purpose without any concessions to the reformers. But it was in vain. The swift conclusion desired by emperor and king was blocked not only by the common interest of the Estates in the reorganization of the empire but also by the disinclination of the Estates to make any sacrifices whatever for the emperor and his dynastic dominions. Thus the proposals for an imperial tax and a cash subsidy met with stubborn opposition. For beyond all the existing misgivings over any kind of imperial subsidy—the fear of a Hungarian reprisal against the empire and the wish for a mutual defense pact against Hungary—there was a particular reluctance concerning taxes to be paid in cash: the Estates distrusted the emperor and harbored the not entirely unfounded suspicion that Frederick III would use their money, not for the struggle against Hungary, but for meeting his personal debts, thus rendering their sacrifice futile. To avoid this, the electors, joined by Duke Albrecht of Saxony and the bishop of Eichstätt,[7] suggested that the contributions of the Estates be handed, not to the emperor, but to special commissioners to be appointed jointly by the emperor and the Estates, who were to bind themselves under oath to disburse the money only for the Hungarian campaign. The princes, however, rejected the idea of a general imperial tax altogether. Even the personal intervention, conducted on March 2 by Count Haug von Werdenberg on behalf and in the presence of the emperor and Maximilian, could do nothing to alter the princes' attitude;[8] thus on March 8 the idea of an imperial tax had to be abandoned.

In its first three weeks, therefore, the diet had made no progress whatever on the question closest to the emperor's heart. On the other hand (though it is not possible to follow the proceedings in detail), the discussions about peace and justice were being continued, and on March 8, the very day on which the draft for the imperial tax was dropped, the talks reached a measure of agreement, for on that day the drafts for the Public Peace and the imperial Chamber Court ordinance were read to the diet. The original plan for the Public Peace remains unknown; I have discovered one draft,[9] but this does not show with any certainty to which stage of the discussions it belonged. Its wording suffices, however, to give us an impression of the most important of its controverted points. The idea of a permanent peace, supported by Berthold of Mainz, among others,[10] still met with opposition. The reform party had therefore to insert a clause limiting the duration of the peace to "the next ten years." Furthermore, the very first attempt to put the reform demands into effect was disrupted by the particular aspirations of the territories, specifically by their concern to preserve intact their privileges and protect the territorial sovereignty which they were then in process of building up. It was probably on the insistence of the territorial princes that the original wording, according to which the peace was in no way to infringe the emperor's authority, was augmented by the addition that the peace should "place no limits on the sovereignty[11] and rights of any party." There also appear to have been doubts as to how the realization of the peace might be better guaranteed than it had been in times past. The first draft seems not to have taken any account of the possibility that a man might forcibly break the peace; at least it anticipated no precautions against such breaches.[12] This attitude might reveal the moral excellence of Elector Berthold of Mainz, but it also brings out his political naïveté, for he seems to have assumed that all men, even the territorial magnates, had the same inclination to accept stable political organization as he himself. The great miscalculation of the reform party, its belief that it would be possible to implement the new regulations throughout the empire without a soundly organized executive power, can be seen even in these preliminary drafts. Only in their later versions was at least the imperial chamber judge given the power of calling up the Estates against those who violated the peace.

Thus the question of the Imperial Public Peace led directly to the draft for the ordinance of the Imperial Chamber Court. The court naturally encroached much farther upon the emperor's powers than the Public Peace, since it touched on his most important right. Even the weakened draft agreed on by electors and princes[13] amounted to a diminution of the emperor's previous arbitrary powers. It may be that too much has been made of the significance of this draft submitted by the Estates. It can hardly be said that they aimed at a fundamental alteration of the location or execution of judicial authority, or at any transformation of the emperor's Chamber Court into a court of the empire controlled by the Estates. At least the plan drawn up by the Estates spoke only of the emperor's court, and the right to appoint the chamber judge was probably to remain with the emperor. But in order to gain some results, to procure a guarantee that the imperial court would function regularly and in accordance with the law, the Estates had separated the court from the emperor; it was to have a fixed location and to exclude the emperor's influence altogether, except for a purely formal connection through the documents recording and promulgating verdicts, which were to be issued jointly. In its verdicts, even in the infliction of the severest penalty, the imperial ban, the court was to be completely independent. In matters of jurisdiction the emperor was not allowed to intervene. While in this way the emperor lost important and profitable prerogatives, the territories gained in internal consolidation. As in the case of the Public Peace, the ordinance of the Imperial Chamber Court brought out not only the tendency to consolidate empire and Estates, but also the particular interests of the individual territories, which felt themselves threatened by the existence of a powerful imperial authority, no matter what form this was to take. For this reason the independent judicial authority of the territorial rulers over their subjects was ensured by the express provision that the imperial Chamber Court was in the first stage of proceedings, competent only in cases involving persons directly subject to the emperor (*reichsunmittelbar*).

Frederick and Maximilian had no choice but to acquiesce in this plan if they wanted to receive the subsidy. The respective attitudes they adopted toward the plan are indicative of their different characters. Maximilian, in his sanguine way, managed to ignore the difficulties of the situation. He attempted to win over the Estates by means of a grandly conceived reform program of his own without, however, meeting them halfway in the matter of judicial organization. In a draft[14] read out on March 16, he only mentioned the organization of the court in passing, while at the same time acceding to the Public Peace in a way which went considerably beyond the expectations of the Estates. What he proposed was to augment the Public Peace with an enforcement regulation. In so doing he not only skillfully avoided any violation of territorial autonomy by making the princes themselves responsible for the Public Peace in the larger territories, but he also tried to tempt some of the more important rulers with the task of preserving and enforcing the Public Peace in the domains of the smaller neighboring powers of counts, knights, and cities, and, at the same time, of supervising the execution of the judgments of the Chamber Court. To be sure, the principal advantages of the enforcement regulation would, under this plan, have fallen to the emperor and, more particularly, to Maximilian himself. By an imperial mandate Swabia was placed under the control of Archduke Sigismund of Tyrol and the count of Württemberg; and along the whole of the western frontier of the empire, all the way from Mömpelgard to Friesland, Maximilian or his deputy (*Hauptmann*) were to be "administrators" (*Handhaber*) of the peace, a role which, in view of Maximilian's perennial involvements with France, could have had questionable consequences for the Estates. We do not, however, know whether the Estates were clear about this aspect of the proposal; all their discussions were dominated by the universal aversion to any restriction of territorial independence through "administrators" of the Public Peace and particularly through imperial deputies, as well as to any curtailment of their right to form free alliances through a unification of the empire as a whole. As a result, Maximilian's plan, including the perfectly sound idea of an organized executive authority over the Public Peace, failed dismally.

Frederick III, however, trusting to his long years of familiarity with the ways of the Estates, followed a different path to try to obtain the subsidy. He did not even attempt to lure the Estates with a promise of reform but relied instead on his personal influence. On March 16, he asked each individual prince whether he would render him assistance.[15] At this point, however, it became evident that the power of the Estates had grown. The emperor was no longer able, as in former years, to frustrate the normal debating procedure of the diet by resorting to personal intervention, and that he now received no straight answer to his inquiry may well have been due to the influence now being exerted by Berthold of Mainz.

Thus, Frederick finally had to meet the Estates halfway in the matter of reform if he did not want to risk forgoing the subsidy, the necessity of which the Estates had, of course, not disputed. But all he would accept in the form proposed by the Estates was the Public Peace, which did not impinge on any of his rights. During the negotiations of Aachen and Cologne in April 1486, which followed upon the Frankfurt Diet, Frederick brought forward objections[16] to the organization of the Chamber Court. He refused any formal or material diminution of his position as sole supreme judge. He reserved the right to pronounce the imperial ban, protected for the future his influence upon the composition of the court by making the appointment of new assessors dependent on his consent, and rejected the proposed form of the court's documents which made the court appear to rank equal with himself. Finally he tightened the reins on the Estates' urge to independence by holding fast to the court's jurisdiction, even in matters concerning the mediate subjects of the empire, who might refer their legal proceedings exclusively to the territorial courts only in virtue of special privileges, not of any general regulation. Moreover, territorial "ordinances, statutes, and customs" were to be binding on the court only insofar as they were compatible with the statutory rights of the emperor.

There was no reconciling these utterly opposed viewpoints. The electors, while declaring their readiness to furnish an imperial subsidy in coin, held fast to their former conditions.[17] They demanded: 1. a written undertaking on the part of the imperial deputy to apply the sums contributed by the Estates only to the war against Hungary: 2. the proclamation of the Public Peace, and 3. the institution of the Chamber Court in the form proposed by the Estates. If the emperor were not to fulfill these conditions the second installment of the subsidy would not be forthcoming. Frederick would not yield, however. Throughout the whole of 1486 he tried again and again to obtain the money through special negotiations with electors and cities[18] (and perhaps also with some individual princes, though this remains unknown), but it was to no avail. For without the Public Peace and the Chamber Court the Estates would not budge, and all the time the danger to the dynastic lands was becoming ever greater. Thus there was nothing left for the emperor but to resign himself to yet another diet in the spring of 1487.

But even at this diet, the Diet of Nuremberg,[19] which went on from the end of March until well into July, the emperor would not alter his accustomed approach. His *Proposition* contained only the request for the imperial subsidy and passed over the demands of the Estates in silence. Despite this the Estates proceeded without further ado with the designs of the preceding diet, and the emperor was soon forced to take a stand on these. He first gave the Estates an account of how the money, obtained as a result of the Frankfurt agreements, had been spent. From this extremely detailed account it appeared that the emperor's expenditures of 64,000 florins were appreciably higher than his revenues of about 40,000 florins, to which, apart from the imperial cities, only the electors of Mainz, Cologne, and Palatinate, Saxony, and Branden-burg had contributed, and only the first installment had been paid. The princes had persisted in their tougher attitude and refused to pay anything at all.[20] Frederick then went on to detail his endeavors on behalf of peace and justice. With the Public Peace he had no difficulty, as he had proclaimed it exactly according to the draft of the Estates. He disclaimed any responsi-bility for violations, but declared himself ready to enter into discussions with the Estates about redress for possible defects in the law or its enforcement. On the matter of the court, however, he came not a step nearer the position of the Estates than in the previous year. He did, to be sure, ask for suggestions as to the choice of assessors, but the draft law setting up the court, which had been submitted to him, and which was the main point at issue, he passed over without mention.[21]

Discussions were interrupted at the beginning of April because the Estates, on account of the limited number of members present, did not want to negotiate, but wished first of all to consult with the most important of the absent Estates.[22] No doubt this was primarily an attempt to postpone the whole session and to put off satisfying the emperor's demands for the subsidy. But it was also significant as a stage in the development of parliamentary reforms in Germany, which were closely connected with the matter of imperial reform. Since resolutions passed at the diets were of increasingly greater moment for the empire as a whole, it naturally became more important for negotiations and resolutions to proceed according to an established order. Two questions stood out above all others: the procedure at the diet itself, and the relationship of the diet to the Estates not actually present at the meetings. It goes without saying that certain fixed forms for dispatching business at the diet had evolved in the course of time. The division into the three curias of electors, princes and cities, for example, had been customary long before the period of imperial reform, as R. Bemmann[23] proved a few years ago. Since, however, the separation of the curias had not always been strictly observed, the whole procedure at the diets in the reign of Frederick III conveys the impression of a lack of order and form. The emperor summoned only such Estates as suited his purposes, while a large number of the Estates ignored their obligation to comply with the resolutions of the diets; and the emperor was frequently able to use the device of the personal intervention as a means of undermining deliberations in the Estates.

But during the period of imperial reform, and under the predominant influence of Elector Berthold of Mainz, all this began to change. The right of the Estates to take part in the negotiations of the diets was no longer to be subject to the emperor's pleasure; during the reform period there was frequent insistence[24] on the requirement, later regularly observed, that all the Estates must be invited to the diets. Admittedly it was still not clear to what extent the cities were entitled to take part in the discussions and to help frame the resolutions; the cities remained, as before, dependent in all essentials on the discretion of the higher Estates. Nor was there any firm decision as to whether the resolutions of a diet should be binding on the Estates which, though invited, had not appeared. The emperor, without any qualification, said that they were,[25] and even the Estates maintained firmly, in theory at least, that the diets could promulgate laws binding on all. In 1487 they conceded that when negotiations with absent Estates came to no agreement the resolutions passed by those present would be final and conclusive.[26] In the terms agreed to in 1495 for the administration of peace and justice, it was laid down that the annual diet should "deliberate and resolve effectively and decisively," and it is probably correct to see in this a recognition of the basic principle that resolutions passed at the diets had binding force. To renounce this right would certainly have rendered any imperial legislation impossible. But it appeared very soon that the principle could not always be observed in practice. Even the Recess of Freiburg applied it only to the following diet. Similarly the Recess of Speier in 1542, occasionally quoted in imperial documents and publicistic writings, according to which the Estates at the diet, "whether many in number or few, shall proceed without delay in the matters under discussion and pass resolutions, and any such resolution shall be no less binding on those absent than if they had themselves been present"—this recess was valid only for the time until the next diet, and only as regards the Turkish subsidy then under way. Again, the Recess of Cologne in 1512 fell short of the principle of binding force, for it decided that the majority resolutions of those representatives of all the Estates who were actually present were to be binding only if passed at diets which took place in virtue of the ordinance of execution, which had recently been agreed upon.[27] In practice things were less stringent still. Even during the reform period the Estates kept to the customary procedure of engaging in special negotiations with the more important absent members. This is what happened, for instance, in 1495; and when, in 1500, Maximilian threatened all those who would not accept the new arrangements with forfeiture of their regalia, fiefs, and privileges, the Estates urged him to try amicable negotiation instead of force.[28]

The question therefore remained open. On the other hand a decisive settlement was reached in the matter of parliamentary procedure. The long customary deliberation on the emperor's *Proposition* in the three curias now took on a new character through the imposition of strict secrecy which applied even to delegates vis-à-vis their principals, and which, to the lasting detriment of historical research, was usually observed. The reason for this innovation was given as the interests of the empire, so that foreign enemies might learn nothing of the campaigns planned against them or the strength of the armies to be drawn up.[29] Such caution was certainly justifiable. But the real reason for the new procedures must have lain deeper. The secretiveness of the discussions not only served the interests of the empire against foreign powers but also those of the Estates against the emperor. Berthold of Mainz told King Maximilian quite openly in 1492 that as long as there was no assurance that deliberations would be kept secret from the king no individual Estate would venture to speak its mind freely.[30] Further, the secrecy was the Estates' way of hitting back at the emperor's practice of intervening with single members and questioning them on their willingness to render him assistance, thus obtaining from individuals what the corporation would have refused. Berthold of Mainz had stood against this device from the very beginning. As early as the Frankfurt Diet of 1486 he had insisted that the emperor grant time for collective consultation, and in the autumn of 1486 the electors agreed among themselves to reply to the emperor's demands only as a body.[31] In all subsequent conflicts with Maximilian, Berthold was similarly at pains to appear before the king not as an individual but as the spokesman for all, whether of the diet as a whole or of the electoral college.

As a result of this self-seclusion of the diet, however, a shift in the whole relationship between emperor and Estates becomes apparent. Formerly the emperor had stood above the Estates, frequently as mediator between the two principal groups, electors and princes on the one side and the cities on the other (this role had been especially evident during the Diet of Eger in 1437). Gradually, however, procedures changed, and since 1469 it had been the practice of the various groups to agree in advance among themselves about the responses to be made to the emperor. As late as the 1480's, however, the emperor was at least able to maintain direct contacts with individual Estates. But once Berthold of Mainz had begun to conduct proceedings in secluded secrecy the emperor, standing alone, found himself confronted with the closed organization of the Estates, which was what the diet had now become.

This transformation of the constitution of the diet may be considered the preliminary step toward that fundamental alteration of the relationship between king and Estates which was to be attempted and achieved at the Diet of Worms in 1495. It was only a preliminary step insofar as it undertook to regulate but one aspect of this relationship and because it probably arose out of practical necessity rather than from considerations of fundamental principles. The reform movement was still in its beginnings. The objective—a realization of understandable and legitimate desires—was to put right the worst defects of the organization of the empire. In the same way, the alteration of the constitution was based ultimately on the Estates' desire to consult freely without being subjected to pressure by the emperor and without being called before him to render accounts. But just as a feeling of suspicion toward the emperor prompted the diet to present a common front against him, so the reform movement aligned itself against the emperor and against his absolute power, which, if not checked, would have made it impossible to achieve anything at all. Thus, a sharp opposition of emperor and Estates existed in the movement from its very outset.

This opposition provided the impetus to constitutional developments in the empire. The more clearly the Estates became conscious of it the more the reform movement began to aim at a fundamental limitation of the emperor's powers and a consolidation of the organization of the Estates. The Diet of Nuremberg in 1487, to which our attention must now return, shows in this respect a definite advance on the two preceding diets at Frankfurt. Not only was there increased unanimity among the Estates now that the electors had adopted the same sharp tone as the princes, but the Estates were beginning to set their sights higher than ever before. They were no longer content with individual reforms whose implementation would depend in all essentials on the pleasure of the emperor; they attempted, rather, to put through an integrated program of imperial reform. To this end they drew up a project[32] based on the previous year's plan for an alliance of emperor and Estates against foreign attack, though expanding it into a general imperial union. It was to be the task of this union to establish and maintain the public Peace, the Chamber Court, and a system of defense against enemy attack. The very idea of combining the various reform demands into a "constitution" marked an advance in the development of the imperial reform movement. No less indicative of the way in which the ideas of the Estates were now moving was the form of this "constitution." The two parties to the new imperial union were to be the emperor, both as supreme head of state and as lord of his dynastic lands, and the Estates; in the document of union both parties were accorded equal status.

It is difficult to believe that the Estates had not deliberately set out to diminish the emperor's absolute power by means of this project.[33] The fundamental significance of their plan, which in modern terms might be described as a change from autocratic to federative rule, certainly did not escape the emperor, as can be seen from both wording and substance of the counterproposal with which he replied to the draft of the Estates.[34] In the emperor's project, the contract between emperor and Estates was turned into an imperial mandate bidding the Estates to render each other assistance against all hostile incursion while carefully avoiding any mention of participation by the emperor himself. A promise, it is true, was made that the Chamber Court would be set up, though not, as in the draft of the Estates, according to the articles which "were heretofore drawn up for this purpose," that is to say, according to the proposals of 1486 but "according to the terms of a special procedure drawn up to that end;" by which the emperor probably meant the old Chamber Court ordinance of 1471 (there is evidence that he referred to this during the Diet of Nuremberg).[35] A further deliberate rejection of the plan of the Estates may be seen in the emperor's insistence that the court not be styled "imperial," in the sense of pertaining to the empire, but "the emperor's and the empire's," in the sense of pertaining to emperor and empire together (*sein und des Reiches Kammergericht*).

In the end, compromise was struck between these two contradictory views. The definitive draft[36] corresponded in its wording to the emperor's proposal, but it expressly included the emperor, along with his dynastic dominions, in the arrangement and thus in the mutual defense pact. Due to the dispute over the question of the Chamber Court everything was left in the vague phraseology of the emperor's draft, which made it possible for each side to interpret it to its own advantage. In this form, then, the union was approved by the reform party, as well as by the emperor. But at this point the principal enemy of imperial reform made its appearance: the territorial princes, who were utterly averse to any kind of centralization, whether under the monarch or under the Estates by means of any compromise between the two, and would enter into no obligations toward the rest. The Elector Palatine[37] rejected the whole constitution out of hand, because it clashed with his own particular alliances, and it would seem that he was joined by other princes,[38] since, in the end, nothing came of the idea of an imperial union.

The failure of the constitution, may, however, also have been due to the fact that the compromise merely veiled the contradictions between the respective views of emperor and Estates, since these emerged again as soon as the Estates expressed their demands with regard to the organization of the Chamber Court.[39] The Estates had based their deliberations on the draft of the previous year and had taken no account of the emperor's misgivings, except in a few points, for example on the appointment of the court assessors. On the main issues concerning the Chamber Court they had either remained firm, as in the form of the court documents and the recognition of special territorial privileges, or else they had taken a middle course. The imposition of the imperial ban was again conceded to the emperor, but he was to be bound to the verdicts of the Chamber Court and must follow them up with the declaration of the ban within four weeks. Jurisdiction over mediate subjects during the first stage of legal proceedings was even now not granted to the court, and only in cases of denial of rights would it be allowed to intervene in the jurisdiction of territorial courts.

The Estates continued to insist on this draft despite all the emperor's protests. And they left no room for doubt that unless their draft were accepted "no fruitful or effective help" could be expected.[40] Admittedly, what they had offered in the way of assistance for relieving sorely oppressed Wiener-Neustadt was not likely to persuade the emperor to meet their demands. Their proposals regarding the subsidy[41] were dominated by deep distrust of the emperor. As they had in the previous year, the Estates refused to hand over their money to him personally, but only to two princes, Duke Albrecht of Saxony and the Elector Johann of Brandenburg, who were to be appointed to lead the campaign. In this way they meant to ensure that the money would be used only for the relief of Wiener-Neustadt. But the Estates did not wish to assume the burdens of the campaign alone and insisted that the emperor should this time pay as much as all the Estates together, or rather, to use their own term, as much as the "empire" (for this distinction between emperor and empire was made at this occasion,)[42] and that his portion should also go to the two designated princes, and his payment precede that of the Estates.

Confronted with these demands the emperor tried the same tactics as in 1486. He came a considerable way toward meeting them in the matter of the Public Peace, for he did not merely renew it but supplemented it with a "declaration"[43] confirming much more emphatically than before the obligation of all Estates to take military action against violators. But this measure offered absolutely no effective guarantee that these obligations would be met and was just as unavailing as the Public Peace itself. As to the Chamber Court, the emperor declared his willingness to institute it, though even now he could not bring himself to accept it according to the ordinance suggested by the Estates. As at the beginning of the diet, he merely agreed to allow the Estates to nominate a number of assessors acceptable to him. On the other hand, he once again attempted to gain the subsidy by means of personal intervention. He did not, it is true, get his way completely, as the archbishop of Mainz managed to secure time for mutual consultation, but the Estates did finally approve the urgent cash subsidy without insisting on their earlier demands for a corresponding contribution from the emperor or on his acceptance of the reform drafts. The sole reservation they made was control over the disbursement of the money; for this purpose they appointed the High Chamberlain (*Erzkämmerer*) of the empire, the elector of Brandenburg, as treasurer and collector, and pledged him to deliver the money only to the commander in chief, Duke Albrecht of Saxony.[44]

Thus, at the end of the lengthy Diet of Nuremberg, Emperor Frederick had managed to maintain his position unchecked against the Estates. Nothing, however, had been achieved. Lack of peace and defective administration of justice—the twin plagues of the empire—remained rampant, and the imperial subsidy was late in arriving and was not paid in full amount. As in previous years the only ones to pay, apart from the imperial cities, were those princes in close personal relationship to the emperor, most of them ecclesiastical princes. Of the temporal rulers only Saxony, Brandenburg, and Hesse paid their dues, while important spiritual Estates like Trier, Magdeburg, Bremen, Salzburg, and Würzburg, all of whom had been assesssed at from 3,000 to 4,000 gulden, were among the missing. Of the 100,000 gulden which had been appropriated, only 51,428 were actually paid in.[45] Moreover, because the emperor's military preparations had been pitifully inadequate, Wiener-Neustadt was lost after all, and the Estates had sacrificed their money in vain.

The emperor apparently considered the fruitlessness of the diets of 1485 to 1487 as a vindication of his old governing principle of coming to special agreements with individual Estates. After the Diet of Nuremberg he kept himself as remote as possible from all imperial business. He discovered a substitute for the empire in the Swabian League. This league had been set up in 1488, originally, to oppose the Bavarian dukes in their aggressive and anti-imperial political activities, but it soon proved to be not only eminently well suited to maintaining the peace in its own territorial sphere but also useful as a source of money and support for Hapsburg politics, far more so, in fact, than its articles of constitution, even in their augmented form of 1500, might suggest. In the history of Germany during this period the league played an important role as a practical power factor; but since its very existence was ignored by the reform party, the historian of the imperial reform movement may leave it out of consideration.

But it was not only the emperor who gave up all attempts to come to an agreement with the diet. The reform party, too, seems to have realized that all attempts to establish a firm central organization for the empire would be frustrated by the emperor's resistance. Thus, the reform movement stalled in its tracks. After the Nuremberg Diet the Estates maintained for a time a completely passive attitude. The emperor's request for money to gain the release of Maximilian (who had been placed in captivity by his own Flemish Estates) was turned down by the electors without even touching on the matter of internal reform. Even at the Frankfurt Diet of 1489[46] the reform question played a remarkably minor part. Negotiations for the help demanded by Maximilian went on for two weeks, and only toward the end of the session was any reference made to peace and justice, but not—as at previous diets—as a precondition for assistance. The restrained attitude of the Estates was reflected also in the final recess, which,

though it did hold out the prospect of help for Maximilian (however insubstantial and heavily qualified) pledged him to do nothing
more than use his influence with the emperor on behalf of the
enforcement of the Public Peace and the establishment of the
Chamber Court in accordance with the earlier drafts.

Now, Maximilian himself was not nearly as averse to the idea
of imperial reform as was his father. At the Frankfurt Diet of 1489
he voluntarily offered to protect the Estates against foreign attack,
which in fact meant assuming the responsibility that the Estates
had long wished to lay upon the emperor in the form of a "union
against foreign attacks." And in 1486, as we have already seen,
he had proposed an extensive program of reform covering the
Public Peace and its enforcement, and the protection from
foreign incursions. Admittedly, even this plan demonstrated the
existence of a considerable cleavage between Maximilian and the
Estates. The important thing for Maximilian was to secure subsidies with which he could carry on his struggle to preserve his
status as a major power. In this regard the Estates failed him
completely. Even those who, like Berthold of Mainz, had a serious
interest in restoring the former greatness of the empire and were
prepared to make some sacrifices on its behalf, thought it possible
to put aside the tasks of external affairs until the internal reform
had been put through. Here was evidence of that parochial narrow-
ness and that failure to recognize the responsibilities of world
politics of which Maximilian was later to accuse his opponent
Berthold. The Estates failed utterly to grasp the nature of political
power and of power politics. Not only did they restrict themselves to "benevolent and gracious" offers of mediation while
Maximilian was imprisoned by his subjects in Bruges, but they
also took it very calmly when their envoy was unceremoniously
sent away and no reply was made to their note. This complete
inability on the part of the Estates to appreciate the necessity of a
strong policy of defense led, as early as the diet of 1489, to a sharp
controversy between Maximilian and Berthold of Mainz.[47] And
in the sphere of internal politics the differences were no less
considerable. While the reform party among the Estates strove

to obtain the greatest possible control over the emperor's exercise of power, Maximilian countered with the idea of a monarchical reform of the empire which, while consolidating the imperial union, would also strengthen the political and financial resources of the sovereign.

These differences dominated the Nuremberg Diet of 1491. Admittedly, much too little is known about it for us to be able to follow the course of the negotiations in detail or even to put all the known projects and drafts into their proper contexts.[48] The main outlines, however, are clear. The diet opened with a request by King Maximilian for an imperial subsidy against his principal opponents, the king of France and King Ladislaus of Bohemia, the latter his rival for the control of Hungary. The Estates did not reply by raising general demands for reform but insisted instead that the differences between the House of Wittelsbach and the Swabian League should be put aside—which shows the attrition to which the idea of reform had been subjected since 1487. Only gradually, between the middle of May and the beginning of June, did this suggestion grow into a plan for replacing the deficient judicial authority of the emperor with a general agreement on procedures for arbitration, and for including in such special judicial arrangements a statement of obligation to mutual defense against foreign incursions. The undated "Proposals submitted at Nuremberg"[49] in which this idea was set forth may perhaps belong to this stage of the negotiations, and they may also have been what Maximilian was referring to on June 14 when he declared that he could hardly venture "to induce the emperor to agree to this project of the Estates."[50] At all events, this declaration of Maximilian's fits the substance of the "Proposals," which amounted ultimately to setting aside the emperor's jurisdiction altogether and replacing it with a judge chosen by the electors and princes alone.

It would appear, too, that Maximilian's declaration made an impression upon the Estates, and that Berthold of Mainz tried to come to some kind of agreement with the king. At least we learn that in the course of the following few days Berthold was earnestly

negotiating with Eberhard of Württemberg, Frederick of Brandenburg, and Albrecht of Saxony—in other words, with princes
known to be in close touch with the emperor.[51] But neither the
course nor the outcome of these negotiations is known, and only
the subsequent events enable us to conclude that they came to
nothing. For the draft,[52] submitted on June 19 by those electors
and princes present at the diet to the delegates of those who were
not, cannot possibly have originated in an understanding between
the king and the reform party because it was immediately
answered with a counterproposal by Maximilian. It must, therefore, have been a unilateral proposal drafted by the Estates. It
contained the outlines of an ordinance "for the increases of the
Holy Empire's honor, advantage and might"; to this end electors
and princes were to agree to support one another in the event of
foreign incursions and violations of the Public Peace, as well as
to settle their mutual differences by means of mediation. Maximilian's counterproposal[53] was in its form and language more
elaborately worked out than the drafts of the Estates, though in
substance it did not go as far, since it completely passed over
foreign relations and confined itself to pledging the Estates to
uphold the Frankfurt ordinance of the Public Peace and to settle
all quarrels through an especially stipulated process of mediation.

But the whole idea of such a special agreement of mediation
met with opposition from the Estates. The electors of Saxony and
Brandenburg joined the councillors of the archbishops of Cologne
and Magdeburg and the Landgrave of Hesse in referring Maximilian to the text of the Public Peace ordinance, according to
which the maintenance of law and order was closely bound up
with the Chamber Court. They therefore rejected emergency
measures such as the mediation procedure and insisted on the
institution of the court on the basis already decided. They proposed petitioning Maximilian to urge his father to set up the
Chamber Court; only after the emperor had refused to do so
would it be time to think of substitutes such as a special arbitration
treaty between Maximilian and the Estates.[54] This proposal was
applauded by the majority of the Estates and on June 24 it was

presented to Maximilian, who thereupon abandoned his mediation project for the time being. At least the final recess of the Nuremberg Diet, drawn up on June 28 and styled "the authoritative recess,"[55] said nothing about arbitration and included merely the resolution "that the Chamber Court be organized in accordance with ordinances and capitularies as determined, approved and accepted at earlier diets." The recess also promised Maximilian a subsidy, though this was still very much hemmed in with provisos and presupposed further negotiations. In any case, the subsidy was probably never paid.

Not until the very end of the negotiations, presumably after the "authoritative recess" had been read out, did Maximilian come forward with a detailed plan of reform. While it is true that this plan had some bearing on the discussions of the diet, particularly in its reference to altercations between Bavaria and Swabia, and though it touched on the demands of the Estates at many points, it was conceived so independently and recast the diet's demands so fundamentally that it could not possibly have brought about an agreement with the Estates.[56] It would be wrong to think that Maximilian, when proposing a written "agreement of union" of emperor, king and Estates, was adopting the idea of union suggested in the earlier drafts of the Estates, for instance in the "constitution" of 1487. He was not accommodating the Estates in any way with this; in fact he was counteracting their plans. He was sacrificing the form in order to save the substance. For his projected reorganization of the empire would have significantly increased the emperor's real power. The emperor would stand to lose nothing at all. Even the Chamber Court was to remain part of the imperial establishment, and no reference whatever was made to the reform drafts of the Estates. On the other hand, the proposed imperial army, to be commanded by imperial captains, would have put a permanently mobilized force at his absolute disposal, ready and able to maintain the peace not only at home but also against foreign attack—Maximilian's two principal enemies France and Bohemia, were named, and the prevention of French preponderance was described as one of the "evident and important" concerns of the empire. To compensate the Estates for the increased payments they would in future have to contribute, they were to be granted a certain share in the imperial government. There were to be annual meetings of the diet with greatly expanded powers and competence. These diets were "to administer the law, the peace and the unity of the German Nation and the Holy Empire." Majority resolutions were to be binding and their implementation was to be entrusted, along with all executive matters, to the emperor, who for this purpose could call upon assistance and subsidies from the empire.

Considering the advantages the emperor and Maximilian would have drawn from this proposed arrangement while the Estates were to be put off with the promise of not much more than regular diets (which, incidentally, many of them regarded as a muisance), it is hard to understand why this only recently discovered project should ever have been considered as an understanding between Maximilian and the reform party. Unfortunately we do not know what attitude Berthold of Mainz and his supporters adopted toward Maximilian's proposal; the diet announced for the late autumn of 1491, at which the new ordinance was to be finally negotiated never took place, because Frederick III, convinced of the futility of all diets, would not allow it to be held. We only know the reactions of the most confirmed opponents of imperial reform, the Bavarian dukes; naturally they were averse to this proposal as well, having no desire to submit themselves to powerful imperial authority nor to an imperial deputy who "will take it upon himself to give orders to us."

But it can be assumed that the other Estates, too, and even members of the reform party, were at least suspicious of Maximilian's draft if not actually opposed to it, since they made it clear during the following year that a rigorous administrative reorganization of the empire was far from their minds. At the Diet of Koblenz in the autumn of 1492 Maximilian laid before the Estates a plan for an improved military and fiscal constitution for the Empire.[57] The whole organization was to be based on the ecclesiastical dioceses, which were eminently suitable for the

purpose since they constituted in fact the only developed administrative framework in the whole empire. The means for implement-
ing the imperial military system were to be obtained through a
direct and general imperial tax, to be raised according to the
number of hearths, though the authorities in the individual
localities had the duty of ensuring that burdens were shared
proportionately by rich and poor. For the supervision and
collection of the taxes in the individual localities, and for the
levying of troops, a commissariat was envisaged for each bishopric,
composed of two imperial deputies and two commissioners
appointed by emperor and king, and two commissioners chosen by
the electors in the name of the empire. Above these diocesan
authorities stood similarly constituted bodies in the archbishoprics,
except that they were staffed by four instead of two electoral
commissioners. At the apex there was to be a supreme imperial
deputy with a number of associates, and these, too, were to be
chosen by the electors on behalf of the empire. In the event of a
military campaign all the imperial deputies as well as two of the
electoral commissioners in each of the archbishoprics were to take
the field, while the remaining commissioners remained behind to
supervise the raising of taxes in their provinces and see to the
regular forwarding of the money to the field. Maximilian had
reserved for himself the ultimate right to supervise the use of the
money by means of personal field inspections; but he also met
the Estates in their legitimate demand for an accounting of what
was being done with their money. A reckoning was to be submitted quarterly by the commissioners to a committee of the
Estates sitting in Mainz.

At one point this draft agreed with the project of 1491. It
created an efficient executive dependent on the emperor alone and
ensured its permanence through an organization, adequate to its
purpose, while the Estates were to be compensated for their
sacrifices with a share in consultation and supervision. But this
share also included the participation of the Estates' commissioners
in fiscal administration—reminiscent of analogous attempts in the
territories—and was therefore considerably more generous than

the proposal of 1491. In the case of this new draft we are in a position to observe the attitude of the reform party, and we also know that Berthold of Mainz had a decisive influence on its formulation.[58] The royal proposal was completely altered by the Estates;[59] half of it—the imperial army with its deputies and the electoral commissioners who were assigned to the field—was struck out. And the tasks of the remaining commissioners were substantially reduced. They were deprived of their supervisory powers over the hearth tax (which has also reduced in amount by one-half) and over the levying of troops. They also lost their duty to dispatch the tax money to the deputies in the field. Instead, the revenue was to be put by "for the needs of the empire." Maximilian's stipulations concerning final negotiations about the entire organization were altered in such a way as to slow them down. While Maximilian was insisting on a binding reply from the individual Estates by Martinmas in order to bring matters to a swift conclusion, the draft of the Estates insisted on a new diet, but not until December. Only the emperor, the king and Archduke Philip, Maximilian's son, were to pledge themselves at once to payment of the imperial tax—the tendency, already noticeable in 1487, to insist on a contribution from the emperor before the Estates would pay anything appears here in a more embracing form. In only one point is the draft of the Estates reminiscent of the demands of the reform party: the obligation imposed on emperor and king to defend the Estates against foreign invasion. Agreement on a union settling the obligation of the Estates to provide reciprocal support was postponed until the next diet.

But since this diet never met, the whole plan for an imperial military and fiscal constitution petered out. The drafts for this constitution were never utilized, so that their significance for the history of imperial reform is very limited. On the other hand, they are valuable for revealing the attitude adopted by the reform party toward Maximilian. In the first place, the Estates struck out everything in Maximilian's plan which could have prejudiced the independence of territorial rulers; this is why the powers of supervision were taken away from the imperial bureaucrats (for the commisariat authorities might well be described as such) and why they were reduced to mere receivers of money. In the second place, the Estates eliminated everything which might have placed resources quickly and surely at the disposal of emperor and king. The House of Habsburg was to help bear the burdens of the other Estates, but the benefits of the payments made by the Estates and their subjects should accrue to the empire, not to the imperial dynasty. We may assume that the Estates would have reacted in a similar manner even to the imperial union of 1491 if there had been any serious negotiations on the subject.

In view of all this, it is impossible to conclude that Frederick III and Maximilian missed an opportunity in 1491 of reforming the empire with the full cooperation of the Estates.[60] Throughout the whole period of reform no such opportunity ever existed, because the differences between emperor and empire had already become much too marked and the divergence of interests much too consciously felt. Even in the linguistic usage of the time a clear distinction was being made between the emperor as proprietor of his Austrian patrimonial dominions, and the empire as the totality of the Estates.[61] But it is certainly true that this distinction (analogous to the dualism of sovereign and estates in the empire's territories) corresponded much more closely to political reality than the various political and legal theories which both then and later set out to derive the rights of the emperor from Roman law. It was the culmination of a long chain of events that the power of the emperor, once deprived of its direct political and financial resources, had to depend on his dynastic possessions and thus must gradually grow away from the empire. As early as 1438 the special status of the Habsburg dominions had become clear, in that both projects for an administrative division of the empire into circles, that of the electors and that of the royal councillors, left Austria and its neighboring lands out of account. The less interest Frederick III took in the affairs of the empire, and the more unrestrainedly he tried to make the resources of the Estates serve Habsburg interests, the wider the gap between the empire on the one hand, and Habsburg patrimonial dominions on the other. Thus Frederick's reign ended with emperor and Estates in opposition, an opposition extending even to matters (such as defense against the Magyars) in which the interests of the empire coincided precisely with those of the dynastic lands.

The Diet of Worms in 1495

The change of sovereign in 1493 served to make the relations between king and Estates worse than ever. There is no doubt that personal reasons played a part in this. Maximilian, the last of the medieval knights, may have been an attractive person and the most popular, perhaps the only popular, monarch in the later history of the empire to the great mass of the people, but he was never able to establish a working relationship with the leader of the Estates, Berthold of Mainz. I have referred elsewhere[62] to this personal difference between the two men and there is no need to go into it here; after all, substantive matters, not personal attitudes, were really decisive, chiefly the divergence of interests between the Holy Roman Empire and the ascending power of the Habsburg-Burgundian complex. The more Maximilian strove to draw the empire into the great struggle for the position of his house the stronger the opposition in the empire became. And the opposition arose not only from territories that had no wish to do anything whatever for the empire, but also from those that supported the idea of imperial reform. Thus it was that under Maximilian the reform movement came to life again.

As in 1485 under Frederick III, so now also it was the failures in the sovereign's foreign policies that enabled the Estates to put forward their demands and programs for reform. At the end of 1494 Maximilian found himself forced to summon the Estates to a diet at Worms.[63] The summons did make some mention of the obligation "to organize both court and justice" in addition to its usual request for an imperial subsidy; but since Maximilian only allowed two weeks for the diet's consultations and commanded the Estates to appear in full military array, it was obvious that his intentions toward internal reform were not serious at this time;

and the *Proposition* with which he opened the diet, late as usual, on March 26, 1495, dealt only with the imperial subsidy. But, as at every diet from 1485 to 1487, the Estates replied to the requests for assistance with their demand for a reform of the empire. A further reminiscence of the earlier diets was Maximilian's attempt to interrupt reform negotiations by demanding a speedy subsidy. But, again as always before, it was to no avail.

But this Diet of Worms was no mere repetition of what had gone on earlier; the demands of both sides, king and Estates, went much further than ever before. Maximilian, firmly convinced that the struggle against the rival power of France must be fought to a conclusion, and utterly determined to end the wearisome, tedious haggling with the Estates, confronted the session at its very beginning with a demand for a permanent subsidy, to be paid over the course of ten to twelve years. With this proposal he now made it abundantly clear that the ulterior motive behind his reform projects of 1486 and 1491 had been to obtain control over the empire's military resources. The Estates, for their part, adopted the same attitude to this new request as they had to all previous demands; they countered his request for a permanent subsidy for the purposes of foreign politics with the idea of a permanent internal administrative organization. And this internal reform, as became apparent at the very start of the Worms negotiations, was to be the condition for any support given to Maximilian against his enemies. The Estates refused to discuss anything else whatever during the first weeks.[64]

The originator of the plan for an ordinance setting up a general and permanent imperial organization was Elector Berthold of Mainz. Unfortunately it happens that the Mainz documents on imperial matters are none too informative on the whole of the reform period and tell us nothing at all about the Diet of Worms; thus even less than usual can be known of what was going on in Berthold's mind. Nor do other available records make it possible to form a clear picture of his plans. The original version of his proposals for the ordinance is preserved only in brief excerpts.[65] But as the first available full draft[66] does not depart in its essentials from these excerpts, it can probably be taken without hesitation as the sum of Berthold's political aims. His conception of a new imperial ordinance (*Reichsordnung*) was a further development of the constitution first projected in 1487. It combines the Estates' demands for the Public Peace, the Chamber Court and the defense against foreign invasion with Maximilian's own request for a subsidy against the Turks. (Berthold seems to have wanted to avoid an open declaration of war against France, though he cannot have doubted that the struggle against France was nearer to Maximilian's heart than the campaigns against the Turks.) The new draft went beyond the earlier project in two ways: first, it sought to provide a financial basis for the new ordinance and, second and much more important, it aimed to procure for the Estates a permanent share in the government of the empire. The organ for exercising this share in government was to be a permanent Imperial Governing Council (*Reichsrat* or *Reichsregiment*), sitting in Frankfurt. Of its seventeen members only one, the president, was to be appointed by the king; the electors were to provide six of the other members, and the remaining ten were to be "taken" from among the territories of the empire and from the cities. Nothing was said about how these ten would first be appointed. Presumably they were to have been chosen by all the Estates acting jointly at meetings of the imperial diet. In any case, in the future the right to fill these places was to belong to the Governing Council itself, while retiring electoral councillors would be replaced as the need arose by the electors who had appointed them. In general, the whole project favored electoral interests and ambitions. One elector, determined by a fixed system of rotation among the seven, was always to serve personally on the Governing Council, and he would also have the right to stand in for the president. Once a year all the electors were to gather at the seat of the council in order to "determine whether all proceedings are being carried out according to the agreed order." Thus they constituted a supervisory authority for the imperial council, to which the council members had to turn in cases of great moment which they could not venture to decide on their own.

This Imperial Governing Council, then, was intended as the supreme central authority in the empire. Its members were to be altogether independent, bound only to the Governing Council's constitution, with no primary or other obligations to Maximilian or any particular Estate. Its competence was extraordinarily extensive. It constituted the imperial government in fact as well as in name, and it made no secret of its intention to assume the place of the king, who, as the council's constitution itself stated, was prevented by the multifarious demands of his foreign interests from giving the necessary attention to the government of the empire and was thus only to retain such insignificant rights as the bestowal of offices and hereditary titles. All remaining administrative business within the empire was to be transferred to the council, which even formally, in its decrees and pronouncements, was to appear as the bearer of the royal authority. Its major task was to be the imposition of a thoroughgoing reform of the empire. It was to supervise the activities and execute the judgments of the Chamber Court, newly instituted, maintain the peace not only within the empire and among the individual Estates but also in respect of foreign powers. Furthermore, it was to make all the necessary preparations for the proposed Turkish war; and by this were meant negotiations with the Christian powers of Europe and the recruitment of an army for the purpose of pressing the campaigns in the field. The financial means both for the war and for the fulfillment of its general duties were to be made available by means of a universal imperial tax.

The effect of the Imperial Governing Council would have been to create a powerful central authority in the empire. It would have required the individual Estates to renounce much of the freedom they had previously enjoyed. They would have been curtailed in their relations with foreign powers, and a measure of control would have been imposed not only over their revenues and of those of their subjects, but also, and most important, over their military resources; for, according to the original working, the council needed the approval of the electors only for the raising of a "general" subsidy, but could raise lesser subsidies on its own authority for various necessities, such as the suppression of the universal nuisance presented by the robber barons.

Maximilian himself was, of course, much more hemmed in than were the territories. The restrictions, in fact, were directed not only against the territorial sovereignty he exercised in his hereditary lands, which was now, like that of all the other Estates, to come under the control of the Governing Council, but against his royal prerogatives themselves. Compared with the Governing Council, he had as good as no authority in any matter whatever. Only if he happened to be in the vicinity of Frankfurt, could he summon the council to his presence, and he was further restricted in his negotiations with the council by the stipulation that he might be advised by no more than four councillors, who must, moreover, all be Germans by birth.

Depriving territorial rulers of the free choice of councillors and forcing them to appoint only native Germans to their councils was a tendency to be found in the public affairs of all the Estates. But the constitution of the proposed Governing Council went much further than the usual demands of territorial Estates. It proposed no mere restriction of royal authority, but represented an attempt to replace it with a formal organization controlled by the Estates. Thus it introduced a new idea into the history of German imperial reform, though, as with all the other demands of the Estates, a precedent can be found for it in the earlier history of the empire. The origin of the whole idea can be seen from the predominance accorded to the electors in the proposed council. Several times in the past the electors had tried to take the government of the empire into their own hands; whenever there had been some failure on the part of a sovereign—under Ludwig the Bavarian in 1338, for example, or under Wenzel in 1399, Sigismund during the early phase of the Hussite Wars, or Frederick III in 1446, and again in the 1450's—the seven electors had joined forces in the attempt to secure a decisive influence over the government of the empire by means of forming an electoral union, setting aside the royal authority altogether. During the reform period this practice developed into the idea of a permanent imperial

Governing Council in which the electors would rule, not along with the king, but above him.

As soon, however, as this plan began to be unfolded there took place a repetition of the old scene that had been enacted at all the previous diets: many of the Estates, while happily joining with the reformers in opposing the king and his requests for subsidies, were utterly averse to any strengthening of central authority in the empire. From the very first day the imperial cities voiced the fear that the planned reorganization of the empire would lead to "perpetual tribute or servitude" and impose permanent burdens upon them.[67] Berthold of Mainz managed to pay little attention to the cities throughout the course of the negotiations over the reform, and the opposition of the cities alone would not have presented too severe a stumbling block; but similar suspicions prevailed among the other Estates, too, probably among a majority of them, as can be seen from the subsequent insertion of a clause imposing a time limit on the new ordinance.[68] The principal opponents of the ordinance were to be found in the Council of Princes. There the extensive powers of the Governing Council and the favored position given the electors aroused such lively misgivings that the electors could not avoid taking them into account. As a result the Governing Council's power of arbitration in disputes among Estates was eliminated and the prohibition on raising "common" subsidies was extended to cover general imperial subsidies. But most of the wishes of the princes were merely noted, without any effort to revise the ordinance or to keep the cities informed of what was going on. The essential intent of these wishes was to put the princes in all matters on the same level as the electors and to prevent the Governing Council from issuing new laws without the consent of all the Estates of the empire. The Landgraves of Hesse, for their part, could not by any means be moved to accept the ordinance and reserved their attitude; the dukes of Bavaria, too, were unalterably opposed to a strong Imperial Governing Council. It seems certain that this aversion to any imperial authority, even though exercised by the Estates, was much more widespread than the available accounts suggest,[69] as can be seen from the attitude of the electors of Saxony and Brandenburg toward the Chamber Court (which will be referred to later on). If this aversion of the Estates to any strengthening of central authority during the negotiations at Worms has usually been underestimated this is due not only to the secrecy in which all the discussions among the Estates were shrouded, but also to the fact that the principal opponent of the organization of the Governing Council was Maximilian himself.

When the plan first came to his attention, Maximilian had declared himself amenable to a permanent imperial constitution and had reserved his supreme authority only in general terms. Even when, during the course of May, the drafts of the Estates concerning the Governing Council, the Public Peace, the Chamber Court ordinance and the Common Penny had been passed on to him,[70] he did not advance his misgivings. Such restraint was doubtless dictated by considerations of the hoped-for subsidy, a matter he was pursuing with fervent tenacity. But the drawing-out of the negotiations which this involved only served to heighten the already existing tension between king and Estates. The latter exacerbated Maximilian with the difficulties they put in the way of the subsidy he so urgently required, and Maximilian's clumsy actions and his inclination to submit constantly changing proposals put them on their guard and reduced even further their already limited inclination to pay. Thus, when Maximilian attempted in the middle of June to reach a compromise with the Estates in the matter of the Governing Council, it was too late. His proposals, in any case, did not go far enough. He simply declared himself willing to appoint, with the advice of the electors and princes, a number of privy councillors (*Hofräte*) who, under his control and at his court, would direct the business of the empire in accordance with the constitution of the Governing Council as drawn up by the Estates, insofar as the council was compatible with the authority of the king of the Romans. He would agree to the separation of these councillors from his court only for such periods as he himself was not in the empire; for such contingencies he wished to appoint a presiding official, but would not tolerate a permanent president above himself.[71] On this basis Maximilian negotiated with the electors and with a number of trusted princes, Duke Albrecht of Saxony, Margrave Frederick of Brandenburg, and Count Eberhard of Württemberg, the same men who, in 1491, had tried in vain to bring the king to some agreement with the reform party. But he achieved nothing. On June 20 the assembled Estates resolved unanimously to maintain the position they had adopted from the beginning of the diet, namely, to approve no subsidy without prior concessions in the matter of internal reform. In fact, they went further at this time. They refused even to continue negotiations as long as Maximilian pursued his accustomed tactics ("every day a new proposal") and delayed coming to any resolution on the Estates' reform drafts.[72]

This incisive declaration on the part of the Estates achieved the desired effect inasmuch as Maximilian did reply to the drafts without any more delay. But as regards the matter in hand, the only result it could have was to magnify the existing differences. Maximilian couched his misgivings about the proposed Governing Council in the form of a counter-proposal,[73] which, as has often been observed since Ranke, took up the wording of the Estates' draft in order to reverse its meaning (a procedure used by Frederick III in 1487 against the constitution). Count Haug von Werdenberg, the adviser of both rulers, may have been the author of this tactic, though nothing is accurately known about the part played by councillors in the politics of either the emperor or the king. Maximilian's counter-project was fully in keeping with the view he had already set forth in his compromise proposal. It sought to turn the permanent imperial Governing Council into a governing body appointed by the king, which might act only during his absence from the empire and on the basis of an "instruction" issued by himself. Even then it would have to leave everything "pertaining to the dignity and authority of the Royal Majesty" to the king himself. The prohibition on autonomous policies was to apply only to the Estates, not to the king. Maximilian criticized the remaining drafts of the Estates as well, but the details need not be given here; it will be sufficient to show the direction in which the king's proposals were pointing. His intentions correspond exactly to those behind his reform plans of 1486, 1491, and 1492, and for that very reason the present proposals were unacceptable to the Estates.

Unfortunately there is a gap in the records between June 26 and July 6, and this is all the more regrettable since during these days a sort of compromise was reached between the king and the reform party. The Estates dropped the idea of a permanent Governing Council and contented themselves with exercising their influence over the government of the empire through the annual diets which Maximilian had already conceded in 1491. On the other hand, they did not cease to insist that any imperial subsidy granted to the king should be contingent upon internal reform, and they held fast to their demand that Maximilian enter into a formal contract with the Estates to bind himself to observe the reform ordinances that were to be rewritten. This contractual obligation upon the king was taken over from the draft proposal for the Governing Council and was now incorporated in a new project called "Administration of Peace and Justice."[74] This administration (*Handhabung*) took the form of an agreement between Maximilian on the one side and the body of the Estates on the other. Maximilian was to pledge himself to execute the ordinances for the Public Peace, the Chamber Court, and the Common Penny not only within his own and his son's hereditary lands, but also and expressly, as king of the Romans. The Estates, for their part, were to commit themselves both to the king and to one another that their conduct would be governed by the ordinances. The Common Penny was not expressly mentioned in this pledge of the Estates, but there can be no doubt that it was one of the ordinances referred to.

But now that an agreement between king and Estates seemed to be in the offing the division among the Estates themselves became clearly apparent: whenever the reform party seemed to be in sight of some positive achievement, its other opponent, the so-called party of "freedom" (*Libertät*) took objection to any strengthening of central authority in the empire and to any attempt to bind the

Estates to universally applicable imperial laws. No matter what ordinance was proposed—the Public Peace, the Chamber Court, the Common Penny—the anti-reform princes revealed themselves intent mainly on reducing their burdens and obligations while the reform party, in order to achieve anything at all, gave in to them on almost every point. Even during the preliminary discussions on the Imperial Governing Council the princes had proved that they wanted no strong executive organ in the empire on the lines of the proposed council. But now they raised objections even to the very modest substitute which the draft of the administration sought to introduce.[75] According to this proposal annual diets were to take the place of a permanent Governing Council in order to supervise the implementation of imperial ordinances, but it was clear from the very start that in many cases of breach of peace or other trouble it would be impossible to wait until the convening of this diet. It had, after all, been one of the principal weaknesses of the empire that the king was often too far away and too occupied with the problems of his dynastic possessions to see that the judgments of the courts were promptly executed, and there was no authority in the empire which might have taken over this task from him. For this reason the first draft of the administration provided that a group of electors, princes, counts, and cities, each to be expressly named, should assemble in urgent cases at the instance of the judge of the Chamber Court and pass the necessary resolutions instead of the diet. It was this provision (which may, incidentally, be seen as a forerunner of the regular imperial deputation (*Reichsdeputation*) created in 1555)[76] that was struck out, at the insistence of the of the "party of liberty," with the result that the empire, now as before, was to remain for the greater part of each year without an assured executive.

This aversion to any established imperial authority emerged again with the new ordinances concerning the Public Peace. This new law was based entirely, even in its wording, on the very first law passed during the reform period, the Frankfurt Public Peace ordinance of March 17, 1486,[77] with only two substantial alterations. The time limitation, which in 1486 had had to be included in the law, was left out on this occasion, apparently without arousing any opposition. This was, to be sure, an important step forward (its significance will be considered presently), but other changes introduced in the regulations concerning the executive authority for the Public Peace represented a further substantial weakening of the mild and, in practice, ineffective provisions of 1486. According to the earlier provisions the judge of the Chamber Court was empowered to call upon the Estates to afford assistance or even, if occasion arose, to take military action against violators of the Public Peace, and the declaration of 1487 permitted even victims of such attacks to request support from the Estates, which might not be refused. These provisions were completely struck out in the new Public Peace ordinance and were only renewed toward the end in the so-called "Recess of the Diet of Worms"[78] as a transitional provision to have effect until the next diet. In general, however, it was determined that the power to call up the assistance of the Estates should be transferred from the judge of the Chamber Court to the annual diet. Only in emergencies could the judge summon a special session of the diet, though not a meeting of the deputation (*Deputationstag*), as the administration had at first envisaged. As a result, the implementation of the Public Peace was withdrawn from the central authorities of the empire and left to the discretion of the Estates.

The differences between the supporters and opponents of imperial reform appeared at their sharpest in the drafts for reorganizing the Chamber Court. Inasmuch as Smend has recently dealt with this subject on the basis of new source material to which I am unable to add anything, it will be enough here to emphasize the main points. The Estates were agreed that the rights of the king over the Chamber Court must be substantially curtailed. The electors as well as the princes based their discussions on the draft proposals of 1486 and 1487, without taking cognizance of the objections raised at the time by the emperor in matters of political importance. On the other hand, they differed in their views on the appointment of the court's assessors and the extent of its legal competence. In the matter of the appointment of assessors, we have an obvious case of envy on the part of the princes toward the electors. The electors wished to have their own appointed assessors in the court, just as they had them on the Governing Council, while the princes demanded that all the members of the court should be appointed by the Estates acting jointly, at the diet. In the matter of the court's legal competence we see most clearly the antithesis between imperial reform and the so-called "liberty" of princes, an antithesis which even split the electoral council where the two most powerful of the temporal electors, Saxony and Brandenburg, were in this instance the keenest opponents of the elector of Mainz, who, in keeping with his desire to strengthen the empire, wished to make the Chamber Court a true supreme court of justice in the empire, with jurisdiction over all princes, exempting none. This idea was decisively rejected by Saxony and Brandenburg, while the Council of Princes proposed a middle way; princes of the empire were not to be arraigned before the Chamber Court but instead before a Court of Arbitration composed of their own councillors; appeals against verdicts of this court might go to the Chamber Court, though this procedure would not infringe any of the privileges of appeal which had already been secured. It is clear from all this that the opponents of imperial reform commanded a majority in the Council of Princes. The reform party, on the other hand, would have nothing to do with any such mutilation of imperial powers of justice, and no agreement was reached among the Estates. Instead, the various drafts were passed on to the king, who attempted to mediate in the matter. Maximilian confirmed the competence of the Chamber Court over the princes but agreed to acknowledge existing exemptions. For the rest, he attempted once again to maintain his rights, though he showed himself ready to go very much further than his father in meeting the views of his opponents, and did not raise any objections to the transfer of the power to impose the ban from the emperor to the Chamber Court. All he demanded was that his jurisdictional sovereignty be recognized and that he might call the Chamber Court to his court while in residence in the empire. He only wished to continue to be governing Roman king in fact as well as in name.

In all these controversial issues the reform party reacted in a characteristic manner both toward the king and toward the opposition among the territorial princes. As regards the king, the reformers stood by their previous demand that the Chamber Court have its own fixed seat in the empire, regardless of where the king might be residing at any particular time. But to the princes they made many concessions. The membership of the Chamber Court was arranged in accordance with their draft, and even in procedural matters the princes had their way almost completely: at the first stage of any legal proceedings imperial princes were to appear not before the Chamber Court but before their own councillors; appeals to the Chamber Court were admitted, and the express reservation of the privileges of appeal, through which the princes had made this concession illusory, was struck out. But since the very next article of the Chamber Court ordinance went on to recognize once again all existing privileges it cannot be said with any certainty that the princes were really willing to renounce their freedom of appeal.

The attitude of the reform party—uncompromising toward the king and yielding toward opposition from among the princes—can also be seen from the negotiations concerning the Common Penny. The four-year time limit mentioned in the July draft of the Estates will probably not be considered as a weakening of the reform idea in view of the explanation attached to it.[79] As the whole imperial reform movement, as well as the Chamber Court in particular, was to be financed by the Common Penny, a standing tax of some kind was presupposed. All the same, the time limit did constitute a serious prejudice. Even more serious, and more revealing of the general aversion to an imperial tax, was the manner in which the tax rate was apportioned. The tax rate was set lower than Maximilian thought expedient in the interests of his foreign policies, and lower even than had been envisaged in the first draft of the Estates; and it was precisely the rich who came off most lightly. The rich were, of course, mainly the princes. They did, to be sure, propose "to do something more," but they were even then going around with the idea of making good the expense, work, and trouble they would incur at the diets on behalf of the empire by balancing it all against their tax contribution. Maximilian, on the other hand, was required to raise the taxes in his hereditary lands prior to the levies of the Estates in their territories, a requirement in keeping with the proceedings at the diets of Nuremberg and Koblenz in 1487 and 1492.[80] And this condition was imposed even though it was not Maximilian himself who was to receive the money; in fact, since the contributions were destined both for the Turkish subsidy and the implementation of imperial reform, it was stipulated that a commission of seven treasurers, one appointed by the king and the remainder by the Estates, was to collect the money and disburse it in accordance with the resolutions of the annual diet.

It was near the end of July before the Estates agreed on all the details; not until July 26 were the various drafts, old and new, for the Public Peace, the Chamber Court, the Common Penny, and the Administration submitted to the king. Not very much was achieved compared with the first versions which he had rejected in June. But Maximilian realized only too well that he could expect no subsidy unless he accepted the conditions of the Estates, and the need for resources for his planned war against France was much too great to leave him in a position to go on battling against their demands. Indeed, the question of the subsidy had determined the whole of the king's conduct at the Diet of Worms; it had forced him to undergo four months of wearisome haggling with the Estates. To continue standing upon his royal authority would endanger all he had hoped for by waiting. He confined himself, therefore, to the most essential objections to the drafts, and he came out with them at once in order to avoid drawing out the negotiations any further. He naturally demanded that the raising of the Common Penny be carried out in all the territories simultaneously, and he also urged that the time during which payment might be made be shortened. Once again he claimed the right to have the Chamber Court attend on him during his sojourn in the empire. For the rest, however, he allowed the Estates' drafts to stand.[81]

Further negotiations taking place in the week from July 28 to August 4 remain once again unaccounted for, as the cities were kept out of them. We know only the result as contained in the final ordinances. Once more the wishes of the territorial princes asserted themselves, and peace and order in the empire were again neglected in favor of their particular advantages.[82] Their aversion to a permanent imperial tax seems to have prevailed. There was no further attempt to shorten the time allowed for payment, and the continued existence of the Chamber Court after the expiry of the tax period was ensured by burdening the king with its costs. But the principal negotiations probably did not take place among the Estates themselves but rather between king and Estates. The greatest difficulties appear to have been presented by the question of the urgent subsidy which Maximilian was constantly demanding with every new proposal. He wished at least to get full value for all the reforms he was having to concede, but he seems to have worried himself very little about the individual stipulations in the various reform drafts, for no further substantial alterations were made in them. The main points concerning the Public Peace had never been disputed; as for the Imperial Chamber Court, the Estates stood firm and refused to let it be attached to the king's residence. As regards the Common Penny, however, they did at least abandon the idea of placing the Habsburg lands in a special category. They allowed the Penny to be paid there at the same time as in the other territories. Admittedly, however, the old prejudice lingered on in the rider that if the payment were made promptly in the hereditary lands "Electors, Princes, and Estates will be all the more willing to contribute." In the administration, too, more consideration was shown to the royal authority than had been provided for in the early drafts. The participation of the king or his representative at the annual diets was accorded equal status with that of the Estates. On the other hand, the restriction on the right of both king and Estates to enter into alliances, originally envisaged in the plans for the Imperial Governing

Council, was written into the new administration, where it was stated that the king, his son the Archduke Philip, and the Estates could not start a war without the approval of the diet or form any alliance with foreign powers which might be disadvantageous to the empire.

Once the matter of the urgent subsidy had been solved by the granting of a loan the new ordinances could be finally proclaimed on August 7, 1495. In the seventeenth and eighteenth centuries it was occasionally asked what had become of the final decrees issued at Worms.[83] There can be no question that what is generally called the "Recess of Worms," an amorphous collection of provisional regulations,[84] was no *Reichsabschied*, or recess, in the later sense, that is to say, an agreement between king and Estates combining all the individual settlements and drawn up in proper legal style. The simple answer is that there were no such recesses until after the imperial reform had gone into effect; the earliest such recess was that of Lindau in 1497. Recesses originated in a trend that dominated the whole of the imperial reform movement: the insistence on a mutually binding contract between king and Estates to ensure that all resolutions were fully implemented. Formal recesses of this sort had not before been known; decisions of the diets which were to remain in force either permanently or at least over a long period had formerly been promulgated as royal mandates, as was the case, for example, with the laws pertaining to the Public Peace. Other agreements were recorded without any special formality. Even the Hussite tax of 1427, the forerunner of the Common Penny, had not been formally drawn up.[85] These conventional practices, then, were employed for the Diet of Worms. Matters of merely transitory importance— such as the appointment of the princes who were to negotiate with the nonrepresented Estates about the acceptance of the new ordinance, or the drawing up of an agenda for the next diet—were collated as before in a *Zettel*, or note. The reform laws, on the other hand, were published in individual documents. The Public Peace and the Chamber Court ordinance appeared as royal mandates under the royal seal, while the ordinance respecting the Common Penny and the Administration, containing mutual commitments on the part of King and Estates, were promulgated as contracts between both parties under the seals of the king and various Estates.

These ordinances of Worms were the first major achievement of the imperial reform movement. The Perpetual Public Peace, above all other measures, gained public notice and popularity; it was undoubtedly the diet's title to fame. It is true that the idea of a perpetual peace had been implicit in all the earlier stages of reform and that an attempt had been made as early as 1438 to turn it into a reality. But now, for the first time, it was universally accepted and permanently retained. Even if more than a generation was to pass before the inhabitants of the empire could confidently rely on the preservation of the Public Peace, it is still the merit of the Diet of Worms to have established the principle that the members of the empire should live in peace among themselves, that they should advance their opposing claims only along the peaceful paths of legal proceedings or arbitration, and that they would come to one another's assistance against all violations of law and order. It is true that this commitment to mutual support was still uncertainly worded and offered no guarantee that it would be honored; the obligation to common defense against foreign invasion was also very vaguely defined. But there can be no denying that an advance had been made on what had obtained previously, and there is a grain of validity in the plan of Justus Möser to begin the history of the later empire with the year 1495.[86]

Care was also taken that the Public Peace should not collapse for lack of an organized legal system. Admittedly the reform party shrank from any suggestion of intervening in territorial jurisdiction (which had still appeared permissible in 1438) such as a directive to all the Estates to pursue justice honestly and fairly.[87] Territorial justice, therefore, remained completely outside the purview of imperial legislation, and, as has been noted, the attempt to subject the princes to the jurisdiction of the Chamber Court proved unavailing. But the Diet of Worms had brought a supreme imperial court into existence, a tribunal which, as a court of appeal, was open to nearly all mediate and immediate subjects of the empire and, in cases of denial of rights, was open as a court of first instance to all men without exception.

Where the reform was least successful in effecting a permanent organization was the realm of imperial finance. Nothing could have been achieved here without directly or indirectly burdening the Estates themselves; therefore the powerful supporters of territorial liberties, whose influence made itself felt throughout the duration of the diet, asserted themselves most strongly in matters of finance. They refused to countenance any consolidation of the empire or the establishment of any central authority, and they were not prepared to make any sacrifices whatever on behalf of the empire. Their resistance to the imperial tax was supported by the aversion of the imperial cities to a "perpetual tribute." Thus the Common Penny was only approved for a period of four years, as has been noted, after which time all the burdens of imperial administration and wars were to fall once more upon the king. But the most grievous deficiency of the new revenue system was the absence of an administrative organization. All that was stipulated in the ordinance was a central authority, the college of seven treasurers already mentioned. These treasurers were to appoint commissioners for each of the territories, but the powers of these officials were very narrowly circumscribed. They were authorized merely to collect the tax contributions of the individual territories and hand them on to the treasurers. They could neither help in the assessment, nor in the raising of the taxes. There is no doubt that this limitation was fully intentional, for whenever in previous years the idea of an imperial tax and its collection had been brought up it had invariably been frustrated by the territorial authorities, who would allow no one a glimpse into the strength and assets of their lands.[88] The organization proposed by Maximilian in 1492 had also been truncated for this very reason by the Estates, as has been seen already. The empire's abandonment of all supervision over the raising of taxes in the individual territories was all the more serious as matters of control were now left exclusively to the discretion of regional authorities. The ineffectiveness of the Common Penny was to prove very soon how serious a mistake this had been. Thus the Common Penny made no contribution to any improvement of imperial finances. All the same, the reform party did serve the empire and its cause well in its attempt to make a reality of the universal obligation to contribute to the expenses of the empire.

The most important part of the imperial reform, however, was the new settlement of the relationship between king and Estates. Rudolf Smend, it is true, has disputed that the Worms reform can be considered as "the realization of definite principles of constitution,[89] but I cannot agree with him. An attempt to determine the ultimate aims of the reform party must begin with the drafts submitted by it, not with the final ordinances, which were compromises negotiated among king and Estates, and as such were considerably weakened compared to their original intentions. There can be no possible doubt that Berthold of Mainz went substantially further in his reform plans at the Diet of Worms than he had at any of the previous sessions. He endeavoured to bring about a comprehensive reorganization of the whole empire; all that had proved itself, over the course of the years, to be in need of political and moral reform was to be firmly regulated at this diet. It was this tendency which gave rise to the proposals for overhauling the monetary system as well as the decree against blasphemies. There were also plans for sumptuary regulations against luxury and extravagance, and concerted action against the encroachments of the Roman curia.[90] These tasks were attempted at ensuing diets, some were broadened in scope and, what is most to the point here, all represented new elements in imperial legislation. But even in the more restricted context of the imperial constitution, Berthold cherished much more far-reaching plans than at any prior time. As has already been observed, it is impossible to maintain that the Frankfurt diets of 1485 and 1486 intended to bring about a fundamental alteration of the imperial constitution. The earliest reform programs contained nothing more than suggestions for the Public Peace, the Chamber Court, and the defense against foreign invasion. When the princes threatened to infringe the emperor's prerogatives in 1486 it was precisely the electors who opposed them in this venture. But at the Diet of Nuremberg in the very next year the reform party went well beyond the draft of the princes which had only just been rejected, and attempted to carry through a comprehensive program of reform by means of a treaty with the emperor. Even this draft, had it been implemented, would have meant a diminution of the emperor's position, and for this reason Frederick opposed it, but it did not involve an infringement of the emperor's powers to govern. Most likely it was during the fruitless sessions after 1486, and as a result of Maximilian's eccentric and seemingly directionless political activity, that Berthold first became convinced of the impossibility of effecting a permanent cure of the empire's weakness without firmly subordinating the monarch to the Estates. At the Diet of Worms he set about his task with energy, fully conscious of its significance. He no longer contented himself, as he had still done in 1487, with the project of a union between emperor and Estates for the preservation of the Public Peace and the Chamber Court and for defense against invasion. He now aimed at taking the implementation of the entire imperial reform project out of the king's hands and transferring it to an imperial Governing Council controlled by the Estates. One might say that he tried to neutralize the dualism of emperor and empire by subordinating the emperor to a securely reorganized empire. But this would probably be too modern a terminology for what he intended, though it might not be inappropriate to describe this idea as the substance of the reform attempted by the Estates. The aim was undoubtedly to reinforce the power of the Estates through a firm mutual alliance and to establish the empire on the basis of a close association of the Estates. The purpose behind this was to develop the permanent organization of the diet which was another work of Berthold of Mainz and one that proved its worth against the king at the Diet of Worms. Maximilian's complaint that at Worms he had to stand outside the door is well known. The capstone of this association of the Estates was to be the imperial Governing Council; there is no need to re-emphasize at this point how high the Governing Council was intended to tower above the king. This move to render the king permanently dependent on the Estates and to transfer to the Estates the government of the empire previously controlled by the king appears to me to be the constitutional principle which Berthold of Mainz wished to realize at the Diet of Worms. In the final days of the Worms negotiations, Berthold could still propose that the originally planned limitation on the king in the choice of his councillors—a restriction which fell through when the whole imperial Governing Council was rejected—ought to be preserved at least formally through the requirement that "his Royal Majesty's councillors should also be pledged to the Empire."[91]

Maximilian may have managed to ward off the imposition of an imperial Governing Council, but the twofold aim of the reform party, to federate the Estates and subordinate the king to them, persisted even after the idea of the Governing Council had been dropped. This aim lived on in the Administration of Peace and Justice, which for that very reason is constitutionally the most important law passed at the Diet of Worms. Its result, first of all, was to give substance to the idea of an organization of the Estates by bringing all the Estates together to implement and maintain the reform laws passed at Worms. The very importance of these laws made the alliance of the Estates significant, though more important still is the fact that the alliance came into being at all. Up to this time, the imperial constitution had suffered most of all from the contradiction between theory and practice. In theory the authority of the emperor was unlimited, but in reality it ended at the borders of the territories. Long ago it had become the custom for emperors and kings, if they wished to carry out a task in some particular territory (the maintenance of the Public Peace, for example) to form leagues among the Estates involved, and occasionally to enter themselves into such alliances with the Estates. Among the Estates, too, the practice of forming unions had become widespread during the fourteenth and fifteenth centuries. Now, it is quite clear that this practice provided a model for the imperial reform movement to adopt. Maximilian's draft alliance of 1491 may have been suggested by the Swabian League.

In the case of the Estates it is possible to follow exactly the development from the desired union to the particular purpose, namely the defense against "alien dangers," by way of the "constitution" of 1487, to the administration. The new element in the movement toward union during the reform period was the tendency to universality and unlimited duration, and in 1495 the Estates were the first to achieve a universal and binding union of this sort in the form of the administration. For this reason they could quite happily do without a special federation to ward off potential foreign enemies; which explains why the Diet of Worms, as opposed to earlier diets, made no effort to bring such a federation into being. Now that the resistance of the king had scuttled the projected Governing Council, the imperial union of Estates evolved for itself an organ of control in the annual session of the diet. It was not until the very end of the Diet of Worms that it was agreed to admit the king or his representatives into the administration. The regular diet was to be the supreme authority in the empire set over all other governing bodies. It controlled the treasurers and decided how imperial taxes were to be spent. It supervised the Chamber Court and was responsible for executing verdicts and maintaining the Public Peace. Finally it conducted the foreign policies of the Estates and even of the king.

Thus the union of Estates served also as a means of achieving the second principal aim of imperial reform, the subordination of the king to the Estates. For however many of the details had had to be struck out from the restrictive stipulations of the ordinances setting up the Governing Council, the Estates had managed to gain their most important point in the administration: not only did Maximilian lose his autonomy in his dynastic lands when his hereditary territories were deprived of their traditional special position and were subordinated to the laws of the empire, but his political freedom as king, his relations with foreign powers, were submitted to the control of the Estates. Even on this point the king was not to enjoy rights exceeding those of the other Estates. And through their power of disposition over imperial taxes the Estates secured an efficient instrument for rendering Maximilian compliant.

This naturally represented a shift of Maximilian's position in the empire, a shift which found its expression in the new constitution of the Chamber Court. True, the king retained the supreme judicial authority in the empire, and for this reason it was customary at the time to speak of a mere "reformation" of the Court.[92] But this does not touch on the essential point. The Chamber Court as set up in 1495 was something other than the old Chamber at the court of emperor and king. The Governing Council, too, was to have governed formally in the name of the king, and yet would have completely ousted him from the rule of the empire. In the same way, the king, despite his position as supreme judicial authority, had nothing to say in the Chamber Court, and it is this fact which is decisive in any estimate of the constitutional significance of the Chamber Court ordinance of 1495. The Chamber Court was separated from the king's establishment and was given its permanent seat in Frankfurt, where, of course, it came under the supervision of the annual diet. Furthermore, the king was to be deprived of all influence over the composition of the court, and this intention was carried out, despite the compromise wording which was finally chosen when his objections were made known. The assessors appointed in the year 1495 were, as Smend has discovered, chosen by the imperial assembly in a manner similar to that of the subsequent "presentation." Smend is of the opinion that this procedure was occasioned by purely practical considerations, and it must be admitted that Frederick III himself sometimes called upon the electors to propose suitable assessors for the Chamber Court. But it is one thing for the emperor, acting from his own authority, to accept councillors put forward by the Estates; it is quite another thing for the Estates to appoint them as a matter of law. As regards the presentation to the Chamber Court, reference may well be made to the universal tendency among the Estates to deputize trusted persons as councillors to the emperor's court and thus also to the sovereign's tribunal of justice. This tendency, which appeared clearly in the ordinance of the Governing Council, also influenced the Estates in the organization of the Chamber Court. In the first drafts they wished to exclude the king altogether from any role in the selection of its members.

Maximilian put up a hard fight against the Estates in an attempt to assert his old position vis-à-vis the Chamber Court. Since Smend was able to show in detail how haphazardly the Chamber Court was designated in the declarations of Estates and emperor alike—Imperial Chamber Court (*Reichskammergericht*), the Emperor's Chamber Court (*kaiserliches Kammergericht*), both together the Emperor's and Imperial Chamber Court (*kaiserliches und Reichskammergericht*)—the customary importance formerly attached to these names is now lost. But it is, perhaps, not totally without significance that Maximilian, in his counterproposals, regularly avoided the expression *Reichskammergericht* and spoke only of the *königliches Kammergericht*, the Royal Chamber Court. At all events the antithesis between the king's court and that of the Estates was consciously felt by both Maximilian and the Estates. Maximilian resisted with the utmost tenacity any permanent separation of the court from his residence, and even after the Diet of Worms he did not cease in his opposition to the Estates' organization of the Chamber Court. It is true that Maximilian and his successors later exercised a rival jurisdiction with the Chamber Court, but this does not seem to me to affect the significance of the Chamber Court ordinance one way or the other. Maximilian was not asked at Worms to promise expressly to refrain from such judicial competition, but this may have been an oversight on the part of the Estates, because they took it for granted that he would not compete in this way and never considered the possibility of a rival royal jurisdiction. The Chamber Court ordinance, unlike that of Brandenburg in 1540, for example, did not envisage the possibility of appeals or supplications to the king. And the resistance which Maximilian set up to the separation of the Chamber Court from his residence may well be an indication that he, too, had not originally thought of circumventing the Estates in this way. But whatever attitude may be adopted to his particular question, there can be no doubt in general that the organization of the Chamber Court is not merely a piece of administrative history but a move of major constitutional significance. It represents a substantial part of the constitutional reform at Worms. The reform in general sought to shift the balance of government from the king to a union of Estates, and the Chamber Court ordinance accomplished just that in the administration of justice.

If this view is accepted it seems hardly appropriate to claim that the imperial reform was "monarchical" in its tendency.[93] The German reform movement, in fact, stood in sharp contrast to developments in other major European states, where royal authority was asserting itself powerfully and thrusting all competition aside. In the empire, on the other hand, the Estates were in the ascendancy. An electoral oligarchy attempted in the Governing Council ordinance to gain the direction of the empire, and as a result of the Administration the supreme political authority belonged no longer to the king, but to the annual diet. Thus the reform party identified itself with the Estates in opposition to the king, but took a centralizing stand in opposition to the particularism of most of the territorial princes belonging to the party of "liberty." In other words, the reform party was for the empire as a whole (reichisch). It wished to set up a firm and established organization of the empire to which the king must submit himself and to which every single Estate had also to conform. It laid down binding laws, required the burdens of the imperial tax to be shared by all without exception, and set limits to all existing forms of autonomy.

King and territories: these then, were the two opposing forces whose power had to be defeated if the reform party was to maintain itself. Even during the Diet of Worms the aversion of both opponents of the new order had come often enough to the fore, but at first the antithesis beween reform and the adherents of "liberty" remained latent because their interests united them against the king. In the years between 1495 and 1500 Maximilian not only perpetually violated the ordinances of Worms but also incessantly demanded sacrifices of money and troops from the Estates for the benefit of his foreign undertakings, thus driving even the anti-reform princes over to the reform side. As a result the reformers were able in 1500 to mark up yet another success, the institution of the long-anticipated Imperial Governing Council controlled by the Estates. At that point, however, it became clear that the reform party was too weak to govern the empire. It lacked real power, because the public spirit which they had assumed for the purposes of establishing their organization was simply not there. The major territories had cooperated only out of opposition to Maximilian, and they now refused to make any positive contribution. Not only, therefore, did the Governing Council fulfill none of the hopes that had been built on it, but it was not able even to remain in existence. It dissolved itself ignominiously after barely a year and a half of life, and the institutions for which it had so laboriously struggled came to nothing.

Taken as a whole, therefore, the imperial reform movement was a failure. It realized none of its aims, neither putting an end to the particularism of the Estates nor subordinating the monarch permanently to the empire. The Election Capitulations to which all German rulers since Charles V had to agree, were but a feeble substitute for the restrictions on the king intended by the Administration and the Governing Council. The actual liberty of the individual Estates had become too extensive, and the particular interests of the major princely houses too strong and too legitimate, for any devotion to the empire or any voluntary surrender of their absolute authority on behalf of the general good to be expected of them. Particularism had utterly destroyed the idea of union. And the royal power, too, had grown much too far beyond the empire to allow itself to be subordinated to an organization of the Estates. The lack of direct resources in the empire had forced the kings ever since the Interregnum to rely on their dynastic possessions; they had become so closely involved with the preservation and advance of these possessions that, by the time of Frederick III, instead of dynastic properties being used to assert sovereign authority within the empire, the government of the empire was used as a means of promoting the interests of Habsburg possessions. This was the origin of the distrust between

emperor and Estates which made their mutual relations so difficult in the final years of Frederick's reign, and under Maximilian
suspicions increased further. Maximilian's politics reaching out in
all directions, going not only far beyond the political horizons of
the Estates, but beyond the interests of the empire itself, were
bound to prompt the Estates to set limits to the king's freedom of
action and to bind him to the will of empire and the diet. All the
same, it was a political mistake on the part of the Estates to try to
place the king under their control. It was, in any case, too late
for this attempt. Maximilian was no longer merely the king
chosen by the electors and pledged to support the empire, nor was
he merely one German territorial prince among others. He was
the head of the growing Habsburg-Burgundian power state and
as such had interests of his own which he could not allow to be
directed by the Estates.

Against these two opponents, king and territories, imperial
reform failed. But it had not failed without bestowing some
benefit upon the empire. One of its consequences was a lasting
revival of the idea of empire. The interest of the Estates in the
empire and their share in ruling it had been growing ever since
the diet had become an effective embodiment of the organization
of the Estates, ultimately constituting a political factor equal to
the king. The Public Peace and the Chamber Court were also
achievements which, in the long term, the empire would not
allow itself to be deprived of. There is no need here to describe
the ultimate significance of the Chamber Court for the empire
and its judicial activities;[94] but it might be well to point out that
it was the reforms undertaken at the Diet of Worms which, in
ordinances concerning the Public Peace, the Chamber Court and
the administration, carried through the idea of solidarity and
peaceful, law-abiding co-existence among the Estates. The union
founded on these ordinances survived even the religious division
of the Reformation. While it is true that the Reformation reinforced territorial particularism and exacerbated the general
aversion to any established authority within the empire—the
reform party had disappeared by that time and the principles

embodied by it found no further support—the basic principles of the ordinances laid down by the reformers held their own.

Another principle that prevailed was the idea of union, of which, to be sure, the reformers were not the discoverers, though they were the first to try to make it a permanent foundation for the entire empire. By the time of the imperial reform movement, of course, it was a bit too late to achieve this, and in the years to come the concept of union would not be strong enough to hold the empire together. The position of the emperor was steadily outgrowing the empire, and the major territories also made themselves increasingly independent. But under the oppressive alien domination of Charles V, and even more during the troubles of 1552–54, it became clear to a great number of Estates that they would never be able to hold their ground alone; they therefore once again learned the value of federation and, in the *Exekutionsordnung* of 1555, transferred the maintenance of the Public Peace to unions of territories, the circles. The idea of union was revived here on a smaller scale than that envisaged by the reformers, though perhaps for that very reason it proved more effective. The confessional schism was only a temporary setback to this unity. The exigencies of the Thirty Years' War called it back to life again; and, kept alive by almost ceaseless wars, the idea of union and common organization against paramount military powers subsequently came to dominate the politics of the medium-sized and smaller Estates in the empire. Admittedly, however strong the urge to unite may have been, the Estates were too weak in themselves. What they had gained in the way of inner cohesion since the principal opponents of the imperial union, the emperor and the large territories, had withdrawn from their sphere, they had lost in vigor and strength. For this reason the system of alliances could assert itself in the history of the empire only when backed up by a strong power. The Confederation of the Rhine of 1658 found its support in France, the associated circles during the wars against Louis XIV were backed by the emperor and the naval powers, the Confederation of Princes was held up by Frederick the Great, and the Confederation of the Rhine of 1806 by Napoleon. But this thought cannot be pursued here, nor do I have space to show how the present German Empire rests on a similar combination of the idea of union on the one hand, and the particular interests of a great power on the other. I should, however, like to end by emphasizing once again that it was the imperial reform movement that attempted for the first time to establish the union of imperial Estates as the bearer and protector of the empire.

NOTES TO CHAPTER 3

1. In his book on the Imperial Chamber Court *Das Reichskammergericht*, Vol. I: *Quellen und Studien zur Verfassungsgeschichte des Deutschen Reiches in Mittelalter und Neuzeit*, ed. K. Zeumer, Vol. IV, Heft 3 (Weimar, 1911).
2. Cf. J. von Minutoli, *Das Kaiserliche Buch des Markgrafen Albrecht Achilles* (Berlin, 1850), p. 63.
3. The only sources are the correspondence and papers of Brandenburg, *ibid.*, p. 60 ff., esp. p. 82 f. (no. 73) and p. 85.
4. The diet records have been printed in part in J. J. Müller, *Reichstagstheatrum Friedrichs III*, Abteilung 3, also in Minutoli, *loc. cit.* Supplements in J. Grossmann's essay on the credibility of the *Reichstagstheatrum* in *Forschungen zur deutschen Geschichte*, Vol. XI, p. 117 ff. It is possible to reconstruct with fair certainty the sequence of the negotiations on the basis of the Bavarian relations, excerpts of which are given by R. Bemmann in his *Abhandlung zur Geschichte des Reichstags im 15. Jahrhundert* (Leipzig, 1907).
5. According to the Bavarian relations in Bemmann, *op. cit.*, p. 43.
6. Printed in J. J. Müller, *Des Heiligen Römischen Reichs . . . Reichstagstheatrum . . . Friedrichs III* (Jena, 1713) Abt. 3, p. 22. According to Bemmann, *op. cit.*, p. 43, note 3, this ordinance originated sometime after February 18. The electors' reply is given in the Bavarian documents (Geheimes Staatsarchiv, Munich, Kasten schwarz 156/12), dated the Wednesday before Oculi (22 February); printed in J. J. Müller, *op. cit.*, p. 22.
7. Cf. the memorandum printed in J. J. Müller, *loc. cit.*, p. 9, and in Minutoli, *loc. cit.*, p. 192 f. The date, Oculi (26 February), appears in the supplement to F. Wagner's "Berichtigungen und Nachträge zu Minutoli," *Zeitschrift für preussische Geschichte und Landeskunde*, Vol. XVIII (1881), p. 336. See also the memorandum of March 1 in J. J. Müller, *loc. cit.*, p. 11 f.
8. Cf. the Bavarian report in Bemmann, *op. cit.*, p. 44, note 5.
9. In the Staatsarchiv, Vienna, Mainzer Reichstagsakten, fascicle 3a.
10. In a memorandum of the Monday after Reminsciere (20 February), *ibid.*
11. Here followed the words (later deleted): "and the right to bring this to bear on his subjects."

12. Paragraph 5 of the final text of the Public Peace (as found in the *Neue und vollständigere Sammlung der Reichsabschiede* [Frankfurt, 1747], Vol. I, p. 277) is lacking in this draft.

13. Printed in Müller, *loc. cit.*, p. 29 ff.; and in Minutoli, *loc. cit.*, p. 274 ff., with Wagner's corrections in *Zeitschrift für preussische Geschichte*, Vol. XVIII, p. 338 f. According to the Bavarian relations (Bemmann, *op. cit.*, p. 45) the draft was read out on March 8 and passed on to the emperor after March 10.

14. All that is known at present of the original wording is a fragment in Müller, *loc. cit.*, p. 23 f. Excerpts are given in H. Ulmann, *Kaiser Maximilian I*, Vol. I, p. 308 f., and F. Hartung, *Geschichte des fränkischen Kreises*, Vol. I, p. 79.

15. According to the Bavarian report in Bemmann, *loc. cit.*, p. 44, note 5.

16. Printed in J. J. Müller, *loc. cit.*, p. 70 f.

17. Cf. their decision of Wednesday after Cantate 1486 (26 April) in Minutoli, *loc. cit.*, p. 218 (also in Müller, *loc. cit.*, p. 72, dated Thursday after Cantate).

18. For the city diets of the winter 1486–87, cf. Müller, *loc. cit.*, p. 76 ff.; for the diet of the Rhine electors at Speier at the end of January 1487, cf. the documents printed in Minutoli, *loc. cit.*, p. 256 ff.

19. Apart from the documents given in Müller, *loc. cit.*, p. 80 ff., information on this diet may be found in the "Akten des dritten Kaiserlichen Buches" of Brandenburg in *Forschungen zur deutschen Geschichte*, Vol. XXIV, p. 484 ff., and in the detailed relations of the cities in Johann Janssen, *Frankfurts Reichskorrespondenz* (Frankfurt, 1863–72) Vol. II, p. 451 ff.

20. Excerpt from the third *Kaiserliches Buch*, *loc. cit.*, p. 485 ff. In view of the doubts expressed by the editor on p. 491 it might be pointed out that this document can also be found in the Archives of Weimar, Registr. E, No. 33, fol. 91 ff. For the date, see the Frankfurt relation of April 19, in which it is stated that the emperor had been required to render his account on April 18 (Janssen, *op. cit.*, Vol. II, p. 463).

21. See the emperor's declaration of April 3, 1487, in Müller, *loc. cit.*, p. 89 ff., and Janssen, *loc. cit.*, p. 476 ff.

22. Cf. the reply of the Estates on April 6, *ibid.*, p. 91 f. and 479 f.

23. In his *Zur Geschichte des Reichstags im 15. Jahrhundert* (Leipzig, 1907).

24. The emperor's practices were already being criticized in 1485, and in 1491 it was expressly emphasized that "it would be fruitless to continue holding imperial diets in matters relating to the empire so long as the imperial Estates were not all summoned to them and the summons were not brought to their attention." (Müller, *loc. cit.*, p. 194.)

25. Cf. Emperor Frederick's declaration of April 7, 1487, in Janssen, *loc. cit.*, Vol. II, p. 480, and Müller, *loc. cit.*, p. 92: It "has therefore been customary in the empire that whatever was resolved at the diets by the electors, princes and the delegates of the princes and cities be made known to those who were not present; these then had to show themselves obedient to such resolutions."

26. See the declaration of April 6, mentioned above. If the absent Estates, despite the negotiations to be opened with them, did not come "then the assembly might all the more readily resolve to come to a decision."

27. Cf. ¶2 of the administration (*Handhabung*) of 1495, in K. Zeumer, *Quellensammlung zur Geschichte der deutschen Reichsverfassung in Mittelalter und Neuzeit* (Leipzig, 1904), p. 236; ¶59 of the Freiburg Recess of 1498, in *Neue und vollständigere Sammlung der Reichsabschiede* (Frankfurt, 1747), Vol. II, p. 52; ¶7 of the Cologne Recess (*ibid.*, p. 137) and ¶121 of the Speier Recess (*ibid.*, p. 463). The other passages, which were later often adduced as proofs of the right of majority of those present (especially during the debates of the diets of 1641 and 1653–54, cf. M. C. Lundorp, *Acta publica*, Vol. V, pp. 252, 321 ff., and Vol. VII, p. 204 f., etc.) prove nothing, since they were only special cases, mostly affairs concerning the circle diets and the deputations (monetary and matricular matters). Thus the city *Votum* of 1653 was correct in stating that the question of majority resolutions "may never be made into a permanent decision"; Lundorp . . . *Des heiligen Römischen Reiches Acta publica*, part VII p. 227 f.

28. Cf. Johann Reysse's report of August 17, 1500 in Janssen, *loc. cit.*, Vol. II, p. 659 ff.

29. Cf. Janssen, Vol. II, pp. 464, 481, 485. In order that "the secrets, resources and resolutions of the empire" might not be divulged, even the recesses when finally printed did not contain any details about the extent of the subsidies to be granted (according to a written communication of the elector of Mainz to the emperor dated Thursday after St. James, 1548 [26 July], draft in the Vienna State Archives, Mainzer Reichstagsakten, fascicle 17L, fol. 86 f.).

30. Cf. Janssen, Vol. II, p. 563.

31. Cf. the recess of the electoral councillors, Frankfurt, Saturday after St. Giles, 1486 (2 September) in *Zeitschrift für preussische Geschichte*, Vol. XVIII, p. 343 f.; also (undated) in Müller, *loc. cit.*, p. 75. For the later period, cf. especially the recess of the Diet of Lindau, ¶7, in *Neue Sammlung der Reichsabschiede* (Frankfurt, 1747), Vol. II, p. 31, and the electoral union of July 5, 1502 in J. J. Müller, *Reichstagsstaat von 1500–1508* (Jena, 1709), p. 248 ff.

32. An excerpt from the third *Kaiserliches Buch* is given in *Forschungen zur deutschen Geschichte*, Vol. XXIV, p. 497 ff. The formulation of this project dates from the beginning of May, see *ibid.* and Janssen, *loc. cit.*, Vol. II, p. 483 ff.

33. But Smend seems to believe this when (as in his *Reichskammergericht*, Vol. I, p. 42) he opposes the generally accepted view that the imperial reform was a "systematic attempt to realize the idea of union."

34. First described by Wagner in *Forschungen zur deutschen Geschichte*, Vol. XXIV, p. 500 ff. Wagner sees in this draft, as I myself do, a counter-project by the emperor, and the content definitely supports this view. But even if the project originated among the Estates, which seems hardly possible from the content, it would still justify my opinion that the differences in principle were consciously being felt.

35. I agree with Smend, *op. cit.*, p. 11, note 1, in holding that Wagner is wrong in his reference to a declaration of 1487. The Chamber Court ordinance of 1471 was mentioned in the emperor's declaration of May 19 (Janssen, *loc. cit.*, Vol. II, pp. 486 f.).

36. Printed in Müller, *Reichstagsstaat*, pp. 113 f.

37. The Elector Palatine was referred to as early as in the first draft as an opponent of the "constitution"; cf. *Forschungen zur deutschen Geschichte*, Vol. XXIV, p. 497. He also rejected the compromise draft, as is shown by his declaration of June 5, in Janssen, Vol. II, p. 490.

38. Evidence that the Count Palatine Otto von Mosbach-Neumarkt was one of those who joined the elector can be found in Janssen, *loc. cit.*, Vol. II, p. 490.

39. Printed in Müller, *op. cit.*, p. 117 ff., and J. H. von Harpprecht, *Staatsarchiv des Kammergerichts*, Vol. II (1758), p. 223 ff.

40. A fragment of this declaration is printed in Müller, *loc. cit.*, p. 121. It was passed on to the cities on May 27, and to the emperor on May 29 (cf. Janssen, *loc. cit.*, Vol. II, p. 487 f.).

41. Cf. Müller, *loc. cit.*, p. 99, for the declaration discussed on June 12 and communicated to the emperor's councillors on June 15. For further negotiations, cf. Janssen, *loc. cit.*, Vol. II, p. 499 ff., and Müller, *loc. cit.*, pp. 99 ff. and 103 f.

42. It was made most clearly in the statement by the elector of Mainz on June 12 (Janssen, *loc. cit.*, p. 494): "That the imperial majesty should give 100,000 gulden and that the empire should also be assessed 100,000 gulden."

43. Printed in Müller, *loc. cit.*, p. 114 ff., and also in the *Neue Sammlung der Reichsabschiede*.

44. Cf. the report on the inquiry of June 28 in Janssen, *loc. cit.*, Vol. II, p. 502 ff. For the declarations of the Estates: Müller, *loc. cit.*, p. 111, and the reply of Eichstätt printed in *Forschungen zur deutschen Geschichte*, Vol. XXIV, p. 509. Information about the conclusion of the diet, which went on until July 17, can be found in the letter of Margrave Frederick of Brandenburg to the archbishop of Cologne, dated July 21, *ibid.*, p. 510 ff.

45. According to the audit made by Dr. Pfotel on Wednesday after Martinmas (14 November), Vienna State Archives, Reichstagsakten (Kaiserliche Serie), fascicle 1.

46. In addition to the city protocol in Janssen, *loc. cit.*, Vol. II, p. 522 ff., I have used that of Mainz in the Vienna State Archives, Mainzer Reichstagsakten, fascicle 3a.

47. Cf. the Strassburg relation in Bemmann, *op cit.*, p. 56, note 10. According to this report, the king described Berthold as "recalcitrant" and "obstinate."

48. We only possess the fragments of the documents in Müller, *loc. cit.*, pp. 188–99, the brief Frankfurt reports in Janssen, *loc. cit.*, Vol. II, p. 549 f. (though these go only up to May 23), and a number of useful details from the third *Kaiserliches Buch* in *Forschungen zur deutschen Geschichte*, Vol. XXIV, p. 548 ff.

49. Printed in Müller, *loc. cit.*, p. 198.

50. Taken from the Bavarian records by H. Ulmann, *Kaiser Maximilian*, Vol. I, p. 315.
51. Ulmann, *op. cit.*, also refers to these negotiations, though I cannot agree with his estimate of the proceedings.
52. Printed in Müller, *loc. cit.*, p. 198 f.
53. *Ibid.* That the draft came from the king can be seen from the memorandum of Saxony. Cf. note 54.
54. This memorandum can be found in the Ernestinisches Gesamtarchiv in Weimar, Reg. E, Nr. 41, fol. 32. It forms the basis of the Estates' reply, Müller, *loc. cit.*, p. 199. The date of this reply is given in the *Kaiserliches Buch* as the feast of John the Baptist (24 June), *Forschungen zur deutschen Geschichte*, Vol. XXIV, p. 551; this invalidates Smend's conjecture (*op. cit.*, p. 12, note 4) that it came before June 14.
55. Printed with this comment but without the date in *Forschungen zur deutschen Geschichte*, Vol. XXIV, p. 551; without the comment but with the date in Müller, *loc. cit.*, p. 194.
56. Printed in *Forschungen zur deutschen Geschichte*, Vol. XXIV, pp. 552 ff. The editor, F. Wagner, as well as Ulmann, *op. cit.*, p. 316, sees the project as an agreement between Maximilian and the reform party, and they have been joined by others, including Smend, *op. cit.*, p. 12. I have attempted to account for my own diverging opinion in my *Geschichte des fränkischen Kreises*, Vol. I, p. 83 ff.
57. Printed in *Forschungen zur deutschen Geschichte*, Vol. XXIV, p. 558 ff.
58. Cf. the city minutes in Janssen, *loc. cit.*, Vol. II, p. 563.
59. The draft of the Estates has often been printed under the heading "Recess of Coblenz," e.g. in J. J. Müller, *Reichstagstheatrum unter Maximilian*, Vol. I, p. 159 ff., and in *Neue Sammlung der Reichsabschiede*, Vol. I, p. 294 ff.
60. This is Ulmann's view, *op. cit.*, p. 319.
61. I cannot agree with R. Smend when (in his essay, "Zur Geschichte der Formel Kaiser und Reich in den letzten Jahrhunderten des alten Reiches," *Historische Aufsätze für Zeumer* [Weimar, 1910], p. 439 ff.) he denies that this view holds good for the period of imperial reform and describes the empire as the permanent and universal force as opposed to the individual sovereign, the emperor. I shall refer here to the words quoted in note 42, above, and also to the provisions in the drafts of 1492 whereby the electors were to appoint commissioners "in the name of the empire" in addition to the imperial deputies. That "empire" here was understood as meaning the totality of Estates is suggested by the fact that the alternative words "for themselves and in the name of the other Estates of the Holy Empire" appear in one place. Even the apportioning of the fines for monetary offenses proposed in 1495 (cf. *Neue Sammlung*, Vol. II, p. 27), by which they should go "half to the Royal Majesty and half to the Empire and its aerarium," seems to fit my view better than Smend's; the same interpretation can be given to those words in the Estates' note of August 1497 (in Janssen, *loc. cit.*, Vol. II, p. 632), where the "general rumor and suspicion" are mentioned that "the (common) penny would benefit the Royal Majesty alone and not the Empire." I would be inclined to

attach the same meaning to the proposal made by Berthold of Mainz in 1495, "that the Royal Majesty's councillors should also be pledged to the service of the Empire." The analogy with the dualism of the territories of the Estates referred to above can, of course, be drawn out so far as to show that emperor and empire could not be sharply separated in principle in the Holy Roman Empire any more than could sovereignty and provincial diet in the territories. But the notion of dualism does bring out the essential features.

62. Cf. my article on Berthold in *Historische Zeitschrift*, Vol. CIII (1909), p. 527 ff., and my *Geschichte des fränkischen Kreises*, Vol. 1 (1910), p. 76 ff.

63. The principal source for the proceedings of the Diet of Worms remains the municipal protocols in J. P. Datt, *Volumen rerum Germanicarum novum sive de pace imperii publica* (Ulm, 1698), p. 825 ff. J. J. Müller, in his *Reichstagstheatrum Maximilians*, Vol. 1, adds nothing to Datt's account of the negotiations. I myself have been able to provide some supplementary details from the Berlin, Weimar, and Würzburg documents. Very useful in this connection is the information drawn from the records by Ulmann (*Kaiser Maximilian I*, Vol. 1) and Smend (*Reichskammergericht*, Vol. 1). The ordinances of Worms have often been printed, and I have made use of K. Zeumer's edition, *Quellensammlung zur Geschichte der deutschen Reichsverfassung in Mittelalter und Neuzeit* (Leipzig, 1904), p. 225 ff.

64. According to the Würzburg reports in the Würzburg Kreisarchiv. Würzburg, Reichstagsakten, Vol. 2, fol. 2. Unfortunately they give detailed information only for the beginning of the diet.

65. Best found in the city protocols for April 28 in Datt, *loc. cit.*, p. 830. The Würzburg protocol (fol. 7 f.) gives a substantially shorter account, though it reports the communication of the draft to the Council of Princes.

66. The oldest version of the Governing Council ordinance of 1495 of which I know is in the Ernestinisches Gesamtarchiv in Weimar, Reg. E Nr. 43. This, after deletions and additions, became the version of the Estates' draft which was printed long ago (e.g. Datt, *loc. cit.*, p. 836 ff.).

67. Cf. the city minutes for the Monday after Laetare (30 March) in Datt, *loc. cit.*, p. 827.

68. This and the following is based on the corrections undergone by the draft mentioned above, in note 66, as well as on marginal notes added to a copy of the draft to be found also in the Ernestinisches Gesamtarchiv in Weimar, Reg. E Nr. 43. Further comments corresponding to some extent to these marginal notes can be found on a leaf entitled "addiciones," which found its way into the Kurbrandenburgische Reichstagsakten of 1500 (Geheimes Staatsarchiv Berlin, Rep. X, fasc. 2K), but must belong to the year 1495. Cf. also Ulmann, *loc. cit.*, Vol. 1, p. 352.

69. Berthold of Mainz expressed himself very optimistically before the cities on the Friday after Ascension (29 May), Datt, *loc. cit.*, p. 843. He glossed over the fact that the "sundry persons" opposing the ordinances were the most powerful among the temporal princes.

70. According to Berthold's account (Datt, *loc. cit.* p. 836) the drafts for "peace, law and order in the empire" were passed on to the king on May 18, though the Bavarian relation referred to in Ulmann, Vol. I, p. 362, note 1, suggests that the Public Peace and the Chamber Court ordinance only reached the king a little before June 10; the dating, however, is not of vital importance.

71. Cf. the undated declaration of Maximilian in Müller, *Reichstagstheatrum Maximilian*, Vol. I, p. 389. That the declaration belongs to the middle of June I conclude from the protocol, unfortunately only fragmentary, in the Geheimes Staatsarchiv, Berlin, Rep. X, Fasc. 1C, where, under the date Friday after Corpus Christi (19 June), mention is made of a "proposed article" which "bases the King's opinion upon three things": 1 "that his Royal Majesty will suffer no President above him, and only when travelling outside the Empire will he appoint one to act and negotiate together with the appointed councillors"; 2 "that they should, together with the Electors, appoint and elect the councillors"; 3 "that the same councillors should be with his Royal Majesty wherever he holds his court in the Empire."

72. All these details from the Berlin protocol mentioned above.

73. Printed in Datt, *loc. cit.*, p. 854 ff., and in Müller, *loc. cit.*, p. 386.

74. The first version is printed in Datt, *loc. cit.*, p. 861 ff.

75. This fact can be seen from the alterations which the Estates proposed to make to the original draft and which Berthold of Mainz made known to the cities on the Friday after St. Mary Magdalen (24 July), Datt, *loc. cit.*, p. 866.

76. I have referred to this connection in my book, *Karl V. und die deutschen Reichsstände von 1546 bis 1555* (Halle, 1910), p. 165 f. I should like to add here that the provision rejected in 1495 was accepted at the Diet of Freiburg in 1498, cf. ¶5 of the Recess in *Neue Sammlung*, Vol. II, p. 40 f. The provision was not, however, implemented.

77. A draft for the Public Peace ordinance of 1495 may be found in the Würzburg Kreisarchiv. Würzburger Reichstagsakten, vol. 2, fol. 15 ff. It begins without preamble with ¶1 of the final version (as printed in Zeumer, *Quellensammlung*, p. 225 ff.), to which it corresponds exactly. Only in ¶9 does the wording form a transitional stage between the version of 1486 and the ordinance of 1495.

78. Cf. *Neue Sammlung*, Vol. II, p. 26, ¶45.

79. Cf. this draft in Datt, *loc. cit.*, p. 864. The explanation that if the arrangement should prove its worth it could be renewed is given *ibid.*, p. 866. For the first draft, cf. Datt, *loc. cit.*, p. 841.

80. Cf. my earlier remarks, above.

81. Maximilian's rejoinder is included in Veit von Wolkenstein's communication to the Estates on the Monday after St. James (27 July) and in the written additions of which the elector of Mainz notified the committee of cities on the following day; cf. Datt, *loc. cit.*, p. 869 f.

82. Cf. Ulmann, *loc. cit.*, Vol. I, p. 367.

83. See Datt, *loc. cit.*, p. 787, and Müller, *Theatrum Maximilians*, Vol. I, p. 664.

84. Printed, e.g., in *Neue Sammlung*, Vol. II, p. 24 ff.
85. Printed in *Deutsche Reichstagsakten*, Vol. IX, p. 91 ff.
86. Cf. Möser's proposal of a new scheme for the history of the empire in his *Patriotische Phantasien*, Vol. IV (1786), p. 153 ff., especially p. 156.
87. This provision is contained in the electors' draft of the July diet of 1438 (now printed in the second edition of K. Zeumer's *Quellensammlung zur Geschichte der deutschen Reichsverfassung in Mittelalter und Neuzeit*, No. 165 A, which appeared immediately before the second part of the present article reached the correction stage and has not been referred to elsewhere). The provision was taken over from the electors' draft into that of the royal councillors (Nr. 165B) and also into the still unprinted draft of the cities.
88. Cf. my notes on the attitude of Archduke Albrecht of Bavaria in 1480 in my *Geschichte des fränkischen Kreises*, Vol. I, p. 147.
89. Cf. Smend's *Kammergericht*, Vol. I, p. 42 ff.
90. For these further reform plans, cf. the observations at the end of the Governing Council ordinance in Datt, *loc. cit.*, p. 840, the negotiations of the Monday after St. James (27 July), *ibid.*, p. 869, and the so-called "Recess," *ibid.*, p. 884 ff. and in *Neue Sammlung*, Vol. II, p. 24 ff.
91. Cf. Datt, *loc. cit.*, p. 869.
92. Cf. Smend, *op. cit.*, p. 46, whose view in this matter I am unable to share.
93. Cf. R. Smend, *loc. cit.*, p. 45.
94. Cf. the work of J. Poetsch (which appeared only after this article had been completed), *Die Reichsjustizreform von 1495, insbesondere ihre Bedeutung für die Rechtsentwicklung* (Münster, 1912).

4 Approaches to Imperial Reform at the End of the Fifteenth Century

KARL SIEGFRIED BADER

Karl Siegfried Bader, author of the following revisionary article on the imperial reform movement, is lawyer, jurist, and legal and institutional historian. He was born in 1905 and has been professor at the University of Zürich since 1953.

I

THE reforms of the constitution of the Holy Roman Empire associated with the reign of Maximilian I and set afoot during the transitional years between medieval and modern times are generally treated with disdain by political historians and do not enjoy an especially good reputation even among scholars of constitutional history. Indeed, having read through the innumerable and vexatiously repetitive negotiations recorded in the records of the imperial diets and related sources, the historian is often reminded of a political tug-of-war, a fruitless and undignified game in which nothing ever changes except the opponents at the ends of the ropes. And if he considers the results of these reforming efforts taking up roughly a century of German constitutional development the historian may find it hard to escape the impression that a huge mountain had given birth to a very small mouse, or at most to a few mice. In the documents of the decades following the reforms of Maximilian's reign he will read the same complaints about the empire's impotence and failings that had been put forward during the struggles before 1495. Listening more closely, however, he may begin to try to differentiate between the voices that appear to

A paper read on October 7, 1952, before the General Assembly of the Görres-Gesellschaft. I have contented myself with giving only such references as seemed likely to be of immediate use.

come from all directions at once. They are many and variegated: genuine grievances from those qualified to speak, from men with a sense of divine and temporal responsibility; endless litanies of lament about the corruption of the age, of the world, and of the church; but also the loud cries of those who used their complaints as a cover for their contentment with things as they were, men who were satisfied with the obscurity and insecurity of the time because these enabled them to pursue their own interests. Qualified and unqualified, responsible and irresponsible, selfish and selfless, all added their voices to the chorus, representing every camp—supporters of the emperor and supporters of the Estates, interests temporal and interests spiritual. But it is precisely because these sounds came from all directions that the historian finds it so difficult to distinguish between them. He must not judge them by their volume, nor even by the sounds they make. He has to listen critically, and must learn to distinguish between what was said and what was thought. For even in that age politics was exercised as an art of concealment, and words did not necessarily correspond to motives and intentions.

Constitutional historians, concerned with institutions and intent on results, have not passed quite so negative a judgment upon the imperial reform movement of the late fifteenth century as have political historians. This is not due, as Erich Molitor has observed,[1] to the attractiveness of the subject as a research problem; the results of the reform movement are by and large well known and the general course of events has been grasped at least in its essential features. But in the last few decades efforts have been made to put matters into more accurate perspective. It has been shown, for example, that measures which at the time were given little or no prominence produced results of more lasting value than did certain other undertakings proclaimed in great triumph.[2] Political historians, on the other hand, notice the absence of the sort of solid framework of institutions on which constitutional historians can rely. Interpretations are more often than not influenced by general historical attitudes or by the political convictions of the particular observer. It seems to me important to demonstrate this truth from the way the imperial reform movement has been assessed in our own times by influential historians. This will show, at the same time, how deeply certain prejudices are rooted in the thought of historians, and it is probably no accident that these historians are mainly specialists in modern history who tend to feel uneasy and insecure when confronted with the civilization of the Middle Ages.

The first point always made in rendering a judgment on the imperial reform movement is the complaint that the Estates lacked any real feeling for, or identification with, the empire. This judgment seems to me to originate in political conceptions arising in the days of the politically weak German confederation, with its dream of German unity and imperial power. Despite Ranke's interpretation[3] and in the face of the judicious assessment of Heinrich Ulmann's biography of Maximilian,[4] the king is represented as a political factor of unity and strength in the sixteenth century. Gerhard Ritter, for instance, although he has little patience with the Habsburgs, especially with the Spaniard Charles V, still sees Maximilian as the "high-minded" German king who, temperamental and "always inclined to adventure," was intent above all on "strengthening the executive authority of the monarchy" and, with this support, conduct a "bold and brilliant foreign policy."[5] Maximilian's opponent among the Estates, the imperial chancellor and elector of Mainz, Berthold von Henneberg, appears in Ritter's interpretation[6] as suspicious, slow, and no less dull than the great mass of the Estates, though admittedly a prudent, tenacious, and strong-willed man in his own person and in the pursuit of the immediate objectives of the Estates. Not in so many words, but between the lines, we can read Ritter's reproach that this level-headed man thought it more important to strengthen the empire from within than to make it externally successful. This is, of course, nothing other than the old *querelle allemande*, the resentful charge that the nation is being slighted in the councils and the power politics of the European states, an attitude which leads logically to the overvaluing of matters of prestige and foreign politics, especially the warlike accomplishments of imperial visionaries with ambitions to military glory like Maximilian. A similar and to some extent even sharper judgment is passed on Berthold by Andreas: that he had no sense for matters of foreign politics, "though the frontier position of his territory should have opened his eyes"; that he had no understanding of the nature of a great power; that he was "narrow in vision, one might almost say a typical representative of the petty state."[7] The fact that the electors under Berthold's leadership labored at imperial reform while the emperor was reaping the political fruits of his extravagance in the Magyar invasion of Austria and the French inroads in the west and the south, is described by Andreas as "a lamentable spectacle."[8]

To my mind, it is not permissible to simplify things in this way and to consider the work of reform merely from the aspect of external brilliance and power. The task of the constitutional historian is different: he must attempt to go more deeply into the constitutional situation of the empire and on this basis alone assess the measures which were thought necessary at the time. In his examination of the domestic struggle between emperor and Estates he must judge whether this struggle resulted in an improvement of the internal situation. Above all, he must ask whether the failure of the reform was not, perhaps, due to a much later constellation of factors and events.

The success of this examination depends, in my opinion, not so much on discovering new evidence as on making a new and more accurate evaluation of the sources. The situation as regards the sources has unfortunately made no advance since the years at the turn of the century when constitutional investigations into imperial reform and its individual aspects were published with great frequency.[9] The expectations aroused by the prospect of continuing publication of the records of the imperial diets could not be fulfilled, because at the beginning of the undertaking it was impossible to envisage the enormous difficulties to be encountered in this enterprise. And so, for the foreseeable future, the vitally important material from the eighties and nineties of the fifteenth century will remain unavailable. Such progress with the sources as has been achieved came mainly in works concentrating on a narrower sector and thus more concrete and modest in their approach, such as the studies of Fritz Ernst[10] and Eduard Ziehen.[11] An understanding of the attitude and situation of the Estates can in many cases be attained only if careful investigation is made into the circumstances and conditions of the individual territories and their rulers.

What we are concerned with here, therefore, is not so much to fill in the picture by adding new features (since only newly discovered sources can accomplish this), but to reopen the debate on the basic questions and especially to reassess the relations between emperor and Estates as regards the reform. "Approaches to Imperial Reform"—this title does not imply an attempt to sort out the respective contributions of the two opposed powers— emperor and Estates—in a society which had become dualistic, but to ascertain, in the light of our knowledge of the late medieval empire, what the Estates accepted as their principle of action and where this clashed with the ideas of Maximilian. It is an attempt to make clear that the thoughts and actions of the Estates were not necessarily signs of political weakness or of hostility to the whole conception of the empire, and that Maximilian's policies were not always vigorous and likely to promote the greatness and glory of the empire. I wish to show that the failure of the reform movement —insofar as it really was a failure—was bound up with the general course of events in the late empire, and in particular with the Reformation, which, after all, eclipsed all attempts at secular reform.[12]

II

There was a general awareness toward the end of the Middle Ages that the character and operations of the empire had, ever since the Interregnum, been undergoing a far-reaching change, though the deeper causes of this change were not recognized. Dante and the Ghibellines, and even the German political documents of the fifteenth century,[13] still saw the empire in the splendor and power of the Hohenstaufen era, but in reality both emperor and empire had in the meantime undergone fundamental changes. Even Rudolf of Hapsburg, probably the most level-headed of the kings who had ascended the German royal throne by this time,[14] and in every way the opposite of what Maximilian saw in him as royal ancestor and founder of the Habsburg dynastic possessions, understood the change that had come about since the end of the Hohenstaufen period and had set himself more restricted goals. He returned to an expedient which had its roots in German legal thought and had long been used by local and regional associations for the purpose of securing the public peace, namely the practice of forming unions for the purpose of securing amicable and peaceful mediation of disputes by means of mutual pacts rather than authoritative judgments. The king's role of protector of church and Christendom was diluted to an arbitrational function in which the monarch placed himself on the same level as the disputants.[15] At the turn of the thirteenth and fourteenth centuries the imperial idea was finally dissolved in the course of the emergence of the king of France as a rival on equal terms with the emperor.[16] The German king became *primus inter pares* among the German princes, and the imperial dignity no longer bestowed upon the king a unique majesty; in fact the two titles of king and emperor became so closely fused that even in the official writings of the time no strict distinction was made between them.[17] A number of emperors and kings—Sigismund, for example, whose character has so often and for so long been misunderstood[18]—had attempted to put new life into the old universal idea of empire, but without any lasting success. All that remained to the king and his house, therefore, was the power over which he disposed in his own domains, a power and resources independent of his election. His personal possessions enabled him to try to improve his position vis-à-vis the other princes in the empire. During the seemingly interminable reign of Frederick III this arrangement came to be generally accepted. In appropriate measure, however, there occurred a shift in the imperial balance of power in favor of the Estates who, together with the emperor, embodied the empire, but who were now increasingly ready to consider themselves the sole constituent elements of the empire.

The idea of union, long disputed as a legislative and juridical factor, is a necessary part of the history of the late medieval empire as well as of the history of imperial reform. Otto von Gierke[19] may have overestimated its importance in legal and institutional history in general; on the other hand, Georg von Below's determined attempt to account for the medieval state in terms of authoritarian and monarchical ideas[20] leaves out a good deal of the reality of medieval history. Since Gierke and Below an effort has been made in German constitutional history to find a middle way; Fritz Hartung's important book,[21] for example, concedes to the system of unions a share in the constitutional developments of the fourteenth and fifteenth centuries. But political historians tend to persist in adhering to Below's depreciatory assessment (and here our chief witness, again, is W. Andreas in his widely read *Deutschland vor der Reformation*)[22] and turn the insistence of the leading reformers among the Estates on forming unions into a reason for censure. In actual fact, things were rather different. The Elector Berthold and his political friends were not the ones who showed themselves to be reactionary, averse to all innovation, caught up in old prejudices. It would be nearer the mark to say that it was the young king, Maximilian, who entertained ideas far removed from political reality.[23] Like many dreamers who indulge only in a kind of literary approach to political life Maximilian was chasing visions. The reflection held before his eyes in the fanciful *Theuerdank*—this was what he accepted as the real article. But none of the romances of this book had anything to do with the reality of day-to-day politics. Just as the imperial court had not since the days of King Wenzel been thought of as the center of the empire[24] the emphasis in practical politics had moved altogether to the large princely territories where the construction of proper state systems had nearly reached its culmination. Decision-making in the empire had, ever since the Golden Bull, been lodged in the electoral college. The emperor was a figurehead, an idol endowed with certain imponderable symbolic rights and powers. His weight in the interplay of political forces began to be felt only when, as ruler of the largest and most extensive territory, he entered on the solid basis of negotiation with his peers.

An objective look of this kind will do away with many distorted judgments and heartfelt complaints of the intolerable selfishness of the Estates. It is a literary sentiment, and perhaps also a rather typically German one—but certainly unsound both politically and historically—to persist in reproaching the Estates for pursuing policies that arose inevitably out of their very nature and existence, namely, the struggle for self-preservation. How ready we have always been, and still are, to accept the *sacro egoismo* of the men of the Italian Renaissance as a phenomenon of the age, and even to accord it a certain measure of admiration; but how little do we understand the reality of a situation[25] as a result of which the empire over the course of about two centuries had been turning into something very different from what the political idealists were imagining. Among the imperial princes there were certainly men who went much too far in their selfish ambitions and who had no other idea in their heads but to enlarge their territorial domains and extend the influence of their own persons and houses. All this is an undeniable fact about the age, and historians are perfectly entitled to record it and, if they wish, pass censure. But it does not mean that everything to do with the Estates is to be taken as harmful and hostile to the empire; nor that every single imperial prince intent on preserving and enlarging his territory, and every imperial city reluctant to open its purse for the benefit of common interests, ought to be accused of freebootery or petty parochialism. That the attempts at reform were not set aside, that they kept the diets busy despite many years of procrastination, and that there were always men who went back to old ideas in order to draw something usable out of the petrified old imperial constitution—none of this speaks against the Estates as a whole.[26] It should also be remembered that the endless to-and-fro of negotiations and recesses, the general business of getting things done, and the almost limitless confusion of protocols and instruments, represented only one aspect of the reform movement. Everyone familiar with the diplomatic history of the time will recognize these procedures as a distinctive feature of the contemporary political style. No great reform decrees may have been passed in the fifteenth century, at least not until its last decade, but a number of individual achievements may nonetheless be recorded. The legal historian who takes the trouble to sift the detailed work embodied in imperial legislation[27] may well come away with the impression that the efforts had not been quite so unavailing after all. True enough, the *reformatio in capite et membris*, a contemporary preoccupation by no means confined to imperial reform, did not begin to be tackled until the very end of the century. The man who made himself the spokesman of the Estates had long been acknowledged as a selfless champion of the cause—the elector and chancellor of the empire, Berthold von Henneberg.

We are still without a complete and conclusive biography of this man who in his time was seen as an honorable and courageous representative of the German princes. His personality lies hidden behind the veil with which the Middle Ages were wont to conceal the person in favor of the type.[28] Yet Berthold—much more clearly than his spiritual master, Nicholas of Cusa—shows the marks of a man living in an age of transition.[29] We have learned a few things about his personal and family background, his activity as a territorial sovereign, his relations with the cathedral chapter of Mainz, and his conduct of pastoral affairs as archbishop and metropolitan. The works of Bauermeister, Weiss, and Ziehen have penetrated beyond the anonymity of his official measures and have shed a little light on his mind and his person.[30] But as yet no biographer has attempted to use the knowledge gained from ecclesiastical and territorial sources in conjunction with imperial history as a whole. The fairest judgment to date on Berthold as the great imperial politician (Ranke himself long ago discovered him as a statesman)[31] was formed by the unsurpassed biographer of Maximilian, Heinrich Ulmann.[32] It has, admittedly, become increasingly difficult to gain an overall picture because our knowledge of Berthold is derived not only from the official correspondence of Mainz and Vienna but also from his lively activities whenever and wherever political threads were being spun for the purposes of reinforcing the empire and its various parts.[33] At all events the task should be undertaken, as a counterpart, perhaps, to a study of Nicholas of Cusa, with emphasis on the practical realization of reforming ideas. Berthold's political work was to some extent an implementation of the *Concordantia Catholica*,[34] making allowances for the distance between the soaring flight of a creative thinker and the measured pace of a practical politician. But since no such account exists, all that can be done here is to draw attention to a number of individual traits as revealed in his political activities on behalf of the imperial constitution.

Raised to the archiepiscopal see of Mainz only after overcoming countless obstacles, Berthold carried considerable weight by virtue of his family connections alone. Though not a temporal lord (secular magnates were not appointed to the see of Mainz because of all the political influence it involved) he did represent a section of the nobility which aspired to territorial sovereignty. His ancestry ensured that he was Estate-minded.[35] All that the young ecclesiastic lacked in the way of insight and experience he was able to pick up with very little difficulty in the shadow of that doughty fighter, Archbishop Diether von Isenburg,[36] who spent a lifetime struggling with the cathedral chapter of Mainz over the formation of an ecclesiastical state. But while Diether was wearing himself out in feud and strife with the neighboring powers, Berthold came to realize that the only way to ensure peace and security for the state in a world made up of many small rival powers was that of flexibility and compromise. At the same time, however, he saw in the connection of the see of Mainz with the chancellorship of the empire not only the dignity and responsibility of office, but also a real and politically decisive function by means of which Mainz could gain a leverage over imperial politics. The ultimate significance of Berthold von Henneberg in the work of imperial reform arose from this combination of territorial power and his specific sense of political responsibility toward the empire. Where he differed from the other reformers (most of all, perhaps, from the two-faced, mercurial Margrave Albrecht Achilles, "the most practical-minded among the princely schemers of the period")[37] was in his consciousness of responsibility toward both sides. The imperial chancellor and archbishop of Mainz was not just another territorial lord, nor even just another spiritual elector, taking the rule of self-assertion as the first commandment, like his contemporaries in Italy and Germany. He possessed sufficient political acumen to realize that the powers of his office, though they had by that time been allowed to fall into disuse, gave him in effect a measure of control over his royal sovereign. The chancellor's authority to add his signature to all documents proceeding from the royal hand[38] contained, if it is permissible to use a constitutional term unknown to that age, an element of what in later periods of constitutional development, was to be the right of countersignature accorded to responsible ministers. Thus, the elector of Mainz, if he took his office seriously, as Berthold did, had in his hand a lever enabling him to guide the politics and constitution of the empire. Berthold grasped this lever more firmly and more deliberately than any chancellor before or after him.[39]

The chancellor obviously possessed to a very high degree the politician's acute feeling for constitutional possibilities, but this gift his royal adversary lacked altogether. Maximilian was not a man of political gifts or insight; his personality was not sufficiently balanced for him to be able to wait and consider, and he had no talent for consultation and negotiation. But even worse than his lack of a clear-headed sense of the realities of political life was his inability to abide by his decisions. Always "making new starts,"[40] countermanding his own orders—such irresolution prevented Maximilian, for all his dreams of knightly prowess, from ever becoming a great strategist. Those who like to see in Maximilian the noble hero and the last of the medieval knights—another recent example of this interpretation is Will Winker[41]—forget that more is needed to make a soldier and a commander than headstrong ambition. Historical researches have made it possible to fill in a number of important features in our picture of this man, who was haunted his whole life long by the specter of his predecessors' incurable inertia. There is now no further excuse for overlooking the fact that the politics of drift, which for so many years Frederick III had not so much pursued as simply allowed to go on, involved his successor from the very start in an inextricable tangle unless he could force himself to take a definite line and follow it up.[42] But the decisive factor was the dismal state of his finances. The second volume of Goetz von Pölnitz's work on Jacob Fugger[43] has so clearly shown the extent of the chronic financial misery of the Habsburgs at this time that all illusions must vanish. Everything Maximilian did to hinder or further the development of the imperial constitution was a reflection of his financial condition. A royal arch-debtor who indiscriminately pawned his own and other people's possessions in order to secure new credits, and who on the most threadbare of pretexts laid hands on the indulgence money while his councillors disputed the papal curia's right to raise it; a king who arrived late at the Diet of Worms because he had been detained by his creditors in the Netherlands together with his wife and retinue:[44] all the information adds up to the suspicion that Maximilian's constant attempts to fling himself into military adventures were simply a form of escapism. In the first years of his kingship he may perhaps for a time have showed a spark of genuine responsibility for the constitutional structure of the empire.[45] But certainly by 1495, and probably as early as the turn of the eighties and nineties, the reforming aspirations of the Estates, which were shared with minor exceptions by all the princes and imperial cities, were ultimately of interest to Maximilian only as a means of extracting the necessary resources from those who were in a position to pay. All the proposals he advanced at the diets between 1486 and 1504 (for example, at Frankfurt, Worms, and Lindau) amounted to the same thing: money to indulge in war and the chase. Behind it all, and abetted by the royal councillors—most of whom were highly disputed personages[46]—was the mental reservation that when the war was won and the coffers filled, he would again rule without the Estates and in opposition to them. The Augsburg Chronicle[47] was not so far wrong when it said of Maximilian: "He was pious and not highly endowed with understanding and he was always poor. . . . He had councillors who were cunning knaves, and who ruled him hand and foot. The councillors grew rich and the emperor became poor." This was how contemporaries saw the German king who, in an hour of supreme embarrassment and intense pressure at Worms granted the empire the Public Peace and the Imperial Chamber Court. Long-term plans and lasting reforms were not to be expected from him as long as he was left to himself. They could only be wrung out of him. And this was precisely what was done by the Estates and their standing spokesman, the elector of Mainz.

III

The picture outlined here is disconsolate and may appear distorted. The constitutional historian would prefer to take another starting point than that offered by the sources, since reforms of the imperial constitution, which were so painfully necessary, would surely have needed to be based on other premises if they were to be of any lasting value. All the more surprising, then, that the reforms of 1495, amplified though perhaps not altogether improved upon during the following decades, were rather more substantial than might appear from the paltry appreciation they gained from contemporaries and later generations. If we wish to arrive at a clear picture of the constitutional elements in the imperial reform there is no other way than to consider all the individual parts separately. But this means that I must regard some well-known facts as axiomatic and must leave out all the merely accessory details, for otherwise we would be going far beyond the limits imposed on this essay.

At the very beginning of the reform achievements stands the ordinance of the Perpetual Public Peace. Even this important product of imperial legislation has suffered the strange fate of being either overestimated beyond all proportion or made to look utterly trivial.[48] A survey of the legislation for the public peace ever since the imperial Public Peace of Mainz of 1235[49] will suffice to show that it is hardly possible to attach much importance to the efforts in that direction made in the fifteenth century.[50] Laws pertaining to the public peace had been constantly renewed and modified, without becoming any more effective or respected. Under Frederick III as good as nothing had been done by the central authorities. In 1486 the Estates, acting with the consent of the young king, had brought about a ten-year peace.[51] What Maximilian had contributed to this up to the year 1495 was not calculated to encourage the placing of great hopes in the royal preservation of peace; the arbitrary extension offered by the king in 1493 at the instigation of his councillors did not satisfy the Estates, because there were no institutions available to ensure jurisdiction and execution. The emperor's Chamber Court barely existed even formally; its chief judge, Count Eitelfritz von Zollern, was far too occupied with his many other offices to put in an appearance on the bench. The only hope of real peace and order lay in a guarantee undertaken by all the Estates, including the imperial knights, the great focal point of unrest during the fifteenth century who, however, held themselves suspiciously and sullenly aloof.[52]

The legal historian who attempts to probe the substance of the Perpetual Peace and its concrete provisions will most likely be disappointed. "Perpetual" leagues and alliances had existed since the fourteenth century, though their "perpetuity" had seldom persisted for longer than a few years. If the new formulation of old ideas now became a real basis for law and justice, this was due to the fact that the peace was combined with concrete institutions set up at the same time, notably the Imperial Chamber Court. Nonetheless, the Public Peace ordinance itself was also important, the indispensable prerequisite for all attempts at constitutional reform. The Public Peace ordinance may have been breached in practice, as happened within a year of its proclamation and with the emperor's approval; but as a principle it was not seriously impugned after 1495. Feuds were not, of course, eliminated, but, as Otto Brunner has recalled in connection with the public peace legislation of the Middle Ages,[53] they no longer counted as a legitimate institution, nor were they now an instrument of constitutional procedure or a substitute for it. The value of the Perpetual Peace lies in its attempt to make a constitutional distinction between what is legitimate and what is illegitimate.[54] It did not achieve pacification, but it did create what was at the time accepted as an indispensable prerequisite for it. That things were understood in this way is shown by the reaction among the imperial knights, especially in Franconia, where the legal basis of the new norms were in all seriousness disputed—and precisely on the grounds that they were to be enforced by the Estates. During the consultations at Worms, Maximilian himself had tried at the last moment to breach the principle by trying to establish as legitimate and proper the right of seizure in cases of just demand.[55] He did not get his way and the Estates rightly stood firm: what constituted just demand and legitimate self-help was not a matter to be left to the convictions of individuals. Any "just" seizure could lead to a "just" war—and what aggressor has ever been known to admit that his war was not just?

The decision as to what was just and unjust could only be entrusted to a court. Thus the Public Peace and the Imperial Chamber Court were institutionally inextricable. But they might take many different forms. Maximilian's proposals, already intimated in no uncertain terms some years before, had undergone important modifications. The most important innovations effected by the Worms resolutions were that places on the Chamber Court bench were to be filled by the Estates and that the court itself was to be separate from the royal establishment. When the king saw that nothing would come of his wish to exercise a decisive influence over the composition of the court he at first stood fast by the principle of the old palace court. But it was to no avail. The kind of judicial procedure customary in the emperor's court, the later Imperial Chamber Court, facilitated, indeed encouraged the warping of justice. Had it been retained, the Chamber Court would have become simply a tribunal controlled by the imperial and Hapsburg-dynastic councillors. The following years showed that Maximilian was not able to accustom himself to the new arrangement; he indulged in all sorts of interventions, which were even worse for the reputation of the new institution than the hasty rotation which Maximilian undertook in the appointments to the presidency of the court. Even the competing imperial privy council, founded by Maximilian as a countermove to the Estates, showed what was at stake. Later on, especially in the eighteenth century,[56] the privy council was to become an important and effective complementary factor in imperial judicial procedures, but this was the result of the new situation created by the Reformation. It is also true that the two imperial courts, the Chamber Court and the privy council, ultimately became mutually beneficial and even supported each other despite their rivalry—as is well known, a pure priority principle was introduced in 1559.[57] But this was only possible because religious parity had been established in the meantime and the Chamber Court had become *de facto* a court for the Protestant Estates, while Catholics kept mainly to the privy council.

It is neither possible nor necessary here to assess the significance of the Chamber Court in any detail. Estimates of this, too, have been in dispute, though in recent years they have become considerably more positive than was usual in the nineteenth century, ever since a clearer picture of the scope of Chamber Court justice began to emerge from the studies of Rudolf Smend.[58] Despite the cumbrousness of its apparatus and proceedings the Chamber Court carried out substantial and important tasks, in virtue more often of its existence than of the quality of its judgments.[59] It was unable to prevent major catastrophes, such as the civil wars following the religious schism. But in the middle of the twentieth century we know only too well that courts of law, even when much better organized and equipped than the Chamber Court, are unable to do anything when men and states are not willing. At all events the Imperial Chamber Court was the cornerstone of the reform legislation of 1495. It proved more viable than could have been imagined by anyone making forecasts on the basis of the situation at the Diet of Worms.

In these institutions, then, the approaches to reform of emperor and Estates took on some definite shape. But everything else done in 1495 was patchwork. This is true of the so-called "Administration of Law and Order" (*Handhabung Rechtens*) with its vaguely formulated executive responsibilities.[60] It is true also of the Common Penny, which proved an altogether impracticable institution,[61] however important the recess itself may have been for the development of the imperial fiscal system.[62] The next step taken during the subsequent course of imperial reform also led on to unsteady ground. The first Imperial Governing Council of 1500, bullied out of the emperor by the Estates and intended as the keystone of the plans for an aristocratically controlled government of the Estates, was a failure. This council was the weakest spot in Berthold's political conception: the whole structure, half of it administered by the Estates, half by a bureaucracy, proved cumbersome and helpless.[63] Berthold may well have overestimated the real influence of the electoral college; the important territorial rulers outside the group of electors could no longer be bound by imperial policies by means of an executive committee in which they had no share. With the death of Berthold in 1504 both the idea and the machinery of the council collapsed. When a new Governing Council arose in a different form seventeen years later at the Diet of Worms, the world had changed. Charles V was not Maximilian; the Spanish Habsburg ruler represented a totally different, and immensely larger, threat to the Estates and their organization than his poor, unstable grandfather. And yet even this Governing Council was unable to assert itself. The empire of the sixteenth century could not tolerate an effective executive, an intolerance that increased as time went on. The Reformation and the division of the empire into confessional partisan camps swept away the last foundations upon which, in theory at least, an imperial government with more than merely representative powers might have been built.[64]

Though the Estates' reform approach clearly failed at this point, it did prove to be a viable foundation for the final effort of the reform movement, the system of imperial circles. Hardly any other aspect of the imperial reforms has received more contradictory assessments among political historians than this division of the empire into administrative circles; and even constitutional historians have not yet recognized that a supremely important constitutional structure had been inaugurated here, even if it was not one clearly visible to the outward eye.[65] The nineteenth century, which generally tended to consider the old imperial constitution as *de facto* nonexistent and to accept literally Pufendorf's characterization of the empire as *quasi monstro simile*,[66] may have judged things from the standpoint of military administration, and therefore found nothing good in the circles. But in reality things were different. There were, to be sure, circles and circles. It is well known that, apart from the Franconian and Swabian circles, those of the Upper Rhine and—following at some distance—Lower Saxony achieved considerable constitutional and political status. Information about the remarkable character and structure of the Burgundian circle and its functions has only recently been made available in the latest publication from the Viennese archives.[67] In itself, however, the idea of an organization of the empire into circles was a supremely significant constitutional principle in an age when the territorial state was attaining its fullest development.

There are a number of doubts surrounding the origin of the idea of circles. This is the place to ask where the respective approaches of emperor and Estates to this problem coincided, differed, or at least overlapped. Beginnings may be sought as far back as the public peace legislation of the fourteenth century, where the way was being pointed to an organization of those regions which clearly formed part of the imperial confederation. But the first concrete start in the direction of the circles came in early decades of the systematic reform era, as, for example, in the drafts for a Public Peace ordinance of 1438.[68] When Maximilian took up the idea in 1486 and attempted to entrust the preservation of the Public Peace to imperial deputies residing in fixed "circles," his project met with an extremely unfriendly reception. The division into circles proposed here, and the choice of peacekeepers, were so ill-considered and inappropriate that the king himself, dismayed by the violent opposition of the Estates, dropped the plan, declaring that he was insufficiently familiar with the territories to carry it into execution.[69] At the Diet of Worms, too, there were negotiations about the administrative division of the empire, but these came to nothing. The Estates placed their hopes in the prospective Imperial Governing Council, while the king wished to entrust the Public Peace to organs independent of this council. This, in fact, was the root of Maximilian's plans for an administrative division.

It was a difficult undertaking. Was it desirable or even possible to go back to the ancient tribal associations and, on the basis of these, establish, side by side with (or perhaps even above) the territories a new system derived in part from imperial authority and corporative in nature, in part associative and derived from the Estates? One thing was certain. As it was to be exclusively under royal authority, the new structure would be placed in sharp opposition to the important territorial magnates. Just as impracticable was a plan mentioned among the electors, by which the electoral college as such, or at least the temporal electors, were to be entrusted with control in certain "circles" or "districts."[70] Thus the scheme only came to maturity when the Governing Council was created in 1500. The Public Peace circles of former years were turned into electoral constituencies for the short-lived Imperial Governing Council, as Fester has noted.[71] And when, in turn, the Governing Council itself had disappeared from the scene, the constituencies gave rise to that strange and constantly fluctuating twilight institution, the imperial circles.

It will not be necessary here to pursue the fortunes of the imperial circles in detail.[72] But it is important for the legal and constitutional historian to determine the structure of this so-called Circle Administration, for on this point the general historical literature is dominated by the vaguest and most warped ideas. As juridical institutions the imperial circles were, according to their constitution, Janus-faced. In part they were institutions of imperial law, regulated by and to an extent dependent on the empire. On the other hand, they were, and increasingly became in the course of time, independent bureaucratic bodies. They contained all the distinctive features of late medieval political authority: that is to say, they exercised the rights of dominion and yet remained associative institutions. I have tried, in my book on the German southwest, to explain these juridical functions in greater detail, using the Swabian circle as an example.[73] It might be said in summary here that the imperial circle was an association exercising political authority (*Herrschaftsgenossenschaft*), that is to say an associative union endowed with and practising rights of dominion[74] derived in part from imperial authority, in part from its own corporative competence. In proportion as imperial authority failed to bring order into conditions like the financial and monetary system, road and transport problems, the roving bands of thieves, and so on, the constitutions and political activities of the circles gained in power and effectiveness. It is therefore hardly surprising that the circles which proved themselves most useful were those which comprised the territorially fragmented areas of Franconia, Swabia, and the Rhineland, where they could assume indispensable political functions arising from common territorial and urban interests.[75]

IV

Thus, one part of the reform legislation, and a part that had in a sense grown up on the edge of the main concerns, became a lasting and, by and large, effective institution which determined for a quite considerable area the character of public life in the empire, especially the enforcement of law and order. In my opinion, this fact is significant for any assessment of the imperial reform movement as a whole. These attempts to graft new constitutional and administrative forms onto ancient and accustomed traditions cannot be understood from the documents alone, nor can they be interpreted simply in terms of their times of origin. One must first gain an understanding of their process of development, and this took a different turn for each of the achievements of the reform attempts. Institutions take on a kind of autonomy of their own. Laws, and institutions created by laws, are apt, once they have been brought into existence, to grow independent of the will and purpose of their creators; they can even run counter to their intentions and turn into spontaneous and autonomous entities. Jurists who are acquainted with the operations of modern constitutions and with the occasionally alarming, but nevertheless undeniable, fact of what has sometimes been called "imperceptible constitutional change"[76] will not see anything unusual, and most certainly nothing improbable, in such a process.

If a conclusion is to be drawn from all this purely in terms of political history (and the deficiencies and distortions of this approach were duly deplored at the beginning of this essay), it is that all judgments *pro aut contra* are partial, monistic, and likely to be politically immature. It would be foolish to dismiss the whole reform venture by asserting that it failed and was at bottom only a symptom of the empire's impotence. But it would be equally silly and, ultimately unhistorical, to lay both the positive and the negative results of the reform movement at the door either of the king or of the Estates. In evaluating the reform plans and their implementation it should be remembered that they were an expression of political power, and as such were products of their age. First of all, no more could be expected of Maximilian's royal authority, enfeebled as his power had become, mostly through his own fault, than he was actually able to deliver. Secondly, since the Estates, in the course of the fifteenth century had become important and powerful formations with a decisive voice in public life, it can hardly be expected that they should have sacrificed themselves for the sake of a nationalistic ideal which, in any case, arose only much later.

If the whole shape of the reform movement was dictated predominantly by the interests of the Estates, as our considerations here would seem to suggest,[77] then this was a consequence of the real power relations of the time and not of the political faults of this or that participant. At all events, the effort of the Estates to create at least an "existential minimum" of internal order and stability in the empire was perfectly legitimate and is not evidence of national weakness or diehard reactionary intransigence. This conclusion is forced on us, among other factors, by the important figure of Berthold of Mainz, of whose character and role historians should now begin to provide a fairer and more carefully balanced assessment. If this means that we will have to look at his opponent, Maximilian, with colder, less romantic eyes, then this, too, will be done for the sake of a more truthful estimate of their respective political significance. A fresh and clearer picture of our history seems to me to be well worth a prudent re-evaluation of the reform work itself and of the main actors involved in it. History must not be measured only against palpable successes, or against the positions which a nation acquires for itself by means of external conflict and the assertion of its power. No less admirable than place and might are the energy and intelligence devoted to the construction of an inner political, social, and moral order based on existing political and constitutional conditions.

NOTES TO CHAPTER 4

1. E. Molitor, *Die Reichsreformbestrebungen des 15. Jahrhunderts bis zum Tode Kaiser Friedrichs III* (1921), p. vii.
2. F. Hartung, "Die Reichsreform von 1485–1495," in *Historische Vierteljahrschrift*, XVI (1913), pp. 24 ff., 181 ff. [Chapter 3 in this book]; *idem, Deutsche Verfassungsgeschichte vom 15. Jahrhundert bis zur Gegenwart*, 5th ed. (1950). See *Ibid.*, pp. 23, 27 for further bibliography.
3. Leopold von Ranke, *History of the Reformation in Germany*, tr. Sarah Austin (Condor, 1845–47), book I.
4. H. Ulmann, *Kaiser Maximilian I* (1884), p. 292 ff.
5. G. Ritter, *Die Neugestaltung Europas im 16. Jahrhundert* (1950), p. 62.
6. *Ibid.*, p. 62 f.
7. W. Andreas, *Deutschland vor der Reformation*, 3rd ed. (1942), p. 242. It might be remarked in passing that, since the territory of the elector of Mainz was almost nine-tenths on the right bank of the Rhine in what are now parts of Hessen, Bavaria, and Thuringia, it is hardly possible to talk of any "frontier position."
8. *Ibid.* Compare against this the carefully balanced judgment of Joseph Lortz, *Die Reformation in Deutschland*, 3rd ed. (1948), p. 37.
9. In addition to the references given in Hartung, *Verfassungsgeschichte*, see also Richard Schröder and Eberhard von Künssberg, *Lehrbuch der deutschen Rechtsgeschichte*, 7th ed. (1932), p. 904 ff. (including supplements in the appendix).
10. F. Ernst, "Reichs- und Landespolitik in Süden Deutschlands am Ende des Mittelalters," in *Historische Vierteljahrschrift*, XXX (1935), 720 ff.

11. E. Ziehen, *Mittelrhein und Reich im Zeitalter der Reichsreform 1356–1504* (I, 1934; II, 1937); *idem, Frankfurt, Reichsreform und Reichsgedanke* (1940). [See also the review essay by Hans Baron, "Imperial Reform and the Habsburgs, 1486–1504: A New Interpretation," *American Historical Review*, XLIV (1939), 293–303. Ziehen's volumes may be consulted for references to the voluminous literature on the German imperial reform movement.]

12. J. Lortz, *op. cit.*, I, 47 f.

13. I do not undervalue the significance of these documents for the history of ideas, ranging as they do from wishful thinking to Utopia. But a constitutional historian, attempting to formulate a view of the constitutional reality of the time, will approach this literature with due skepticism. See the list of titles in Hartung, *Verfassungsgeschichte*, p. 23.

14. Cf. my remarks in *Der deutsche Südwesten in seiner territorialstaatlichen Entwicklung* (1950), p. 62 ff.

15. K. S. Bader, "Probleme des Landfriedensschutzes im mittelalterlichen Schwaben," *Zeitschrift für Württembergische Landesgeschichte*, III (1939), 42 ff.

16. Heinrich Finke, *Weltimperialismus und nationale Regungen im späteren Mittelalter* (1916), p. 22 ff.; Robert Holtzmann, "Der Weltherrschaftsgedanke," *Historische Zeitschrift*, 159 (1939), p. 255 ff.

17. Cf. Hermann Krause, *Kaiserrecht und Rezeption (Abhandlungen der Heidelberger Akademie der Wissenschaften*, phil.-hist. Klasse, 1952), p. 23 f.

18. This has rightly been emphasized by Hermann Mau, *Die Rittergesellschaft mit Sankt Jörgenschild in Schwaben* (1941), p. 38 ff.

19. O. von Gierke, *Das deutsche Genossenschaftsrecht*, I (1868), 220 ff.

20. G. von Below, *Der deutsche Staat des Mittelalters*, I (1914), 32 ff.

21. *Verfassungsgeschichte*, p. 26.

22. P. 241 f.

23. This is also the opinion of W. Goetz, *Propyläen-Weltgeschichte*, IV (1932), 443, who rightly rejects the view that Berthold was "the reactionary advocate of the past."

24. Erich Brandenburg in the preface to the *Deutsche Reichstagsakten* (ältere Reihe), Vol. VII, 1 (1935), p. vii.

25. I cannot agree with Lortz when (*op. cit.*, I, p. 39) he speaks of an "unnational egoism" and expresses the opinion that this was present "to an extent possible at that time only in Germany."

26. A view adopted by and large also by Molitor, *op. cit.*, p. 79.

27. So far as I can see, no serious attempt has been made to accomplish this beyond some individual details. A number of observations can be found in Molitor, *op. cit.*, p. 15 ff. Cf. also Thomas Wütenberger, *Das System der Rechtsgüterordnung in der deutschen Strafgesetzgebung seit 1532* (1932), p. 9 ff.

28. F. Hartung, "Berthold von Henneberg, Kurfürst von Mainz," *Historische Zeitschrift*, 103 (1909), p. 528.

29. Cf. Martin Honecker in *Historisches Jahrbuch*, 60 (1940), p. 124 ff.

30. K. Bauermeister, "Berthold von Henneberg," *Historisches Jahrbuch*, 39 (1919), p. 731 ff.; J. Weiss, *Berthold von Henneberg, seine kirchenpolitische*

und kirchliche Stellung (1889); Eduard Ziehen, *Mittelrhein und Reich*, Vol. I, pp. 166 ff. All the older literature is given by Ziehen in *ibid*, I, p. 353, note 190.

31. J. H. von Wessenberg, *Die grossen Reichsversammlungen des 15. und 16. Jahrhunderts*, III (1840), p. 550, was one of the first to describe Berthold "as a statesman who deserved well of the Holy Roman Empire for his constant efforts to provide a solid basis for the administration of justice."

32. Ulmann, *op. cit.*, I, pp. 294 ff.

33. Cf., for example, the verdict on the Frisian question (September, 1493) in *Urkunden und Aktenstücke des Reichsarchivs Wien zur reichsrechtlichen Stellung des Burgundischen Kreises*, I (1944), 7 ff.

34. Ziehen, *Mittelrhein und Reich*, Vol. II, p. 541.

35. For this and the following, cf. especially Ziehen, *Mittelrhein und Reich*, Vol. I, p. 167 ff.

36. Cf. K. Menzel, *Diether von Isenburg, Erzbischof von Mainz* (1868); also, A. Kirnberger, *Diether von Isenburg* (1950), a book which makes no claim to original research.

37. Ulmann, *op. cit.*, I, p. 299.

38. Molitor, *op. cit.*, p. 21, agrees that the position of imperial chancellor could have been turned into something more effective, especially in connection with imperial administration.

39. Ulmann, *op. cit.*, I, p. 293. P. Kirn, *Urkundenwesen und Kanzlei der Mainzer Erzbischöfe* (1929) does not go into this aspect of governmental activity in Mainz.

40. Ulmann, *op. cit.*, I, p. 334.

41. *Kaiser Maximilian I* (1950); cf. also the largely affirmative interpretation of Maximilian in Lortz, *op. cit.*, p. 39 f.

42. As E. Molitor rightly pointed out in the discussion on the present paper, it is important to note the Burgundian streak reflected in Maximilian's personality. So far there has been a great shortage of preliminary studies on this subject. The literature has been concerned almost exclusively with the question of Burgundian influence on the Austrian administrative organization. J. Huizinga's works on society and culture under Charles the Bold (especially his *The Waning of the Middle Ages*) should stimulate German historical research to a more thoroughgoing investigation of the effects of this overrefined culture upon the circle of German princes, beginning with King Maximilian himself.

43. *Quellen und Erläuterungen* (Tübingen, 1951); cf. my review in *Historisches Jahrbuch*, 71 (1952), p. 418 ff.

44. Ulmann, *op. cit.*, I, p. 336. For Maximilian's financial management cf. also K. Kaser, *Deutsche Geschichte im Ausgang des Mittelalters, 1438–1519* (1912), p. 181 ff.

45. E. Ziehen, *Frankfurt, Reichsreform und Reichsgedanke*, p. 36 ff.

46. G. von Pölnitz's book also provides a good deal of information about the councillors, even though it seems to me that, compared with Ulmann, he tends to treat the emperor's financial wizards somewhat leniently.

47. Quoted from Ulmann, *op. cit.*, I, p. 805.

48. It was given little credit for promoting peace in Schröder and von Künssberg, *Lehrbuch*, p. 863. See, however, *ibid.*, p. 968, where the Public Peace ordinance is considered as the "basic law of the empire." For a more positive interpretation see Hartung, *Reichsreform*, p. 197, and *Verfassungsgeschichte*, p. 28. Hartung is followed by H. E. Feine, *Deutsche Verfassungsgeschichte der Neuzeit*, 3rd ed. (1943), p. 20.

49. For the earlier period, cf. Joachim Gernhuber, *Die Landfriedensbewegung in Deutschland bis zum Mainzer Reichslandfrieden von 1235. Bonner rechtswissenschaftliche Abhandlungen*, 44 (Bonn, 1952).

50. Cf. K. S. Bader, *Probleme des Landfriedensschutzes*, p. 44 ff.

51. Hartung, *Verfassungsgeschichte*, p. 28.

52. Ulmann, *op. cit.*, I, pp. 394 f.

53. O. Brunner, *Land und Herrschaft*, 2nd ed. (1942), esp. p. 47 ff.

54. The same conclusion is reached by Feine, *op. cit.*, p. 20.

55. Ulmann, *op. cit.*, I, p. 375.

56. Oswald von Gschliesser, *Der Reichshofrat, Bedeutung und Verfassung. Schicksal und Besetzung einer obersten Reichsbehörde von 1559–1806. Veröffentlichungen der Kommission für neuere Geschichte des ehemaligen Österreich*, vol. 33 (Vienna, 1942).

57. Feine, *op. cit.*, p. 23.

58. R. Smend, *Das Reichskammergericht*, I (1911).

59. Thus Hartung, *Verfassungsgeschichte*, p. 51. The same conclusion is reached by E. Molitor, *Grundzüge der neueren Verfassungsgeschichte* (1948), p. 29.

60. Cf. Ulmann, *op. cit.*, I, p. 379.

61. Ziehen, *Mittelrhein*, II, pp. 491 f.

62. Schröder and von Künssberg, *op. cit.*, p. 923; cf. also Johannes Sieber, *Zur Geschichte des Reichsmatrikelwesens 1422–1521* (1910), p. 22 ff.

63. Feine, *op. cit.*, p. 21; Hartung, *op. cit.*, p. 29 f.

64. *Ibid.*, p. 31 ff.

65. *Ibid.*, p. 51, rightly refers to the inadequacy of the relevant works. The significance of the imperial circles had already been recognized by Richard Fester, *Franken und die Kreisverfassung. Neujahrsblätter der Gesellschaft für fränkische Geschichte*, I (1906); his suggestions were followed up by Hartung, *Geschichte des fränkischen Kreises, Darstellung und Akten*, I (1910). But the comprehensive book of Ernst von Simmern, *Die Kreisverfassung Maximilians I. und der schwäbische Reichskreis* (1896), despite its abundance of material, failed to grasp the wider constitutional context.

66. It is always worth rereading the passage in Severinus de Monzambano, i.e., Samuel von Pufendorf, *De statu imperii Germanici*; but all it comes to is that Pufendorf had to give up the attempt to provide a clear constitutional definition of the imperial constitution. For the whole problem, cf. Erik Wolf, *Grosse Rechtsdenker der deutschen Geistesgeschichte*, 3rd ed. (1951), p. 325 ff.

67. *Urkunden und Aktenstücke des Reichsarchivs Wien zur reichsrechtlichen Stellung des burgundischen Kreises*, I–III (1940 ff.).

68. For a detailed treatment of this, cf. Hartung, *Geschichte des fränkischen Kreises*, p. 35 ff.

69. Ulmann, *op. cit.*, I, p. 310.
70. Cf., for instance, the so-called "Recess of the Spiritual Electors" of 1456, excerpts of which are printed in Karl Zeumer, *Quellensammlung, zur Geschichte der deutschen Reichsverfassung* . . . , I, p. 269.
71. Fester, *op. cit.*, p. 10 ff.
72. Cf. Hartung, *Verfassungsgeschichte*, p. 52 f.
73. K. S. Bader, *Der deutsche Südwesten in seiner territorialstaatlichen Entwicklung* (1950), esp. p. 191 ff.
74. This concept, only apparently contradictory, was formulated by von Gierke, *Das deutsche Genossenschaftsrecht*, I, p. 155.
75. Hartung, *Verfassungsgeschichte*, p. 53. Cf. also Hans Planitz, *Deutsche Rechtsgeschichte* (1950), p. 213. E. Ewing, *Die geschichtlichen Grundlagen des Landes Rheinland-Pfalz* (Mainz, 1953), p. 2, rightly points out that "the major territories and the imperial circles were the real constitutive associations in modern times."
76. F. A. Freiherr von der Heydte, "Stiller Verfassungswandel und Verfassungsinterpretation," *Archiv für Rechts- und Sozialphilosophie*, 39 (1951), p. 461 ff.
77. This would seem to be the unanimous opinion of constitutional historians. It is often regarded as a matter of regret that the reform originated among the Estates and did not emanate from the monarchical head; but this attitude seems to me to result from a wrong approach to the matter.

5 Humanism and the Development of the German Mind

PAUL JOACHIMSEN

Paul Joachimsen (1867–1930), a leading intellectual historian, wrote this famous summary essay in 1929. It proved so influential in Germany that it had the effect of stifling for a considerable time the scholarly discussion on the nature and provenance of German humanism. Joachimsen writes intellectual history in the German manner: *Geistesgeschichte*. That is to say, he sees intellectual history as posing "problems" and striving toward solutions. His rather abstract and not infrequently opaque language is due to his attempt to "condense the known facts into a clear idea: *zu einer Anschauung verdichten*." By no means all of Joachimsen's interpretations of German humanism are accepted today (cf. the essay by Werner Näf cited in note 48, below), but it remains the most important single contribution to the course of the discussion. I have filled out Joachimsen's sketchy footnote references and have added the titles of recent works on many of the subjects mentioned in the text. I have, however, eliminated most of the quotations from the sources given in Joachimsen's original notes.

ANYONE who sets out to discuss the relationship between humanism and the German mind is aware of being confronted with two different and rather vaguely defined quantities whose respective scope and significance are matters of controversy. An analysis of the terms would be difficult and would not put an end to the controversy anyway; let it suffice, then, to say what I shall mean

An expanded version of a lecture given before the Philological Conference at Salzburg, September 1929. References will be given only to works which have directly advanced my study.

by humanism in the following pages. Humanism will be taken to mean an intellectual movement rooted in the attempt to revive classical antiquity, and to revive it is the strictest sense of this word. It will be assumed that antiquity had in fact died, but that it was capable of revival and, as far as those who spoke about the question were concerned, in need of revival. Such men must necessarily have sensed that there existed a gap—a chasm even—between them and the ancient world. Furthermore, they must have seen antiquity as a unity complete in itself; unique and not repeatable, yet at the same time containing principles which would enable those who were moving toward, or were committed to, some kind of humanism to give form and standards to their own cultural world.[1] Finally, it is assumed that this intellectual attitude was not confined to a few individuals but was characteristic of an entire period, which, in turn, means that humanism as an historical movement was only possible where men were aware that something was lacking in their lives and turned to a revival of antiquity as a means of making good the deficiency.

I must add here that, given this awareness, there existed two attitudes toward the problem of humanism. These two attitudes might be termed the romantic and the classical. The romantic attitude felt the revival of antiquity as a kind of nostalgia which could never be completely fulfilled because it longed for a genuine palingenesis; indeed, its true merit lay in the very impossibility of fulfillment. For the classical attitude, antiquity meant a set of eternally valid ideas that served to justify present existence, and the revival of antiquity was recalling to memory, an *anamnesis* in the Platonic sense. In both cases, however, the task of humanism was the same: giving form and laying down standards. As far as form was concerned the emphasis was primarily aesthetic, though ethical values were considered to be contained within the aesthetic. When these two elements—the aesthetic and the ethical—became divorced the notion of humanism underwent its first change of meaning, a change which, as will be seen, was extraordinarily significant historically and of decisive importance for the whole problem of German humanism.

If this is correct, then there was no humanism in the Middle Ages, whether Carolingian, Ottonian, or Norman.[2] There had been a greater or lesser degree of emphasis on such elements of antiquity as Christianity had incorporated as a result of its confrontation with Greek philosophy and its entry into the Roman Empire. There had also been manuscript hunters and collectors of inscriptions, letter writers who strove after a purer Latin style, schools where ancient authors were read. There had been a medieval Aristotelianism and a medieval Platonism. But there had been no medieval humanism in the sense of an historical movement exerting a creative influence on European culture and values. Humanism begins with Petrarch, and I shall not be able to deal adequately with my subject without first saying something in detail about him.

In Petrarch[3] all the essential features of humanism appear at once, though admittedly only as a problem of individual psychology. Petrarch was the first in the history of Western thought to build his life on aesthetic sensibility. Even as a child, before he could understand the meaning of Latin words, he had an ear for the beauty of the periods of Cicero and the verses of Virgil. Just like his contemporaries, he noted down the ancient *sententiae*, to which the teaching methods of the grammar and rhetoric schools had reduced the cultural treasury of the ancient world. Unlike others, however, he did not do this in order to gather useful turns of phrase for the enrichment of his letters and his conversation; rather, he felt himself spoken to by voices from a world of the past.[4] For him they confirmed a spiritual dichotomy that drove him into isolation and set him apart from his contemporaries. He felt himself old before his time; even in his youth he entertained thoughts of death. These arose from a sense that he was unable to become what he would so dearly have liked to be.[5] They were the first onsets of the *Weltschmerz*, his ἀχήδεια which increased as the years went by. He never escaped this mood, whether as a law student in Montpellier and Bologna, or as a dandy and benefice-hunter in Avignon. His love for Laura released his poetic genius, but his *Canzoniere* was a single variation on the same theme. If

his effect on the modern reader (especially the non-Italian) is one
of monotony, it is due to this pervasive strain of melancholy. But
that is not all. Although his love was essentially a troubadour's
love, a love that evaporated with the possession of the beloved,
two things distinguish Petrarch from the troubadours. First, he
saw life in all its variety, nature in all its hues, and men in all their
differentiated individualities. Thus Laura herself was saved from
becoming a philosophical abstraction, as did Dante's Beatrice.
Second, he was marked by his numerous urges to get away from
it all. These urges expressed themselves in two, apparently contradictory ways: one, his journeys, which took him through France,
to the Rhine, and to Rome and Naples for no other purpose than
that of sightseeing,[6] and the other his longing for solitude, which
drew him to Vaucluse. In both cases reminiscences of antiquity
reinforced the natural penchant of a discontented man, ever
yearning for the true reality and never finding it. Petrarch's travels
became voyages of discovery after classical manuscripts, and his
solitude an aesthetic idyll embellished in the colors of the ancient
world. Petrarch was the first to create for himself an aesthetic
environment in which he might live *procul ab hominibus, non ab
humanitate alienus*: far from men, but no stranger to humanity.

What was still lacking, however, was the composition of the
disiecta membra antiquitatis, with which he was preoccupied, into a
philosophy of life upon which his mind could come to rest. This
he achieved in a roundabout way, through his attempt at a religious conversion.[7] Here St. Augustine served him as example and
father-confessor to help the better part of his nature overcome the
worse, the part driven by love and ambition. The attempt was
not successful. But while building up a picture of St. Augustine
based on his personal needs, Petrarch came to believe that Augustine had lived by the wisdom of the ancient world in exactly the
same way as he himself wished to do.[8] This recognition had two
consequences of great importance. By setting himself beside
Augustine, Petrarch became the first to gain that view of the
ancient world which Augustine had been the last to possess.
Augustine offered him the link between Christ and Cicero which

he had so long been seeking.[9] Secondly, Petrarch gained the ability—again the first to achieve this—not to overcome the ancient world, like the real Augustine, but to live in it as he imagined his own Augustine to have done. The flight into antiquity became for him a means of flight from the world.

The final step occurred in Rome. Even on his first visit to the Rome of the barons and the Gothic towers, Petrarch rediscovered the Rome of the Scipios and of Peter and Paul. The fantastic adventure of Cola di Rienzo had taught him that a real revival of this Rome was impossible.[10] But he now found in the Rome of his imagination the ideal background against which to set the *avara Babilone*, the Avignon of the popes.[11] He gained a sense of spatial contact with an ancient world peopled by poets, heroes, and saints, a world he could not find in the present.

With this he had arrived at his goal. The voices from the distant past, which in his youth had seemed to him those of a bad conscience, now sounded to him like the expression of his deepest being.[12] He wrote letters to Cicero, Seneca, and Livy as though they were personal friends, and appended these to the collection of his letters to his contemporaries. He gathered round him the *viri illustres* of the past, the great Pantheon of heroism, morality, and achievement. At last he had found that other world in which he could live, and by doing so had brought the two parts of his nature into harmony. But the chasm between past and present yawned more unbridgeable than before: he could be borne across it only on the wings of his longing.

But something else should be noticed about this process. Petrarch's striving after antiquity as another and better world was not, in its very essence and as Petrarch himself conceived it, different from the striving of the soul for repose in God. Had Petrarch been another kind of man he would have followed countless others both before and after him into the cloister. He himself looked on his task of self-cultivation much as the medieval monk regarded his search for perfection in the service of God. Such was Petrarch's religion, a subject on which so much has been written. This religion was not a lie, not even a self-delusion. His flight from the world took the shape of a flight into antiquity, and it was religion as far as so purely aesthetic a man could be religious. But this very transposition of the religious impulse into the aesthetic, of the sense of sin into *Weltschmerz*, of the surrender to God into the cultivation of the soul as an end in itself—all this, seen in relation to antiquity as a better world, gave rise to humanism as an historical movement in its earliest form, that of individual psychology; indeed it enabled humanism to become a creative cultural force in the Christian world.

But if humanism was from this moment able to set out on its victorious advance into the world of western culture, this was due to two factors which will also be found in Petrarch. The first is Petrarch's sense of reality, the faculty that kept him from turning Laura into a symbol and which opened his eyes to a thousand tiny enchantments of nature in Vaucluse and to men and things in all their variety on his travels. This same sense also rendered his picture of antiquity more truthful and precise than any hitherto known. The men of the ancient world with whom he lived as with his peers he saw as men of their own times. He extricated the "real facts" of antiquity from the fairy tales with which the *Mirabilia*, *Physiologi*, and *Bestiarii* of the Middle Ages had encrusted them.[13] The sense of spiritual distance between himself and the ancient world which he had felt as a boy now became historical distance. With Petrarch we arrive at the beginning of the critical and historical study of antiquity, perhaps at the beginning of historical thinking itself. The second factor can be seen in the rejections by means of which Petrarch sought to buttress the position he had reached: his struggles against scholasticism, jurisprudence, medicine, and Averroism. In scholasticism and jurisprudence he attacked the Aristotelian dialectic which he found so uncongenial to his own nature. In Averroism he fought a rationalizing contemplation of the world that went against his own mystical outlook and was, at the same time, as pagan as his own antiquity was truly Christian. In medicine he saw a superstition that presumed to know unknowable things and purveyed a distorted view of man's relationship with nature.

All this, of course, was nothing more than the dilettantism of a humanist romantic. But it turned out to be the way to an altogether new relationship between life and learning.

The Italian Renaissance was the first to be affected by the formative and normative influences of this new humanism. By Renaissance I do not in this case mean an artistic trend, nor do I take it as just another word for humanism, nor as the name of a particular form of culture. I simply mean a period of Italian history roughly extending from 1250 to 1550. Its distinguishing social and political feature, which, since the term is being used historically, is all that matters here, is the rise of the city-state. Thus it is possible for us here to retain the word Renaissance in an historically meaningful sense quite apart from its traditional artistic usage. For what was then being reborn in Italy, and only in Italy, was the ancient polis. Like the polis, the city-state was based on the absorption of the estates into the concept of citizenship. As a result of this, and of this alone, the city-state of the Renaissance achieved a special place within the hierarchical order of the Middle Ages. Like the ancient polis the Renaissance city-state aimed externally at autonomy and self-sufficiency, and internally at a rational organization of communal life based on something beyond custom and tradition. Thus the Renaissance polis became the first individualistic structure in the western world, that is to say, one which, within the transcendental organization of the medieval world, set its way of life according to its own internal interests rather than by its position as a link in the system. At the same time there developed in the Italy of the communes a new individualistic human type, to be found first of all in the tyrants of the Renaissance. This is not to say that these men were in some sense "individuals" while medieval men had not been "individuals," but rather that the tyrants ventured to affirm their own egoistic individuality and make it the measure by which they lived their lives. This is what Jacob Burckhardt meant when he said that thirteenth-century Italy saw cities and despots "whose existence was simply a matter of fact" (*deren Dasein rein tatsächlicher Art war*); and also when he said that here, for the first time, a veil woven of faith, childish prepossession, and illusion was blown away, a veil through which men had previously seen the world and which had allowed them to think of themselves only in terms of race, people, party, corporation, family, or some other general grouping.

Despite all modern misinterpretations, these words, to my mind, are perfectly apt and give the only fitting description of what might be called the spirit of the Renaissance—here taken as a cultural epoch. All the same, it should not be thought that this "individualist culture" means that earlier there had been fewer or lesser individual personalities and structures, nor that this individualism implied a break with the organic system of the Middle Ages. On the contrary, the individualism of the Renaissance, like any other individualism, presupposed the system. It needed the system if its purely matter-of-fact otherness was to develop into a conscious attitude. This conscious attitude led to those elements which distinguish the individualistic Renaissance from the purely instinctive self-assertions to be found in all early periods of national development; it led to a rationalization of the immediate environment; it led to the first theory of life to divide the world into the two domains of *ratio* and *fortuna*; it led, finally, to the first attempt to render this purely *de facto* existence within the system meaningful through the idea of *virtù*.

The history of the Renaissance polis can be divided into epochs of social and political development, and these correspond to the divisions made by contemporary Italian historians into the periods of the communes, the signories, and the principates. It can also be organized into epochs of economic development, characterized by the permeation of the communities with the institutions of capitalism. Finally—and for us the most important—there are epochs of ideological justification, made necessary by the fact that the polis continued to form part of the militant sacerdotal community of western Christendom and by the relationship of the new *ratio* to the tradition and authority of the transcendental system.

The Renaissance polis found its first justification in the modification of Roman law as shown by the practice of the notaries to be seen most clearly in the remarkable figure of Master Boncompagno of Bologna;[14] and in astrology, which, springing from the hybrid Sicilian and Arabic culture of the last Hohenstaufen court, was intended to make even the sphere of *fortuna* calculable and thus bring it under control.[15]

This development filled the first period of the Italian Renaissance, the time of the communes and of early capitalistic institutions, roughly from 1250 to 1350. This period had come to an end by the time humanism was ready to set about giving form and standards to the Renaissance, thus to provide it with a new and permanently valid justification. The age of the communes was replaced by that of the signories. It was with these and with the *principati* that humanism was concerned, in other words, with the fully developed Renaissance state. Thus—and this is important for the subsequent course of events—humanism did not encounter the old polis with its free citizens but rather the new state dominated by its ruler. Two apparent exceptions existed to this: Venice and Florence. I say apparent, for even in Venice, where a merchant oligarchy had risen to eminence, and in Florence, where a form of democracy had attained supreme power, the theoretical equality among the citizens had long ceased to correspond to the realities of life within the state. And only in Florence was humanism still concerned with the formation of a spirit of citizenship.[16] In the main humanism was now confronted with the problems of an aristocratic culture, to which it was to give a classical shape. Ambition was good, for Horace and Virgil had sung its praises. Enjoyment of life was no sin, since Ovid and Epicurus had commended it. Yet throughout all this the ancient polis continued to make itself felt, for these virtues were not those of a social estate but of a new type: the new *humanitas* understood as a sense of life and a desire for learning. This new type received its most distinctive development in Florence through Lionardo Bruni. And Florence, too, kept alive the idea that there were civic virtues which could vie with the spiritual ones, since Cicero and Aristotle had praised them.

From the point of view of the humanists, then, there was a gradual uncovering of the traditions of antiquity. From Augustine who, as we have seen, had still been the focal point of Petrarch's view of antiquity, they moved on to the late classical schools of the Epicureans and the Stoics, and then further still to Plato and Aristotle. Plato was a completely new conquest, while Aristotle was set free from the bondage into which scholasticism and the Arabs had placed him. From the point of view of the Renaissance there was an increasingly pronounced shaping of public and private life on the pattern of the ancient world, and everywhere this formation had the practical effect of establishing standards as it progressed. It was precisely this which enabled the individualistic way of life of the Renaissance to fit itself into the transcendental system of the Middle Ages. The *virtù* of the men of the Renaissance, as time went by, took on more and more the characteristics of the Roman *virtus*, and before long those of the Greek ἀρετή. The paganism of which the Renaissance made great display was in almost all cases a veneer, an outward show. Even with Petrarch, antiquity had been set not against Christianity, but against scholasticism; and the further humanism progressed in giving shape to the Renaissance, the more the revival of antiquity came to look upon itself as being Christian, as being, in fact, a religion.[17] In Florentine Platonism, it really did become a religion for a group of aesthetically minded men; though here the impulse came no longer from any romantic nostalgia, as it had with Petrarch, but from the attempt to vindicate something whose possession had already been secured.

For one result of the humanistic formation of the Renaissance was that the two great opposites which scholastic doctrine had brought together in an ingeniously constructed hierarchy of values reaching beyond the present world, the natural and the supernatural, came to be considered as united in an ultimately aesthetic harmony centering on the limitlessly perfectible human being. The other result was that this human being entered into a new social bond with his fellow beings by creating the first modern society. The characteristic feature of this society was its *consensus opinionum*, a tacit agreement about the forms and institutions of life, whose standards were based on supreme principles assumed to have been accepted by all those with a "humane" culture and no longer a matter for discussion. The new society was not a community resulting from natural ties and necessities, nor a society of estates with special ceremonies of admission (like the chivalric society of the Middle Ages whose place it took). It was based on pure convention. Ariosto was both its product and its most brilliant portrayer.

This Renaissance society represented the new cultural unity of Italy which Lionardo Bruni had been the first to sense. It survived the collapse of Italy's political independence—as in ancient Greece—and brought about an Italian cultural hegemony in Europe which was to last nearly two centuries.

It should be noted, however, that the historical problem of the Renaissance cannot be reduced entirely to the question of the humanist formation of society.[18] What has got left out can be seen from two names figuring in the last generation of the Renaissance, Machiavelli and Michelangelo, which can be coupled with two others from preceding generations, Lorenzo Valla and Leonardo da Vinci. Valla raised the question whether a *consensus opinionum* was possible without a discussion of the forms of thought itself, through mere agreement on what was spoken about and the way it was to be expressed. From him there runs a straight line of development to Peter Ramus and Descartes. Leonardo asked whether the mastery over nature was possible purely in terms of aesthetics, without any exploration of its underlying mechanical principles. Machiavelli asked whether the humanist accommodation of *ratio* with transcendence, as provided in the Platonist solution, means very much when confronted with the purely existential individualism of the Renaissance. He referred back to the basic problem of the polis, which he then proceeded to build up in terms of *ratio* alone, thus creating the new science of politics in which aesthetic man had no place. Michelangelo went straight from the artistic problem of the contradiction between idea and appearance to the question of whether the humanist individuality could indeed be the ultimate form which the human personality could attain to. But all these men were descended from the humanistically formed culture of the Renaissance and would have been inconceivable without it. To appreciate this it will be sufficient to try to imagine them against the spiritual background of the Middle Ages.

On the other hand, these four names bring out clearly the problems raised by humanism within the history of ideas. Humanism undertook to provide a cultural form and establish standards by referring to a culture of the past, a culture that was considered valuable precisely because it *was* of the past. It gathered these forms and standards together under the idea of learning (*Bildung*), in a sense of this term previously unknown. This new learning with its independent existence in the ancient past interposed itself between men and the life they lived; it surrounded them, and it was the tradition from which they took their origin. It would have to be broken through every time something radically new was to be created. The new human types produced by the Renaissance were the empirical investigator, the politician, the *homo religiosus*, and the subjectivist critic. Humanism produced the aesthetic man of letters who transformed life's problems into objects of thought. Petrarch was his prototype.

It may appear as though I have dealt with all this in more detail than my subject requires. But just as it is impossible to treat German humanism without some knowledge of Italian humanism,[19] so also is it quite impossible to recognize the problems that were to arise from the encounter of humanism with the German mind, without having first condensed the known facts about the Italian Renaissance and its humanistic formation into a clear idea. This is so not only because Germany had to come to grips with the Italian Renaissance, but also because the humanistic formation of the Italian Renaissance represented the first appearance of humanism as a matter of cultural psychology, whereas with Petrarch it had been only a matter of individual psychology. The most important reason, however, is that in Italy a concept of learning seems to have absorbed the entire historical existence of a nation. This was possible only because, in the Italian Renaissance, humanism as an historical force met with conditions closely akin to itself. The worldliness of the Italian national spirit, to be seen even in so spiritualized a figure as Saint Francis of Assisi, the open receptive attitude to the realities of life as shown so delightfully by Salimbene of Parma, the concern for immediate aims which made the Italians just as little at home in the world of chivalry as in that of scholasticism and the Gothic, and finally the possibility of recognizing in ancient Rome one's own past—all these factors combined to make possible the unique phenomenon we have called the humanist formation of the Italian Renaissance.

Of all this there was no trace in fifteenth-century Germany, where humanism was now to begin its second victorious advance. The German state of the late Middle Ages would appear to have been the very opposite of the ancient polis: instead of a fusion of the estates into a real community, we have a complete collapse of the idea of citizenship; instead of increasing rationalization in public and private life, a tenacious traditionalism which was due equally to the preservation of old ideas about the Teutonic community and to a complete identification with the hierarchical character of the Christian world. There was one exception— the Bohemia of Charles IV. Here both ruler and state bore very striking analogies with ruler and state in Renaissance Italy. Here there was a deliberate fostering of culture which combined native and foreign elements into a new unity. Here, too, the remarkable contacts of the ruler and his chancery and court with Cola di Rienzo and Petrarch, seemingly pointing the way toward a humanistically influenced culture. But Bohemia was a foreign body in fifteenth-century Germany, and its ruler's achievements remained without any effect upon the course of German culture as a whole. Symbolical of this is the fact that its most significant literary product, the *Ackermann aus Böhmen*, was an isolated phenomenon. Any formative tendency on German development as a whole was limited to the chancery schools, where it merely bore two equally questionable fruits, the so-called chancery style (*Kanzleistil*) of written German and the theory of the Master-singers. Whatever really formative elements might have developed in the hybrid colonial culture, for such it was, of Bohemia, were destroyed by the Hussite revolution which wrecked the integration of the German and Czech peoples without which such a culture would not have had any substance.

To find out how the native propensities of the German mind revealed themselves after the collapse of the high forms of the Middle Ages it will be best to look not so much to the Bohemia of Charles IV as to the period of Ludwig of Bavaria which immediately preceded it. Neither the personal inadequacy of this ruler, nor his fantastic conduct of politics, nourished, as it was apparently, on reminiscences, should obscure the fact that his epoch evidenced characteristic stirrings of the German mind in many very different fields. German mysticism, for example, evidenced the beginnings of a German philosophy; mysticism was, in fact, the first intellectual tendency in Germany which was not merely passively receptive. There was, further, a movement to describe the natural world; also a respect for historical context which went beyond the composition of mere chronicles and novelistic tales; furthermore, an attempt to reconstitute a system of laws for the German Empire; and, finally, a remarkable attempt to relate the old literature of chivalry to current actuality by filling it with contemporary ideas.

However, these encouraging initiatives came to grief in the political disorder brought on by internal struggles among the cities and the Estates, by the schism and the period of the first council. At the beginning of the fifteenth century German intellectual life appears everywhere confused and unsettled. It is true that Germany was represented in the great discussion on the restoration of church unity by men like Heinrich von Langenstein and Dietrich von Niem, who were certainly conscious of being German; all the same, their cultural sources lay in Paris and Rome, not in Germany. At the Council of Constance, Germany was intellectually passive in comparison with France and Italy.

But immediately after this, at the Council of Basel, there appeared a man in whom the characteristic propensities of the German mind emerge methodologically trained, independent, and fully versed in the whole range of western culture. Nicholas of Cusa was, even when judged by his external activities alone, a universal man. Jurist and theologian, naturalist and speculative thinker, historian and statesman, his ideas in every field formed a continuity with the past and pointed boldly toward the future. As can be imagined, he attracted much attention among his contemporaries, and esteem for him has been growing ever since.[20] Every history of German thought must place him at the beginning of that important period of transition which separates the new German era from the Middle Ages. If Germany can boast a Renaissance mentality, it will be found more than anywhere else in him; he was certainly the first to express it. And if he is compared with his Italian contemporaries it will be hard to name anyone else who gave such clear expression to the sense of living at the beginning of a new era as Cusa did in the introductory words to his principal political work, De Concordantia Catholica.[21] With equal clarity, however, he revealed the specifically German "problems" of the Renaissance, and it can be seen immediately that these were altogether different from the Italian ones. In Germany there was no question of marking out the sphere of ratio in the life of individual, state, or society; nor was there any concern for war or the state as works of art. Interest centered, rather, on the human mind which, as the measure of all things, conferred value not only on the empirical world but even on God,[22] and on man who found his life's happiness precisely in his awareness of this faculty and of the never-ending task it opened up for him.[23] This rational faculty of the human mind had to be integrated with the purely intuitive certainty that the universe was organically integrated within itself and with the individual personality; the problems of theological and mathematical infinity had to be dealt with; and finally it was necessary to reflect this theory of life in a political and social structure which was ultimately transcendent and yet had to be based on the natural rights of all members of the community.

It is perhaps characteristic of the German mind that such a man should have a very lively share in the intellectual curiosity of contemporary Italian humanism, and yet at the same time feel not the slightest need to draw from the contemplation of antiquity any standards for the human personality or its social and political existence. The form of his writings remained essentially scholastic, and his ultimate goal was a specifically catholic one (in the etymological sense of that word), the *coincidentia oppositorum*.[24]

I do not here intend to ask whether this position might not also have led to the development of humanist culture based perhaps on Christian antiquity, the importance of which for the history of German humanism will be seen later. Suffice it to say that this did not happen, and that while Cusanus may have embodied a new mentality in the history of German thought, he did not introduce new principles of education and culture, such as the Italian Petrarch had created and developed into a new form of life.

German humanism as an historical movement begins with a confrontation with Italy, and in this sense its real apostle in Germany remains Enea Silvio Piccolomini.[25] He it was who first set things moving. He brought with him to Germany the narrative art of Poggio, the methods of historical and biographical presentation of the school of Bruni and Biondo, and especially the new rhetorical and epistolary arts cultivated by Filelfo. His first sphere of influence was the chancery. Among notaries, clerks and, later, jurists he found his first supporters and disseminators, and, also, his opponents. Subsequently, however, his influence extended to the whole range of interests of a generation striving for new objectives. Much against his own will he succeeded in educating the Germans to embark on rivalry with Italy.

The differences between the Italian and German paths of development were described by Enea with all the perspicuity of a born observer of men and peoples. Among the Germans he found a sort of freedom which he missed in Italy,[26] and they seemed to him to live more according to nature than to "opinions."[27] Thus, for him, Germany lacked both the political and social development which had been effected by the Renaissance

polis and given a meaningful form by humanism. Nevertheless—
and this is of decisive importance for the progress of the movement—Germany at once took over the humanistic ideals cultivated by Italian humanism- the ideal types of the *orator*, the *poeta*,
and the *philosophus*. These types were distinguished just as sharply
in Germany as they had been in Italy from the old products of the
"trivial" schools and the arts faculties. Orators, poets, and philosophers are not made by the learning of rules. Each must have an
inborn aptitude, an *ingenium*, and in each resides a moral element,
or even a divine spark. The *orator* is the *vir bonus, dicendi peritus* of
Cato; above all he is a statesman and a man versed in practical
politics.[28] The *poeta* is a prophet, an intimate of the divine
mysteries.[29] The *philosophus* is learned in both divine and natural
things; he is the natural rival of the *theologus* and might better be
called *theosophus*.[30] But side by side with these features shared with
Italy, Germany showed certain peculiarities of her own. The ideal
types reflecting the ideal of humanity, for example, were rendered
much more concrete: for instance, the poet, who came almost
always to be called *historiographus* as well. Most important, the
ideals were almost all converted to pedagogical purposes. The
reason for this lies in the first place in the lack of a German state or
society in the Italian sense. For the *orator*, the *poeta*, and ultimately
also the *philosophus* worked, at least in principle, in the public
sphere, something which in the ancient world had really existed
and which the Italian city-state at least pretended to have. In
Germany things were different. And even though the German
humanist found as many opportunities as the Italian to adorn
great occasions and public affairs with fine rhetorical flourishes, it
cannot be said that his speeches had any effect on public life.
Indeed, it is characteristic that the most powerful political talent
of German humanism, Johann Sleidan. left only a collection of
formal addresses, while a naturally declamatory man like Wimpfeling never got any further than pedagogical exhortation.

Thus German humanism made its first effects felt in the schools,
and especially the universities. Here it discovered a more favorable
field than elsewhere, for the German universities were princely

foundations. The second period of university foundation in Germany, beginning in 1456, was increasingly determined by the courts, which had begun to turn to the new learning, and German humanism found that its concern with princely education gave easy entry into the institutes of learning. There was another factor which favored the humanist conquest of the universities. German universities lacked the established scholastic tradition of French and English institutions. And even if the struggle between the ancients and the moderns was less important for the general history of learning in Germany than has long been supposed,[31] it is nevertheless clear that it offered much scope to the humanists' attacks. Much more lay behind all this, but that will become apparent later.

The humanist movement in Germany was therefore confronted with a number of special phenomena. The universal inclination toward reform left over from the councils of Constance and Basel appeared very powerfully and distinctively in Germany. Plans for a reform of the church, already to be seen in Nicholas of Cusa, were combined with plans for reforming the empire. The Hussite threat gave these projects an immediate urgency, and a remarkable little tract, *The Reformation of the Emperor Sigismund*, shows how easily and naturally they became mixed with popular democratic tendencies. What humanism brought about here can be seen from the Grievances of the German Nation. In their original version these complaints represented a move on the part of the higher German clergy, dictated by the interests of the ecclesiastical establishment. But in the version they were given by the chancellor of Mainz, Martin Mair, a pupil of Gregor Heimburg, in his controversy with Enea Silvio, they appear as the outcry of nation which had fallen from its earlier greatness and was now defenselessly abandoned to the mercy of an alien power, The Roman curia. The great theme of national humanism had been sounded, and its reverberations were to continue right down to Ulrich von Hutten.

Besides this general reforming trend we have the imperative of monastic reform. This, too, was a result of the councils and was a general phenomenon in western Europe. The intention was to reform at least the most important member of the church, the monastic estate, after the attempt at a *reformatio in capite et membris* had come to nothing. In Germany this monastic reform brought with it something of special significance: the revival of the ancient Benedictine culture.[32] For the first time, an epoch of the German past—the age of Charlemagne, with Charlemagne himself at its center—was examined and evaluated. An outstanding figure in this context was the singular Abbot Trithemius, the first great collector and scholar of documents from Germany's distant past.

Matters were taken a step further by the Alsatian School of Geiler, Brant, and Wimpfeling,[33] who stood in some opposition to monasticism, and even came into conflict with it, mainly because they were reluctant to acknowledge that there was any "wisdom under the cowl." But they shared the monastic ideals: seclusion from the world (all three repeatedly considered becoming hermits in the Black Forest) and at the same time exhibited the missionary urge to spread their influence in the world. Spiritually they were disciples of John Gerson, whose *theologia mystica et negativa* with its mysticism diluted by rationalism nourished their own religious thought. They interested themselves in Gerson's lesser-known works. Geiler made a pilgrimage to France to visit the centers of his activity, and it was the Alsatian circle which first brought out a complete edition of his works. But in addition to all this they had some definite ideas for the reform of the ecclesiastical estate and the whole of ecclesiastical life, and their guiding principle here was learning. Hence their reference to the Fathers of the church and, to a lesser extent, to the Bible itself. Hence, too, their attempt to come to grips with the new resources of humanist rhetoric and poetics, which in the case of Wimpfeling resulted in a—really quite old-fashioned—"new way" for learning.[34] On top of this came a lively patriotism, springing from a strong sense, unknown before then, that Alsace was border territory. For this purpose Charlemagne, considered as a German, became very important. Finally there was renewed evidence of an unbroken link with the older mysticism; thus Tauler took on a new lease of life. But most important of all, perhaps, was the vital contact these men had with the world in which they lived—Geiler availed himself of it to create the vivid human types who filled his sermons, Brant used it to form a primitive theory of life, and Wimpfeling, scatterbrained though he was, had a keen nose for all contemporary issues and knew how to give them a controversial edge.

What immediately comes to mind here is an element which not only distinguished this German humanism from the Italian brand, but also caused it to stand apart from the concept of humanism as I have described it. Nothing suggests that antiquity was here being used as a means of providing norms. Even though Brant and Wimpfeling (but not Geiler) knew their Italians and their classics, their aesthetic ideas were never at any time inspired by antiquity. Yet it is a fact that Brant's *Ship of Fools*, a work which seems anything but humanist, was enthusiastically acclaimed by the humanists, translated into Latin, and even compared with Dante's *Divine Comedy*.[35] This comparison is instructive. In the early days of the German humanist movement, the *Ship of Fools* represented a first attempt to impose a rational pattern on the motley spectacle of contemporary events, the sheer senselessness of which was weighing more and more heavily on people's minds. It was also an attempt—admittedly a naïve one—to provide a psychology of human passions, and it took its distinctive character from the essentially humanist idea that even sins and vices are follies, that is to say, a backsliding from the natural exercise of human reason. The fact that this composition, like almost all the Alsatian productions, was also a satirical polemic serves to bring out the problematical attitude of these men to their age. It might even be said that this Alsatian group reflects the whole problematical situation of the great spiritual and temporal commonwealth which, at that very time, was beginning to style itself as the Holy Roman Empire of the German Nation. It expressed a growing consciousness of national peculiarities, a humanist optimism which, however, found itself embattled with all the utter impossibilities of contemporary life; and a strong feeling that the fundamental issue of the age was religious—that it was necessary, as the older mystics had insisted, to break loose from the trammels of externalized religion and find the most direct, the shortest way to God. Here, then, was a first plan for a *restitutio Christianismi*, guided by an as yet somewhat vague idea of Christian antiquity but it remained an attempt, advancing no further than toward an educational reform, and attacking not the evils it recognized, but merely its symptoms.

It is not easy to see where all this might have led. In any case the future course of the German humanist movement was not in the hands of these semi-humanistic theologians but in the care of another group of men, the poets.

It is among these poets that the impact of Italian humanism is to be seen most clearly. For all the members of this group the journey to Italy was not simply a period of study which might be spent just as well in Paris as in Bologna, but an experience. Among them alone the aesthetic element was uppermost and became their sole starting point. Again, it is characteristic of the German setting that these men were wandering scholars, that is to say, that they had no place in the German social structure. In Italy, lyric poetry drawn from personal experience had never quite lost its function in society and had, indeed, secured a sure footing through Dante and Petrarch; but in Germany it had fallen into decay along with chivalric poetry. The poetry of the Master-singers, which had taken the place of that of the Minnesingers, did not merely restrict invention to certain approved subjects but also made of the poet himself an essentially bourgeois figure. It was therefore natural that humanist poets in Germany appeared as social outsiders. It was they who showed the clearest signs of that striving to realize the humanist personality which in Italy had produced the *uomo singolare* and the *uomo universale*. But the social environment which the Italians had been able to take for granted had first to be created in Germany; hence the typically humanist urge to travel, which had obsessed Petrarch and which was usually defended by means of analogies to Orpheus or the ancient Rhapsodists or even to the Apostles, took in Germany the form of

Vagantentum—the wandering scholars of the Middle Ages. The poets resurrected some of the spirit of this *Vagantentum*. They sallied forth to drive barbarism out of Germany and to "polish the *ingenia*." It was they who fought the real battle of humanism against scholastic methods in schools and universities and led it, often ruthlessly and unscrupulously, to victory.

There was at least one personality of genius among them, Konrad Celtis,[36] the German "arch-humanist," as D. F. Strauss has well described him. He was a genuine poet, and had he written in German there might perhaps be fewer zealous attempts to seek signs of poetic inspiration in Hans Sachs. At all events, these signs can certainly be found in Celtis, and the subject of his poetry was his own life. There were no grand themes in it—adversaries, women, and debts provided much of the substance. But there was more. Celtis was an itinerant poet, and he rediscovered Germany, both the current scene and the historical past. He rummaged through libraries for historical documents; these he studied with an attitude vastly different from that of Trithemius and the other humanistic monks. He was not a researcher so much as a finder who looked on his research expeditions in much the same way as a knight might have looked on his adventures. But he discovered the famous Roman itinerary map (the so-called Peutinger Table); he rediscovered the works of Hrosvita and the *Ligurinus* [a German heroic poem in praise of Frederick Barbarossa], which confirmed him in his opinion that the ancient German historical tradition had been poetic in form. As a lecturer in Ingolstadt and then in Vienna he outlined and championed a new academic program in which poetry was conceived as aesthetic and philosophical omniscience. He was speculative in his conception of the relationship between nature and humanity, patriotic in his pronounced dissociation of German culture from the Italian, and religious in his search for contact with the ancient "druidical" wisdom of the Germanic tribes.

It was Celtis, too, who brought into being the combat troops of the new learning, the humanistic sodalities. These associations were modeled on the Italian academies, and as such were fellowships of like-minded men drawn from the cultivated layers of society. But here again, in Germany, there was no direct line of tradition, no linking up with medieval lyric poetry or with semi-erudite discussions in the courts of local princes such as had been the case in Provence and in lower Italy. Nor did the German sodalities organize themselves into schools of disciples under particular masters, as happened in Naples, Rome, and Florence. Instead, they became organizations for propagating the new *humanitas* as a model of life and learning, and, especially, the contents of the new learning.

Once again, therefore, we make the observation that for German humanism the two problems of formation and valuation became divorced from one another. Antiquity may have appeared much more clearly and compactly as an aesthetic ideal for the members of Celtis' sodalities than it had for the Alsatians; Plato's birthday may have been celebrated in these circles as among the Florentines; and statutes may have been drawn up to make admission to the new intellectual circles dependent on a knowledge of the three sacred languages; Latin, Greek, and Hebrew. All the same, the realm of moral values and norms was settled in terms of *German* national life for German life had a past of its own to be revived, and this past was no longer the Benedictine culture of Charlemagne but the ancient Germanic tribal world opened up by the rediscovered *Germania* of Tacitus.[37]

German humanism now entered on its period of national romanticism. For the history of German thought, at least as far as the influx of new ideas is concerned, this new period was even more important than the later, second Romantic movement, the name and definition of which is being used analogously here. And what enormous innovations there were to be made! In the first place, German history was to be linked with the ancient Germanic world, a connection obscured for the Middle Ages by the notion of the *translatio imperii*. Questions had been raised before about the beginnings of the empire, about the origins of the Franks and the Swabians, but never about the origin of the German people as such.

Secondly, the concept of a German nation came to have an ethical connotation. Previously "nation" had only been a collective term for men hailing from the same countries, and as such it was used at the universities and then at the great councils. We have already observed the work of the jurists, in extending the meaning of "nation"; the poets now carried this work a step further.

Thirdly, an attempt was made to delineate an ideal type of German, for which purpose Tacitus' *Germania* provided nearly all the essential ingredients. Contemporary aspirations soon created their own nostalgic image of the past. One of its results was the idea of German simplicity. This was not entirely new, since there had long been a feeling that the Germans were somehow different from devious and crafty Frenchmen and Italians. Now, however, the image was divested of the sense of inferiority that had formerly clung to its root and took on significance as a fundamental ethical principle for contemporary life.[38] The words of Tacitus, *"plus apud eos boni mores valent quam alibi bonae leges"* (among them more importance is attached to good conduct than elsewhere to good laws), were ingeniously taken by one of the leaders of the poets, Heinrich Bebel, the son of a Swabian peasant, to account for the absence of philosophers and lawgivers among the ancient Germans. From this he went on to show that Germanic political and practical wisdom of the past had been expressed in proverbs and verses.

Fourthly, the medieval concept of *imperium* was given a new foundation. The *imperium*, it was said, belonged to the Germans, not because Roman popes had bestowed it upon German emperors, but because the Germanic peoples had inherited the Roman Empire and taken possession of their heritage. A young follower of the school of Celtis, Franz Irenicus, elaborated this point of view into a singular and highly fanciful work,[39] but the line of thought is already clearly recognizable in Bebel.

All these ideas became joined together in the interpretation of Tacitus' assertion: *Germani sunt indigenae.* Herein the concept of German nationhood was discovered. Here was an antiquity in its own right, to be set beside that of Greece and Rome. Like classical antiquity it had vanished and become separated from the contemporary world by a wide chasm. It contained the moral and political standards for a new German nation. It was to be understood and portrayed by the exponents of the new learning who were to gather in a grand confederation of sodalities which, as Celtis intended, should reach from the Alps to the Baltic, from the Rhine to the Danube. The result was to be a *Germania illustrata*, a cultural history of Germany which would seek and reveal the roots of the Germanic past in the features of contemporary Germany. Of all this only a few preliminary sketches were actually produced—notably Celtis' own—but the basic idea and general plan can be reconstructed with certainty.[40]

We are thus presented with a very clearly defined national romanticism. Its prospects looked very good, especially since at the center of it all was no less a person than the Emperor Maximilian. This man, whose character and political significance have so long been controversial issues, is of indisputable importance for the development of German thought under the influence of the humanist movement in Germany. Although his "random excitability"—this expression of Lamprecht seems to me to sum him up best—may have made him a political dilettante, it also made him receptive to all the vital movements of the age and, what is more, made him draw these movements to himself and let them radiate from his own person in a way that none of his successors ever could, and perhaps none of his predecessors either. As a patron of humanistic romanticism he had a number of forerunners. Perhaps the most important is Johann von Dalberg, bishop of Worms,[41] a liberal and open-minded man, who liked to act and plan on the grand scale, but was basically a princely dilettante. Maximilian's own capacities did not go much further, but his very circumstances preclude all comparison between them. He inherited the ambition of the Habsburgs, the chivalry of Burgundy, and the traditions of the old empire. All this was united in a mind possessed of a rare zest for learning and an even rarer ability to keep things moving. Through the proclamations and speeches which accompanied all his actions Maximilian helped create public opinion in Germany, which was put to use by the humanists and also helped to foster the first stirrings of the Reformation. The outward form of Maximilian's reign was chivalric, but all his efforts were directed at rallying nothing less than the whole range of the nation's energies. The most forceful demonstration of this intention was his salient creation, the "new order" of *Landsknechte*. There was a quality of adventure about his life, fully in the spirit of chivalry. The world of Arthurian romances defined even his diplomatic transactions.[42] In his *Weisskunig* and his *Teuerdank* he portrayed his life in terms of the old chivalric poetry. But the underlying aim of these works—as can be seen from the plans which his scholars worked out for it—was that great Renaissance problem, the struggle between *ratio* and *fortuna*.[43] From Italian Renaissance princes he took the idea of fame, with the desire to be remembered by later generations and to become a Maecenas with all the trappings of Augustan Rome. To give concrete shape and official recognition to the educational ideas of Celtis he set up the *Collegium mathematicorum et poetarum* "after the example of our predecessors, the Roman Emperors." Was this not like Petrarch, who had fancied that his coronation as poet on the Capitol was an ancient Roman ceremony?

From the point of view of the humanist movement it might perhaps be said that Maximilian was less important for what he himself learned from humanism or what he did to further it than for what was expected of him. And there are unmistakable indications that the emperor came to be considered as a sort of second Charlemagne. It was assumed that he would lay down a German grammar and a German law, complete the *Germania illustrata* as a history of Germany and, perhaps most important, resolve contemporary ecclesiastical and religious questions by fostering a German form of ecclesiastical life. The first steps toward the fulfillment of these hopes can be found in Maximilian's own projects and exertions. Among these the highly fanciful ideas about religion prevailing at his court deserve special attention. The detailed researches carried out by Giehlow, Saxl, and Panofsky[44] have shown that a very definite system of ideas lay hidden behind even the jumbled allegory of the great woodcuts which the emperor commissioned for the purpose of giving an emblematic description of his life and works. In this system there are to be found significant traces of Egyptian hieroglyphic art blended with Pythagorean ideas and Eastern mysticism. If the significance of all this is to be properly understood it must be remembered that Johannes Reuchlin moved in this world of ideas; indeed, at that time, when German humanist romanticism was in full flower, Reuchlin was generally looked on as the real leader of the humanists. Reuchlin's revival of Hebrew, accepted without misgivings by a limited number of humanists, was intended not only as a means of going back to the original text of the Old Testament, but also as a way of unlocking the secrets of the "wonder-working word," which, in actuality, was taken to be a wonder-working symbol. As Reuchlin himself said in the important foreword to his principal scholarly work, *De arte cabbalistica*, his aim was to raise up a new Pythagorean philosophy to stand beside Florentine Platonism and French Aristotelianism as a third, and distinctively German, philosophy.[45] Indeed, this might have enabled the romantic and mystical stirrings of the German soul to link up in a singular way with the humanist world of ideas. It might have become the culmination of humanist romanticism, a distinctive development of Celtis' "Druid religion," enabling both to come to grips with the great intellectual systems of the ancient world. There is no doubt that these endeavors to make the German spirit independent of the Italian were helped on by certain characteristically German habits of thought. Even in Nicholas of Cusa the theological and mathematical problems of infinity had stood side by side. It was to be characteristic of the first period of German humanism that the mathematicians were set beside the poets. Mathematics and geography were to become distinctively German sciences, evidence of that blend of imaginative speculation and technical application so typical of the Germans. In the lively intellectual culture of the city of Nuremberg this blend can be seen opening the way to a new concept of order quite independent of the Italian attempt at harmony through symmetry.

It is regrettable, though at the same time understandable, that this wealth of ideas did not produce a single definitive work to fill out our mental image of the romantic phase of German humanism. One might be tempted to suggest Aventinus' Bavarian Chronicle for the purpose if it did not, in fact, reflect a later stage of development which remains to be considered. The best summary of the romantic spirit of the *aetas Maximilianea* may have to be sought in the work of a visual artist, in the "Melencolia" of Albrecht Dürer.

It is important in this context to get away from all attempts to see the "Melencolia" as part of a trilogy with the "St. Jerome in his Study" and the "Knight, Death and Devil." Let us look at the sheet on its own. This powerfully built woman is at first nothing more than a heavy German female figure, seemingly taking a rest from her housework, However, she rises above the things of the everyday world, not only by means of the wings on her shoulders and the garland on her head, but also through her faraway gaze, which seems to be penetrating into the realm of infinity, and through the curious paraphernalia all about her. Whatever interpretation may be offered, it is clear that more than an ordinary daily task is going on here; the implements, at all events, are for some sort of research, and the whole picture only starts to become understandable through the title. It is melancholy as the Florentine Platonists had understood it, the temperament of the "Saturnian" nature, of the creative genius.[46] But no Florentine could even have conceived anything like Dürer's creation, let alone execute it. It is German weightiness and depth, the spiritual preoccupation with both the divine and the created, a repose which results not from satiety but from fulfillment, the human mind sensing itself to be really the measure of all things.

While Dürer was occupied with his "Melencolia," national romanticism was no longer the sole, nor even the dominant, form of German humanism. In that same year, 1514, there appeared the *Clarorum virorum epistolae*, published by Reuchlin as a means of associating himself with the humanist movement while waging his battle against the German Dominicans over the question of Jewish books. In the following year appeared the first part of the *Epistolae obscurorum virorum*, and with this volume we encounter a completely different spirit from that of national romanticism under the aegis of the Emperor Maximilian: the spirit of religious enlightenment. Here we have the second form of the German humanist movement. Its originator and leader was Erasmus.

From the point of view of German humanism and its effects upon the next generation and, particularly, upon the Protestant Reformation, there is no figure who can compare in importance with Erasmus. For this reason his essential ideas and aims have become central to any discussion of German humanism. But this is an extraordinarily complicated question, which cannot be solved by a consideration of the previous development of German humanism or by a study of German intellectual history alone. For Erasmus did not come from this setting. The question of Erasmus is, in fact, a problem in the whole history of western ideas at the close of the Middle Ages. On the other hand, even in this context again, it cannot be properly grasped without some prior mention of the general significance of Erasmian humanism.

I shall try to give an answer by starting from the general question set out at the beginning of this exposition. It goes as follows:

With Erasmus, the problem of using antiquity as a means of providing forms and establishing standards for a given cultural background entered its second stage, or, perhaps, its third. It was no longer, as it had been with Petrarch, a question of individual psychology resulting in the first instance in a personal ideal of life and learning. Nor was it any longer, as with the Italian Renaissance and German romantic humanism, a matter of providing forms and standards for a cultural tendency determined by national aspirations. The question now was the reorganization of the entire western cultural community as represented in the *respublica christiana*—in other words, European culture *as a whole*. The lifework of Erasmus was directed toward the transformation of this *respublica christiana* in all three of its forms—a hierarchy, a sacramental institution, and an organic society—into a community of learning. The hierarchy was to become an institution for educating men to Christ, the sacramental institution a genuine Christian community, and the organic society a social ethic based on general agreement about the Christian purpose of society. All this was to be achieved by means of a fresh representation of Christ's teachings set against the background of the new understanding of antiquity. *Humanitas*, as a conception of life and learning, was to be related to a view of Christianity freed of all distortions and accretions. It was to become *humanitas christiana*.

For this purpose Erasmus had first of all to mark off Christian antiquity as a sphere within the ancient world and give it a special place in his intellectual system.[47] Christian antiquity, as Erasmus saw it, stretched from Origen to the Latin Fathers. Its truest representative was St. Jerome. Christian antiquity provided the context within which Christ's teaching could be properly understood. It furnished the weapons with which Erasmus was to attack the whole of scholasticism as a distortion of true Christianity, without at the same time directly impugning Christian dogma and its philosophical consequences.[48] Christian antiquity formed, as it were, an inner circle enclosing the teachings of Christ. Around this, in turn, was an outer circle, the secular wisdom of humanism, classically formulated by the thinkers of pagan antiquity, and furnishing the Christian with all that was necessary for practical life in the world. This outer circle of ancient learning could be related easily and naturally to Chirst's person and teaching, for even though it was seen, as it were, rotating free and independent about the inner circle of Christian antiquity, its center was the same: the person of Christ himself.

In the present context it is neither possible nor necessary to trace the individual ingredients of Erasmus' intellectual structure to their sources, nor to demonstrate how they fitted into the system as a whole. Even the important question of the relationship between Erasmus' Christian philosophy and medieval theology can only be touched on briefly. The important thing is to realize how Erasmus himself reached these ideas; in other words, to

determine the historical position of his activities within the history
of European thought. The question is first of all a biographical
one. No final and authoritative biography of Erasmus has as yet
been written, though this may well become possible now that the
classic edition of his correspondence by P. S. Allen is nearing
completion.[49] There will always remain, however, the difficulty
that it is scarcely possible any longer to form a satisfactory mental
picture of the intellectual and spiritual atmosphere in which
Erasmus lived; and it is especially hard for the German mind to
think its way back into it.[50]

All the same, one may confidently say the following: In
Erasmus' spiritual and intellectual development there are two
negative and two positive elements. The negative elements are
the time he spent in the monastery of Stein and his period of study
in the College of Montaigu at the Sorbonne in Paris; the positive
ones are his visits to England and his journey to Italy. The sojourn
in the monastery marked the point at which Erasmus turned his
back on monastic piety, and the period of study in Paris the point
at which he broke once and for all with scholasticism. In England
he found something with which to replace scholasticism: Colet's
practical and Platonically inclined Christianity. In Italy his association with the Aldine academy in Venice brought him to a clear
perception of Greek antiquity, while his contacts among the high
official circles in the Rome of Julius II familiarized him with the
possibilities of *humanitas* as a social ideal.

These assertions, however, cannot be made without a number
of qualifications and reservations. Erasmus is supposed to have
become hostile to monasticism while in the monastery and
opposed to scholasticism while in Paris: but these were notions
he himself held in his later years, while trying to recall the events
of his early life and explain them in pragmatic terms.[51] The direct
evidence from Erasmus' sojourn in the monastery and from his
years of study does not confirm these views, or at best only in
part. In the same way, although it can be shown that he was
influenced first by John Colet and then by his Italian experiences,
this is insufficient to account for the particular character of

Erasmus' mentality, which was basically a piety with a mystical turn and yet working within the rationalistic intellectual categories of and motivated by enlightenment aspirations. Even if account is taken of the most important influence upon the rational side of Erasmus, that of Lorenzo Valla,[52] the question immediately and rightly suggests itself whether his very distinctive mentality may not have to be explained in terms of tendencies native to the Netherlands or of particular forms of intellectual and spiritual development there.[53]

In fact, even today the mentality of the Netherlanders reveals those same features which are to be found in Erasmus—a powerful urge to mystical piety side by side with a sharply rationalist turn of mind. As early as the fifteenth century both tendencies had received literary development. Side by side with *Reinicke Fuchs* there existed a body of religious poetry which could rival any other in depth of feeling, and which was certainly more deeply rooted in popular sentiment. For an account of Erasmus' specific mentality, however, there is an even more important question, namely, the significance of the Brethren of the Common Life.[54] There is sufficient justification for raising this question in connection with Erasmus, because he had attended their school in Deventer, and he often spoke proudly of having had Hegius and Agricola as his masters. But, as is well known, the question goes further than this: Can the Brethren of the Common Life be considered of general importance for the development of humanism? Is it possible to speak of a northern root of humanism equal in importance to that of Italy? If the answer is yes, then it would be necessary to set beside the humanism of Petrarch, as described above, another and independent humanism originating in Geert de Groote. Here, too, the argument would not be whether a greater or lesser number of ancient authors had been read, copied, or subsequently printed, but again only whether antiquity had played the special part of providing forms and establishing standards for the cultural values which the Brethren had set before themselves as an ideal of life. The answer to this, at least as far as Christian antiquity is concerned, and with a certain measure of

caution and reservation, is in the affirmative. However certain it
may be that the foundations of Geert de Groote and his disciple
Florentius Radwijns were at first nothing other than offshoots of
the great tree of monastic reform, and however important it may
be that the schools founded and influenced by the Brethren kept
at first to the paths of scholastic tradition, and even later instituted
no fundamental reforms,[55] it can be stated with certainty that
Geert de Groote's original intention—to imitate the life of the
Apostles without being bound to a rule, and to live in the midst
of the world without becoming immersed in it—had itself been
the fruit of conscious opposition to the monastic way of life.
Furthermore, the resulting *Devotio moderna*, with its combination
of practical activity and mystical contemplation, implied at least
a relegation, if not a rejection, of scholasticism. On both issues,
contemporary attacks on the Brethren's new foundations bring
out most clearly what was new and what was felt to be in contradiction to the spirit of the age in which they lived. Two things
were found most objectionable: a reluctance to agree that a
community could live the *vita communis* without rules, and a
disapproval of the Brethren's practice of mutual confession.

So far, however, nothing more has been said than that there
was a point in the life and thought of the Brethren where Christian
antiquity could be received as a normative and formative element.
Furthermore, it is difficult to see how anything more could have
come out of it than a "reformation" in the medieval sense, which
was always a kind of *ridurre al segno*; in other words, a recollection
of the early Christian ideal of life and an attempt to revive it.
Nonetheless, it might be sufficient simply to say that a basis of life
had here been created, like a field which needed only to have its
surface broken up a little in order to produce a new growth
incompatible with all that had gone before; and the means of
breaking the soil, as with Petrarch, would have to have been an
interest in the aesthetic. In this way a longing after *Christian
beauty* might well have enabled the humanist enlightenment of
Erasmus to break forth from the *Devotio moderna*. This seems a
probable assumption.

It may, indeed, be possible to give this assumption some further support. On the way from the piety of the Brethren of the Common Life to the enlightenment of Erasmus we encounter two figures who merit our special attention—Rudolf Agricola and Conrad Mutianus.

Agricola[56] is one of the most extraordinary figures of German humanism. One cannot assign him intellectually to his own generation, for although he was contemporary with such early itinerant humanists as Peter Luder and semi-humanist jurists like Gregor Heimburg he had nothing whatever to do with either type. He was more advanced in his thinking than the Alsatian theological group with which he had some connections and the Dalberg circle, where he was for a short time a member. His real intellectual and spiritual peers were the men and women of that cultivated and mature Italian humanist culture among whom he lived at the court of the Este in Ferrara—such as Poliziano and Codro Urceo. With an energy and talent hardly typical of contemporary Germany, Agricola turned himself into an *uomo universale* and *singolare*, that is to say, into a gifted dilettante. The Petrarchan ideal of the cultivation of the soul as an end in itself was embodied magnificently in Agricola, though with him, as with contemporary Italians, it was completely secularized. It is of no slight importance that he wrote a biography of Petrarch in which autobiographical features can be traced without too much difficulty.[57] And this man was now to spend several years of his life as schoolmaster and town clerk in his native Groningen and to leave a work whose express purpose was to replace the Aristotelian-scholastic logic with another based on the humanist philosophy: his *De inventione dialectica*. In this work Agricola resumed Valla's attempt to revise the logical principles of scholasticism and to create a system of experiential concepts which, by means of their self-evident interconnections, would form the basis for new discoveries. Everything in it was related to the world of antiquity, and the aim was to promote a general conviction that life was good and had values of its own. Here was the humanist social ideal in a characteristically German pedagogical form. It would have been fascinating if Agricola had carried out the plans of the last years of his short life and applied himself to the study of Hebrew and theology. The result would have been, even at this stage, a theology of enlightenment. But it was not to be, and even the *De inventione* remained unprinted for a time. But then certain Dutch followers of Erasmus brought it to the public. It had an influence on Erasmus himself, also on Oecolampadius, on contemporary jurists, and on Melanchthon. And his system of *loci* as finding places for concepts formed the basis for a humanist system which, as will be seen, had an important bearing on the Reformation. Whether and to what extent Agricola was responsible for the penetration of humanist ideas into the schools of the Brethren of the Common Life is a matter calling for examination. The fact that Hegius was his pupil suggests that he was.

Another variation of this problem can be seen in Mutianus.[58] He had been a schoolfellow of Erasmus at Deventer, then gone to Italy. His youth seems to have followed the paths of humanist itinerancy; on the other hand, he was a man of a fundamentally contemplative turn of mind. At first sight his case seems to be little different from that of Petrarch. The cultivation of the soul as an end in itself led him to seek *beata tranquilitas* at the cathedral of Gotha. A lively desire for learning, purely aesthetic in inspiration, turned his retreat there into a center of literary activity which was universal in its interests and highly critical in its attitude toward the contemporary world.[59] The difference between Mutianus and Petrarch, however, can be seen from the respective intellectual environments in which they lived. With Mutianus it was no longer a matter of a world infatuated with scholasticism and the spirit of chivalry, and most certainly not of an antiquity which remained to be rediscovered. What Mutianus was trying to escape from was the staleness and triviality of life which confronted him first in his own monastery and then wherever he went in the world. He sought the divine, which remained unchanging throughout all ages. This accounts for the many notorious elements of free thought and pantheism in his utterances, for his criticism of the churchly ceremonies (which, however, he could not bring himself to deny) and his esoteric religion. Mutian's interest in the Reuchlin controversy[60] was not aroused until he believed himself to be witnessing the creation of a new "sect." Finally, he constructed his own highly individual brand of religious worldliness. "*Longe melius est,*" he once wrote, "*ab ignorantia ad scientiam consurgere quam sperare futura. Si animum tuum noveris, in celo es.*" (It is far better to rise from ignorance to knowledge than to hope for things to come. If you know your own soul you are already in heaven.) Mutianus indicates clearly the form which aesthetic religiosity might take in Germany. He also shows that life and consciousness in Germany were capable of harmonization by means of a religious enlightenment. These were foundations on which Erasmus could build.

With Erasmus, the question of a Christian philosophy infused with humanist values was a problem no longer of individual but of social psychology. The significance of this can perhaps be seen all the more clearly from the fact that Erasmus attempted to reform a whole world, the *respublica christiana*. This attempt has been called a "Christian Renaissance," though it should be noted that Erasmus himself never used the expression but spoke of a *restitutio christianismi*. Just as frequently, however, he spoke of the *renascentes litterae*. The two expressions bring out the true state of affairs. The "Renaissance of learning" was Erasmus' starting point. It was already there when he appeared on the scene. He became its leader by gathering together the various streams of the movements. Christianity, however, was still to be restored, and this restoration was his life's work.

If he appears to have met with such a rapid and astonishing success it is primarily because this new Christian philosophy satisfied so many different aspirations. It responded to the contemporary mystical impulse that aimed at a religion of sentiment without ceremonial and ornament. It indicated the mystics' direct way to God but set out to make this way easy rather than hard for men of good will, as can be seen from the *Enchiridion militis christiani*. This militant Christian whom some have thought to detect, though surely wrongly, in Dürer's famous engraving of the Knight, had very little to do with Death and the Devil. His fearlessness was not that of a fighter who felt himself threatened, but that of a wise man who had already gone through his own interior struggle and now wished to teach others the "art of piety." It was an *Imitatio Christi* with scarcely a mention of the cross.

But this Christian philosophy of Erasmus also satisfied the claims of aesthetic culture. It was based on philosophic erudition and strove to attain aesthetic beauty and dignity. Moreover, this philosophy gathered together all the enlightenment tendencies of the age while at the same time stripping them of all personal shortcomings. *The Praise of Folly* did not set out to satirize the various manifestations of human folly in the manner of Sebastian Brant's *Ship of Fools* and the comedies of Wimpfeling and Reuchlin. It was, instead, an imposing attempt to understand folly as the irrational element in the world, and on this basis to regard the world rationally so that we ourselves, in turn, might be regarded rationally. It was significant, however, that Erasmus intended, or at least declared it to have been his intention, to follow up the *Laus stultitiae* with a *Laus naturae*, and this with a *Laus gratiae*.[61] Here we have the hierarchical world of Aquinas over again in Erasmian terms.

Likewise, the Erasmian philosophy was now to prove helpful to the spirit of anti-ecclesiastical criticism. There was surely no more effective counterblast to the scholastic quillets on which so much theological energy was spent, or to monastic sloth, or popular superstition, priestly humbug, or a religion which had become reduced to a ceremonial, than those brilliant pamphlets which brought Erasmus fame. But this same spirit of heartfelt and principled opposition to the contemporary shape of church and Christianity is also evident in the New Testament paraphrases and the famous *Methodus*. In all these (and Erasmus himself emphasized this again and again) there was no naming of names, no attacks on personalities. This lent all the more force to his challenge to institutions. And if an institution's most dangerous enemies are not those who stand outside it and deny it altogether but those from within who point to the contrast between idea and reality, then the church had no more dangerous enemy before the Reformation than Erasmus.

In this way, as Ranke has said, Erasmus became the first great critic in the modern sense. But he also became the leader and unifier of all the trends in German humanism. Conservative, theologically oriented humanists of the Alsatian type, cultivated scholars from the Peutinger-Pirckheimer circles in Augsburg and Nuremberg, products of the Viennese school of Konrad Celtis such as Aventinus, Vadian, and Cuspinian, members of Mutian's circle—all of these saw their own aspirations developed more brilliantly by Erasmus. As the Swiss chronicler Johannes Kessler said in his *Sabbata*: "His name has become a byword. Whatever can be called artistic, prudent, learned and wise is now said to be Erasmian, which is to say infallible and perfect."

For the present purpose of setting all this in the context of the history of ideas, the most important thing is to see how the Erasmian enlightenment joined forces with the nationalistic spirit in Germany, and with German humanist romanticism. A theoretical consideration will help to make this context clear. It has been seen how strong the religious element was even in those aspects of romantic humanism which appeared to be purely secular. The nationalistic aspirations of the Celtis school, too, had been based on a religious ideal. When Celtis appropriated the ancient druids for his tribal Germans he meant not merely to refute the suggestion that the ancient Germanic peoples had understood nothing of art and science, but also to prove that they had had priests who, unlike those of the present age, did not have to be bribed with "gifts of eggs and cheese" before they would impart their blessings.[62] And even where these religious ideas bore pagan trappings, the intention was always to effect a *restitutio christianismi*. These nationalistically conceived aspirations fitted into the general scope of Erasmian philosophy; and when Erasmus issued the call to battle against monkish barbarism the Germans felt themselves summoned to be in the vanguard.

But the union of these two trends of humanism might not have been effected so rapidly or so completely had it not been for an event of major importance: the Reuchlin affair and the literary feud into which it developed in the *Epistolae obscurorum virorum*.[63]

For, in itself, the occasion of the controversy—whether the holy books of the Jews should be burned or used for the study of Hebrew—was as futile as it could possibly be, and Reuchlin was anything but a crusader. There are also clear indications that the humanist groups surrounding Maximilian, as well as Mutian's circle and probably even Pirckheimer, were all rather chary of becoming involved in the issue. Few humanists shared Reuchlin's aesthetic enjoyment of the Hebrew language, and in his tolerant attitude toward the Jews Reuchlin stood quite alone. But as soon as the Dominicans of Cologne stepped in behind the accuser Pfefferkorn and thus threatened to turn the controversy into a heresy trial, the whole affair became in effect a battle between humanism and the party of monks and scholastics. It now became evident that humanism in Germany was itself an organized party. Celtis' sodalities revealed themselves as the cadres of a united fighting force such as no other country at that time could have mustered. It was the peculiar blend of judicial litigation and erudite polemic, which had long been a feature of humanist struggles, which was decisive in keeping the principles of the matter in the forefront. This was the importance of the *Epistolae obscurorum virorum*. They were, and are still, the finest examples of topical satire which humanism has produced. They have rightly been described as combining three elements: traditional scholastic derision of the religious orders with its comfortable delight in self-mockery; popular German satire pointing its finger at what was ridiculous in each of the Estates; and the Renaissance art of characterization imported from Italy, with its power to concentrate mere typical figures into clearly delineated individuals. And if it is an essential part of satire that it should spring not only from a feeling of intellectual superiority but also from a sense of social commitment, then here is yet another reason for placing the *Letters of Obscure Men* in the very first rank.

In the present context, however, the important thing is that in this event the two humanist trends—the enlightened and the nationalistic—were united. For it has long been realized, and recent researches have established it virtually beyond doubt, that the two parts of the *Letters* are the products of two different spirits. In the first part the satire is directed at the ignorance and narrow-mindedness of the *obscuri* and always takes a secret delight in its victims, whereas in the second there is an anger which, though kept within the limits of satire, speaks of an impending reformation whose shining lights Reuchlin and Erasmus were to be. We know, too, that the spirit of the first part is that of Mutian, while the spirit of the second is that of Hutten.

An attempt has recently been made to belittle the human, intellectual and historical importance of Hutten, or to deny it altogether. It can now be said that the attempt has failed. The only good thing which came out of it was the impetus it gave to further study of Hutten; and Hajo Holborn has provided us with a biography of this remarkable man which satisfies modern requirements and has superseded the older, though in its own way still admirable, work of D. F. Strauss.⁶⁴ Most of the essentials are now fairly clear.

It is the unity of Hutten's life and activity that makes him so attractive a personality to the unprejudiced observer. He stormed his way through the brief years allotted to him; it should not be forgotten that he died when he was only thirty-five. A personality such as his needed many more years to develop fully. And his life was that of an adventurer. He never ceased to be a knight errant; the fact that he combined with this the conduct and way of life of the wandering poet was to turn out not exactly an advantage to him. But he was not a knight who followed in the train of *fortuna*; his life was, rather, an unremitting struggle with *fortuna*. And his poetic activity was not merely the search for a lyrical form into which to pour his life, as Celtis had succeeded in doing, for Hutten was no poet; it was the quest for values. Here the significance of the humanist outlook in general can be seen clearly. For what was it ultimately that lifted the life of Hutten

above that of a Goetz von Berlichingen and of a Sickingen? It was
nothing other than his attempt to cleanse the idea of German
freedom of its association with the unbridled self-indulgence of the
German nobility and give it a higher intellectual and spiritual
meaning.

It is possible to show the stages in this process, though, for the
sake of their underlying significance, the order in which they are
presented here is thematic rather than chronological. First of all
there are the impressions he gained from his two journeys to
Italy, and they are completely different from those of other
humanists who crossed the Alps. His impressions were formed
during Maximilian's struggles with the French and the Venetians
and gave a definite coloring to Hutten's romantic patriotism. On
top of this, however, came his observation of the papal court
under both Julius II and Leo X. This marked the beginning of
Hutten's battle against the "Romanists." The constrast between
German guilelessness and Italian imposture now seized his mind
powerfully. Next, his dealings with Ulrich von Württemberg,
who had stabbed his cousin Hans Hutten to death; this helped to
root in Hutten's mind the typical features of the tyrant. Then his
acquaintance with Erasmus in Mainz in 1514. It was the most
important association of his life: Hutten, a man born to devote
himself to others, had now found a master whom he could serve.
He wished to play Alcibiades to Erasmus' Socrates. The classical
idea of friendship, for Petrarch one of the means of reflecting his
own ego, and for most of the humanists merely a phrase, found
with Hutten a firm ground in his native ideas of Germanic alleg-
iance.[65] Then there was his bond with Sickingen, made in 1519,
and tested on the battlefield in the campaign against Ulrich von
Württemberg. In Sickingen he found the aggressive drive which
would help bring German freedom to victory over the Roman
tyranny. And before long the newly discovered Tacitus enabled
him to cast even this idea into humanist form, in the person of the
Germanic hero Arminius. Then the Reuchlin controversy, which
had been going on all the while. For Hutten the Reuchlin affair
provided the opening for an attack on the Romanists in their

double capacity as corruptors of the ancient German virtues and as enemies of the new intellectual freedom. Hence his interest in the *Epistolae* and his continuation of them in a very different spirit, although satire was not strictly congenial to his ardent nature. He tried to win Sickingen's aid in this literary quarrel and thus turn it into a knightly feud. When Reuchlin seemed to be giving way, his wrath knew no bounds. Finally, his intervention in high politics at the imperial Diet of 1518, where the figure of Cajetan yielded for him a distorted picture of Roman pomp and arrogance, and where, with a strange mixture of love and anger he described the gluttonous and guzzling German princes in the words of Tacitus' tribal warriors. Here, as the orator of the German nation, he tried to stir emperor and princes to a Turkish war. It was to be a national undertaking, harnessing popular energies, which were now being wasted in internal strife, and to continue the fight against the enemy of the Christian faith—all in the spirit of the deeds of Barbarossa and the old German emperors. Here, too, he wrote that famous letter to Pirckheimer in which he depicted the dawn of a new, humanistically enlightened century and identified his own special place in the struggle against barbarism. It may well be said that, so far as it was ever possible to combine the two manifestations of German humanism—national romanticism and religious enlightenment—they found their union in Ulrich von Hutten.

But how long could this union be expected to last? As we have seen, the real advantage of humanist romanticism was that it was specifically national and rooted in popular sentiment, while its greatest defects were its limitation to the Italian ideals of *orator*, *poeta*, and *philosophus*, and its inherent divorce of the formative and the normative principles. Erasmian enlightenment had overcome these defects. Its presupposition of a harmony between the concentric rings of classical *humanitas* and the new Christianity was undoubtedly the most original solution of the problem possible within a Christian civilization. But for this triumph, the Erasmian enlightenment had to pay a price: albeit unwillingly, it turned itself into an aristocratic religion of erudition. No matter how eloquently Erasmus expressed the hope that all women would read the Gospels and the letters of Paul, that the peasant lad would sing scriptural verses while walking behind his plow, the weaver repeat the words of the Bible to his loom, and the traveler shorten his weary road with stories from sacred history—these hopes were in fact vitiated by the very premises on which the Erasmian enlightenment was based. For to know the Bible as Erasmus wished it known it was necessary to have mastered the three sacred languages and to have become expert in the philological and, especially, the allegorical exegesis of scriptural discrepancies. Only the optimism of the humanist enlightenment could have supposed that this erudite religion could ever have become a popular creed.

All this escaped Erasmus, for to admit anything of the sort would have imperiled his whole life's work. On the other hand, he had a strong sense of the differences which separated him from the Germans. The Alsatians had extorted from him an admission that he was a German. In 1521 he had shifted his residence from the Low Countries to Basel; there, as before in the Netherlands, he continued to receive the pilgrimages of his German supporters, who by now constituted nearly the largest segment of his following. Through his presence Basel became the center of the European humanist movement. But Erasmus could never shake off his fear of the *furor Teutonicus*. He pointedly sent his Alcibiades, Hutten, a character sketch of his English friend Thomas More, a model of refined and balanced *humanitas*. He, too, had taken sides in the Reuchlin affair, but his object was to prevent a "tumult" arising out of it, for this he saw as one of the most serious dangers to the progress of the new erudite religion. In the great preface to the new edition of the *Enchiridion* in 1518, addressed to the Alsatian abbot Paul Volz, he may well have intended to lay down for his German friends a sort of program of the humanist movement as he wished it to be. The humanist conviction that truth works best in tranquility was deeply seated even in this perpetual activist.

The Germans, however, were not aware of any such contradiction. The vast majority of them had an almost naïve faith that their struggle against hierarchy, Romanism, and papal pomp made them Erasmus' partisans in his great battle against barbarism, and that the front rank in this battle belonged by right to Germany.

But there was one man among them who betrays at least the internal contradiction between the romantic and the enlightenment tendencies. This is Aventinus.[66] Admittedly, a judgment of his character and work must take two qualifications into account: first, the fact that he was a Bavarian to the very core. His main characteristic was that earthy and clannish touchiness which arises from the peasant's instinctive suspicions. In him this trait for the first time took on a literary form. Secondly, Aventinus' life stretched from the era of Maximilian into the age of the Peasants' War and religious struggles, and these brought deep disappointments to all practitioners of a scholarly and humane culture.

These two facts explain the biting and carping elements in Aventinus' criticism and the resignation in his philosophy, though even behind these one can discern the deep trends of the age, without which Aventinus would not have become an historian at all; and their underlying relationship can be seen all the more clearly since they are mirrored in an historical work whose principal feature is its imposing moral pragmatism. For in this moral pragmatism romantic idealism and the topical criticism of humanist enlightenment were brought face to face. How odd Aventinus' Germanic pantheon, within which were to be found all the great legislators, heroes and sages admired by the humanist nationalist, when contrasted with the contemporary world, where virtue and morality were to be found only in the common man. How strange, too, Aventinus' pride in the new learning, which had revealed the whole of scholasticism as nothing more than "squabbling and tilting at shadows," when set beside his furious outbursts at the ignorance of priests and monks. Most remarkable of all, perhaps, the contrast between his love for Erasmian pacifism (Ninus, the inventor of idolatry, was, in his "mythology," also the inventor of wars of conquest) and his naïve delight in the warlike tempers of the ancient Teutons, whose campaigns he narrates with the most obvious relish. Aventinus achieved neither the enlightened mental culture of Beatus Rhenanus, who in this point was a true disciple of Erasmus, nor the withdrawn religious individualism of Sebastian Franck, for whom the world was simply "God's carnival play" exemplifying by contrast the essential other-worldliness of man's spiritual life.[67] Aventinus castigated the Germans of his day with all the vehemence of a penitential preacher, while at the same time prescribing for them a new military organization on the Roman pattern, as Machiavelli had done for the Florentines. He sketched a plan of scholarly production which put the humanist disciples into an ingenious and meaningful order; yet he had absolutely no faith in the rationality of events in the world. In his presentation of history he found himself hard put indeed to see how the coarse and ignorant German tribes, who were pagans into the bargain, could ever have subjugated the great Roman Empire, the refuge of the arts and sciences and at that time also the seat of Christianity. His explanation assigned to his own people no better role than that of a scourge in God's hand, the same role which was, in his own day, ascribed to the Turks.

One could interpret these contradictions simply as the utterances of a passionate mind struggling in vain to find its way through a mass of ideas crowding in from all round. But that would be to underestimate them. It is nearer the truth to say that they are the very signature of the age. They represent, in fact, the state of mind of the German people on the eve of the Reformation.

And now to the Reformation itself, the greatest intellectual and spiritual upheaval ever experienced by any European nation. It brought literally a transvaluation of all values. Everything that had existed before had now to adjust itself anew. And it also confronted the humanist movement with a new problem, the last to be considered here.

To appreciate the significance of the Reformation for the German mind it must be remembered that the original intention behind it was not ecclesiastical reform but a renewal of faith. Furthermore, this renewal of faith was in a unique way the act of a single individual and must be accounted for by the spiritual distress and need of this individual. In this spiritual distress, it is true, Luther was fully in tune with one of the deepest emotions of his times, the fear of sin—otherwise the effects of his actions could hardly have been so far-reaching. All the same, the challenge he issued to religious traditions was utterly at odds with the confident spirit of enlightenment of his age, just as the anguished way along which he sought, and ultimately found, his gracious God was out of keeping with the way along which popular religious instincts were seeking to find satisfaction. This uncharacteristic element in Luther must be strongly emphasized if the problems raised by the Reformation as an historical movement are to be rightly understood. This is especially true for the problems rising out of the relationship between the Reformation and humanism.

We have seen that the humanist creed in its final and most fully developed, that is to say, in its Erasmian state, set out to humanize religion. It aimed to make the way to God easy rather than difficult, to change the imitation of Christ into an educational process, and to show that moral requirements were the substance even of an essentially redemptive religion. Above all, it aimed to create a new balance between the spheres of faith and reason, based on a pre-established harmony of the two. With the aid of Allegory it undertook to give the word of God a rational meaning valid for all men.

But now came Luther, who had gained his first religious assurance in the paradoxical recognition that divine justice was identical with divine grace. With Luther's God we return to the *deus tremendus et absconditus*. Luther's Christ was not the humanists' Christ, the wisest of all philosophers, nor again the true 'Ἐπίκουρος whose followers were to be no more "melancholy" than he himself; he was simply the redeemer from sin and death. Luther constructed his theology on the absolute antithesis of reason and faith, and he based his idea of the unity of Scripture on the assertion that God's word speaks of nothing other than the process of redemption, the antithesis of sin and grace, law and gospel.

The contrast with a religious *humanitas* based on the dignity of man and the perfectibility of the human mind and spirit could hardly be crasser. Luther's awareness of this contradiction had been one of his earliest theological perceptions.[68]

Yet this is only one side of the relationship between the Reformation and humanism. It is well known, and can be demonstrated, that the Reformation as an historical movement was carried a good part of its way by humanism. Without romantic patriotism and the resulting national irritability, the Reformation would hardly have become a great movement, or at least not so rapidly. Without its connection with Erasmian tendencies it would not have taken hold so firmly on the European mind. But even when Luther was formulating his religious experiences into a theology—in other words, during the Wittenberg years from 1512 to 1517—there existed a number of contacts with humanism. The nearest thing to Luther's struggle against Aristotle as the adulterator of theology was the Erasmian enlightenment. Even in purely religious questions there was a sort of natural alliance between Luther and the Erasmian enlightenment. This can be proved from Luther's direct borrowings. Equally unmistakable is Luther's appeal to the older German mysticism, the contribution of which to earlier German humanism has already been mentioned. In 1518, when he published for the second time the *Theologia teutsch*, that remarkable little work produced by the Rhenish circle of the Friends of God in which the doctrine of the subduing of the will received such special emphasis, he called himself fortunate to be able to trace his theology back to that of this ancient German author, and find that God had for once spoken in the German tongue, and more clearly than ever in Latin, Greek, or Hebrew.[69]

As is well known, Luther's relations with both the romantic and the enlightenment trends of humanism were at their closest between the time of the Leipzig debate and the Diet of Worms. This *rapprochement* was reciprocal. It was the time when Erasmus told the Elector of Saxony in Cologne that Luther was being persecuted because he had struck at the pope's crown and the monks' bellies, and that it would be impossible to suppress the truths he defended by means of fire. It was the time, also, when Hutten was ready to join forces with Luther and when the ideas of German and of evangelical freedom seemed to be about to enter into a mutual covenant.

But then, inevitably, came the break. It turned out that the freedom of the Christian preached by Luther was something quite different from the Germanic freedom embodied in Arminius. More clearly still, it was shown that the Hieronymian theology of Erasmus was worlds apart from the Augustinian theology of Luther. Even when his enthusiasm for Luther was at its height, Hutten realized that, while his own aims were strictly human, Luther moved among things divine. In one of his last writings he altered the Lutheran *ex fide vivere* to *ex conscientia vivere*. But it was Erasmus who got to the heart of the difference between the humanist creed and the Lutheran religion when, after long hesitation, he wrote his *De libero arbitrio* against Luther. He may thereby have achieved nothing beyond giving Luther the occasion to write his magnificent reply; all the same, the dialogue between these two eminent and utterly incompatible minds was to remain the classic document of the relationship between humanism and the Reformation. In itself it offers sufficient proof of how foolish it is to think that the Reformation might be considered an offshoot of humanist tendencies.

On the other hand, the help given by humanism to furthering the Reformation was not a purely external and political matter. Humanism also undertook to provide a form for the new principle which the Reformation had introduced.

There were two possible points of contact for this undertaking. The first was Luther's appeal to primitive Christianity, which implied the existence of intellectual and spiritual conditions similar to those of primitive Christianity. A faith conceived entirely in terms of the transcendent world had therefore to try to give norms to the secular world of cultural values. The significance of the "Renaissance of learning" was that it was once again able to present these cultural values in the forms of Greek philosophy and Roman legal theory.

The second point of attachment was Luther's "Bible experience." When Luther rediscovered in Paul's Epistle to the Romans his own perception of the identity of divine justice and divine grace, the problem of certitude in faith was lifted to a new plane. A personal experience was turned into an appeal to the fundamental credentials of the Christian religion. Faith was now no longer a matter of placing trust in something, but a matter of holding it to be true. And it was implicit in the very nature of this Bible experience that Christian truth was bound up with a right understanding of the Scriptures and with a satisfactory proof that they were unequivocal and homogeneous. Luther himself never doubted that such a proof would be possible only through "the languages." In a famous passage in his address to the councillors of German cities in 1529 he gave classic expression to this. But even his first plans for reforming the University of Wittenberg (perhaps the germ of all his projects of political reform) started out from this conviction, and the same idea can be seen at the close of his *Address to the Christian Nobility of the German Nation*.

An attempt to provide a humanistic form for the new faith could start from these two points. Zwingli started from the first, Melanchthon from the second.

Zwingli's[70] transition from Erasmian humanist to reformer was, as is well known, so gentle that he was even able to deny Luther's decisive influence on him. In the same way he could be a Swiss patriot and also a churchman without doing violence to either. He might well have ranked William Tell and Arnold von Winkelried among the Fathers of evangelical freedom along with Nicholas von Flüe. At all events, he was convinced that this freedom could have arisen nowhere more naturally than in free Switzerland.[71] Thus, his activities as a reformer were immediately relevant to his community, in a way unequaled elsewhere, even in the reformations of the German cities. Only with Calvin do we meet this phenomenon again, though at a higher level. Zwingli's Zürich, it may be said, shows a German municipality taking on the character of a polis, that is to say, attaining to the same sense of autonomy and self-sufficiency as the Renaissance communes in Italy. This was due to social and political factors as much as to intellectual ones: the separation of Switzerland from the empire, the attempts of the larger cities, Zürich and Bern, especially, to conquer large territories. To these one must add Zwingli's campaign against the enlistment of Swiss mercenaries in foreign armies and against the French subsidies. Among the spiritual and intellectual factors there is, first of all, the Reformation itself. It is, after all, remarkable that, at the first religious colloquy in Zürich, a municipality dared do something never ventured by the imperial diet: to decide for itself the question of religious truth. This was to set the example for Nuremberg, Strassburg, and many other cities. But side by side with this declaration of religious autonomy stand, at least in Zwingli's view, the civic virtues in their classical form and a firm theory of society. The ideal society was a Christian democracy. Its origin is the Aritotelian definition of man as a social animal. Zwingli as "prophet" watched over it to ensure that the will of God was not adulterated by the will of the community. This Christianized polis gave birth to a spiritual and religious absolutism in which the Christian, civic and "classical" freedoms of the individual were effectively fused into one.[72] The result, as a Swiss historian has said, was a church directed by the state, a Christian theocracy deriving its *raison d'être* from the sovereign decision of the people.

Let us observe the combination of these elements in Zwingli's *Weltanschauung*, and especially in its specifically religious form, by considering Zwingli's *De providentia divina*, the revised version of a sermon given before Philip of Hesse on the occasion of the colloquy of Marburg in 1529. It is connected, at least in its fundamental ideas, with the principal theme of the colloquy, the sacramental controversy. Whereas Luther derived the proofs of faith at least to some extent from the reality of symbols, Zwingli deduced them from his ideas about God and the structure of the world. He thus gave rise to a world picture in which the most important problem was the relationship between the processes of the natural world and divine grace, an ancient problem which had first been posed by the collision of the early forms of Christianity with Greek philosophy and had kept the whole of the Middle Ages occupied right up to Thomas Aquinas. But whereas Aquinas had solved it in Aristotelian terms, Zwingli solved it in Platonic ones: by constructing a cosmos whose supreme principle was the goodness of God. This supreme quality subsumed all his other attributes; it was at once light, righteousness, simplicity, and totality, that is to say, truth. All creation was permeated and governed by this divine goodness; all things had their true being in God—inasmuch as they exist they are divine. This meant that divine providence was seen as the ultimate ground of all created existence, including that of man. Zwingli's train of thought is completely philosophical. "What does it matter," he asked, "if we call the divine and the religious philosophical?" It is well known how strongly the Florentines, especially Pico, had influenced him on this point. This cosmically conceived providence only turned into predestination in the religous sense through the question of the position held by man, the recipient of God's special law, in this providentially ordered world. Zwingli could not have answered this question at all if, like Luther, he had considered the law simply as a means to the recognition and acknowledgment of sin. Zwingli expressly disputed this. Law was for him simply another expression for the unchanging will of God. God had given the law to men for two reasons: to know the divine essence more clearly, and to make it possible for them even on earth to enter into a state of friendship with him.

This is to say, surely, that the problem of law for Zwingli was identical with the platonic problem of δικαιοσύνη (righteousness), and that the solution in both cases was a pedagogical one: the whole course of the world was an education of mankind toward God. This is how Erasmus had seen it, too, and this is the idea prevailing throughout the religious enlightenment right up to Lessing.

But Zwingli bent this idea back into the fully religious sphere by relating it to the fall of man, a fall, however, not only of man but also of the angels and of all creation. God had permitted it in order that we might see His righteousness even from examples of unrighteousness and wickedness. This conclusion forced Zwingli to make the redemption part of God's original plan of creation.

There is a passage in which Zwingli summed up his notion of divine providence. "To whom it is granted to contemplate profoundly the works of Providence, what joy he will feel when perceiving everywhere the goodness and wisdom of God, so that the observation of the whole world, beautiful as it is, must lose its charms compared with the rapture which overpowers us when we rise up to God and contemplate the architect of the whole world." Here we have the *amor intellectualis Dei* of Spinoza. We do not require Zwingli's explicit acknowledgments of the Erasmian faith in the pious pagans of antiquity, Socrates, Plato, and all the other Christians before Christ, in order to recognize this humanized Christianiy in his life and thought.

Melanchthon, too, was an Erasmian when he arrived in Wittenberg.[73] He took up his professorship in Greek there with a discourse on the improvement of education for the young in which he laid down a purely humanistic program. There was only one way to all that was great and worthwhile: the study of the humanities, the true philosophy based on a knowledge of nature, ethics, and the great paradigms of morality. *Humanitas*, Melanchthon said it clearly, was the inculcation of moral values and the knowledge of nature. It was "learning" in exactly the sense elaborated by humanism over the course of one and a half centuries. But soon after this Melanchthon, under the influence of Luther, was converted to Paul and his doctrine of justification. The conversion must have been a tempestuous affair, turning this naturally gentle man inside out. He now saw it as his first task to give a systematic presentation of Luther's conviction that Scripture was concerned solely with sin and grace, law and gospel. The outcome was the *Loci communes*. The means of proof were the categories of humanist rhetoric assembled by Agricola, along with the hermeneutic principles of Erasmus, who had converted the fundamental concepts of logic into theology, and had turned the *loci* of Aristotle into *loci communes* in the Ciceronian sense. The result was a theory of internal experience closely related to the concerns of the Reformation and undertaking to transform this experience into a generally valid system of logical deduction.

The *Loci communes* had enormous influence. It would hardly be going too far to assert that the whole scientific spirit of early Protestantism was determined by it. The influence was twofold. In the first place, the system of the *Loci*, as developed out of the scholarly reflections of humanist criticism, seemed well suited not only for proving the unity of Scripture but also for providing a doctrine of values applicable to all aspects of secular life. This is what Melanchthon himself did in his later editions of the *Loci*, and also in his textbooks of ethics, physics, and so on. Secondly, the *Loci* were not intended as a commentary, interposing itself between reader and Scripture, but as a "method" offering both a sure way to the Bible and a defense against "prophecies" presuming to speak with tongues or appeal to an inward illumination in order to set the spirit of Scripture against the letter. In this way, the *Loci* became an intellectual scheme no less rigid than the scholastic system they opposed. Zwingli's ideas were quite different. He created a "prophecy" for himself in which by means of a philological discussion of the words of Scripture he made a remarkable attempt to transform the humanist *consensus omnium* into a method of gaining religious certainty. This was Erasmianism in the form of the Reformation.

But it was Melanchthon's solution which carried the day. His system prevailed in Germany throughout the sixteenth century and was overthrown only after a long struggle. Not that it was entirely consistent or beyond arousing criticism even during its ascendancy. In the long run religious experience and logical deduction proved unfusable. Melanchthon himself was eager to return to his earlier moralism and intellectualism, which had been suppressed only by his first tempestuous enthusiasm for Luther's doctrines. He came to accord more and more autonomy to philosophical ethics, an ever broader infrastructure for theological morality. A new Protestant scholasticism came into being with a place for Aristotle side by side with Cicero, both *propter certitudinem principiorum*. The doctrines of natural illumination and innate ideas became ever more important within the system itself as time went on,[74] and finally burst it asunder.

Melanchthon's scientific system was the final product of the encounter of mature humanism with the German mind. By about 1550 the humanist movement had come to an end. What survived in scholastic drama and courtly poetry were simply shells without new content. At the same time the German mind lost its ability to absorb and Germanize foreign elements. The second half of the sixteenth century may not have been so intellectually sterile as is often claimed, but it was certainly a time of imitation and dissolution. The new trends pointing to the future, Ramism, Cartesianism, Pietism, must be studied from an altogether new point of view.

What, then, is the end result of the humanist century which we have surveyed?

It has been said that humanism separated German society into two camps, the educated and the uneducated, and thus destroyed the earlier unity of national culture. This accusation has been made by Friedrich Paulsen, and there is an echo of it in the declamations of those modern Gothicizers who, with their usual confusion of ideas, have asserted that the so-called Renaissance was responsible for the decline of German thought. It is strange that such an opinion could ever have arisen. Where, one might ask, was the unity of national culture around 1450, when humanism began its penetration of Germany? There was, indeed, a unity of national inclinations, stronger at that time than ever before. But it can in no sense be said to have been a national culture. A striking proof of this can be taken from the chronicles of German cities. These contain extraordinarily attractive depictions of contemporary life (the finest example is probably the chronicle of Burkhard Zink of Augsburg). But whenever they tried to advance from description to a proper historical view of things, they failed.

An exception, significantly enough, was Switzerland. For the rest, however, the chronicles wavered uncertainly between collections of notices, family records, and world chronicles with local pre-occupations. Further search for spontaneous expressions of an indigenous popular tradition during this period will yield principally the folksong and the popular chap book. It was a sound instinct on the part of the Romantics that they explored those with such love and enthusiasm. But by the end of the humanist period neither had died out or even declined. On the contrary, the folksong experienced its first stage of flowering between 1450 and 1550. Not until then did it take up the great subjects of world events; not until then did it become capable of depicting German life—all this has been shown by Rochus von Liliencron. Chap books continued throughout this whole period to pass on the traditions of medieval fable and storytelling. They also succeeded, however naïvely, in assimilating new elements taken from classical antiquity and, in the form of the Faust saga, taking up a contemporary and specifically German subject. Around 1550 Germany could boast several publishers who specialized in this type of literature.

But if we compare the intellectual state of Germany at the beginning and at the close of the humanist century we find no room for doubt about the extraordinary widening of the spiritual and intellectual horizon. We find a German approach to history, even though there was still no German history; we find German cosmography, even though it was only a limited version of the *Germania illustrata*, German natural history, celestial physics, the beginnings of an independent movement to sift and organize law and legal thought, a varied and vigorous literature of lay theology, and a somewhat naïve but solidly national German philological school. And in all these products there was evidence of a sense of self-reliance such as could not be found anywhere at the beginning of the humanist period. Together with this we find a general broadening of mental horizons. To have a taste of this expansion, one needs only to thumb through the alarmingly lengthy catalogue of books processed at his poetical workbench by Hans Sachs.

Not that the accusations directed against humanism are altogether unjustified. As I have tried to show in these pages, humanism did create a new concept of learning which interposed itself between men and their lives and claimed to be entitled to provide forms and establish standards for life in accordance with its own scholarly and intellectual principles. But this was a general process throughout Europe. Its effects can be seen much more clearly in the natural philosophy of the Italians, and skepticism and rationalism of the French, the empiricism of the English, and the philology of the Netherlanders than in the Germany of the late sixteenth and early seventeenth centuries, where preoccupations remained decidedly theological. It is not likely that anyone would ever have thought of looking for such an effect in Germany if Goethe had not given classical formulation to it:

> *Wer Kunst und Wissenschaft besitzt,*
> *Der hat auch Religion.*
> *Wer diese beiden nicht besitzt,*
> *Der habe Religion.*

(He who possesses art and learning has religion as well. He who possesses neither, must have religion.) But this is a formula typical of the second, later humanism, which proceeded from a new concept of humanity; and even then it related only to an exalted and highly intellectualized view of man. The humanism of the sixteenth century had never possessed this view, had not even aspired to it. No humanist of the earlier period can be shown to have espoused it.

The really fatal result of the first attempt to shape the German mind according to humanist principles was of another kind. It was the utter split between thought and form. This can be seen most clearly in Fischart, doubtless the greatest imaginative talent of the outgoing sixteenth century. Relate the thought content of his works to traditional cultural values and you will see that he inherited both the romantic and the rational tendencies of humanism and was intent on continuing them. But when it came to creating a form to hold and organize this substance, he showed himself a complete failure. This is all the more shattering when one considers those parts of his work where he took an equally formless genius, Rabelais, as his model.

But even in this point humanism served only to hasten a long-established process which was going on independently of it and, as it were, at a lower level. Let us take Paracelsus as an example. So far as his life and his influence are concerned, Paracelsus belonged to the humanist age. In another era and another spiritual and intellectual setting he could never have conceived the notion of turning medicine into a pan-scientific philosophy, let alone attempt to put it into effect. But that did not make him a humanist. He wanted to be an individual, standing alone, owing nothing to any tradition, and he succeeded. He called himself a "philosopher in the German manner," and that was precisely what he was. He was the first German since Cusanus to aim at a genuinely universal theory of life, and in this he had an influence reaching well beyond his own age. The "spirit of Paracelsus" was something to be reckoned with in Germany before the Thirty Years' War, when Johann Valentin Andreae, himself a man receptive to all contemporary trends and ideas, accorded Paracelsus a niche in the Palace of Fame, the dwelling place of supreme thinkers, in company with Cardanus, Peter Ramus, and Copernicus. But the very comparison with Nicholas of Cusa reveals the fatal transformation which the German mind had undergone in the meantime. Was Paracelsus, in his *Paramirum*, really able to rise above the fanciful, or, in his *Paragranum*, above the fragmentary? Did he carry his *Monarchei* to an intellectual level as high even as that much lesser genius Giordano Bruno? In my opinion he did not; and I believe that it would have required the genius of an artist of more recent times for the greatness of the man to emerge from behind his life's work, which, after all, amounted to no more than a collection of "aphoristic treatises."[75]

But one thing more may be said. If the encounter of the German mind with European humanism ended in a series of half-solutions, this was not due to any intellectual deficiency but to the very copiousness of the German mind—a depth and breadth so abundant that it resisted every attempt to provide forms which were at the same time norms. Surely it is something more than an external fate which always brings the Germans face to face with this problem, a problem clearly revealed to us for the first time in the confrontation of the German mind with humanism.

NOTES TO CHAPTER 5

1. This will not, I hope, be taken as a piece of original wisdom. Cf. the following passage from Ranke, written in 1874: "One of the most important factors (for the new trends in civic, artistic, and commercial development at the turn of the fifteenth century) lay in the new direction taken by general studies: this was the period of early humanism. And it was not just a matter of language and grammar. The interest in classical antiquity led to an awareness of the great ideas which underlie human life in society, as expressed in law, religion, and civic society." Leopold von Ranke, *Preussische Geschichte* [ed. Willy Andreas (Wiesbaden-Berlin, 1957), I, 157].

2. Even as regards the terminology I depart here fundamentally from the studies of Konrad Burdach. For my objections to these, see [Paul Joachimsen, "Vom Mittelalter zur Reformation," *Historische Vierteljahrschrift*, XX (1920–21), 426–70. My views] will be elaborated shortly in the same journal in the light of the recently published volumes of Burdach's great work.

3. Very instructive is the work of Hans W. Eppelsheimer, *Petrarca* (Frankfurt, 1934). In addition, though, it would be well to read the criticisms of Paul Piur in *Deutsche Literaturzeitung* (1927), p. 61 ff., and especially those of Calcaterra in *Giornale storico della Litteratura italiana*, vol. 91, p. 92 ff.

4. Cf. *Epistolae de rebus familiaribus* (Florence, 1859–63), Vol. XXIV, 1 (Vol. III, p. 251).

5. Cf. F. de Sanctis, *Saggió critico sul Petrarca* (Naples, 1869).

6. *Epistolae*, Vol. I, 3. Cf. *Ibid.*, Vol. III, 2. [On Petrarch see now the works of E. H. Wilkins, especially *Studies in the Life and Works of Petrarch* (Cambridge, Mass., 1955) and *Life of Petrarch* (Chicago, 1961)].

7. Cf. Petrarch's *Secretum* . . . *De Contemptu mundi* [English translation: *Petrarch's Secret*, by W. H. Draper (London, 1911)].

8. The decisive passage, in the first book of the *Secretum*, gives rise to a remarkable observation: Petrarch had praised his father-confessor Augustine for his book, *De vera religione*, which had been for him a revelation, and Augustine accepted this praise and remarked that he had been inspired to write it principally by a line from Petrarch's own beloved Cicero; on further questioning he named the line as *Tusculan Disputations* I, 16. In itself this passage might well have been a program for Augustine. But I myself have checked on this and made inquiries of eminent Augustine scholars, and it appears that nowhere did Augustine say anything of the

sort. Where Petrarch got the idea I do not know. He repeats the assertion in *De vita solitaria*, Lib. I, sect. 9, chapter 8. Petrarch may have made it up himself or simply read it somewhere; in either case it is quite clear that he was contemplating Augustine only against the background of the ancient world and naturally had thus misunderstood him. Cf. Konrad Burdach's account of this connection, *Vom Mittelalter zur Reformation*, Vol. v (1926), p. 72.

9. Cf. *Epistolae*, Vol. XXI, 10.

10. This is the real significance of the Rienzo episode for humanism. In accounting for it Petrarch acknowledged that his projected epic on Rienzo, for the sake of which he had shelved his *Africa*, would have become a satire.

11. Much of value will be found in the new edition of [Petrarch's so-called "Liber sine nomine" by] Paul Piur, [Petrarca's '*Buch ohne Namen*' *und die Päpstliche Kurie* . . . (Halle, 1925)].

12. *Epp. famil.*, Vol. XXII, 2.

13. To see this it would be well to compare his picture of Cicero with that of Fra Guidotto of [Bologna . . . *la elegantissima doctrina* . . . *chiamata rethorica nova traslatata* . . . (Bologna, c. 1472)], or with that of his friend William of Pastrengo in the latter's work *De originibus rerum* [Venice, 1547].

14. Cf. C. Sutter, *Aus Leben und Schriften des Magisters Boncompagno* (Freiburg, 1894). Also Friedrich Baethgen ["Rota Veneris"] *Deutsche Vierteljahrsschrift für Literaturwissenschaft und Geistesgeschichte*, Vol. 5 (1927) p. 37 ff.

15. A good account of this is given in Robert Davidsohn, *Geschichte von Florenz*, Vol. 4, "Die Frühzeit der Florentiner Kultur" (Berlin, 1921).

16. On this cf. now Hans Baron, *Lionardo Bruni Aretino: Humanistisch-philosophische Schriften* (Leipzig, 1928). In the introduction there are some useful details about Florentine "civic humanism." On the concept of *humanitas*, cf. also K. Brandi, *Das Werden der Renaissance*, a discourse given in Göttingen in 1908. [Also Hans Baron, *The Crisis of the Early Italian Renaissance: Civic Humanism and Republican Liberty in an Age of Classicism and Tyranny* (Princeton, 1955; 2nd rev. ed., 1961).]

17. This was true even of Lorenzo Valla, as can be seen from a careful analysis of his treatise *De voluptate ac de vero bono*.

18. Very useful, though approaching the subject from a different angle, is E. Zilsel, *Die Entstehung des Geniebegriffs* (Tübingen, 1926).

19. This has been clearly emphasized and demonstrated for one particular field by E. Fueter, *Geschichte der neueren Historiographie* (Munich, 1911), p. 137 ff.

20. For biographical information, cf. E. Vansteenberghe, *Le cardinal Nicolas de Cues* (1920) [also Henry Bett, *Nicholas of Cusa* (London, 1932); Paul E. Sigmund, *Nicholas of Cusa and Medieval Political Thought* (Cambridge, Mass., 1963), and Morimiche Watanabe, *The Political Ideas of Nicholas of Cusa* . . . (Geneva, 1963)]. Most useful for the ideas being pursued here is Ernst Cassirer, *Das Erkenntnisproblem in der Philosophie und Wissenschaft der neueren Zeit* (Berlin, 1922), Vol. I, p. 3. *Idem: Individuum und Kosmos in der Philosophie der Renaissance* (Leipzig, 1917), p. 203 ff., [*The Individual and*

the Cosmos in Renaissance Philosophy, tr. Mario Domandi (New York, 1964)], which includes a critical edition and translation of the Liber de mente [the English translation does not include this]. Somewhat opiniated but very stimulating is Rudolf Stadelmann, Vom Geist des ausgehenden Mittelalters. Studien zur Geschichte der Weltanschauung von Nikolaus Cusanus bis Sebastian Franck (Halle, 1929).

21. Cf. A. Meister in Annalen des historischen Vereins für den Niederrhein, Vol. 63.
22. "De ludo globi" (cf. Cassirer, Erkenntnisproblem, p. 58, note 1).
23. Complementum theologicum, chapter 2 (cf. Cassirer, op. cit., p. 26, note 1).
24. For this, cf. also Stadelmann [op. cit.] 38.[1]
25. On him, very little has come to supersede the great monograph of Georg Voigt (Berlin, 1856 ff.). [Also C. M. Ady. Pius II . . . ; The Humanist Pope (London, 1913) and W. Boulting, Aeneas Silvius . . . Orator, Man of Letters, Statesman and Pope (London, 1908).] A few preliminary attempts to determine his position in the history of ideas can be found in Max Mell's introduction to the translation of the letters (Jena, 1911).
26. Cf. Enea Silvio Piccolomini, Germania [in Opera (Basel, 1551)].
27. Cf. Enea Silvio Piccolomini, Pentalogus de rebus Ecclesiae et Imperii.
28. The most easily readable summary of the arguments for the orator are to be found in the Vallum humanitatis of Hermann von dem Busche [Hermanni Buschii Pasiphili Vallum humanitatis (Cologne, 1518)].
29. G. Bauch, Geschichte des Leipziger Frühhumanismus (1899), has dealt with this in an amusing and readable, though highly idiosyncratic way in his discussion of a Leipzig quodlibet of 1497. In addition, see the as yet unassessed Poetics of Vadianus [De Poetica et Carminis ratione liber (Vienna, 1518)], and the magnificent summary of the humanist idea of the poet in Aventinus, Bavarian Chronicle [Johannes Turmairs Sämmtliche Werke (Munich, 1880 ff.)], Vol. IV, p. 422.
30. On this, cf. especially my remarks on Mutian, infra.
31. G. Ritter, Studien zur Spätscholastik I and II (Sitzungsberichte der Heidelberger Akademie, 1921 and 1922); J. Haller, Die Anfänge der Universität Tübingen (Stuttgart, 1927).
32. Cf. my own work, Geschichtsauffassung und Geschichtsschreibung in Deutschland unter dem Einfluss des Humanismus, I (Leipzig, 1920), p. 40 ff.
33. The best work is still Charles Schmidt, Histoire littéraire de l'Alsace, 2 vols. (Paris, 1879).
34. Despite the many efforts to be found in the pedagogical literature there is still no satisfactory study of the Isidoneus. [Isidoneus Germanicus ad R. P. D. Georgium de Gemyngen Spirensem prepositum . . . (Strassburg, 1498).]
35. Cf. the Prologus in Narragoniam of Brant's translator, Jacob Locher Philomusos. For a comparison of ideas it is interesting to note that a story was going the rounds in fourteenth-century Paris that Dante, during his stay there, had resolved to compose his Divine Comedy on the lines of the Roman de la Rose (F. A. Huhn, Jahrbuch der kunsthistorischen Sammlungen des allerhöchsten Kaiserhauses, Vol. 31, p. 1).
36. Still the best on him is the essay by Friedrich von Bezold, originally in Historische Zeitschrift, vol. 49, now in the collection of Bezold's essays,

Aus Mittelalter und Renaissance (Munich, 1918). [Also Lewis Spitz, *Conrad Celtis, the German Arch-Humanist* (Cambridge, Mass., 1957).]

37. Cf. my own work, "Tacitus im deutschen Humanismus," *Neue Jahrbücher für das klassische Altertum* (1911), 1. Abt., Vol. xiv, 697 ff. [Also Gerald Strauss, *Sixteenth-Century Germany; Its Topography and Topographers* (Madison, Wisc., 1959,) chapter 2.]

38. A first stage in the humanistic formation of these ideas is Gregor Heimburg's address at the Congress of Mantua in 1459, where Heimburg, as an excuse for the rough edges of his address, said to the Pope: "*Ignosce theothonico ritui, qui etsi a stilo romano paululum declinet, tamen a pietate naturae non abhorret.*" Cf. Voigt, *Enea Silvio*, 3, 782. A more highly developed attitude is to be seen in Hutten's *Arminius*, in which Arminius refused to proclaim his own deeds, since to do so would go against German modesty.

39. Cf. my *Geschichtsauffassung* (note 32, above), p. 167 ff.

40. *Ibid.*, p. 155. Cf. A. Werminghoff's edition of the *Norimberga: Conrad Celtis und sein Buch über Nürnberg* (Freiburg, 1921).

41. Karl Morneweg's monograph [*Johann von Dalberg ein deutscher Humanist und Bischof*] (Heidelberg, 1887) is out of date and the views it expresses are often faulty.

42. H. Ulmann, *Kaiser Maximilian I* (Stuttgart, 1884), Vol. 1, p. 573 ff. [R. W. S. Watson, *Maximilian I, Holy Roman Emperor* (London, 1902).]

43. Cf. Cuspinianus, *Vita Maximiliani* [in Johann Cuspinian, *De Caesaribus atque Imperatoribus Romanis opus insigne*].

44. K. Giehlow, "Die Hieroglyphenkunde des Humanismus in der Allegorie der Renaissance besonders der Ehrenpforte Kaiser Maximilians I," *Jahrbuch der kunsthistorischen Sammlungen des allerhöchsten Kaiserhauses*, Vol. 32 (1915), Heft 1. F. Saxl and E. Panofsky, *Dürers Melencolia, 1, Studien der Bibliothek Warburg* (1923).

45. [Cf. Lewis W. Spitz, *The Religious Renaissance of the German Humanists* (Cambridge, Mass., 1963,) chapter 4: "Reuchlin, Pythagoras Reborn."]

46. Giehlow may well have been the first to see the connection with Ficino's doctrine of the temperaments; *Mitteilungen der Gesellschaft für vervielfältigende Kunst* (1903). [Cf. N. A. Robb, *Neoplatonism of the Italian Renaissance* (London, 1935).]

47. The exemplary edition of the correspondence by P. S. Allen, Oxford, begun in 1906, has opened a new era in Erasmus studies. The most recent work on him is J. Huizinga, *Erasmus* [English translation by F. Hopman: *Erasmus of Rotterdam* (London, 1952),] is packed with gifted individual observations and shows a particularly sympathetic appreciation of the Dutch elements in Erasmus' nature. Excellent on Erasmus, sojourn in Basel is R. Wackernagel, "Humanismus und Reformation in Basel," in *Geschichte der Stadt Basel*, Vol. iii (1924).

48. On this and all subsequent points, cf. the essay of Gerhard Ritter, "Die geschichtliche Bedeutung des deutschen Humanismus," in *Historische Zeitschrift*, Vol. 127 (1923), p. 393 ff. [The course of the conceptual discussion of the nature of German humanism to Joachimsen and beyond may

be followed in Hans Rupprich, "Deutsche Literatur im Zeitalter des Humanismus und der Reformation," *Deutsche Vierteljahresschrift für Literaturwissenschaft und Geistesgeschichte*, XVII (1939), *Referatenheft*, 83–133, and Werner Näf, "Aus der Forschung zur Geschichte des deutschen Humanismus," *Schweizer Beiträge zur allgemeinen Geschichte*, II (1944), 211–30.]

49. [Allen's great edition was completed with volume XII, the indices, in 1958.]

50. Cf. especially Allen, no. 1436 [Erasmus to Gerhard Geldenhauer, April, 1524] and the remarks of Huizinga.

51. Hitherto the best on this point has been Paul Mestwerdt, "Die Anfänge des Erasmus," *Studien zur Kultur und Geschichte der Reformation* (Leipzig, 1917), p. 29 ff. [Also A. Hyma, *The Youth of Erasmus* (Ann Arbor, Mich. 1930).]

52. The very solid *Vita di Lorenzo Valla* of Girolamo Mancini (Florence, 1891) looks at things too much from the viewpoint of (the then) modern Italian liberalism.

53. Cf. in general the excellent presentation in H. Pirenne [*Histoire de Belgique* (Brussels, 1909–32,) Vol. III, book 2, chapter 3, "La Renaissance"].

54. An exhaustive discussion of the older notions about the Brethren of the Common Life has been provided by L. Schulze in *Realenzyklopädie für protestantische Theologie und Kirche*, 3rd ed., vols. 3 and 23; also, once more, Mestwerdt. For the wrong-headed new book of Hyma, *The Christian Renaissance* [Grand Rapids, Mich., 1924]. Cf. the review of Hans Baron in *Historische Zeitschrift*, Vol. 132 (1925), p. 413 ff.

55. This also emerges from the information Erasmus gave about his education, esp. Allen, Vol. I, p. 48.

56. For biographical information, H. E. J. M. van der Velden, *Rudolphus Agricola* (diss., Leiden, 1911); for his place in the history of ideas, cf. my study, "Loci communes," in *Lutherjahrbuch* (1926). [Also Charles G. Nauert, *Agrippa and the Crisis of Renaissance Thought* (Urbana, Ill., 1965).]

57. Cf. the critical edition by L. Bertalot in *La Bibliofilia*, ed. Olschki (1928), p. 382 ff.

58. Evidence for this can be found in Mutianus' own correspondence, which has been edited twice, by Krause and Gillert. [C. Krause, *Der Briefwechsel des Mutianus Rufus* (Kassel, 1885); K. Gillert, *Der Briefwechsel des Conradus Mutianus* (1890).]

59. *Briefwechsel*, ed. Gillert, no. 93, p. 134.

60. Documentary material for the controversy in Boecking, *Opera Hutteni, Supplementum*, Vol. II (Leipzig, 1869–70). The most recent account to be found in the introduction to the critical edition of the *Epistolae obscurorum virorum* by Aloys Boemer (Heidelberg, 1924). A critical examination of the individual phases of the controversy would be more than desirable (cf. note 63).

61. Cf. Erasmus' autobiographical sketch: Allen, Vol. I, p. 19.

62. Amores, book II, no. 9 (Nuremberg, 1500): *Ad Elsulam a priscis et sanctis Germania moribus degenerantem* [*Quattuor libri Amorum* . . . , ed. F. Pindter (Leipzig, 1934)].

63. W. Brecht, *Die Verfasser der Epistolae obscurorum virorum* (Strassburg, 1904), p. 76. The conclusions of this excellent discussion have been corrected only in minor details by Boemer. Cf. note 60 above. [Cf. also *Epistolae obscurorum virorum: Latin Text with an English Rendering, Notes, and an Historical Introduction*, by F. G. Stokes (London, 1909).]

64. Hajo Holborn, *Ulrich von Hutten* (Leipzig, 1929) [English translation by Roland Bainton (New Haven, 1937)] which also provides information about earlier researches and the sources. [Also Harold Drewinc (i.e., Richard Newald) *Vier Gestalten aus dem Zeitalter des Humanismus* (St. Gall., 1946,) pp. 215–84.]

65. Cf. W. Kaegi, "Hutten und Erasmus: Ihre Freundschaft und ihr Streit," *Historische Vierteljahrschrift*, 22 (1925), pp. 200 and 461 ff.

66. There is no satisfactory biography. The best that can be found has been provided by Sigmund Riezler in the concluding remarks to his edition of Aventinus' *Annales* in Vol. III of *Johannes Turmairs Sämtliche Werke* (Munich, 1891 ff.), and in Vol. 6 of his *Geschichte Baierns* (Gotha, 1903), p. 389 ff. [Also Gerald Strauss, *Historian in an Age of Crisis: The Life and Work of Johannes Aventinus* (Cambridge, Mass. 1963).]

67. I have dealt with this in *Blätter für deutsche Philosophie*, Vol. 2 (1928), p. 1 ff. [On Sebastian Franck, see Will-Erich Peuckert, *Sebastian Franck. Ein deutscher Sucher* (Munich, 1943).]

68. Cf. the famous letter to Spalatin of 19 October 1516 in Ludwig Enders, *Luthers Briefwechsel*, Vol. 1, no. 28. For the general differences between Renaissance, humanism, and Reformation, cf. my essay ["Renaissance, Humanismus und Reformation"] in *Die Zeitwende* (1928), p. 402 ff.

69. The preface is printed with my notes, in *Luther, Ausgewählte Werke*, ed. H. H. Borcherdt, Vol. 7 (Munich, 1925), p. 343 ff.

70. Fundamental: the biography by R. Stähelin, *Huldreich Zwingli, sein Leben und Wirken nach den Quellen dargestellt*, 2 vols. (Basel, 1895–97); also the numerous works of Walther Köhler [*Huldrych Zwingli* (Stuttgart, 2nd ed. 1952); *Zwingli und Luther . . .* (Leipzig, 1924).]

71. Further characteristic details may be found in Zwingli's "Archeteles" [*The Latin Works . . . of Huldreich Zwingli*, ed. S. M. Jackson (New York and London, 1912–29), Vol. 1, pp. 197–292].

72. Especially important in this connection are the prefaces to the 1531 Commentary in Isaiah and Jeremiah.

73. For what follows I must once more refer to my essay on the *Loci communes* [cf. note 56 above].

74. Very useful here are the investigations of Wilhelm Dilthey, now in *Gesammelte Schriften*, Vol. II (Leipzig, 1914), especially *Das natürliche System der Geisteswissenschaften*. However, Dilthey now stands in need of considerable correction on these points.

75. Fr. Gundolf used this expression in his *Paracelsus* (Berlin, 1927), though he was very much inclined to apply it to all the products of humanist thought. But to my mind there is a difference between finding in this form an appropriate expression of one's ideas, as Montaigne did, and merely adopting it for want of anything better.

6 Administrative Reforms in Electoral Saxony at the End of the Fifteenth Century

HANS-STEPHAN BRATHER

The following essay by Hans-Stephan Brather, an East German scholar, is the kind of monographic study based on exhaustive archival investigations that is needed if historians are to advance to more confident conclusions about the development of the "modern" state in the fifteenth and sixteenth centuries. First published in 1956, it has been brought up to date by the author.

COMPARATIVE studies in the history of administrative and governmental developments in the German territories during the fifteenth and sixteenth centuries received their fundamental impulse from discussions on the origin of the Tyrolese collegiate council (*Ratskollegium*), particularly from the controversies over the claim made by Eduard Rosenthal, that territorial princes modeled their collegiately organized administrative bodies after the administrative bureaucracy of the Habsburg rulers. In recent times, the gap between interpretations had been narrowed by a number of monographic examinations, especially Theodor Mayer's scholarly and judicious book on the administrative organization of Maximilian I.[1] In 1921, encouraged by the results of Mayer's work, Fritz Hartung,[2] in a summary discussion, took up Konrad Burdach's demand that " . . . one must know the paths of intellectual culture and their alterations in the course of time. Constitutional history can contribute a good deal to this knowledge. Many such paths can be established for sixteenth-century Germany. One of them led from Austria via Bavaria into southwest Germany, another through Saxony to north

Germany. In the general conception of the state, as well as in ideas governing administrative organization, legislation, and the constitution of territorial Estates, we can point to a spiritual traffic taking place on manifold levels, from mere copying to extremely subtle touches of influence. . . . The consideration of this process in all its spatial and temporal ramifications appears to me to be one of the most important, though also one of the most difficult, problems yet to be solved by constitutional historians."

Scholarship in administrative history has usually followed the so-called "Bavarian path" and has tried to gain a general impression of the traffic that once frequented it. One of the questions left open by this traditional approach concerned the position occupied by electoral Saxony in the process of administrative and governmental organization in the time of the emerging modern governmental systems. In reviewing developments in the German territories most scholars were impressed with parallels to changes having taken place in the Tyrol (early independence of the financial administration at the court at a time of considerable increase in mining revenue),[3] as also by the collegialization and the closing of the council as a result of the direct reception of Maximilian's constitution of his *Hofrat*.[4] In actual fact, however, developments in the Wettin lands proceeded in a strikingly rectilinear fashion. They are to be explained, in a much stricter sense than has been assumed until now, from the conditions of the territory itself. The Austrian influence must be held significantly less important than it has hitherto been taken to be. Where it can be established at all, it must be seen as the temporary consequence of existing obligations between the Saxon elector and Emperor Maximilian. Austrian influences may have refined the Ernestine Conciliar Regulation, but they did not provide the impetus for its reorganization.

The elaboration of modern administrative patterns in electoral Saxony was the work of the princes and their officials; as Hartung[5] has shown with reference to the general development in German territories, and Rudolf Kötzschke[6] with reference to Saxony. Once the elector of Saxony had suppressed the opposition movement of the Estates in the civil wars of 1446–51,[7] it became essential to undertake the reform of the totally destroyed financial system, the reorganization of domain management, and the creation of a local administration encompassing the entire territory. The consolidation of the sovereign's power, a process scarcely obstructed by the Estates, thus advanced from two sides: from the extension of local administration and from the organization of the financial bureaucracy.

From about the middle of the fifteenth century the properties of the feudal nobility, the cities, and the monasteries had been placed under the jurisdiction of the local administration—a development not as yet fully understood, but one which continued down to the end of the sixteenth century. The distinction drawn from about the 1440's between bailiwick and chancery subjects (*Amts-und Kanzleisassen*), between nobles, cities, and monasteries bound to obey the bailiff (*Vogt* or *Amtmann*)—that is to say the central government—and those obligated only to the chancery is most likely an expression of this development. Next to his jurisdictional, police and military authority, the bailiff's most important duty became the extension of the sovereign's realm of jurisdiction and the curtailment of the powers of the Estates. Besides the bailiff himself, the bailiff's assistant, a man charged with specific responsibilities, gained ever-increasing importance in the direction of local management and accounting procedures.

At this point the reform of 1456 commenced, associated with Chancellor Georg von Haugwitz. In 1456 the control of local activities was taken from the bailiffs and given to their assistants, the *Schreiber* or *Schösser*.[8] At the same time Haugwitz eliminated two major evils standing in the way of an orderly financial administration: the system of making payment by bill of exchange and the itinerancy of the court. From now on, all surpluses in local treasuries were to be handed over to the chamber, evidently the only treasury located at court. Secondly, the electoral court could in future take up residence at only three sites, for seventeen weeks each: Torgau, Meissen, and Leipzig.[9]

With the exception of the removal of the *Anweisungssystem*, Haugwitz had not created anything new. The office of the *Schösser* had existed in some bailiwicks before him, while the elector had for some years been diminishing the number of his residential stopping places. Nor was Haugwitz able to put his reforms into immediate effect. *Anweisungen* continued to be issued throughout the following decades, though in decreasing numbers, and in some bailiwicks the *Schösser* were not installed until the end of the century (for example, at Plauen in 1489, at Vogtsberg around 1491). But Haugwitz's measures were insistently advanced in the following years by the electors and their officials. Financial conditions improved slowly but noticeably. Permanent residences proved decisive for the administrative consolidation at court; from the 1470's it became common to speak of a "usual" or "principal" court.[10] Furthermore, the fact that the reform of the local and financial administration owed its impetus to the chancellor led to a significant transformation of his office.[11] Since the last years of the fourteenth century the princes had tended to appoint learned and, usually, legally trained ecclesiastics to head their chancery. The implementation of the reform lay first of all in the hands of the clerical chancellor Haugwitz, a man who proved himself thoroughly equal to his administrative tasks. When Haugwitz retired in 1463, his position was filled by officials coming from burgher classes, men who had risen from commercial origin or as local officials to posts such as that of master of the kitchen and had proven themselves as capable and influential persons with special skills in the management of administrative affairs. The responsibilities of the chancellor shifted more and more into the realm of finance, for, following the change of ruler in 1464, the extensive political activity of the young Elector Ernst (1464–1486) and his brother Duke Albert (1464–1500), necessitated the availability of considerable financial resources.

This shift, as well as the heavy work load placed on the chancellor, led in 1469 to the emancipation of the financial administration. The princes entrusted Chancellor Johann von Mergenthal with the newly created post of *Landrentmeister*.[12] It was the duty of the *Landrentmeister* to control administrative matters and the management of accounts in local governments,[13] as well as the expenditures of the ducal household. Accounts were now examined annually by a commission of councillors, the composition of which changed frequently, the *Rentmeister*, as special representative of the prince, being the only permanent member. At the same time Mergenthal assumed direction of the chamber, though not with the title of chamberlain (*Kammermeister*). In this capacity he absorbed all surplus revenues of local administrations and furnished funds for the ducal household, for soldiers' pay, servants, provisions, construction, etc. As ducal treasurer, as administrator of the chamber, and also as ducal councillor, Mergenthal managed within a few years to bring order into fiscal affairs, inaugurate an exemplary system of book-keeping, turn excises into a regular tax, and extend his sovereign's credit.

When the aged Mergenthal relinquished the command of the chamber in 1477, and a year later retired from his treasury office, the administration of the chamber was given to the former clerk of the chamber, Hans von Gunterrode. The princes did not appoint a new treasurer. The formation of this office had been too much the personal work of Mergenthal and a successor equal to him could not be found. Moreover, the years after 1480 are marked by a general air of tentativeness in the central administrative organization, which may have been due to the Thuringian attack of 1482, as well as to the growing estrangement between the elector and his brother (in 1482 there occurred the split in their formerly jointly conducted household).

This estrangement led in 1485 to the Leipzig partition, which divided the territorial state of the Wettins into two badly defined sections. The major part of Meissen, as well as northern Thuringia, fell to Duke Albert, while Elector Ernst took the electoral lands (subsequently the Wittenberg circle), western Meissen, Vogtland, the Ortland of Franconia and the greater part of Thuringia (which was, however, crossed by a strip of land not in Wettin hands). The former administrative organization was retained in both new territories, though it was weakened in the first years by transitional difficulties such as change of officials and new appointments. The Ernestine branch was thrown into temporary confusion by the sudden death of the elector in 1486.

Soon, however, Duke Albert felt pressed by his increasing need for money (resulting largely from his Hungarian and Flemish campaigns in the service of the Habsburgs)[14] to undertake renewed large-scale reforms in his financial administration. From the seventh decade of the fifteenth century—that is to say toward the end of Mergenthal's administration—the dukes had been gaining a significant source of income after important new ore deposits had become economically productive. From 1472 on, an official called *Oberzehntner* (and from 1485 two *Oberzehntner*, one Ernestine and the other Albertine), relieved of the technical and jurisdictional supervision of the mines by specialized officials, sold the mined ore to merchants in Leipzig and in upper Germany (particularly to Hans Umbhawen of Nuremberg). Responsible solely to the prince, and directing his own treasury, the *Ober-zehntner* controlled all revenue from ducal mining properties. In 1487–88 Duke Albert eliminated the overlapping functions of the chamber and *Oberzehntner*'s treasury, entrusting to his *Ober-zehntner* Jakob Blasbalg the administration of both. The central treasury of the *Rentmeister*, as Blasbalg's follower was designated in 1493, had its permanent seat in Leipzig.

From now on the chamber disbursed only the sums needed for the maintenance of the ducal household, but had no revenue of its own, the master of the chamber depending on payments made to him by the central treasury. No longer part of the central treasury, the chamber had become a mere treasury of expenditure for the maintenance of the court (hence its seat at Dresden).[15] The position of *Rentmeister* had been fundamentally altered. He did continue to be a member of the commission charged with checking the accounts of officials, and in this capacity he exercised supervisory accounting authority in the entire territory. But his most important function from now on was as first treasury official for the treasuries of both the *Rentmeister* and the *Oberzehntner*.[16]

A few years later the Ernestines—the Elector Frederick the Wise (1486–1525) and his brother and co-ruler Duke Johann (1486–1525), Elector 1525–1532)—imitated the model of their cousin in Dresden. In 1490/91 they named their *Oberzehntner* Hans von Leimbach[17] *Rentmeister*, and in the spring of 1492 entrusted him with the administration of a newly created central treasury, from the competence of which they removed the chamber, which became a travelling disbursement treasury for household expenses. Leimbach, who held office until 1509, was one of the richest citizens of Leipzig, related by kinship to great Saxon financial officials such as Johann von Mergenthal, Hans von Gunterrode, and Kunz Funcke. He was a progressive representative of the Leipzig business community. Nowhere does one find evidence that he had gained his wealth through real estate speculations or mercantile enterprises, as Blasbalg and his immediate successor had done.[18] He invested his capital in mining and smelting operations in eastern Germany (Rammelsberg, Schneeberg, Gräfenthaler and Hasenthaler, Mansfeld), acquiring at the same time imposing landed properties—among them the estates Dabrun near Wittenberg, Zschepplin near Eilenburg, and Pernstein in Moravia. Repeatedly he helped his princes with large sums of money,[19] even though he could do so only by withdrawing capital from his own enterprises.

In the persons of their *Oberzehntner* both Saxon states had found access to the great sources of capital in their time. These men were invaluable as skilful bankers capable of attaining a precise grasp of ducal financial affairs, and willing to lend their personal wealth as security to their princes' creditors. Hugo Grosse goes so far as to see Leimbach's position as a semicommercial contractual relationship between prince and *Rentmeister*: "not a territorial treasury in the proper sense at all, but a semiprivate institution under ducal control."[20]

However, Grosse failed to notice the extraordinary scope and energy Leimbach devoted to the control of local administration. Grosse's view in this matter is too much determined by his interest in the institutions and procedures of early capitalism, as well as by modern concepts of business administration. Both Mergenthal and Leimbach were responsible to their princes for the administration of the central treasury, the latter as *Rentmeister* and the former after he had taken over the chamber through a cumulation of offices.[21] Both men took their task of exercising control over local administration and local accounts with the utmost seriousness. Both men—Mergenthal through plurality of functions, Leimbach through a change of office—managed to combine accounting and administrative responsibilities in one powerful office.

With the successors of Blasbalg and Leimbach great merchants disappeared from the central financial administration. Their places were taken by financial bureaucrats. After Leimbach's retirement in 1509 the offices of *Rentmeister* and *Oberzehntner* were separated, though the central treasury was retained. The *Oberzehntner* credited his revenues to the *Rentkammer*, which was presided over by Chamberlain Degenhart von Pfeffingen[22] and Marshal Hans von Dolzig. The chamber, directed by the clerk of the chamber, remained purely a treasury of disbursement for court expenses, though it was moved from Leimbach's residence in Leipzig to the main site of the court and therefore ceased to be ambulatory.

We have not yet fully examined a third central treasury, that of the masters of the chamber (*Kämmerer*). In 1488 the Franconian knight Hans Hund von Wenkheim,[23] a man skilled in financial affairs, entered the service of the elector as keeper of the door (*Türknecht*), an office that gave him control over the privy purse of Frederick the Wise. The revenue of this purse came solely from the gambling profits of his master. Since these, however, were usually lost again at dice, the main income came from special payments made by ducal treasury officials such as chamberlains, *Rentmeister*, *Schösser*, and officers in charge of escort, as well as from the interest from outstanding loans. The significance of this office grew rapidly, as the keeper of the door was always in the vicinity of the elector while Leimbach, presiding over the central treasury in Leipzig, visited the court only occasionally.

Gradually, however, Hans Hund lost his personal influence to his successor, the hereditary marshal Degenhart von Pfeffingen. "Pfeffinger," as he is always called in the sources, took Hund's position in 1496;[24] in 1499 he styled himself master of the chamber. This office was no more than that of the *Rentmeister* the product of the "chamber," by which, as late as 1500, was understood the agency for disbursing court expenses, with its attached silver chamber (the management of ducal plate and of the candles required at court). It developed, rather, from the closest personal associates of the elector. The fact that Pfeffingen constantly accompanied the elector, and on his behalf carried out important financial undertakings, that he was in frequent touch with humanists, artists, and merchants in southern Germany, particularly in Nuremberg—all this won him a high place and made him an influential figure at court.[25]

The principles of government professed and practised by the Wettin princes at the beginning of the fifteenth century can scarcely be distinguished from those of other territorial lords of their time. In typical late medieval fashion most governmental business still passed through the hands of the itinerant prince, at whose side there was ranged a series of councillors and "privy officials." As late as the first three decades of the fifteenth century every one of the duke's vassals might still be summoned to court as a councillor. Gottfried Opitz[26] has made an attempt to compile from witness rolls a list of those members of the old council, who seem to have been the constant associates of the prince and, "as it were, constituted an élite that stood at the disposal of the prince and thereby acquired greater administrative experience."

But such an attempt is made suspect by the notion of a regular élite accompanying the prince through the length and breadth of the territory. As an examination of the procedures of prince and councillors it has no value at all, because it leaves unacknowledged as council members all witnesses who only appeared occasionally or appeared only in a particular place. There seems no room for doubt that in the "councillors" brought into such prominence by the elector we may see the origins of the future *Ratskollegium*, the collegiate council. But at this time, when the prince was always under way, moving about his land, the advice of local officials, vassals, representatives of towns, and ecclesiastics exercised a powerful influence on ducal decisions. The bounds of functions were still extremely tenuous, the circle of men close to the sovereign nowhere near as closed as Opitz's thesis would like to have us believe.[27]

Since the establishment of permanent residences in the 1450's, councillors—among them numerous jurists—were compelled to spend a significant part of their time at the site of the court. Still they were often moving, particularly once the consolidation and centralization of local offices had been accomplished. They were commissioned—a separate commission was granted for each case—to scrutinize on the spot and conduct hearings of inquests and suits. As diplomatic activity increased, councillors departed on external missions and participated in meetings with foreign princes or their representatives in order to settle disputes or to make their skilled counsel available to them. At first, all councillors were equally called upon for such activities. The presence of a narrower circle of preferred councillors remaining at court for extended periods cannot be established until the 1460's.

From among the ranks of councillors there gradually emerged the chancellor and other holders of important court positions, men who stayed put at court or in the vicinity of the princes, and were consequently more thoroughly acquainted than other councillors with the tasks of court and provincial administration. These men were the major-domo, the marshal, and the master of the kitchen. The positions of these functionaries had long before emanicipated themselves from their original household responsibilities. The extent of their new activities was by no means clearly delimited, so that the influence of a given official was determined by his personal qualities and by his relationship to the prince. In electoral Saxony in the fifteenth century, as in numerous other German territories, now one functionary, now another, became the dominating personality at court.

As early as the beginning of the fourteenth century the source of the influence of the major-domo and the marshal lay in their activity as princely councillors. Before long, the major-domo was relieved of the routine duties of court management by the master of the kitchen, while the marshal turned his military responsibilities over to the captain of mercenary soldiers. It appears, however, that the judicial authority of the major-domo gave him an edge over the marshal[28] until the marshals of the first third of the fifteenth century (the time of the Hussite Wars and the opposition movement among the Estates) succeeded in repressing his influence at court. It even happened that the post of major-domo remained vacant for a time,[29] while the marshal took the title of marshal-in-chief and turned his duties in the administration of the court over to a submarshal. Under Elector Frederick II this process seems to have been concluded. In 1445 Apel Vitzthum, the energetic spokesman for the opposition movement of the Estates and, at the same time, the duke's major-domo, resigned from court. The office of major-domo remained vacant down to the death of the elector in 1564.[30] The marshal-in-chief stepped into his place.

The court administration, in the narrower sense of the word, now devolved upon the submarshal. The master of the kitchen at first saw himself restricted to the management of the ducal household, but he was gradually able to exert a strong influence upon financial administration. The capable chancellors Johann Stadtschreiber and Johann von Mergenthal (later to be *Rentmeister*) had both been masters of the kitchen. After the creation of the office of *Landrentmeister* in 1469, however, the masters of the kitchen and their assistants held responsibilities only for the court kitchens and for the provision of the court, but not for the stables.

At about the same time the princes began to summon jurists from neighboring universities and towns to be their councillors, and to appoint jurists with training in civil law as chancellors. The political and legal side of the office of chancellor now moved increasingly into the foreground, as financial administration began to be dissociated from the responsibilities of the chancery.[31] An interesting development now took place. As the chancellors turned to legal and political activities, they became estranged from the chancery personnel, which, though formerly tied to them by their emergence from the clerical ranks, now sank to the level of subaltern officials. The gap was filled by ecclesiastics with lesser academic degrees and by experienced clerks who had risen from service as scribes, become scribes-in-chief, and slowly moved up to a position which, from 1479, was given the title of secretary. Thus the chancery in about 1480 seems not to have been in a state to give a chancellor inclined to a legal and political view of his responsibilities the kind of support he required. The enormous increase in chancery business called for rationalization[32] and for a practical man to take charge.

It appears to be a reflection of this situation that the post of chancellor was, from 1480 to the Leipzig partition (in the case of the Ernestine branch until 1499–1501) occupied by nonuniversity men, who had worked their way up from the position of scribe.[33] The explanation of this lies, in part, in the general organizational slackness, which prevailed before the partition. But it should be added that the powerful High Marshal Hugold von Schleinitz suspected that the appointment of a new chancellor would lead to a diminution of his own influence at court.[34]

The Elector Ernst and Duke Albert had appointed Hugold von Schleinitz High Marshal (*Obermarschall*) immediately upon their accession in the year 1464. Schleinitz was practically omnipotent at court; he determined electoral politics to a degree that can scarcely be exaggerated. Next to him stood a major-domo (the office was filled again after an almost twenty-year-long cessation): Dietrich von Schönberg zu Schönberg, the former submarshal (*Untermarschall*). Schönberg could not be compared with Schleinitz in influence, but he was extraordinarily active in financial administration. He came from a family in Meissen whose members had occasionally occupied the bishoprics of Meissen and Naumburg and gained considerable fortune through investments in mining operations in the ore mountains.

Following the partition of Leipzig, Schleinitz and Schönberg entered the service of Duke Albert. In the Ernestine branch, appointments to court office were not properly made until 1487. The office of high marshal seems to have lapsed.[35] In 1487 Hans von Doringberg[36] appears as major-domo. Heinrich von Ende zu Lohma, the former marshal, succeeded him in the same year. The major-domo had thus stepped into the position of high marshal. In rank and influence, he was now foremost among the officials of electoral Saxony. A contributory factor in the formalization of the office must have been the fact that Heinrich von Ende—a man, incidentally, of enormous industry and skill—enjoyed during fourteen years of service the unqualified trust of his princes as he held the management of local administration and justice firmly in his hands. The marshal and the chancellor, respectively, controlled only the supervision of the ducal household and the chancery. The formerly powerful marshal had been reduced to a court marshal (*Hofmarschall*), as he was called after the turn of the century.

It is difficult to establish the number and activities of all the ducal officials to whom the designation of councillor (*Rat*) was applied. No sharp distinction was as yet being drawn between "servants" and "councillors." The princes took on as servants numerous persons of varying geographical and social origin. By means of granting service wages, assigning payments in kind or pensions, or giving assurances of additional princely protection, the Wettin princes secured from nobles in and outside their duchy, pledges of service for fixed military aid, either for a few years or for a lifetime. Legal scholars from the neighboring universities of Leipzig and Erfurt were likewise employed for the political purposes of the Wettin, as were officials of foreign rulers, bishops or cities. They were called upon as jurists, for the implementation of ducal jurisdiction, entrusted with embassies, or summoned to pass on news and information. Frequently such "servants" were given the title of "councillor," and asked to do the duty of "serving and counselling." Determining criteria for the choice of such persons were rank and reputation. The princes went by their judgment of individuals, their juristic capabilities, or their political acumen. In many cases such men were chosen with the aim of frequent or permanent employment in the central administration. Letters of patent, of assignment, of declaration, or reversion, and of gratuity reveal in their wording, that the boundaries between servants and councillors were still flexible.[37] So do treasurers' accounts with their entries of receivers of service money or annuities, of quarterly payments and provision costs. These are found as late as the first third of the sixteenth century. Still, it can be proven for the last decade of the fifteenth century, that Elector Frederick drew only a few of his regular councillors from this group of men. The remaining councillors were only occasionally called for consultation or for participation in administrative and judicial duties.

There are two extant letter books from the Ernestine chancery (*Landeshauptarchiv* Weimar, *Copiale* F 20, for the period February 22 to May 24, 1492, and *Copiale* F 21, a fragment for the period December 25, 1492, to December 22, 1493), containing all the outgoing letters from the elector's residence (or, in his absence, from Duke John) with the names of the officials in charge of the matter which is the subject of the letter. An examination of these letter books makes it possible to determine the number of councillors as well as the duration and nature of their activity. Insofar as both registers record only outgoing letters from the actual place of residence of the elector, clear references to councillors are encountered only for the time of the elector's presence at court, not for their activity at court during his absence.

In the last decade of the century, the main residence of the court (the *wesentliche Hof*) was at Torgau during the first half of the year (December/January to June/July) and at Weimar during the second half (June/July to December/January). In unusual circumstances the court met at Coburg, as in 1495 for the sake of a shorter distance to Worms, where the elector attended the imperial diet. Vacant residences were administered by a councillor or another court official, who had sufficient authority at his disposal.[38]

Major-domo, marshal, chancellor, doorkeeper, and master of the kitchen remained in permanent residence at court, as departmental officials, unless they were employed in special assignments abroad or accompanied the elector on his journeys. The *Rentmeister*, on the other hand, had his seat in Leipzig and appeared only when summoned. To this group were added four or five local officials (*Amtsleute*) and, for a time Heinrich Reuss zu Greiz, who had also risen from the local administration.[39] However, these local officials were never employed at court for more than a few weeks. They returned, in constant rotation, to the provinces in order to carry on the administration of their offices.[40] The duration of their activity as councillors to the central government or to the person of the elector fluctuated; it is not possible to find evidence for an orderly turn of duty. When needed again, they were recalled; thus no time was set for their return. A councillor seems always to have been called, when the work load demanded it, or when the person in question was required because of his special knowledge (for example, the bailiff from Weida Heinrich Mönch, who was frequently summoned for the reading of accounts), or to replace another councillor who was leaving the court. Often the elector departed from court to ride through his land and personally settle complaints and wrongs, administer justice, supervise local administrators, review the accounts of the *Oberzehntner* on the Schneeberg, engage in financial transactions at the Leipzig and Naumburg fairs, meet with other princes, or go hunting. The elector, as well as his brother, made good use of this opportunity to exercise personal control over local administration and maintain personal contacts in the land. On such trips he was accompanied by the doorkeeper, by one of more councillors (among them the major-domo) and by secretaries. Several councillors remained behind at court, but there was a steady exchange among the councillors remaining at court and those traveling with the elector. There was no narrow circle of favored councillors who, through constant association with the elector, might have attained a superior position above the other councillors.

Disregarding relatively unimportant exceptions, the councillors were kept busy day after day. The largest share of the work, however, was done by the major-domo. In 80 per cent of all commissions it is his name that is mentioned. By comparison, the number of dispatches handled by the elector himself is strikingly small.[41] Not infrequently the major-domo rode through the land, sometimes accompanied by councillors, saw to the affairs of local administration, negotiated with regional officials, or examined, as the elector's representative and in conjunction with Albertine councillors, the accounts of the *Oberzehntner*. When he was absent the elector did not relinquish his duties to another councillor, but became, it might be said, his own interim major-domo.

The extent to which councillors were called upon varied considerably. When the major-domo was present they were employed in conjunction with him. During his absence the elector handled affairs by himself or with the aid of councillors. Duke Johann in particular, when carrying on governmental business in place of his brother, tended to dispatch matters jointly with the councillors. This was no doubt due to his lack of administrative experience, compared with his brother.

In the individual commissions one finds that only one or two (rarely three) councillors were active together. In a few cases one comes upon formulations that suggest the presence of a collective of councillors: "Major-domo and other councillors." "Prince and other councillors," "Count Siegmund and other councillors." At the same time one may speak of sessions of all the councillors present. In 1493, while travelling, Duke Johann and Elector Frederick wrote to "the councillors" or to "the major-domo and other councillors" at the court in Weimar. Even more clearly: when Duke Johann sent Councillor Heinrich von Einsiedel to Linz to negotiate with King Maximilian about the renewal of the bill of enfeoffment he sent a copy of his instructions to Einsiedel to his major-domo at Weimar, "to give his and the councillors' advice whether it is appropriate and, if so, to send a messenger after Heinrich to Bamberg and Nuremberg; but if not, to write to Heinrich to turn about and return."[42]

We may conclude that the councillors assembled daily under the chairmanship of the major-domo (and in his absence the prince) and deliberated on matters presented to them by the major-domo or by a member of the chancery. The meeting determined which councillor had to undertake the *commissio*, that is, to assume responsibility for drafting the formal decree in compliance with the decision made in substance by the council. (Why else should the chancery have given the names of all commission bearers in its register?) Whether or not the final copy was presented in the council meeting before its formal execution must remain open. Likewise it can no longer be determined whether the elector or the major-domo exercised the *commissio* of certain transactions without the councillors having advised or concluded thereupon.

In important transactions the major-domo or the elector, either alone or with the aid of one or two councillors, carried out the *commissio*, though by no means exclusively. A division of work according to geographical or material criteria did not take place. The councillors were called upon to handle all matters without differentiation, partially also for tasks that fell in the province of departmental officials (marshal, treasurer, master of the kitchen, cup-bearer, though not the doorkeeper).[43] However, these officials were, a few exceptions apart, entirely limited to the stated duties of their office. Chancellor Johann Flehinger[44] is never mentioned as having undertaken a *commissio*. He was confined to the direction of the chancery. Only in bills of enfeoffment or injunctions issuing from the councillors' jurisdiction over property or litigation is he frequently mentioned.

Numerous councillors[45] were regularly called upon for diplomatic missions, but were only occasionally asked to participate in the sessions of the council. Only sporadically are Albertine officials[46] named to handle commissions for both of the Wettin houses.[47]

It is interesting to note the composition of the council according to Estate. Permanent councillors were almost exclusively members of the lower feudal nobility, but not the chancellor and the jurists. Jurists, who came almost without exception from the universities of Leipzig and Erfurt, or were canons trained in canon law from neighboring cathedral chapters, were called only for occasional judicial sessions (as a rule for several consecutive sessions at Torgau, Wittenberg, or Weimar,[48] occasionally at other places, too), or for participation in conferences or meetings, for negotiations with other princes or their representatives. Precisely the fact that the favored inner group of councillors, the college of councillors, consisted solely of the holders of court positions, the *Rentmeister*, and a few local officials, appears typical for the transitional phase in which the college of councillors still found itself in 1492–93.

Inasmuch as an intimate contact had been opened between Emperor Maximilian and the Elector Frederick the Wise following the great Diet at Worms, Frederick assumed in the autumn of 1496 the imperial vicariate (*Reichsvikariat*) for the remainder of the emperor's stay in the north Italian theater of military operations—the first Saxon elector to do so.[49]

Within a few weeks Frederick and his brother departed for south Germany at the command of Maximilian. The elector entrusted the maintenance of his vicariate prerogatives to the councillors left at home at Altenburg,[50] met Maximilian at Innsbruck at the beginning of January 1497,[51] and remained, with his household servants, for eight months at Günzburg in western Austria. During this time Frederick remained in constant contact with the emperor;[52] he also put himself at the disposal of Maximilian's policy, attempting to negotiate with the French.[53]

Even before the end of the year 1497, Maximilian hurried to complete the political edifice he had built on such good foundations.[54] He had already organized the composition of the intermediate bureaucracy in his hereditary lands. Now he created in the *Hofrat* and the *Hofkammer* two central authorities for the empire and the hereditary lands, which were organized collegially and which deliberated and decided independently of the emperor, though they remained tied to his place of residence. The establishment of the *Hofrat* was undertaken in direct opposition to the reform party among the princes and to Berthold von Mainz' claims as imperial arch-chancellor.[55] In the order of February 23, 1498, Frederick the Wise was named as the emperor's permanent deputy over the *Hofrat* though not over the *Hofkammer*.[56]

Frederick did not meet the expectations which the emperor had attached to his nomination, neither in his position against the reform party among the Estates, nor in his efforts at a large-scale settlement of the hostilities between the houses of Habsburg and Valois. Other men now began to gain in influence.[57] On September 12, 1498, Maximilian issued a new order for the imperial chancery,[58] transferring the execution of all imperial business to the imperial chancery under Berthold of Mainz, thus withdrawing it from the court chancery (*Hofkanzlei*) for whose immediate supervision Frederick must have been responsible. Restricted in his competence, disappointed at the failure of his attempts at reaching a settlement with France and at Maximilian's renewed military projects, the Elector Frederick and his brother Johann[59] left Breisgau in November 1498 and, after a two-year absence, returned home.[60]

The imperial *Hofrat* presumably "became moribund about halfway through the next year."[61] In the electorate of Saxony, however, the Elector Frederick and Duke Johann ended the deputyship of their councillors, and, a few weeks after their return, issued in March 1499 an order,[62] the stipulations of which were taken partially from the wording of the constitution of the imperial privy councils of 1498.

This conciliar constitution of 1499 appointed that "four of our councillors are to be always" at the principal court or at a "convenient part of our land," and instructed them to participate in daily sessions with a precisely regulated procedure under the chairmanship of the major-domo,[63] to deliberate and determine in the order of their arrival[64] all matters concerning the princes and the territory. There was no provision for a participation at these meetings of either the elector or of his brother. But "grave and difficult matters" were to be presented, together with their "advice,"[65] to the princes for decision.

The appointment of principal councillors signified no innovation; it merely legalized a situation that had existed for several
years. This fact is made apparent in one place in the constitution,
where the regular councillors are named as "our councillors, who
are now present at court." The fact that the councillors had for
two years governed the land and were thereby entrusted with the
determination of important measures, can thus have been only of
secondary importance. By "principal" court we are to understand the residences of Torgau and Weimar, at which the elector
customarily spent six months each, and by "convenient part of
our land" probably other places at which court was occasionally
established, as for example Coburg in 1495 or Jena and Altenburg
at the time of the deputyship of the councillors in the years 1497
and 1498. The regulation of the procedure of daily council meetings was, however, new. For these, the provisions of the imperial
constitution of 1498 were adopted almost verbatim.

Henceforth all business, incoming and outgoing, was subject to
the authority of the college of councillors. Its decisions were
made by majority rule, to which the major-domo was now also
bound. The practice of reserving decisions on "grave and difficult
matters" to the prince was adopted from the *Ratsordnung* of the
emperor, but it also conformed to procedures in other territories
and was to lead in later decades to the formation of a central
exchequer.[66] However, even these "grave and difficult matters"
were first of all deliberated in the college before they were presented to the prince. Even the instruction issued to councillors sent
on foreign missions was to take place only in the presence of the
prince or before the councillors; the councillors thus instructed
were to be given sealed information which had been ratified by
the majority of the college. After the councillors' return, "such
emissaries" had to report back to the college. Their reports were
kept in the chancery along with the instructions.

Quite different from these explicit stipulations are those articles
which defined the competence of the college of councillors in
supervising local administration and justice. They did not outline the entire sphere of activity, but merely restated a group of

stipulations that heretofore had been part of customary law. One detailed article obligated councillors and the *Rentmeister*[67] to inquire regularly into the defects of offices, particularly at the annual review of accounts, and to see to their speedy rectification. The participation of a jurist in the drafting is possibly indicated by the following provision, which may have been intended to alter proceedings used until now in compliance with Roman law: "We also desire that everyone who has business before us or our councillors transmit his matter in the form of a supplication; and where anyone cannot or will not put his matter in writing, his case is nonetheless to be heard by the council, so that all matters may be the more solemnly deliberated and decided."

At the same time the procedural competence of the councillors was outlined in a negative way. They could accept no litigation brought to them by the subjects of local officials unless it had beforehand been heard at the local level.[68] Matters which required more information were to be deliberated preliminarily, while additional facts were gathered from the local administration. Litigation between subjects and bailiffs came before the councillors as a matter of principle.

In contrast to the imperial constitution, the Ernestine conciliar organization affirmed the strict subordinance of the chancellor to the college of councillors. While Maximilian's chancellor, Dr. Konrad Stützel, clearly represented the learned community and participated in the emperor's reform program, the Ernestine order of 1499 barely mentioned the chancellor. He, along with two secretaries,[69] was obligated to participate in the meetings of the college of councillors. He was to be responsible for keeping the doors of the chancery closed to all who had no business there. He had the key to one of the three seal chests.[70] However, no provision was made for countersignature of outgoing documents. Letters and other documents continued to leave the chancery without a chancellor's mark or subscription.[71] The main responsibility of the Ernestine chancellor continued to be the direction of the chancery.

Several explicit and detailed directions—taken from Maximilian's *Ratsordnung* of 1498—were to assure the compliance of all outgoing business ("grants, confirmations, recesses, decisions, missives, and other matters") with the advice of the college of councillors. Nothing could leave the chancery without the councillors' approval. The *Munda*, or fair copies, were read aloud before the councillors, and then sealed in their presence. Locks were put on the seal chests in order to prevent illicit use of the seals by chancery personnel. Chancery papers not founded on a council decision were generally declared invalid. Documents, or their copies, could be inspected only with the council's permission —a provision, incidentally, not found in Maximilian's order. Letters of enfeoffment could be granted only quarterly and were regulated by means of explicit directions.

Compared to Maximilian's chancery, the electoral office had had to do its job with significantly fewer staff, whose members, however, distinguished themselves as expert administrators and managers, as surviving registers and copy books still show. This may explain the fact that the electoral instructions for the two conciliar secretaries, the registrar,[72] and the chancery clerks, were not adopted from the imperial conciliar order, though surely these instructions must have been accessible to the elector at the imperial court.[73]

A comparison of the two conciliar constitutions, the elector's and the emperor's, emphasizes the differences between the two conciliar colleges. On the one hand, we find a political tool in the hand of the Habsburg ruler, always concerned with the great political questions of the time and relieved by bureaucratic organizations in the hereditary lands from the constant involvements with local administration and subjects. In Saxony, on the other hand, we have the councillors of a territorial prince—albeit an important one—who, in their daily work, were confined to the narrow circumference of their land and to matters of justice and of administration.

The extensive verbal and technical borrowings from Maximilian's model in no way signified a novel organization of the electoral council or its chancery. Among the Ernestines the transition to a regular *Consilium formatum* had taken place many years before; its origins may reach back to the time before the Leipzig partition.[74] The fact that a conciliar college existed in Saxony may have facilitated the adoption. The conciliar constitution of 1499 was linked with existing conditions to an extent which cannot be understood from the adopted terms and formulations. Borrowings tended to be of provisions that might serve the technical development of the council procedures and of the chancery. Here undoubtedly lies the meaning of this so-called reception.

Whether the consolidation of government accomplished at the electoral Saxon court shortly before the turn of the century could be maintained in the following decades, and whether the provisions of the conciliar constitution of 1499 remained authoritative henceforth—these are questions that can be answered only with difficulty without intensive research into the sometimes scanty materials.

The advanced organization of the conciliar college around 1500 was, in part at least, the consequence of personal circumstances, of the close understanding and sympathy between the elector and his brother,[75] and the personal ties of both princes to their councillors,[76] who were all representatives of the same social and political stratum, and who almost without exception had had extensive administrative experience for many years. Other factors also helped: the lack of jurists, the ability of *Rentmeister* Leimbach and of Major-Domo von Ende, a man able to dominate the council through his strong personality.

Even if the paucity of sources makes this circle of persons appear more homogeneous to us than it actually was, it remains noteworthy that its administrative activity did not proceed in a less formal, less thoroughly organized manner.

However, as this circle dissolved in the course of the first years after the turn of the century, it lost its social and collegiate homogeneity. The noble and juristically untrained Major-Domo Heinrich von Ende (last cited in the documents in 1501) was replaced as a figure of primary influence by the new and juristically learned chancellor (Dr. Johann Mogenhofer is mentioned from 1501).[77] From the time of Mogenhofer's chancellorship, the learned element increased continuously. Learned men turn up as councillors from 1510, and particularly from 1520. Local officials disappear from the council. From then on, also, a distinction is made between court councillors (*Hofräte*) and household councillors (*Räte von Haus aus*).[78]

Any further development was interrupted at the point that, on the basis of the separation of power of 1513, two separate territorial administrations came into being: the electoral lands and Meissen under Friedrich, and Thuringia, Franconia, and Vogtland under Johann, with the residences of Torguau[79] and Weimar. The fragmentary records of the separation negotiations[80] reveal that the provisions of the conciliar constitutions no longer possessed self-evident validity. The conciliar system became considerably less efficient before the end of the separation, which came with the death of the Elector Friedrich in 1525. Each brother had his own chancery and his own councillors, who were remunerated only by him, though they were obligated to both brothers. Both the number of councillors and the extent of their activity decreased at both courts. Johann's growing indebtedness,[81] his lassitude in the control of offices, the fact that he tended to leave foreign affairs to his brother, above all his mediocre administrative talent, worked against a strengthening of the collegiate conciliar system. In addition, each brother was inclined to call upon the councillors of the other for special assignments.[82] The sources are even thinner for the councillors of the elector, but even here one can no longer speak of a uniform council.[83]

Later, under the single rule of Johann (1525–1532) the number of councillors increased; jurists from the ranks of the burgher class were called to court as standing councillors and gained considerable influence. The chancellor, a jurist, replaced the major-domo as presiding officer of the council sessions.[84] The greatly increased range of business of state as the result of church-state tensions and of the new administrative tasks facing a Protestant territorial state tended to separate the councillors from the handling of "important matters." In 1531, shortly before the death of Johann, the first mention of "privy councillors,"[85] signals the beginnings of the future chamber government.[86]

At court everything tended toward organizational rationalization—this was a fact recognized by Johann Friedrich (1532–1554) while still heir to the electoral title. The formulations of his conciliar orders of 1536, 1539, and 1542 still show the after-effects of the constitution of 1499.[87]

In any case, this much may be said: the conciliar constitution of 1499 lost much of its applicability as the social composition of the standing councillors changed, as the learned element began to predominate, as the territorial administrations became separated as a consequence of the division, and as the increased tasks of the territorial state brought about a detachment of the government from the person of the prince. The constitution was known at court; it was cited now and then, but its vital provisions were no longer observed. Many habits of daily procedure were perhaps scarcely recalled as directives remaining from 1499. But when Johann Friedrich caused the management of governmental business, which had until then been running in a quite unregulated fashion, to be ordered anew, he reached back to 1499 for certain technical provisions which had originally been derived from the conciliar constitution of the emperor.

The conciliar constitution of 1499 appears to have influenced only slightly the collegialization of councils in other territories. The case of Mecklenburg[88] seems to be most instructive. Under the strong personality of Duke Magnus II (1477–1503) (the father-in-law of Duke Johann of Saxony) regular councillors were established at court in the 1490's. At the same time a high court of justice was set up. In 1504, immediately after Magnus' death, his sons (Johann's brothers-in-law) issued a court regulation.[89] They designated three fixed residences and ordered daily conciliar sessions, in which the councillors were to deliberate on all matters relating to the princes and the land.

Kurt Dülfer has pointed out that in Hessen the "gradual transformation of an originally informal conciliar procedure into a firmly united *Consilium formatum*—a development noticeable since the end of the fifteenth century and especially in the time of the regency councillors from 1509 to 1514—" may have been impelled by an Ernestine influence. However, it has not been possible to prove a conscious acceptance of the influence of electoral Saxony by the Hessian conciliar organization."[90]

About the archbishopric of Magdeburg, whose governmental organization in the late medieval period has not yet been studied, no precise statement can be made. Although Archbishop Ernst (1476–1513), the brother of Elector Frederick and Duke Johann, resided only two days' distance from the Ernestine residence at Torgau, and there is frequent mention of conferences between the three Ernestine brothers and their councillors, the *Hofordnung* of the archbishop[91] reveals the existence of a rather primitive administrative organization. The provisions made for the marshal prescribed daily sessions of councillors under the chairmanship of the marshal (and, in the case of partisan matters, of the chancellor as well). The councillors could not, however, make independent decisions, The archbishop had to agree. The *Hofordnung* was therefore probably prepared independently of the Ernestine conciliar constitution, although possibly much earlier, toward the beginning of the reign of the archbishop.

Nor can it be proven that the Saxon reform of financial administration contributed decisively to the development of bureaucracies in other territories.[92] It was, after all, in the realm of financial affairs that the historical moment and the extent of organizational development depended more than any other sphere of state activity on financial needs, on the person of the prince, on the influence of the Estates, on the size of the territory, and on the abundance of existing or exploitable sources of money. Generally speaking, it was not before the middle of the fourteenth century that a group of special financial officials established themselves in the south and west German territories to direct financial administration and take over the management of domain lands. They bore varied designations, such as *Rentmeister, Kellner, Kastner.*[93] This process began, indigenously, in the electorate of

Saxony in the first half of the fifteenth century and was expedited by the reform of 1456. In the larger territories of the north, too, waxing sovereign powers tended to appoint *Rentmeister* in the second half of the fifteenth and at the beginning of the sixteenth centuries.

As early as the first half of the fifteenth century Bavarian county courts were presided over by *Rentmeister*, who collected the courts' surpluses and were responsible for the accounts of local adminis-trations.[94] The *Rentmeister* thus excercised, in the middle echelon, the duties of the principal electoral Saxon *Rentmeister* for the entire territory, with the exception that the latter not only exer-cised control, but also kept accounts in his capacity as director of the exchequer. The strong similarity of these two functions sug-gests that there had taken place a transfer of the office of *Rent-meister* from the middle echelon of Bavarian administration to the central government of the Wettins. Personal relations may also have played a role. The Saxon princes frequently met with the Franconian Hohenzollern and the Bavarian dukes, and the Elector Ernst had been married since 1460 to a daughter of Duke Albrecht III of Munich, and was furthermore related through marriage to Duke Ludwig the Rich of Landshut. Numerous conferences of councillors from both sides also took place, and are well docu-mented.

But the many changes affecting the office of *Rentmeister*, around the end of the century, caused the electoral Saxon central financial administration to differ basically from that of other territories. In these other territories, the old unified exchequer, or chamber, had split into the prince's "privy purse" (headed by a *Kammer-knecht, Türknecht, Kämmerer,* etc.) and into a "general" treasury for an undifferentiated court and territorial administration (under a *Kammerschreiber, Kammermeister, Rentmeister, Landrentmeister,* etc.). In Saxony a central treasury inserted itself between the two some time after 1487: the treasury of court expenditures (*Hofausgaben-kasse*) under the clerk of the exchequer (*Kammerschreiber* or *Kammermeister*).[95] If, since the beginning of the last decade of the fifteenth century, *Rentmeister* are encountered also in

Braunschweig-Wolfenbüttel (1493), Mecklenburg (1493–95), Braunschweig-Calenberg (1530) and Henneberg-Scheusingen (beginning of the sixteenth century),[96] the princes of these lands may well have had the Saxon example in mind, but only in the sense of a consolidation of financial responsibilities at court under a special official. On the other hand, a tripartite structure on the Wettin model may have been taken over in Brandenburg (in the first decades of the sixteenth century),[97] in Braunschweig-Calenberg and Braunschweig-Wolfenbüttel (in the 1530's or 1540's) and in Anhalt (in the 1540's).[98]

A direct influence or adoption of Saxon administrative institutions at the beginning of the sixteenth century cannot be proven with certainty. It may be argued, however, that, compared to northern and northeastern territories, both Saxon states were in an advanced state of development insofar as governmental organization, commercial life, and cultural affairs are concerned. Saxony also provided a paradigm for the construction of an effective sovereign authority, though the precise nature of this influence is difficult to trace in the sources. But we are able to identify many of the men active in aiding the princes in their shaping of a more vigorous bureaucratic organization. We meet them as "unlearned" (that is, legally untrained) burghers from Leipzig and from numerous middle-sized and small cities of central Germany. We also meet a number of jurists who had studied at Leipzig, Erfurt, and later also Wittenberg.[99] Finally, there are professors of law, who were regularly called in by the Wettin princes to advise the councillors in their judicial responsibilities, or to assist the high courts, thus taking their places near the dukes' residences and near the site of both the *Rentmeister* and highest territorial court.

While the provincial courts (*Hofgerichte*) declined in importance from about the middle of the fifteenth century, the highest territorial court (the *Oberhofgericht*), which sat in Leipzig, the seat also of the territorial university and the economic center of both Wettin territories, emerged as the most important judicial body. Though temporarily dissolved in 1485, it was reconstituted in 1488 for the Albertine lands, and in 1493 for the entire Wettin domain. Until 1547 it met alternatively at Altenburg and at Leipzig.[100] When Dr. Wolfgang von Ketwig (who hailed from Leipzig) drafted a Chamber Court Regulation for Brandenburg in 1516,[101] he closely followed the Leipzig court regulation of 1493.[102] An influence in Mecklenburg is, on the contrary, scarcely probable.[103] However, when the Albertine Duke Frederick, after he was chosen Grand Master of the Teutonic Order in 1498, established a high court of justice in Königsberg, much against the opposition of his Estates, he modeled its constitution closely upon that of Leipzig.[104]

Bureaucrats did not tend to remain long in Ernestine service. From the third decade of the sixteenth century on, Ernestine officials transferred into the service of neighboring territorial rulers in increasing numbers. But by that time the Saxon electoral state had become the predominant Protestant power in the empire, and had preceded the other north German states in the establishment of a state church and in the organization of territory-wide system of taxation.

NOTES TO CHAPTER 6

1. *Die Verwaltungsorganization Maximilians I., ihr Ursprung und ihre Bedeutung* (*Forschungen zur inneren Geschichte Österreichs*, 7) (Vienna, 1920).
2. Concerning the problem of the Burgundian influence on the administrative organization in Austria, see: *Historiche Zeitschrift* 124 (1921), p. 264. Fritz Hartung expressed his opinion again in "Der französisch-burgundische Einfluss auf die Entwicklung der deutschen Behördenverfassung," *Historische Zeitschrift* 167 (1943), p. 3 ff.
3. Andreas Walther, *Die Ursprünge der deutschen Behördenorganisation im Zeitalter Maximilians I* (Stuttgart and Berlin, 1913) pp. 9 f., 21, 65, 67. Cf. Theodor Mayer, *op. cit.*, p. 74.
4. See the comment of Georg Mentz, *Johann Friedrich der Grossmütige 1503 bis bis 1554*, III (Jena, 1908) p. 126, note 3.
5. *Deutsche Verfassungsgeschichte vom 15. Jahrhundert bis zur Gegenwart* (Stuttgart, 1954), p. 81 ff.
6. Rudolf Kötzschke and Hellmut Kretzschmar, *Sächsische Geschichte*, I (Dresden, 1935), p. 167.
7. Martin Naumann, "Die wettinische Landesteilung von 1445," *Neues Archiv für sächsische Geschichte*, 60 (1939), p. 171 ff. On the problem as a whole: Herbert Helbig, *Der wettinische Ständestaat: Zur Geschichte des Ständewesens in Mitteldeutschland bis 1485. Mitteldeutsche Forschungen* 3

(Cologne, 1955.) An unsatisfactory account is given by Martin Luther, *Die Entwicklung der landständischen Verfassung in den wettinischen Landen (ausgeschlossen Thüringen) bis zum Jahre 1485* (diss., Leipzig, 1895.)

8. The introduction of the *Beschiede*, or salary notices, in which the duties and rights of officials were stimulated seems also to go back to Haugwitz, and not to Mergenthal. Cf. Otto Oppermann, *Das sächsische Amt Wittenberg im Anfang des 16. Jahrhunderts, Leipziger Studien aus dem Gebiet der Geschichte*, Vol. IV, 2 (Leipzig, 1897), p. 8.

9. Hugo Grosse, *Die kursächsischen Finanzen am Ausgang des Mittelalters* (typescript diss., Leipzig, 1914), pp. 5 ff., 47 f., and 85 ff.; Rudolf Goldfriedrich, *Die Geschäftsbücher der kursächsischen Kanzlei im 15. Jahrhundert* (diss., Leipzig, 1930), pp. 23 and 40 ff.

10. Goldfriedrich, *op. cit.*, p. 41. Leipzig and Meissen could not prevail permanently as capitals. Besides Torgau, Dresden served as the residence (in the 1470's) as did Weimar (after the Thuringian attack of 1482) and from the beginning of the sixteenth century Wittenberg as well. It is necessary to distinguish between the seat of the court and the temporary residence of the prince. They frequently do not coincide.

11. Cf. the chancellor lists in Gottfried Opitz, *Urkundenwesen, Rat und Kanzlei Friedrichs IV., Markgraf von Meissen und Kurfürst von Sachsen (1381–1428)* (diss., Munich, 1938), p. 97 ff. and Goldfriedrich *op. cit.*, p. 125 ff. Goldfriedrich was the first to draw attention to the development of the chancery (*op. cit.*, p. 22 ff.).

12. Hellmut Schramm, *Johann von Mergenthal, der erste sächsische Landrentmeister (1469/78)* (diss., Leipzig, 1938), p. 41 ff.; Alexander Puff, *Die Finanzen Albrechts des Beherzten* (diss., Leipzig, 1911), p. 18 ff.; Grosse, *op. cit.*, p. 6 ff.

13. See the promulgation of Elector Ernst and Duke Albrecht, December 13, 1469. Commissioning Mergenthal to be *Landrentmeister*, printed in Schramm, *op. cit.*, p. 46 f.

14. Woldemar Goerlitz, *Staat und Stände unter den Herzögen Albrecht und Georg 1485–1539, Sächsische Landtagsakten*, 1 (Leipzig and Berlin, 1928), p. 390 f.; Puff, *op. cit.*, p. 160 ff.

15. The clerk of the exchequer retained supervision of the princely silver chamber. On Albertine financial reforms see Puff, *op. cit.*, p. 42 ff.

16. Puff, *op. cit.*, p. 45 ff.

17. Emperor Frederick III raised Hans Leimbach to the nobility in 1478 and gave him a coat of arms of a blue shield, two yellow lions facing each other on a double graded yellow mountain. The seal arrangement shows that Leimbach descended from neither the noble families of von Limbach near Oschatz, Otto Posse, *Die Siegel des Adels der wettiner Lande*, Vol. 4 (Dresden, 1911), p. 86, von Leimbach near Salzungen, nor the Herren von Wenkheim (who also called themselves "von Leimbach" after their seat at Unterlaimbach). For the same reason, he cannot be identical with the homonymous Hans von Leimbach, who from 1471 to 1473 was a mercenary in the service of the city of Nuremberg, and who in 1472 appeared before the Saxon prince with credentials from the Nuremberg city council.

One Dietrich Leymbach is mentioned as the chaplain of the dowager princess Margarete; this man, subsequently made treasurer, lent 2,000 florins to the city of Leipzig in 1474, and in 1475 moved from Colditz to Leipzig. This suggests that Leimbach probably progressed at the dowager's court through a mercantile connection or through an administrative function and from there was directed to Leipzig. There is some biographical information in the unsatisfactory sketches of Karl Leimbach, *Hans von Leimbach, kursächsischer Landrentmeister und Bürger zu Leipzig. Schriften des Vereins für die Geschichte Leipzigs*, 11 (1917), p. 51 ff., and Ernst Kroker, "Leipziger Studenten auf der Universität Wittenberg im Reformationszeitalter," in *Neujahrsblätter der Bibliothek und des Archivs der Stadt Leipzig*, 4 (1908), p. 20 ff. As treasurer Leimbach also exercised important functions in the city administration of Leipzig.

18. Puff, *op. cit.*, p. 42 ff.
19. On Leimbach cf. *Copiale C 2*, fol. 23–24, perhaps also *Reg.* Aa 20; Staatsarchiv Nuremberg, *Nürnberger Rchn.-Bel. Urkunden und Briefe*, no. 82.
20. Grosse, *op. cit.*, p. 40.
21. Grosse, *op. cit.*, p. 5, first called attention to Mergenthal's accumulation of offices.
22. On Pfeffingen: Albert Gümbel, *Der kursächsische Kämmerer Degenhart von Pfeffingen, der Begleiter Dürers auf der "Marter der zehntausend Christen"* (Strassburg, 1926, *Studien zur deutschen Kunstgeschichte*, 238) and Paul Kalkoff, *Die Kaiserwahl Friedrichs IV und Karls V* (Weimar, 1925), p. 725, note 2.
23. On his family see H. Neu, "Die Familie der Hund von Wenkheim," *Archiv des historischen Vereins von Unterfranken*, 45 (1903) p. 63 ff.
24. *Reg. Aa.* 1121.
25. Even during the time of separate provincial administration Duke Johann had his own "doorkeeper," who remained, however, without influence in financial administration.
26. Opitz, *op. cit.*, p. 49 ff.
27. Contrarily Hans Spangenberg, *Hof-und Zentralverwaltung der Mark Brandenburg im Mittelalter* (Leipzig, 1908) (*Veröffentlichungen des Vereins für Geschichte der Mark Brandenburg*), p. 71 ff., has collated in the council lists (from the thirteenth to the end of the fifteenth centuries) nearly all evidence from the documents of the Margrave, whose appertaining to the council seemed evident to him. He did not, however, note the frequency or the places of their appearance, nor their positions in the local administration.
28. Heinrich Bernhard Meyer, *Hof-und Zentralverwaltung der Wettiner . . . 1248–1379* (Leipzig and Berlin, 1902) (*Leipziger Studien aus dem Gebiet der Geschichte*, IX, 3), p. 29 ff. On the position of the *Hofmeister* in general, see Gerhard Seeliger, *Das deutsche Hofmeisteramt im späteren Mittelalter* (Innsbruck, 1885).
29. According to Opitz, *op. cit.*, p. 86 f., at least from 1423 to 1428.
30. Naumann, *op. cit.*, p. 177 and 179 f.

31. Goldfriedrich, from whose explanation I diverge in particulars, *op. cit.*, p 25.

32. *Ibid.*, p. 27.

33. The administration of the chancery was assumed in 1479 by the chancery clerk Peter Arnold under varying titles (*Kanzleiverweser, Sekretär, Oberkanzleischreiber*). After the Thuringian attack in 1482 he was joined by Johann Seyfried (Siffridi) the chancellor of Duke Wilhelm. The relationship between the two cannot be exactly determined. (Goldfriedrich, *op. cit.*, p. 25 f.) Seyfried, who had acquired considerable property in and around Weimar, was Ernestine chancellor from 1485 and until 1490–91. His successor was Johann Flehinger: 1487 secretary, declared chancellor March 4, 1496 until December 4, 1499. He may be identical with Johannes Flechingen de Suterburg, who matriculated at Heidelberg in 1458.

34. Goldfriedrich, *op. cit.*, p. 25.

35. The Albertines did not eliminate the office of *Obermarschall* until 1518. Cf. Goerlitz, *op. cit.*, p. 416. The same competition between *Hofmeister* and marshal can also be demonstrated in other territories.

36. *Copiale* D 4, fol. 255. He may be identical with Hans von Dörnberg from upper Hessen. On this individual see Franz Gundlach, *Die hessischen Zentralbehörden von 1247 bis 1604*, Vol. 3 (Marburg, 1930) (*Veröffentlichungen der historischen Kommission für Hessen und Waldeck*, 16), pp. 48 f., 325.

37. The same was true in Württemberg: Irmgard Kothe, *Der fürstliche Rat in Württemberg im 15. und 16. Jahrhundert* (Stuttgart, 1938) (*Darstellungen aus der württembergischen Geschichte*, 29), p. 19 f.

38. For example 1493 Weimar (first half of the year) by Hauptmann Caspar Metzsch of Weimar; Torgau (second half of the year) by Heinrich XI Reuss.

39. Heinrich Loser was provincial governor in Saxony. Caspar Metzsch was in 1487–88 bailiff at Gotha, Tenneberg, and Wachsenburg (perhaps also in Eisenach), in 1491–92 marshal; 1492–1501 bailiff at Weimar; 1501–04 at Plauen. Heinrich Mönch: 1481–88 bailiff at Jena; 1488–1505 at Weida. Hans von Obernitz: 1492–1500 bailiff at Altenburg; 1493–1500 Ernestine chief justiciar. Dietrich Spiegel: bailiff at Gräfenhainichen. Heinrich XI Reuss: 1479–82: Lieutenant (*Statthalter*) for the elector of Mainz on the Eichsfeld; 1483–85/87 governor in Coburg.

40. Thus Heinrich Mönch, because of his frequent absences, was replaced in this office at Weida by his son.

41. See the tables in the original German article, omitted here, pp. 285–86.

42. *Copiale* F 21, fol. 74–78.

43. Specifically mentioned as councillors were Michel von Denstedt (marshal), Hans von Leimbach (*Rentmeister*), Hans Hund (Doorkeeper).

44. See note 33 above.

45. Götz von Ende (brother of the Hofmeister), Caspar von Obernitz (former bailiff at Weimar), Götz von Wolframsdorf and, above all, the learned Heinrich von Bünau at Teuchern. Bünau was electoral spokesman at the imperial diet of Freiburg in 1498 and in the *Reichsregiment* in Nuremberg; he was also one of the emissaries of the imperial government to the

French king (1500–1). Cf. Victor von Kraus, *Das Nürnberger Reichs-regiment* (Innsbruck, 1883).

46. Chancellor Dr. Johann Erolt, *Obermarschall* Hans von Minckwitz.

47. For example, the Swabian knight Caspar Spet (1499–1500 Ernestine marshal, 1500–47 in the employ of Württemberg, cf. Kothe, *op. cit.*, p. 120), Caspar von Vestenberg (from 1493 bailiff in Königsberg in Franconia), the physician Dr. Martin Polich von Mellerstadt, Hans Talner (former Albertine *Kammermeister*, Puff, *op. cit.*, p. 28, formerly a soldier in the service of the city of Nuremberg).

48. Perhaps for sittings of the provincial high court of justice at Wittenberg and Weimar.

49. Writ of Elector Frederick of September 29, 1496 (*Copiale* F 7, fol. 96–97). Shortly before at the Diet of Lindau the electoral Saxon ambassador directed Archduke Philipp from his place as lieutenant of the king to that of an Austrian archduke. Eduard Ziehen, *Mittelrhein und Reich im Zeitalter der Reichsreform, 1356–1504*, Vol. 2 (Frankfurt am Main, 1937), p. 524. According to the Golden Bull the vicariate belonged to the Saxon elector only for the duration of the Interregnum, not during the time of royal journeys across the Alps. Since 1496 the lieutenancy through absence was exercised, in the confusion of both institutions, jointly by the Palatinate and Saxon electors. Adolf Rossberg, *Sachsens Kampf ums Reichsvikariat* (diss., Leipzig, 1933), p. 44, and, more far-reaching in its conclusions, Wiltrud Wendehorst, *Das Reichsvikariat nach der Goldenen Bulle; Reichsver-weser und Reichsstatthalter in Deutschland von König Wenzel bis zu Kaiser Karl V* (typescript diss., Göttingen, 1951), pp. 85 ff. and 109. For 1496 the outgoing correspondence of the Saxon elector in his capacity as imperial vicar has been collected in copy in *Registratura officii vicariatus ducis Saxonis* (*Copiale* F 7, fol. 94–100), used by J. J. Müller, *Des Heiligen Römischen Reichs . . . Reichstagstheatrum . . . unter Kaiser Maximilian I*, part 2 (Jena, 1719), p. 4 f., and the same author's *Reichstagstaat . . .* (Jena, 1709), p. 723.

50. It was provided that, for the duration of the absence of the elector and his brother, his vicariate rights were to be assumed by the councillors remaining at home under the chairmanship of Count Burkhardt von Barby (*Copiale* 7, fol. 99–100'). The *Hofmeister*, who was passed by for this function because he belonged to the lower feudal nobility, stood at the peak of the commissioned councillors, since the vicariate lapsed upon the return of the emperor. All the commissioned councillors are named in their writ of January 4, 1498, printed in: *Ernestinische Landtagsakten*, Vol. 1 (1487–1532), compiled by Carl August Hugo Burckhardt (Jena, 1902) (*Thüringische Geschichtsquellen*, 8), p. 28.

51. On January 5, 1497. Konrad Fischnaler, *Innsbrucker Chronik*, Vol. 1 (Innsbruck, 1929), p. 34.

52. What sort of contact this was we do not know exactly. Therefore the question, whether and to what extent Frederick took part in the working out of the conciliar constitution of 1498 cannot be answered. Only the following meetings with the emperor are confirmed: July 24, 1497, on the field of Stambs near Imst (H. Ulmann, *Kaiser Maximilian I*, Vol. 1,

[Stuttgart, 1884], p. 574); August 14, 1497, at Innsbruck; before the end of April, 1498, at Innsbruck (Cornelius Gurlitt, *Deutsche Turniere, Rüstungen und Plattner des 16. Jahrhunderts* [Dresden, 1889], p. 10). The travel journals for 1497–99 are not preserved, while the travel accounts of the elector (Reg. Bb 5523) give only the residence of his followers.

53. Ulmann, *op. cit.*, p. 577.

54. Maximilian to Berthold of Mainz, Ziehen, *op. cit.*, p. 557.

55. Gerhard Seeliger, *Erzkanzler und Reichskanzleien* (Innsbruck, 1889), p. 78 ff.

56. These drafts are printed in their best versions in Seeliger, *op. cit.*, p. 193 ff., and in Thomas Fellner and Heinrich Kretschmayr, *Die österreichische Zentralverwaltung*, Vol. 1, 2 (Vienna, 1907), p. 6 ff., in their oldest versions. The first draft is dated on December 13, 1497; the *Ratsordnung* according to royal will was proclaimed on February 23, 1498.

The chairmanship of the *Hofrat* did not rest with the Saxon elector but with the *Hofmeister* (Duke Georg von Landshut). Vis-à-vis the *Hofrat* Frederick assumed the position of general representative of the emperor. His newly created dignity served, from the outset, mainly the political purposes of the emperor and aimed less at an institutional establishment of the *Hofrat*; in fact, the position remained vacant after Frederick's departure. The supervision over the *Hofkammer* (created simultaneously) was not given to Frederick; it remained directly under control of the king. The constitution of the *Hofkammer* of 1498 does not mention Frederick. It is reproduced in Sigmund Adler, *Die Organisation der Centralverwaltung unter Kaiser Maximilian I* (Leipzig, 1886), p. 515 ff.; the members of this college were also called lieutenants (*Statthalter*). The *Hofkammer* received its instructions directly from the king; outgoing document transactions were signed personally by the members of the chamber.

57. Report of the electoral Saxon councillor Heinrich von Bünau to Frederick regarding his audience with Berthold von Mainz, December 5, 1498: *Reg.* E. 45, fol. 10 f. Cf. Ulmann, *op. cit.*, p. 610, note 2.

58. Printed in Otto Posse, *Die Lehre von den Privaturkunden* (Leipzig, 1887), p. 209 f.; Seeliger, *op. cit.*, p. 208 ff.; Fellner and Kretschmayr, *op. cit.*, p. 48 ff.

59. Johann had accompanied the emperor on his expedition through the Franche-Comté and Lorraine; in October 1498 he rode from Metz to Louvain. He departed hastily from there at the end of October and met his brother in Freiburg in the middle of November. Travel accounts of Johann, *Reg.* Bb, 5525. This action must have been taken on the basis of information from Frederick; Frederick's decision must have been reached shortly after the promulgation of the organization in the imperial chancery.

60. For their service fee (30,934 gulden) and in return for their loan, Maximilian assigned to Frederick and Johann on August 6, 1498, the manors and castles Cormona, Belgrado, and Castel-nuovo (redeemed in 1535 by King Ferdinand) *Reg.* Aa, 725a. See also Albin von Teuffenbach, *Geschichte der Graftschaft Görz und Gradisca bis . . . 1500* (Innsbruck, 1900), p. 41 f.

61. Ulmann, *op. cit.*, p. 827. Cf. also Adler, *op. cit.*, p. 55 ff.; Oswald von Gschliesser, *Der Reichshofrat* (Vienna, 1942, *Veröff. der Kommission für neuere Geschichte des ehemaligen Österreich* 33), p. 2.

62. *Urkunde* No. 5621, printed by Gustave Emminghaus in *Zeitschrift des Vereins für thüringische Geschichte und Altertumskunde*, 2 (1857), p. 97 ff.

63. The marshal remained restricted to his courtly function and was unnamed in 1499—in contrast to 1498.

64. In 1498 only supplications were to be taken up in strict order of their arrival.

65. In Brandenburg, on the other hand, *Ratschläge* were "written transactions with the Estates, especially their petitions to the territorial ruler, their proposals and complaints." Martin Hass, *Die Hofordnung Kurfürst Joachims II von Brandenburg* (Berlin, 1910, *Eberings historische Studien*, 87), p. 107.

66. Friedrich Beck, *Zur Entstehung der zentralen Landesfinanzbehörde im ernestinischen Sachsen im 16. und 17. Jahrhundert*, p. 288 ff.

67. *Rentmeister* may be understood as a plurality (Grosse, *op. cit.*, p. 65 f.). In 1494 the councillor and bailiff at Weida, Heinrich Mönch, was appointed *Rentmeister* of Thuringia, Vogtland, and Franconia (*Reg. Rr. S*, 1–316 No. 1205). Mönch was regularly called for the reckoning of accounts, hence, *Rentmeister* in the original sense was purely the title of a control official. His district of control coincided with the territory ruled in 1513–1525 by Duke Johann. Mönch's post remained unoccupied after his death, probably in 1505. The co-existence of two chambers (from 1513) was retained from 1525 to 1547 (cf. the pertinent accounts in *Reg*. Bb). See also Mentz, *op. cit.*, p. 187.

68. I have encountered the designations *refir* and *refirer* only in the conciliar tax promulgations of 1498 (cf. note 50) and in the conciliar order of 1498; they include all local officials who in any way exercised the authority of the sovereign over subjects (bailiffs, *Schösser*, customs officials, etc.).

69. Since the time of Flehinger's, the previous secretary's chancellorship, secretaries were apparently appointed only in the second decade of the sixteenth century.

70. The two other keys were in the keeping of the *Hofmeister* and two councillors. Outgoing correspondence was to be readied with "our usual seal and title." Whether "great and difficult matters" were provided with the privy seal cannot be determined without closer examination of the documents.

71. Though during Frederick's reign the sovereign's signature still appeared on princely letters.

72. See note 41, above.

73. Against this interpretation we may point to the interest which Frederick showed even in later years in the Habsburg administrative organization. For example, the Ernestine archive holds contemporary copies of the major part of the Lower Austrian governmental constitution (*Regimentsordnung*) of 1501 (*Reg*. Rr. S., 332 No. 33) and an undated regulation of Maximilian for councillors, court servants, and parties appearing before

the councillors for the duration of his stay at Linz (*Reg.* Rr. S., 333 No. 4 39 a).

74. The Albertine court constitution of 1488–96—printed in *Deutsche Hofordnungen des 16. und 17. Jahrhunderts*, ed. Arthur Kern, Vol. 2 (Berlin, 1907, *Denkmäler der deutschen Kulturgeschichte*, II, 2), p. 27 ff.—appointed "four regular councillors," "four councillors at our councillors' table," and three councillors "which we, when traveling abroad leave behind." Times were established for daily meetings. The court constitution has been erroneously dated 1470–80 until now. Our *termini a quo* and *ad quem* result from the facts that Hans von Minckwitz is named as steward (from 1488) and Duke Georg as unmarried (married 1496). By means of a closer examination of personal history the dating can undoubtedly be made more precise. Goerlitz, *op. cit.*, p. 422, did not know this constitution. The Albertine conciliar constitution is still quite undifferentiated. From this and from the number of regular councillors corresponding in Ernestine circumstances, one may suggest that this simple form of conciliar constitution existed before 1485. Unfortunately, the monograph of Hans Hofmann, *Hofrat und landesherrliche Kanzlei im meissnischalbertinischen Sachsen vom 13. Jahrhundert bis 1547–48* (typescript diss., Leipzig, 1920), was not at my disposal. I was referred to the abstract in *Jahrbuch der philosophischen Fakultät der Universität Leipzig*, 2 (1920), p. 174 f.

75. Paul Kirn, *Friedrich der Weise und die Kirche* (Leipzig and Berlin, 1926, *Beitr. z. Kulturgeschichte des Mittelalters und der Renaissance* 30), p. 17.

76. Abundant evidence exists for this. The fact that many of the higher official families were members of a close-knit circle must have contributed to the homogeneity of their group, though one cannot find in electoral Saxony a "homogeneously formed great family," of official class, as has been claimed for Hessen by Karl Ernst Demandt, "Amt und Familie. Eine soziologisch-genealogische Studie zur hessischen Verwaltungsgeschichte des 16. Jahrhundert," *Hessisches Jahrbuch für Landesgeschichte*, 2 (1952), p. 79 ff.

77. Doctor of both laws, but a canon lawyer, 1493–99, active as chancellor of the archbishop of Magdeburg. See also Emil Friedberg, *Die leipziger Juristenfakultät* (Leipzig, 1909), p. 125.

78. The same distinction was made in Dresden.

79. Perhaps also Wittenberg and Coburg.

80. *Reg.* Rr. S, 317 No. 1b *Reg.* D. 468.

81. Cf. the compilation by Burckhardt, *op. cit.*, p. xxxiv f. Burckhardt's other claims about Ernestine finances are partially uncertain, partially false.

82. For example: Dr. Georg Brück, since 1520–23 Johann's chancellor, was frequently called to the elector's court or sent on foreign assignments.

83. Cf., for example, the frequent consultation of Wittenberg professors.

84. The appointment of Hans von Minckwitz as chief privy councillor, *Hofrat* and high marshal (1532, several months before Johann's death) appears to be a last reaction to this development. After Minckwits' death, the office of *Hofrat* probably remained vacant; from 1542, the chancellor became chairman of the council. Cf. Mentz, *op. cit.*, p. 137 and 126.

85. In the memoranda of several councillors (March 19, 1531), going back to the demands of the Estates for reduced court expenditures. Staatsarchiv Coburg, Loc. F4; excerpts of which appear in Burckhardt, *op. cit.*, p. 218 ff.

86. One of them must have been Chancellor Brück, well known from Reformation history. The further development of the personal government proceeded from the chamberlain, cf. Beck, *op. cit.* Among the Albertines, where there was only one residence in Dresden, the development was the opposite; in 1491 Albert's former doorkeeper Georg von Weide assumed the *Rentmeister's* office with his seat in Leipzig. Actual financial policy-making was in the hands of the duke himself, with the aid of favored councillors. The chamber at Dresden was restricted to the keeping of accounts; the doorkeeper there was apparently without any significance. The guidance of finances finally lay with the duke and his favored councillors. We have no information on conditions until 1547. Goerlitz, *op. cit.*, p. 417 ff.

87. Mentz, *op. cit.*, p. 126 ff.

88. For the following cf. Paul Steinmann, "Finanz-Verwaltungs -Wirtschafts- und Regierungspolitik der mecklenburgischen Herzöge im Übergang vom Mittelalter zur Neuzeit," *Jahrbuch des Vereins für mecklenburgische Geschichte und Altertumskunde*, 86 (1922), p. 107 ff., and C. A. Endler, "Hofgericht, Zentralverwaltung und Rechtsprechung der Räte in Mecklenburg im 16. Jahrhundert," *Mecklenburgisch-Strelitzer Geschichtsblätter*, 1 (1925), p. 118 ff.

89. In the Landeshauptarchiv Mecklenburg at Schwerin.

90. K. Dülfer, "Fürst und Verwaltung. Grundzüge der hessischen Verwaltungsgeschichte im 16.-19. Jahrhundert," *Hessisches Jahrbuch für Landesgeschichte*, 3 (1953), p. 160. In regard to the Hessian council under Wettin guardianship (1509–1514), cf. Gundlach, *op. cit.*, Vol. 1 (Marburg, 1931), 135 ff.

91. Landeshauptarchiv Magdeburg, *Rep.* A 2 No. 4. This may be only a clear copy in draft.

92. See Elizabeth Bamberger, "Die Finanzverwaltung in den deutschen Territorien des Mittelalters (1200–1500)," *Zeitschrift für die gesammten Staatswissenschaften*, 77 (1923), p. 168 ff., an unsatisfactory general treatment.

93. Cf. Georg von Below, "Die städtische Verwaltung des Mittelalters als Vorbild der späteren Territorialverwaltung," *HZ*, 75 (1895), p. 435 f.

94. Eduard Rosenthal, *Geschichte des Gerichtswesens und der Verwaltungsorganization Baierns*, Vol. 1 (Würzburg, 1889), pp. 291 ff. and 316 ff.

95. In the sixteenth century both treasuries were often designated as *Rentkammer* and *Hofkammer*.

96. For Wolfenbüttel: Helmut Samse, *Die Zentralverwaltung in den südwelfischen Landen vom 15. Jahrhundert bis zum 17. Jahrhundert* (Hildesheim and Leipzig, 1940, *Quellen und Darstellungen zur Geschichte Niedersachsens*, 49), pp. 11, 205 and 316. For Calenberg: Samse, *op. cit.*, pp. 19, 274 and 320. For Mecklenburg: Steinmann, *op. cit.*, p. 103 f. For Pomerania: Martin

Spahn, *Verfassungs- und Wirtschaftsgeschichte des Herzogtums Pommern* . . .
(1478-1625) (Leipzig, 1896, *Staats-und sozialwissenschaftliche Forschungen*
XIV, 1), p. 87 note 3, and Herbert Koch, *Beiträge zur innerpolitischen
Entwicklung des Herzogtums Pommern im Zeitalter der Reformation* (Greifs-
wald, 1939, *Pommern einst und jetzt*, 3), p. 74 ff. For Henneberg: Ulrich
Hess, *Die Verwaltung der Grafschaft Henneberg 1584-1660*, (typescript diss.,
Würzburg, 1944), p. 53 ff.

97. Gerhard Schapper, *Die Hofordnung von 1470 und die Verwaltung am Berliner
Hofe zur Zeit Kurfürst Albrechts* (Berlin 1912, *Veröffentlichungen des Vereins
für Geschichte der Mark Brandenburg*), pp. 102 f., 106 f., 117, and 120. Hass,
op. cit., p. 219 ff. On the doorkeeper and chamberlain in Brandenburg see:
Hass, *op. cit.*, p. 165 ff.; Otto Hintze, *Hof-und Landesverwaltung in der
Mark Brandenburg unter Joachim II*, reprinted in *Gesammelte Abhandlungen*,
ed. Fritz Hartung, Vol. 3 (Leipzig, 1943), pp. 241 f. and 277 ff.

98. Ulrich Schrecker, *Das landesfürstliche Beamtentum in Anhalt* . . . *1200-1574*
(Breslau, 1906, *Untersuchungen zur deutschen Staats-und Rechtsgeschichte*, 86),
p. 97.

99. The present state of research does not allow suppositions as to the role of
jurists from central German universities (above all Leipzig) in the introduction and reception of Roman law.

100. The history of the provincial *Hofgericht* in Wettin lands has been totally
neglected, with the exception of Gerhard Siller, *Das Hofgericht zu
Coburg* (typescript diss., Erlangen, 1951). for the *Oberhofgericht*, see K. G.
Günther, *Das Privilegium de non appellando des kur-und fürstlichen Hauses
Sachsen* (Dresden and Leipzig, 1788); Christian Gottfried Kretschmann,
Geschichte des churchfürstlich sächsischen Oberhofgerichtes zu Leipzig (Leipzig,
1804); Alfred Lobe, *Ursprung und Entwicklung der höchsten sächsischen
Gerichte* (Leipzig, 1905). Cf. also Goerlitz, *op. cit.*, p. 182 f.

101. Adolf Stölzel, *Die Entwicklung der gelehrten Rechtssprechung*, Vol. 2
(Berlin, 1910), p. 568 ff.

102. The constitutions of the *Oberhofgericht* of 1488 and 1493 are printed in
Kretschmann, *op. cit.*, pp. 27 ff. and 45 ff.

103. Cf. Endler, *op. cit.*, p. 119, ff.

104. Hans Spangenberg, "Die Entstehung des Reichskammergerichts und die
Anfänge der Reichsverwaltung," *Zeitschrift für Rechtsgeschichte (Germanistische Abteilung)*, 46 (1926), p. 273 note 3; Kurt Forstreuter, *Vom Ordens-
staat zum Fürstentum* (Kitzingen, 1951), p. 22 f., with bibliography and a
careful consideration of the activities of Frederick and his Saxon councillors. Frederick's court constitution has its parallel also in the Dresden court
constitution of 1502 (cf. note 74).

7 The Reception of Roman Law in Germany: An Interpretation

WOLFGANG KUNKEL

A noted legal historian, Wolfgang Kunkel was born in 1902 and has taught at the universities of Freiburg, Göttingen, Bonn, and—from 1956—Munich, where he is Professor of Roman and Civil Law and Director of the Leopold-Wenger Institute of the History of Ancient Law. Kunkel has made a specialty of the history of the impact of Roman law on European legal ideas and institutions, and has published a number of books and articles on ancient and medieval law and on Roman jurists. There is an English translation of one of his books: *An Introduction to Roman Legal and Constitutional History*, trans. J. M. Kelly (Oxford, 1966).

THE historical process known as the reception of Roman law in Germany has long been an object of research and scholarly discussion. The fact that, toward the end of the Middle Ages, the indigenous German law in all its abundant and various manifestations went into decline, to be replaced by alien legal theory and, to a very large extent also by alien legal norms and institutions—a fact of great importance for the subsequent course of the development of law in Germany—has time and again fascinated legal and general historians, especially after the Romantic movement had rediscovered the values of medieval culture and had surrounded them with an aura of poetic mystery and national pride. Hardly any other branch of legal history has aroused so many passions as the history of this reception. There have been bitter incriminations of Germany's national past, and "guilty parties" have been portrayed in blackest hues, all to the detriment of unbiased historical assessment.

The actual process by which Roman law came to prevail in Germany has been known in its essentials for over three hundred years. A substantially accurate account of it was provided as early as 1643 by the Helmstädt professor Hermann Conring in his treatise *De origine iuris Germanici*. Conring opposed the then widespread opinion that the validity of Roman law was based ultimately on its introduction in the ninth century by Emperor Lothar II, the great-grandson of Charlemagne. He showed that this was a legend, that in fact Roman law had never been imposed by imperial decree either in Italy or in Germany. Before the fifteenth century, Conring argued, Roman law had hardly been known in Germany, and in any case had never been put into practice. Then, in the course of the fifteenth century, it had begun to prevail in law courts and in princes' councils due to the influence of jurists trained in Roman law. These were the men responsible for its proliferation. Soon the law was being taught at universities, and the imperial Chamber Court, newly set up in 1495, was expressly obliged to apply it. Furthermore—so Conring—Roman law had found its way into other German courts, not by means of imperial statutes or decrees, but simply through tacit adoption or in virtue of particular prescriptions issued by territorial rulers or cities.

Conring's account of the course of the reception has been considerably filled out and emended by later scholars, especially during the nineteenth and twentieth centuries, but its main outlines have remained intact. The object of the—often rather heated—scholarly discussions was not so much the *course* of the reception itself, as its interpretation and historical evaluation, its causes, its nature, and the question of whether it was historically inevitable or merely a historical accident. But in recent years these old problems have been approached from a somewhat different and, to my mind, more promising point of view, which tempts me to take them up once again and to offer a synthesis of the ideas that have emerged from the most recent literature, as well as a few which have occurred to me from my own work with the materials of the reception.

Two technical objections must nowadays be raised against all earlier attempts at interpretation. First, the older views saw the reception as an isolated event in the history of German law, and, secondly, they placed far too much emphasis on the institutional aspect of the reception.

As regards the first point, it is, of course, true that the reception of Roman law has always been seen as the incursion of a European movement into Germany. Even Conring was aware that Roman law had come to Germany from Italy. It was scarcely possible to overlook the fact that the teaching and the practice of Roman law had also secured a foothold in France and Spain, and even as far afield as Poland and Hungary. All the same, much too little thought has so far been devoted to developments outside Germany, and this has resulted in a number of mistaken ideas. It has simply been assumed that the reception in Germany was in some way extraordinary, that Germany had suffered a catastrophe while other countries had managed, somehow, to avoid it.

More important than this is the second point. Nineteenth-century positivist scholarship approached the reception chiefly as a problem of the legal sources. Its main interest was to find out whether, when, and to what extent the norms of Roman law had become known and established in Germany and elsewhere. This was taken as the measure of the scope of the reception, but such a limitation kept the question superficial and obscured the real nature of the phenomenon and its underlying causes.

Nowadays, however, a start, at least, has been made toward the reassessment of the problem. Ever since the publication of Koschaker's important work, *Europa und das römische Recht*,[1] it has come to be understood that the reception as a whole was essentially European in character, a movement of which the German reception was simply a part. Moreover, the reception is now known to be principally a transformation in the categories of legal thought, involving the sudden appearance within the medieval legal world of a "scientific", rational or academic view of law. Changes in the actual content of the positive law, however important these may have been in themselves, now appear to be secondary, explicable only from the vantage point of the basic intellectual metamorphosis. This latter idea is a specially distinctive feature of Wieacker's brilliant treatment of the reception in his *Privatrechtsgeschichte der Neuzeit*,[2] a book with which my own considerations will have numerous points of contact. Nonetheless, Wieacker seems to me, on the one hand, to push his basic idea rather too far in assessing the material consequences of the reception, and on the other hand not to go far enough with it when discussing the connections among its causal factors. In these points, then, I shall be taking issue with him as sharply as with the older view that has prevailed hitherto.

According to a doctrine that has been traditional since the nineteenth century and is strongly emphasized even by Koschaker today, the reception took place in two stages. There was first a "theoretical" and then a "practical" reception. The theoretical reception was the emerging conviction that the *Corpus Iuris Civilis* was binding upon the medieval Holy Roman Empire because its emperor stood as the successor of the Caesars. This "theoretical reception" was then followed by the practical reception, the realization of this idea in the actual adoption of Roman law in Germany. But since the notion of the continuity of the *Imperium Romanum* had flourished as early as the tenth century under Otto III, and then again under the Hohenstaufen, the theoretical reception—at least as far as Germany was concerned—must have come several centuries before the practical reception. The second, or practical, stage could not begin until the basis of the first stage—the medieval ideal of the Holy Roman Empire—had been weakened by the realities of political life. This would indeed be a strange case of retarded ignition, unparalleled in history. Furthermore, as Wieacker rightly points out, Roman law established itself not only in the empire, but also, and roughly at the same time, in countries that had long disclaimed any connection with the *Imperium Romanum*. Then again, as Hermann Krause showed in his *Kaiserrecht und Rezeption*,[3] the medieval German sources do not associate the concept of imperial law with the Roman legal sources (that is to say, with the *Corpus iuris*), even in passing, as the supporters of theoretical reception had always supposed. It is this fact which seems to me to prove once and for all that the concept of a "theoretical reception" is a false historical construction. The sole element of truth in it is the view that the encouragement received by Roman law from the twelfth century onward in medieval Italy found intellectual and political support in the notion of the *Imperium* current in the time of the Hohenstaufen. But other factors must have been ultimately responsible for the spread of this Italian-inspired science of juris-prudence throughout western and central Europe, and thus for the reception in Germany, too. True enough, German jurists, following the traditional teachings of the Italians, endeavored to justify the application of Roman norms by reference to the *Imperium*; they spoke—for the first time in Germany—of the *Corpus iuris* as "imperial laws." Yet in France and Spain, where the supremacy of the emperor was no more than a myth and had been expressly disputed for a long time, and where—for that very reason—the reception ran counter to prevailing political ideas, it managed to establish itself nonetheless, and in so doing created the odd necessity of using Roman law to refute the Italian doctrine of the emperor's supremacy, a doctrine which was itself based on Roman law. A considerable number of prominent French and Spanish jurists of the sixteenth century applied themselves with great dedication to this task. It is this which makes it especially clear that the process dividing the Middle Ages from the modern world in the field of law was set in motion by forces far more elemental and irresistible than the crumbling idea of the *Imperium Romanum*.

The process in question was the diffusion of a scholarly discipline which had been flourishing in Italy ever since the end of the eleventh century. The law schools where it was taught were renowned throughout Europe as early as the twelfth and thir-teenth centuries. They attracted students from the whole of western and central Europe, not least from Germany. At the more important Italian law universities—especially at Bologna, the oldest, and at Padua, which had the largest German attendance of all during the late Middle Ages—the Germans had formed their own corporation of scholars, the *natio Germanica*, whose importance can be inferred from the fact that it possessed privileges not enjoyed by other nations. Among the law schools in southern France, established in the twelfth and thirteenth centuries as offshoots of the Italian universities, Orléans at least had a *natio Germanica*. Thus, even during the high Middle Ages there was no shortage of German jurists who had studied Roman law abroad and taken their knowledge home with them. This fact immediately prompts the question why Roman law did not make its way into German legal life then and there. It seems that the German jurists of the thirteenth and fourteenth centuries, judging from what we know at present of their lives and activities, were for the most part members of the clergy. Even the sons of princes and noblemen then studying at Bologna, Padua, and other universities in Italy or France were probably destined in the main for a clerical career. The academic degrees brought home by these jurists were taken almost exclusively in canon law, though such degrees, to be sure, presupposed a certain familiarity with Roman law. Back in Germany, the legally trained cleric found employment in the service of the church or of a prince or city; or, again, he worked as a lawyer in church courts, where academic law had already come into use. The important part played by these men in preparing the way for the reception has been repeatedly emphasized, though it continues on the whole to be underestimated. Those clerical jurists who had been working ever since the thirteenth century as chancellors and councillors of princes or as town clerks and advocates in the larger cities were the forerunners of the men who, from the middle of the fifteenth century onward, were to intervene decisively in the development of the reception. The older councillors and advocates probably served their masters mainly as diplomats or as legal advisers in litigation before ecclesiastical courts; but they would certainly have taught princes and municipal councillors to value the study and practice of academic law. Ecclesiastical courts, too, inasmuch as their claims to competence went far beyond the sphere of ecclesiastical law proper, exercising a far-reaching influence on the legal life of the nation, familiarized larger circles of the population with the nature and function of Roman canon law as well as with the responsibilities of academically trained lawyers. This has been clearly brought out in a recent article by Erich Genzmer[4] on the accusations directed by Hugo von Trimberg, a schoolmaster in Bamberg, against the jurists—he used that word, in about 1300—in his clumsy didactic poem entitled "Der Renner." In an episcopal city like Bamberg the learned lawyer (and the semi-learned, money-grabbing advocate as well) must have been familiar figures indeed. Thus the foreign law and its learned adepts came before the eyes of the German public well before the fifteenth century.

All the same, I cannot agree with Genzmer that these and other possible traces of learned law provide sufficient grounds to allow us to speak of an "early reception," occurring in the twelfth and thirteenth centuries. All this "early reception" came to, in effect, was the use of canonical and Roman law in ecclesiastical courts. Neither learned jurists nor their law penetrated into the non-ecclesiastical sphere, where, apart from various isolated influences which cannot be considered here, German law continued undisturbed right up into the fifteenth century. It should also be realized that until the middle of the fifteenth century it was largely only canon law that was taught at German universities. The older German universities—Prague, Vienna, Heidelberg, Cologne, and Erfurt, all founded in the fourteenth century— were centers of theological study on the lines of Paris, not law schools like the Italian universities. Masters and students were almost without exception clerics. The discipline of Roman law, whenever it was taken up, mostly in passing, therefore served merely as an adjunct to canonistic training.

There was no change in this situation until the fifteenth century; but when change did come the pace was almost precipitous. Several of the universities newly founded in the second half of the fifteenth century, Basel (1460) and Tübingen (1477), for example, were endowed from the very start with chairs of Roman law; the remainder, and even the older universities, were quick to follow. By the turn of the century the study of Roman law was beginning to force canon law very much into the background. Masters and students tended now to be laymen; not clerics. Most of the early teachers were foreigners, coming from Italy, southern France, and even Spain. At about the same time more and more Germans went to study at Italian and French universities, but now it was mostly the sons of the nobility and the city patriciate who went across the Alps. Simultaneously, Roman law began to make inroads into the courts and into the legal records of the territories and the cities.

The process of this adoption of Roman law into legal life in Germany extended over a long period of time and took different forms in the various parts of the empire. It has not by any means been fully investigated. The traditional view holds that the reception was completed in principle with the *Reichskammergerichts-ordnung*—the organization of the Imperial Chamber Court—of 1495, according to which half the assessors must hold a doctorate, and the court was instructed to reach its verdict "in accordance with the common laws of the empire." But this is a dangerous oversimplification of the historical facts. It is true that the Imperial Chamber Court came to be a model for territorial high courts, and probably even hastened their institution or reform, since this was the only way the electors and other major territorial sovereigns could guard their *privilegia de non appellando* which exempted them wholly or in part from the *Kammergericht*. But it can hardly be claimed that developments in the territories would have been essentially different had it not been for the institution of the Imperial Chamber Court; they were under way before 1495 and were to go on for a long time afterward. It is particularly important to discard an idea obvious to the modern legal mind, namely, that the court's jurisdiction must have had a determining and concrete influence upon other courts in the realm. The scope of the court's work was much too narrow to have accomplished this feat, and its jurisdiction was concerned predominantly with the sort of cases that offered no occasion for the direct application of Roman law. Moreover, there did not then exist a means for the wider dissemination of the court's judicature. It was not until the second half of the sixteenth century, when selected verdicts came to be published, that the court's jurisprudence began to gain esteem and influence, though this impact could not have been much greater than that of the collections of learned opinions published by individual jurists.

A distinctive feature of the development in the individual territories and cities was often—though by no means always—the publication of more or less comprehensive collections of laws, and these now contained mainly Roman law, preserving German law only in a number of points, particularly as regards marital property and real estate, though even here the style was more or less Roman. It is worth noting that the cities of southern Germany took the lead in this development; the princely territories did not follow until appreciably later, most of them only during the second half of the sixteenth century. The significance of these "reformations" of city and territorial law, which were the work of the learned city syndics and princes' counsellors, seems to me very often to have been wrongly assessed. It goes without saying that, seen from the political perspective, they were expressions of the newly consolidated power of the state, as were the princes' high courts and the centralization of territorial administrative organizations. But judged from the point of view of legal history, they represented on the whole not so much an advance of academic Roman law as a measure designed to cope with an emergency in legal practice resulting from the chaotic and peculiar way in which the reception had come about. For the most part they signify not a deliberate, systematic attempt to put the reception into effect, but simply the recognition and acceptance of the reception by the sovereign power.

This can be clearly demonstrated in the case of one city codification belonging to the early families of urban reformations: the Frankfurt reformation of 1509. Thanks to the particularly fortunate archival circumstances in Frankfurt it was possible for Helmut Coing[5] to investigate the penetration of Roman law into judicial practice in Frankfurt with an accuracy which would be difficult, if not impossible, to achieve elsewhere. Coing was able to show that right up to the beginning of the 1480's no traces of Roman law are to be seen in the Frankfurt court documents, despite the fact that the city had long employed procurators and municipal advocates who were more or less versed in Roman law. It was the function of these jurists to represent the imperial city in litigation before the ecclesiastical court in Mainz and in political negotiations with the empire or other territorial authorities. This was all they did, even in later years. Only from about 1482 on did aspects of Roman law begin to appear, at first merely occasionally and marginally, in the court documents—not in the verdicts as yet, but in the presentations of litigants. After about 1489 or 1490, however, a number of verdicts can be found to conform so closely to the Romanist elements in the presentations that it becomes reasonable to suppose that an academically trained lawyer had had a hand in them. In these cases the *Schöffen*, or jurors, must have turned to the city advocate for advice.

Around 1495 the use of Roman law by the litigants began to increase considerably. Law professors from the neighboring legal faculty at Mainz and procurators of the Imperial Chamber Court (established that year in Frankfurt) appeared as attorneys, and these men insisted that the hitherto purely oral proceedings be replaced by a written one. As soon as this written procedure was admitted the gates were open to the substantive Roman law as well. From then on until the beginning of the sixteenth century Roman law rapidly succeeded in establishing itself. The outcome was sheer confusion. Written and oral procedures existed side by side. Untrained jurors understood neither the procedural rules of written trials nor the substantive provisions of Roman law. The old principles of Frankfurt law, mostly an uncodified, unrationalized customary law applicable only in concrete cases, became uncertain and indistinct. It could not for long resist the dialectic of the learned jurists. This was the state of affairs which the Reformation of 1509 was intended to set right. Its most important innovation was the establishment of a trial procedure based on the principles of Roman and canon law and comprehensible even to laymen. In particular, oral trial procedure was restricted to disputes involving sums of less than thirty gulden. Above this level, written procedures became obligatory. This procedural reform was the most important and far-reaching item in the new statute book; as regards substantive law, the jurors might seek the city advocate's advice before reaching their verdict, but the trial procedure had to be conducted from the very outset according to the correct forms. For the rest, revision was limited to matters relating to private law, especially those which had recently been disputed because of the conflict between traditional law and the principles of the new jurisprudence. These involved mainly wills, marital property, guardianship, and lien. The legislator generally clarified the legal position in these matters by energetically Romanizing the traditional local law—this, incidentally, was in contrast to reforms, elsewhere, which tended to preserve the older accustomed institutions.

A review of these events seems to me to show that the authorities tended to be passive in their attitude toward the reception. The influence of academic jurisprudence and the consequent acceptance of Roman legal principles became established in the courts essentially through the activities of the litigating parties and their advocates. Municipal government did not intervene until traditional trial procedures had become completely unhinged and a considerable degree of confusion had arisen in substantive law. The legal principles decided upon in this predicament were intended as a means of coping with a distinct emergency. Their strongly Romanizing tendency is probably explained by the personal influence of the city advocate Schönwetter, a soundly trained, energetic jurist, but a man utterly preoccupied with the categories of his discipline. No one seems to have thought of the possibility of reforming the judicial organization through the appointment of trained judges: the traditional court of jurors, composed of laymen (the councillors of the first two benches), was still in existence in Goethe's time.[6]

It is obviously impossible to draw general conclusions from the experience of an imperial city such as Frankfurt and assume without further argument that things were the same in the princely territories. In the territories there were often particular conditions and tendencies favoring the reception which did not obtain in the cities. It is difficult for us today to imagine the utterly fragmented condition of the late medieval legal system with its myriad local jurisdictions; given this situation, the attainment of some measure of uniformity in legal norms and administration must have seemed a vital necessity to sovereigns in their attempts to consolidate their political powers. And such attempts could hardly fail to result in a more or less strongly pronounced Romanization, not only because the creation of this legal unity lay in the hands of the princes' legal advisers, but also because the extremely fragmentary provisions of customary law rarely assured a basis for unity. Formal uniformity and Romanization, particularly as regards the conduct of trials, was also urged by the princely high courts, which, as courts of appeal, found themselves obliged to quash all verdicts wherever the conduct of a case had not followed their own norms and complied with regulations provided in Roman law. There is therefore good reason to assume that in the princely territories the reception was promoted by the authorities to a far greater extent than in the cities, that is to say, by princes who were bent on extending their sovereignty and by their councillors who were charged with responsibilities in political and legal administration. But it is surely going too far to claim—as Wieacker has now done, renewing arguments advanced by others before him—that the ultimate reason for the reception was the political transformation at the beginning of the sixteenth century, with its systematic and rational extension of territorial authority. According to this view, princes entrusted their academic advisers with the administration of justice, as well as with political administration; thus the reception was primarily the task of these trained jurists, though indirectly it was the work of the princes. There is certainly a measure of truth in this view, but it looks at the matter too much from one angle. In princely territories, just as in cities, there existed a powerful movement from below, so to speak, from the litigants, in favor of the learned law. One need only gather together the scattered traces of this movement to see what really happened. We see some of these traces in the realization, gained as long as seventy years ago by Stölzel in his work with Hessian sources,[7] that during the course of the reception the litigants gradually turned from the untrained courts of jurors to the learned or semilearned officials of their territorial sovereigns. One appealed to these officials as *Güteinstanz*, as arbitrators, because the litigating parties (or at any rate their legal advisers) expected a more rational verdict from them than from the traditional courts, which as time went on found their work drying up. A further indication in this direction can be taken from the frequent complaints about the activities of semilearned, or sometimes even pseudo-learned, lawyers who exploited the litigiousness of their clients for their own profit and impudently humbugged the untrained jurors. Melchior von Ossa, a councillor of the electorate of Saxony, who died in 1557, referred pointedly to this widespread abuse in his so-called "Testament," a memorandum addressed to the elector. Melanchthon, too, complained about it.[8] A good deal, in fact, of the criticism which arose during the sixteenth century, and which earlier scholars often interpreted simply as a protest against Roman law as such, was really directed against abuses of this sort in legal practice. It can doubtless be assumed from these expressions that the litigants themselves were very largely responsible for calling in the learned, or apparently learned, jurists, and with them the Roman law. This, however, would mean that the reception was not promoted in sovereign territories by the authorities alone, but rather that activities in high quarters were either complemented or—as the relatively late origin of many territorial codifications would suggest—in many cases even anticipated from below. Indeed, the reform of the courts and the standardization of territorial law does not seem to have been felt by all the sovereigns to be a particularly urgent part of their responsibilities. Legal reform did not yield higher revenues, as did administrative rationalization, and one would have to credit the princes with an unusual farsightedness to think that they foresaw the growth of power that it would one day bring to them. Moreover, demands for legal reform and standardization sometimes came from the territorial diets rather than from the princes. And in a number of territories no reform took place at all.

It will be necessary, for all these reasons, to set the problem in a wider context, though this is not to deny that the reception was most certainly bound up with political developments separating the Middle Ages from the modern world. The penetration of professional, academic jurisprudence and its law into Germany was not solely the work of the princes and a relatively small number of counsellors and city syndics. It was the product, if not of a popular movement, then at least of a trend that must have seized broad sections of the population. This is the only possible explanation of a number of characteristic phenomena: the sudden expansion of the study of law at universities both in Germany and abroad, the widespread abuses of semilearned charlatans, and the great success enjoyed by the popular literature on Roman law which began to appear at the turn of the fifteenth and sixteenth centuries.[9] It all suggests an open-minded attitude, and a faith in the value and usefulness of professional, academic jurisprudence, and anyone wishing to grasp the real nature of the reception of Roman law must try to understand this faith.

We have seen that such a faith could never have been founded on the fading notion of the *Imperium Romanum*. Nor could it have been advanced by merely practical considerations rising from an impression that Roman law had proven more workable than traditional German law; in particular that it had shown itself more suitable for practical legal requirements in the age of early capitalism. The commercial world of the late Middle Ages had long since created institutions of its own, and it was only by means of bold analogies that Italian jurists had managed to connect these with Roman law at all. Important centers of trade and industry, like Lübeck and Nuremberg, had proved much more resistant to the inroads of positive Roman law than smaller cities and essentially rural territories. In any case, it was not Roman law as such which established itself, but jurists and their professional, that is, rational, approach to law. If there was a connection between early capitalism and the reception, then it is simply that both were products of that rational mentality which set the fifteenth and sixteenth centuries apart from the Middle Ages.

Much the same can be said for the relationship between the reception and humanism. It may be true that the growing number of young men from noble and middle-class families studying at Italian universities assisted the spread of humanism in Germany; and conversely it may also be true—as Coing has shown in the instance of Frankfurt—that the humanist proclivities of some urban patricians furthered the cause of Roman law. But on the whole Wieacker[10] must be right in asserting that the two movements were basically at odds with each other. Humanists abhorred legal dialectic for its essentially medieval methods and its swollen, cumbersome language. Nonetheless it seems to me that both movements were simply different expressions of one and the same process: the growing secularization of learning. It is striking how the spread of Italian jurisprudence occurred not only in Germany, but also in France and England, at the very same time as the expansion of humanism.

In southern France, to be sure, offshoots of Italian law schools had existed as early as the thirteenth century, and in the Provence Roman law had remained in force throughout. This, together with the proximity of the universities of upper Italy, serves to account for the early acceptance of Roman jurisprudence there. As a result of the studies of the Dutch scholar E. M. Meijers[11] it is now known that at Orléans, the most northerly of the French law schools, professors and scholars were almost exclusively clerics right up into the fifteenth century; Orléans lay in a part of France where Roman law had had just as little practical influence during the Middle Ages as in Germany. At Paris, the leading school of theology in the West, the teaching of Roman law was interdicted in 1219 by a Bull of Pope Honorius III, because many of the students, penurious and supported by monasteries or ecclesiastical foundations, seemed more than ready to give up theology for the more lucrative study of law.[12] Secular jurists obtained general recognition in France at about the same time as in Germany: during the second half of the fifteenth century, the time of the rise of humanism in France. They then proceeded to Romanize legal life to a scarcely lesser extent than in Germany, and at any rate no less than, say, in Saxony, where, due to its codification, the indigenous law had secured as sound a position as in northern France. In England, as is well known, Roman law never established itself at all, though it had been taught at Canterbury and Oxford as early as the twelfth century. Practitioners of English law had formed a professional organization as early as the fourteenth century, and their resistance proved an effective bar to a reception. But in England, too, Romanist jurisprudence made its most powerful and, for the continuity of the indigenous legal tradition, most dangerous advance at the beginning of the sixteenth century, which were the years of early English humanism and the time of the reception in Germany.[13]

Like the humanist movement, therefore, the spread of Italian jurisprudence in the fifteenth and sixteenth centuries was evidently part of a general European transition from a theologically committed intellectual culture to the principle of independent secular learning. Jurisprudence and its method of rational conceptualization, however much it may still have been based on medieval categories of thought, advanced along the same lines as the claims of the sovereign state and, even more importantly, the spirit of the urban bourgeoisie—the class which had not only assumed a dominant role since the decline of feudal culture, but had matured sufficiently to unfold its own intellectual culture, as had long been the case in Italy. The sudden diffusion of Italian jurisprudence throughout western Europe served to unleash pent-up forces, and was not unlike the wildfire spread of the Reformation and its ideas. There can be little doubt that it was the invention of printing that made it possible for such movements to spread so far and to have so profound an effect on the lives of entire nations.

Wherever Italian jurisprudence established itself, it had the effect of overthrowing medieval legal thought. In places where medieval law still had a vital part to play or, as in northern France or Saxony, where it had become firmly rooted by means of codifications, it gained a new respect as "statutory" law. But in the process it became entangled in the conceptual categories of Roman and Italian law, and thus was torn from its original context and frequently altogether reinterpreted in its meaning. On the other hand, wherever the medieval legal system had withered because of its splintering into conflicting areas of jurisdiction—as in southwestern Germany—Roman legal concepts and procedures soon introduced the positive norms of Roman law as well. Nineteenth-century scholars, with their positivist methods, tended to overestimate the variations in the extent to which the content of the indigenous law was preserved because they overlooked the structural alterations experienced by the German law itself. Postivistic scholarship placed excessive emphasis on transformations in concrete legal norms brought about by the reception; but when Wieacker claims that few changes were actually introduced into the older German law itself he seems to me to fall into the opposite extreme of reducing the reception to nothing more than a rationalization of thought about law. Practical jurisprudence is always tied to a particular set of norms, and cannot easily be detached from it. The professional discipline of the Italian jurists was especially closely bound to such norms, inasmuch as the maxims of Roman law were to them the very embodiment of rationality and truth. The adoption of their discipline inevitably involved the adoption of this legal rationality, which left very little scope indeed to the indigenous law.

There can be no denying, then, that the reception involved a total break with the past, and not only as regards the development of law in Germany. Medieval law and legal practice, rooted though it was in the feelings and ways of the people, now disappeared, to be replaced by legal experts, abstract concepts, Latin formulations, Roman norms, and the *communis opinio* of Italian legal doctors. Many elements of the declining medieval system had long been in a state of decay, but much that was still vital, too, was swept away in the general turmoil. This, to be sure, cannot have been unusual in the course of history. Academic jurisprudence brought to Germany the rational approach to law, clad in foreign garb, and with it—though as yet imperfectly implemented—ideas that legal verdicts might be based on evidence, calculation, and revision. To many contemporaries, not merely to jurists, this seemed like progress; indeed to us nowadays it appears as a necessary step.

Above all, the reception marked Germany's entry into a continental legal community which was effective into the seventeenth century and whose consequences have remained perceptible up to the present day. We may no longer enjoy the common bond of a Latin tongue, which enabled a sixteenth-century German jurist to ponder the opinions of a Spanish or French jurist along with those of the leading Italians or of his own compatriots. All the same, Europeans are still to some extent familiar with the principles of legal thought prevailing among their neighbors. The underlying unity of European legal culture is a vital heritage of our own age, and it is one that we should learn to cherish and maintain.

NOTES TO CHAPTER 7

1. Paul Koschaker, *Europa und das römische Recht* (Munich, 1st ed., 1947; 2nd ed., 1953).
2. Franz Wieacker, *Privatrechtsgeschichte der Neuzeit* (Göttingen, 1952). Cf. the present author's review in *Zeitschrift der Savigny-Stiftung, Röm. Abt.*, 71 (1954), p. 509 ff.
3. H. Krause, *Kaiserrecht und Rezeption (Abhandlungen der Heidelberger Akademie der Wissenschaften, Phil.-hist. Kl.*, 1952), 1.
4. E. Genzmer, "Hugo von Trimberg und die Juristen," *L'Europa e il diritto romano, Studi in memoria di P. Koschaker*, 1 (Milan, 1954), p. 279 ff.
5. Helmut Coing, *Die Frankfurter Reformation von 1578 und das Gemeine Recht ihrer Zeit* (Weimar, 1935); *idem, Die Rezeption des römischen Rechts in Frankfurt am Main* (Frankfurt am Main, 1939).
6. Cf. Goethe's description in Book 1 of *Dichtung und Wahrheit*.
7. Adolf Stölzel, *Die Entwicklung des gelehrten Richtertums*, 1 (1872).
8. The relevant passages are reproduced in Roderich von Stintzing, *Geschichte der deutschen Rechtswissenschaft*, 1 (1880), p. 71 f.
9. This literature has been recognized as a special type and thoroughly treated by von Stintzing, *Geschichte der populären Literatur des römisch-kanonischen Rechts in Deutschland am Ende des 15. und am Anfang des 16. Jahrhunderts* (Leipzig, 1867).

10. Franz Wieacker, "Einflüsse des Humanismus auf die Rezeption," *Zeitschrift für d. ges. Staatsrechtswissenschaft*, 100 (1940), p. 423 ff.; *idem, Privatrechtsgeschichte*, p. 75 f.
11. Eduard M. Meijers, "De Universiteit van Orléans in de XIIIᵉ eeuw." in *Tijdschr. v. Rechtsgeschiedenis*, 1 (1918), pp. 108 ff., 443 ff.; 2 (1920), p. 460 ff.
12. Cf. E. Genzmer, "Hugo von Trimberg und die Juristen," in *op. cit.*, p. 303 ff.
13. Cf. Paul Koschaker, *op. cit.*, p. 217 ff. [For several new titles of relevance to this topic, see R. J. Schoeck, "Recent Scholarship in the History of Law," *Renaissance Quarterly*, xx, 2 (1967), 279–91.]

8 On the Reception of Roman and Italian Law in Germany

GEORG DAHM

Georg Dahm is the author of numerous books on law and legal history, particularly the history of criminal law. He was born in 1904 and has taught at the universities of Leipzig, Strassburg, and Kiel. The article translated here was published without bibliographical notes; the editor has thought it proper to fill out Dahm's references. Of the works mentioned in Dahm's article, the latest editions are given, including some printed after the appearance of the article.

IT must be admitted from the start that a discussion of the reception of Roman and Italian law is a difficult, even a questionable undertaking. Few subjects seem so completely to defy summing up as that enigmatic process which, from the fourteenth century to about the middle of the sixteenth, appears so radically to have transformed the German people's attitude toward its own legal ideas and institutions. The reception—so the objection might run —is too complex a process to be surveyed in its entirety. Roman law did not rush through Germany in one mighty stream but— to continue the metaphor—split into countless small rivulets. The reception mirrored the empire's disunion in that it took varying forms in different places. It developed differently in the empire from in its localities, differently in the cities from in the territories, differently in the south and west from in the north and east. Even where external conditions were identical, variations occurred

---

The present article, with minor alterations, was originally given as a paper. It was therefore not practicable to include references to the literature. No new source material has been opened up here, but the extent to which individual points depend on the work of others will be immediately evident to the scholarly reader.

from city to city and from region to region. In some places the foreign law triumphed almost overnight by means of codification; in others it had to overcome centuries of resistance on the part of the indigenous law. Even where the new law entered through administrative practice and juridical procedure it is possible to find considerable variations not only in the actual process of reception but also in the degree of resistance to it. Furthermore, the picture offered by the reception is different in civil law from in criminal law. In civil matters, the developing legal science in Germany influenced the reception during its earliest stages. In criminal law, on the other hand, the reception was consummated—in the empire—with the introduction of the *Carolina* (the first general German criminal code, made law at the Diet of Regensburg in 1532, and named after its instigator, Charles V) at a time when the German science of criminal law had only just begun to develop.

In the face of this bewildering array of manifestations, there would appear to be much to support the view that it is pointless and, in the present state of our knowledge, actually impossible to try to form a synoptic picture of the reception. It might well be said that further progress can only be expected from monographs on particular aspects of the reception. This purpose, too, would seem already to be sufficiently well served by a whole series of important recent studies: Coing's investigation of the reception in Frankfurt, complementing such older studies as Stölzel's of the reception in Hesse and Brandenburg or of Stölzel's and Below's of the reception in Jülich and Berg, and critical editions of sources for the more recent history of private law in Germany, such as that of Kunkel, Thieme, and Beyerle.[1] It is true enough that the only hope for a future synopsis lies in individual investigations of this type—though more attention than heretofore should be given to medieval Italian law as well. Nonetheless, it is permissible—I think it is even necessary—to attempt a provisional stocktaking and undertake to interpret the reception as a whole. Monographs, after all, are ultimately meaningful only in terms of a general interpretation, and occasional attempts to stand back and consider the phenomenon in its entirety can often suggest useful new approaches. The present essay may make a modest contribution by bringing out some essential aspects of the reception and, more especially, by directing attention to a process which might be claimed to be of decisive importance. This is the encounter, occurring some time before the actual reception, during which German and Italian law were methodically brought closer to each other. It is this process which, insofar as it is possible to talk at all of single causes, enables us to understand the true character of the reception.

I

To begin with, it is an important fact that the process of reception was closely bound up with the transformation and dissolution of the German judicial system and legal procedure, and that Italian law came to Germany precisely as a modern "justiciary law." As a rule, transformations in the internal structure of law manifest themselves in changes in judicial organization and in the character and composition of the organs by which justice is administered. It is probably true in all ages that great movements in legal and constitutional history have had their causes in the history of procedural law. In Italy the re-emergence of Roman law in the course of the Middle Ages had accompanied the constitutional transition from consuls to the office of podesta, a transition that involved a transformation of judicial organization. In Germany, too, the reception began as a problem of judicial organization—at all events, it is only comprehensible in terms of the dissolution of judicial organization in Germany and the supression of the *Volksrichter*, or popular judge, in favor of the academically trained professional jurist. The old *Schöffengerichte*, tribunals of lay jurors where justice was administered by men of high local standing, superior wisdom, and practical experience— men, that is to say, who embodied in their own persons the legal consciousness of the community—gave way to a rational legal science in which the passing of judgment was placed in the hands of professionally trained academics and learned legal experts.

This development, which in the course of the fourteenth, fifteenth, and sixteenth centuries, led to a transformation of judicial organization and procedures, is not all that remote from modern experience. In our own day, too, there has been an attempt to alter the administration of justice, particularly to bring it more effectively under the control of the administrative organs of government. Thus the manner in which the medieval judicial organization was being altered was, to some extent at least, the same as in our own day.

To proceed from the general to the particular, two aspects of this transformation require our special attention. First, lawyers established their influence *outside* the realm of legal affairs. The strengthening of territorial sovereignty and the concentration of public authority in the cities—in other words, the emergence of the state in the modern sense—had the consequence of replacing older popular courts by the administrative organs of sovereign rulers or municipal governments, or at least placing these organs in a position of rivalry with the traditional institutions. Courts came to be supplemented or replaced by the ruler's chancellery, the privy councillor, or by ordinary councillors. Municipal courts existed side by side with the city's Governing Council or its individual councillors, magistrates, bailiffs, or city advocates. Rural courts coexisted with the *Amt* in its capacity as a country court. This development was further advanced by the preferences of the litigants themselves. They either agreed to recognize the competence as arbitrator of the political authority and its councillors, or else they addressed unilateral petitions to them. This practice of mobilizing the sovereign's judicial officials by means of independent petitions naturally came up against opposition on the part of the Estates, as may be seen from Below's investigations of the history of the reception in Jülich. These investigations also reveal, however, that the sovereigns, despite their sensitivity to protests of this sort, were in fact often moved to action on the basis of such petitions. There must have been an initial period of indecision during which the competence of traditional popular courts was at first complemented, then increasingly undermined, by newly created competences of extrajudicial bodies. This, of course, gradually dislodged the popular courts or at least narrowed their scope. It goes without saying that a court tied to tradition-bound procedures and encumbered by ancient conventions must inevitably lose out in competition with a modern administration which is more or less free to develop its own procedures. In this way, then, governments increasingly took over the functions of the courts, to produce, as time went on, a new judicial system staffed and developed by academically trained officials. It is well known that, from the end of the fifteenth century, governments were largely responsible for promoting the creation of the new academic status. Medieval aristocratic notions of social standing were losing ground to the modern, rational idea that academic learning was a substitute for rights acquired by birth and blood. The idea—taken over from Italy—that an academic degree placed a man on a level with persons of noble birth, opened the higher administrative and judiciary positions to academics, and enabled many able men to become members of city councils even though they did not belong to the great patrician families.

At the same time, however, a change was going on within the judiciary itself. The government did not only usurp functions that had previously belonged to the courts; it also established its influence within the actual administration of justice. The first change to make its appearance was a new and indirect method of arriving at the verdict. Officially appointed, academically trained councillors, while not formally taking over the office of popular judge, began to influence verdicts materially. The way to this development was prepared by an earlier and far-reaching change in procedural law: the emergence of written proceedings. Coing has given a detailed account of this in connection with his studies of the reception in Frankfurt, where, so it would seem, oral proceedings were being replaced by written ones round about 1500. This change in the outward form soon brought on a change of substance as well. Oral assertion and contradiction in the pressing of claims was now replaced by a logical and established sequence of written statements in which the facts were set forth and the law—now increasingly Roman law—applied to them. Here, too, the reception began with the litigating parties and their legal counsel, and it was also the litigants who, by means of arbitrational agreements and petitions, made it easier for political authorities to meddle in judicial affairs. Proceedings now having become written ones, and Roman law now being employed, it follows that the conduct of cases must have fallen increasingly to the learned advocates, who, while not actually appearing in court, advised the parties and drew up the required written statements for them. Trials were thus guided by persons who did not even appear on the scene.

This process repeated itself in the courts. Popular judges, finding themselves in some embarrassment when confronted by unfamiliar written statements, either tried to evade having to pass judgment altogether, or else attempted to bring the parties to an amicable settlement. If they could not end the matter in this way, they turned for expert advice to learned or semilearned jurists—legal consultants, syndics, city advocates, or town clerks—who were thus drawn into the discussions and took it upon themselves to prepare an authoritative draft verdict. This system of discussion, or consultation, and mediated decision through persons and institutions outside the actual courts, was a distinctive feature of justice at that time. In Germany, as earlier in Italy, it became customary not only for the litigating parties, but also for the courts and the governing authorities and their chancelleries to seek the expert opinions of jurists. From the middle of the sixteenth century on the practice of forwarding court documents to legal faculties assumed great importance. In addition to this, so-called *Schöppenstühle* made their appearance, tribunals of learned adjudicators staffed by legal scholars, some of them actually identical with faculties of law, as for example in Wittenberg and Jena. The purpose and functions of these *Schöppenstühle* has been investigated by Ernst Boehm in his study of the *Schöppenstühle* at Leipzig. Thus, in the sixteenth and seventeenth centuries, and even as late as the eighteenth, legal faculties of the great universities exerted a considerable influence over the practical work of the courts.

Even where faculties were not invested with immediate jurisdiction in criminal matters—the University of Greifswald for example—they fulfilled the function of a kind of supreme court. This was of major significance not only for the practical administration of justice, but also for the development of jurisprudence in both Italy and Germany. Theory maintained close touch with practical problems, a fact of considerable moment for the accomplishment of a successful fusion of the old law with the new. On the other hand, such a close association with practical affairs was to lead academic jurisprudence into some very dangerous trends. It tempted it into an excessive, barren casuistry and made it over-emphasize concrete details, which in turn created difficulties in grasping legal problems systematically and developing a body of sound theory. And this, conversely, had deleterious effects on the practical application of the law. What is more, the encroachment of practical concerns led to a crisis in legal study and teaching. Professors were so busy writing opinions on current cases that they had little time left for their pupils. And this, in turn, ruined legal scholarship, which thrives on theoretical formulation and synthesis as called for in the academic lecture.

Thus the judicial function of the courts became more a matter of appearance than of substance. Behind the litigants and the judges were ranged the influential authorities of advocates, law faculties, legal consultants, and all the rest. The court itself turned into a forum for announcing the decision, a mouthpiece for legal scholars and other professional jurists. The factual investigation of the matter at hand, and the passing of verdicts, were now in separate hands. Men who made the material decisions saw only the documents; they had not heard the facts of the case, or seen the litigants. Proceedings ran in two or three distinct written stages; cases were prepared in the written propositions of the litigants, advice and verdicts were requested by the court or some higher authority, and were rendered from a distance on the basis of the documents. As time went on the obvious happened: officially appointed jurists with academic training themselves became judges; material influence and formal competence had now been merged. Of special significance in this connection is the fact that jurors and the judges passing judgment were no longer kept separate, as had always been the case under the old law. The judge appointed by the political authority began during the sixteenth century to share the responsibility for rendering verdicts with the popular judge—a transitional arrangement which can be found even in the *Carolina*—until finally the jurors were pushed into the background altogether. Thus the court turned into a bureaucratic tribunal. The officially appointed judge was now alone responsible for giving verdicts. At the same time courts of jurors also began to assume a direct official status. From the beginning of the sixteenth century election of jurors was increasingly replaced by appointment on the part of the sovereign. Instead of being chosen they were now imposed from above. Though not every judge was academically trained, the emergence of officially appointed judges did give increasing importance to academic lawyers. As time went on more and more judges, and even jurors, were products of the new university learning. so that eventually high courts and courts of jurors came to be composed of professional legal experts, while the "unlearned courts" were left with a very restricted competence. A final point of significance was the extinction of the old idea that a man ought to be tried by his peers. The sovereign's councillor and the urban magistrate had little, if any, personal connection or concern with litigating parties. Finally, various courts were now able to arrange themselves in ascending order and form a hierarchy. This in turn provided the necessary condition for the system of appeals, which appeared during the second half of the fifteenth century. Verdicts might now be submitted for revision through a higher court with superior powers, and appeals could be made to the sovereign, or his chancellery, to the city council, the high court, or the territorial court. This procedure replaced the older appeal to the high court of justice, which had been based on another idea altogether. It was now no longer a matter of seeking counsel from people with greater knowledge of the law. Under the new arrangement the verdict of a lower court was referred to a higher court composed of more eminent experts, where it was examined for its correspondence to the binding legal norms. For the old high courts it was a matter of either turning straightway into courts of appeal, or gradually losing all their importance.

Thus in a number of ways and in a great variety of forms territorial and municipal government became influential in the courts. The older view, according to which justice had been considered as having its ultimate ground in the consciences of the people, where it was recognized as law by the community and by the judges, who were considered the embodiment of the community's conscience, appears to have been dealt a decisive blow by the end of the fifteenth century, giving way to an authoritarian concept of law. The emerging state was beginning to cast its shadow. It is true that the sovereign was still bound to some extent by the concept of the judicial community and the judges as its representatives. But the work of making laws and administering justice was increasingly assumed by the sovereign, who felt himself personally responsible in this sphere. At least this is what appears from Below's account of the situation in Jülich, where the Estates had expressed their wish to the duke that "no one be allowed to depart from the customary laws or remove himself to other courts;" to which the duke countered that, although he himself was not enthusiastic about the frequent petitions addressed to him, he could not reject them: "For the law and many judicial persons are not above suspicion of partisanship, furthermore matters arise which touch closely on the person of His Grace, the Duke and his prerogatives, and finally, the Duke feels responsible for poor and sick and ignorant folk, also widows and orphans, who do not know the law and cannot themselves defend their rights." Here the sovereign thought himself to be responsible for upholding the law even vis-à-vis the courts, not merely as the highest political authority, but as a supreme judge, invested with the fullness of judicial authority. Thus anyone who wished to appeal against the verdict of a court would turn either to him directly, or to his chancellery or high court. In any case, the courts themselves speeded this development. They recommended the sovereign's councillors as the best arbitrators, or sought legal advice from the council, or from the chancellery.

But the greater the power acceding to the sovereign, the more it was felt that the splintering of German law at the end of the Middle Ages, with its abundance of different jurisdictions and competences, was intolerable. Thus the desire for a law that would overcome local diversities and the claims of different Estates, and for a judicial organization applicable equally to society as a whole. As a result, judicial administration came to be concentrated in a small and easily controllable number of progressively higher courts all under the authority of the sovereign. Uniformity of law was achieved by forwarding of court records and by a system of appeals. On the other hand, however, direct appellation of extra-territorial superior courts was felt to be a threat to legal uniformity within the territory, and the practice was fought with prohibitions which at the same time established the forwarding of records and the system of appeals as an alternative.

Circumstances such as the ones described were favorable for the adoption of Roman law, though it should not be thought that the connection between these developments and the reception was anything other than subtle and complex. It is plain that the re-fashioning of judicial organizations and procedures had to occur before the adoption of the Roman law from Italy could come about. The reception is not cause, but effect of these developments. Italian law did not have to face a firmly established and close-knit juridical organization which then proceeded to crumble under its onslaught. Rather, when the foreign law began to make its way into the empire, German judicial organization was already in a state of dissolution, its associative character being replaced by the claims of an authoritarian system. The struggle against the old high courts had begun as early as the fourteenth century; even written procedures had established themselves before the recep-tion. The intrusion of political authorities into the administration of justice, the suppression of popular jurors and their replacement by appointed judges preceded the appearance of academically trained jurists. The fifteenth century, though the transformation of judicial organization was then well under way, had not as yet felt the need for the services of learned jurists, who, right up to the end of the century, were seldom to be found in the lower courts. Officials made responsible or co-responsible for giving verdicts were not, at first, experts in Roman law; even judges occupying the bench in large cities did not require legal training. Where academics were brought into service their appearance did not necessarily signify that Roman law had been adopted. Even cities averse to the adoption of Roman law, Lübeck, for example, had had academically trained syndics from an early date. Wherever Roman law was received jurists had made their appearance long before the reception. In Frankfurt jurists were the city's diplomats and consultants as early as the late fourteenth century— in other words about a century before the adoption took place.

As time went on, however, elements favoring changes in the judicial organization began to join forces with the movement toward reception. On the one hand, the unity of judgeship, that is to say, the concentration in the hands of an official appointed by the sovereign of the activities of trial judge and verdict-maker, and the centralization of the administration of justice by means of the system of appeal could be, and were, based on the authority of the Roman law. On the other hand, it was inevitable that academically trained jurists, now increasingly occupying higher administrational and judicial positions, should prefer the universal Roman law over the indigenous, traditional law. This, in fact, is what gave such significance to the rulers' employment of extraterritorial officials, a practice deplored by the Estates, as the "foreigner" would be neither familiar nor sympathetic to the indigenous law. In Italy, too, the tendency of cities to appoint a podesta to rule over their citizens had been one of the essential reasons for the emergence and rapid spread of Roman law. Endowed with judicial authority as well as administrative powers, the alien podesta brought his own judges and notaries with him, and the law came in their train.

Roman and Italian law provided useful help also in the struggle of the territorial *raison d'état* with the notorious fragmentation of law and judicial responsibilities. Emphasis has frequently been laid on the importance of this chaotic judicial fragmentation for the reception. It is true that the lack of unity in the empire and the utter impotence of imperial legislation turned out to be fatal to the old Germanic law. Apart from constitutional and criminal law and from regulations concerning public order, no uniform imperial law was ever able to develop in Germany, and even in criminal law unity was defeated by the so-called saving clause appended to the *Carolina*. No less fatal is the fact that, up to the time of the reception, there existed no imperial court endowed with anything approaching comprehensive authority; the Imperial Chamber Court of 1495 was organized after the reception. The law establishing the Chamber Court did mention some "honorable, just, and commendable ordinances, statutes and customs" along with the laws common to the whole empire; but as a general rule there was no scope for the observance of these traditions, if only for the simple reason that the members of the court did not known them. The chaotic state of German law was therefore, and without any doubt, one of the main causes of the adoption of the alien law in the German territories. Admittedly, this does not apply to the cities, which had no need of Roman law as a means of ensuring legal uniformity. Yet the cities, particularly in the west and south of the empire, were active centers of the reception movement. At the same time, they were also pacemakers for new authoritarian political ideas. In German cities, no less than in territories, there could be found determined efforts to concentrate public authority and to secure a uniform and rational operation of legal and political administration. There, too, the principal proponent of this persuasion was a new officialdom, which no longer had any affinity with the traditional courts and the old legal ways.

All this, of course, raises once more the frequently discussed question concerning the relationship of reception and absolutism. There seems to be a general tendency nowadays to lay rather less emphasis on this connection. It is probably true to say that the development of German constitutional law was not decisively influenced by Roman constitutional law, that such maxims as

princeps legibus solutus or *quod principi placuit, legis habet vigorem*—
principles which had been given an absolutist interpretation ever
since the Dominate—did not affect German political ideas. Italian
jurists used to apply maxims of this kind to emperors who availed
themselves of Roman law in their struggle against the papacy,
but they did not attach them to territorial rulers, whose claims
found little favor in the legal opinions of the fourteenth, fifteenth,
and sixteenth centuries. On the other hand, it is true that German
absolutism was not imperial but territorial; furthermore it developed only after the reception. In the sixteenth and seventeenth
centuries it was the Estates that exerted their influence upon
government and legal matters. Indeed, in many cases, as in Jülich
or in Württemberg, it was actually the Estates that urged the
territorial sovereigns to accept Roman law and make the indigenous law correspond to the judicial forms of the Imperial Chamber
Court. All the same, an indirect connection between absolutism
and the reception can be clearly discerned, and it was brought
about by the circumstances described above. Even before the
reception, the emerging territorial state had begun to wrest the
traditional German judicial organization from its moorings, and
promoted a new judicial order which prepared the way for the
alien law. The territorial state created the need for legal uniformity
and rational judicial and political administration. This need was
filled by the foreign law and was thus responsible for its reception.

II

Now, the jurists brought with them a new conceptual and
jurisprudential style of thought. Law was no longer seen to reside
in the conscience and feeling of jurors; law was instead the end
product of learning and logical thought. Law became rationalized.
The judge's verdict must be capable of rational explanation and
may be reviewed by superior experts. The facts of the case and the
legal norm, once forming a single unity, were now separated;
facts must be demonstrated, then to be subsumed under the
appropriate legal concept.

Jurisprudential thought as it developed in Germany under the influence of the reception did not originate in Roman law. Its sources are to be found in medieval Italian jurisprudence. Italian jurists did not take over Roman law as a living, historical law; the *Corpus iuris*, the principal sections of which were rediscovered in the eleventh century, was received originally as an initially alien and unfamiliar object of intellectual study. They then transformed it with the aid of their own scholarly methods, as indeed classical Roman law had itself been radically transformed through contact with the learning and civilization of late antiquity and Hellenistic civilization.

It will be necessary at this point to include a few observations about Roman law. The present writer is aware of his own lack of technical competence in this field and is more than ready to submit to the judgment of those more expert. Nonetheless, what follows may be taken as appropriate. Law may either be based upon conceptual and systematic reasons, or it may rest upon experience.[2] The first type is represented by medieval Italian and modern continental European law, the second by Roman and modern English law. This should not be taken to mean that the Romans had no concepts on which to base their decisions; but these concepts, though they exist, remained, so to speak, latent. Exceptions such as the systems of Gaius and the *Institutes* only go to confirm the rule which emerges at every turn in the *Corpus iuris*: that Roman society was very little concerned with the construction of systems and the formulation of abstract concepts. The decisions of Roman law were not built up from abstract propositions but were based on the nature of each individual case. The *Digest*, to be sure includes a title on *regulae iuris* (D 50, 7); but it is preceded by the motto, *non ex regula ius sumatur, sed ex iure quod est, regula fiat* (right is not taken from the rule, but the rule takes its being from the existing right). Romans were not systematizers in legal matters, but empiricists. Law was for them not a science but part of the business of living. Along with this went another characteristic, brought out very clearly by recent investigations, especially those of Kaser and Wieacker[3]—the tendency of Roman jurists to compartmentalize their ideas. Roman law was firmly rooted in Roman life as a whole, but not in such a way as to offer a reflection of it.

It is natural for us, in keeping with the German legal tradition, to see law as an expression or a representation of national life and to frame it in such a way as to make it correspond to this desired image. Roman law, on the other hand, was only one aspect of national life. Law was a sort of isolated realm kept separate, even at a very early date, from such other spheres of life as ethics, religion, and politics; and even within the body of the law itself there were clearly demarcated departments—profane and sacral law, public and family law, and so on. Law was not intended to contain or to reflect life, nor to impress it with a distinctive character. Law, as a product of highly technical expertise, was reduced to its simplest form. If this is not borne in mind a false picture will emerge, and the main impression conveyed by Roman law will be one of crass individualism. In classical times the Roman concept of property would seem to have granted a boundless dominion over things, all imaginable rights of possession, use and disposition, to the extent of precluding all ideas of joint ownership or collective use. The law never so much as suggests the ties of family, neighborliness, or public order. No less individualistic would appear to be the *patria potestas* of the father, the *manus* of the husband, or the law of inheritance, which seemingly granted boundless powers of disposition in virtue of death and treated joint inheritance as nothing more than a connection among individuals. This, however, is by no means an adequate picture of Roman life as it was in reality. In actual fact, the Roman was subject to many ties, with obligations both to the state and to the community. But these ties, though not non-legal in character, were such that the law was unable to incorporate them, for example the binding force of the *mos maiorum*, also obligations guarded by the censor: morality, religion, and political discipline. These ties arose from the Roman feeling for tradition and authority, for subordination and form, state and family. Thus the seemingly individualistic concept of property was perfectly compatible with various forms of conditional use of land or property and with the bonds of family or neighborliness. Again, the individualistic law of inheritance was complemented by definite customs, which would, for instance, have channeled the testator's freedom to bequeath as he saw fit in the direction of accepted views of entailment. As long as such ties existed, and because of them, law could be content with simple and concise formulations. Law could curb its activities because outside its own sphere there were active the vital motives of *religio* and *pietas*, *disciplina* and *auctoritas*, *fides* and *humanitas*, *constantia* and *gravitas*. The essential presuppositions of the law were contained in the aristocratic order of life, the self-discipline of a community which did not abuse the forms of the law, of a society which observed the rules of the game.

But most of these ties and rules disappeared in the later days of the Roman Empire, and, of course, in medieval Italy. The Middle Ages received the Roman law without its complementary institutions and without those social and moral ties which alone had given it its legitimation. It was taken over like an empty husk. Something new and different had to be made of the raw material provided by the Roman sources. It was no longer possible to discover the original purpose and meaning of the ancient rules and case decisions contained in the *Corpus iuris*; a comprehensive intellectual effort was now required to utilize them under completely different conditions and bring them into line with the legal ideas of a very un-Roman age. This task was achieved by the Italian jurists, the so-called legists who had been active ever since the eleventh century. Their path took them from glosses to the commentators, from exegesis and textual studies to the grand synthesis of theory and practice, ancient and medieval law, Roman and Germanic law, and finally to the magisterial systematic achievements of the sixteenth century. In this great creative effort of medieval jurisprudence lie the beginnings of western European legal thought. Medieval jurisprudence did not interpret the ancient sources in terms of an extinct Roman life and society. It took them as an intellectual unity, discovered, ordered, classified on the basis of scattered, and often misunderstood passages in the *Corpus iuris*.

As a criminal lawyer I may be permitted to illustrate my point by referring to the criminal law. The Justinian code contained the principle of culpability, but gave it no precise definition. By the time of the commentators however, a tightly knit doctrine of guilt had been elaborated, which differentiated the concept of guilt into *dolus, culpa, casus*, and *vis maior* (and that of *culpa* into *culpa lata, levis* and *levissima*), and which even incorporated the category of negligence into criminal law. Another example: a remote passage in the *Digest* (D 29, 5, 1, 124), referring to the *Senatus consultum Silanianum* and dealing with aspects of the law of inheritance, was utilized to furnish the doctrine of *corpus delicti*, a theory of great importance for the development of the common-law trial, especially as regards the use of torture, and indirectly also for the modern theory of evidence. Along with all this went a remarkable readiness to discard what was not wanted. A great deal of legal rubble was cleared away, for instance the Roman penal code, no longer in keeping with contemporary conditions, and laws relating to slavery and the *patria potestas*.

Despite an objection raised recently by Engelmann (but not substantiated by him)[4] there can be no doubt that this momentous recasting of Roman law could only have been achieved by means of certain specifically medieval methods of scholarly thought, methods that appeared first and foremost in theology. Historically speaking, Western jurisprudence is a secularized theology, and its scholarly methodology is a secularized theological methodology. These links between juristical and theological hermeneutics, which may well have been characteristic also of late Roman law and the law under Justinian, have been pointed out by Stintzing, Genzmer, Dilthey, and others,[5] and also by Karl Michaelis in his penetrating study of the transformation of German legal thought following the incursion of foreign law. In the high Middle Ages juristical and theological thought must have arisen out of the same psychological ground. Law, as well as theology, was an expression of the divine ordering of all existence. Jurisprudence, like theology, possessed a definite, revealed text on which to found its ideas and opinions, an immutable word whose meaning had to be explained. The procedure adopted to accomplish this was significantly influenced by the scholastic method. Scholasticism took the doctrines of the church as unassailable truths, but sought to make them intelligible to discursive reason, classifying and summarizing them in such a way as to bring natural philosophy and revelation into harmony. At the same time scholasticism had developed definite techniques of exegesis. Not only was the original, revealed word unchanging, but the competence to interpret it was clearly and unmistakably established as well. All this applies equally to jurisprudence, both as to exegesis and as to the juristic gloss from which the legal commentaries were developed. Theologians explained not only the Bible, but also conciliar and papal decrees and the writings of the Fathers; jurists associated with the *Corpus iuris* the writings of the glossators and especially the *glossa ordinaria*. As in the church, the exegete's authority, that of the gloss and of the *communis opinio doctorum*, came to take the place of the text. *Quidquid non agnoscit glossa, nec agnoscit forum* (what is not recognized by the gloss will not be recognized by the courts). Thus the text became encrusted with a mass of authorities. "I would rather be supported by the gloss than by the text," said Raphael Fulgosins. "If I appeal to the text advocates and judges will retort: 'Do you think that the gloss has not examined the text as well as you have, or understood it as well as you?'" Definite metaphysical assumptions, including the idea of the world as an organically constructed, logical cosmos without irrational contradictions, therefore gave rise to a methodology of scholarly thought. As the realm of traditional truths and authorities held no contradictions, but merely problems of interpretation, the great task to be achieved was a *concordantia discordantium canonum*. The aim was to show that discrepancies between authorities were merely apparent. The object was to harmonize them with one another by means of a dialectic which aimed at a *solutio* on the basis of prior opposition of *pro* and *contra*. Belief in authority thus became a veritable breeding ground for distinctions. In both theology and jurisprudence the *quaestio* and *distinctio* were widely and successfully employed methods. To keep authorities from falling into mutual contradiction, all "apparent" contradictions were reconciled by distinguishing either the term or the object under discussion. This, in turn, led inevitably to conceptual analysis and systematic thought. The method of *distinctio* taught jurists to think conceptually; but it also preserved them from the excesses of abstraction for, always concerned with particular instances, it ensured that their thought remained in touch with concrete reality.

As far as its methods and categories are concerned, therefore, the law coming to Germany was not Roman at all, but medieval. All the same, no discussion of the significance of the reception for jurisprudential method will be complete in the reception movement. It is probably accepted in all quarters today that humanism was not among the fundamental causes of the reception of Roman law in Germany. By the time humanism began to exert its influence, the reception had to some extent already taken place. Far from promoting the reception, humanism was in fact decidedly hostile to the adoption of Italian law and endeavored to guide the process along different paths. German humanists, like the Italians before them, had stood in opposition to the jurists and had tried to make them objects of ridicule. The point at issue can be seen very clearly from the following words of Ulrich Zasius:

I have very little jurisprudence of the kind taught by Bartolus and Baldus. For if you disregard their errors, not much else remains. Barbarism has smothered the pure law like a giant creeper, so much so, indeed, as to become firmly rooted. If the jurists had not always adhered so blindly to the authorities of the Gloss and Bartolus, the true meaning of the law would now be seen more clearly and in greater purity, and most of those obnoxious commentaries, stuffed as they are with errors, would vanish. The only genuine and true interpreters are those who endeavor to explain the sources themselves and who expound only what is true and useful in the Gloss and the Commentaries, so that the understanding is not darkened by the whirlwind of many learned opinions.

The objection raised here against the Italian jurists quite plainly hits at the very heart of their method: their tendency to allow the text to recede in favor of the gloss and the opinions of other learned jurists, and to settle once and for all the question of who was competent to interpret the text. Humanists wanted to discard all authorities who got in the way of the sources in order to make a direct approach to the meaning of the original texts. Here we have another evident parallel between judicial and theological thinking, a similarity which has often been pointed out. Just as the Reformation disputed the authority of the Fathers and proposed to return directly to Scripture, so the humanists, in their turn, appealed to the undiluted word of Justinian. Looked at from this viewpoint the scholastic method of the Italians, its ways of distinguishing, of quoting, and even of speaking must have seemed both bewildering and barbaric. Humanism was the ulti-mate protest of elegant form and enlightened learning against an obtuse, bombastic and circumstantial erudition which had been losing all creative power since the end of the Middle Ages. It was a protest directed principally against hitherto accepted methods of academic study. The deepest concern of humanists was decidedly pedagogical: a reform of teaching and learning. They criticized the waste of students' time and energy caused by the excessive reliance on competitive authorities, and they sought fresh and simpler teaching methods which would allow the law to be taken in as an intelligible whole. Hence there was a close link between humanism's pedagogical efforts and its great aim of systematic classification. Indeed, the significance of humanism for the recep-tion lay in its systematizing bent. Influenced by French thought, humanists confronted the practical, empirical and analytical method of the Italians—the *mos Italicus*—with a new method of systematic thought—the *mos Gallicus*. There was a disadvantage in this: the characteristic humanist contempt for the practical, and the mistaken but constant notion that it was desirable and possible to return to an undefiled classical law, regardless of modern needs and modern prac-tical problems. On the other hand, the humanist approach did have the effect of returning jurisprudence to theoretical questions and of guiding systematic legal thought along new paths. It would, however, be wrong to draw too sharp a contrast between the humanist and scholastic methods, between the *mos Gallicus* and the *mos Italicus*.

Juristical humanism is in itself evidence that in intellectual matters nothing is ever rendered completely obsolete. This can be seen from the eighteenth-century phase of humanism, where the constantly attacked natural law remained very much alive and effective. In the same way, a good deal of scholastic tradition was still at work in humanist thought during the sixteenth century. Nor did the tendency toward system represent an abrupt and sudden break in development. Without a highly articulated systematic sense the Italians could never have evolved their characteristic technique of comparing passages from the *Corpus iuris*, nor, for that matter, their method of distinction and classification. Quite apart from this, their *Brocarda*, *Summae* and tractates show some significant moves in the direction of systematic thought. All the same, the humanists went very much further, as emerges clearly from the history of criminal law. The significance of humanism for the development of systematic thinking is brought out by Schaffstein's investigations into the history of the common criminal law,[6] especially as regards the influence of Tiberius Decianus [Tiberio Deciani, 1509–1582, Italian humanist, advocate, and legal scholar, author of a *Tractatus criminalis*]. The foundations of a classified general section of criminal law were laid in the sixteenth century under French and Italian influence. For reasons which it would certainly be rewarding to follow up, medieval jurisprudence achieved nothing more than a classification of *individual* matters, and its concepts, too, were largely specific. Ideas such as *dolus* and *culpa* had been worked out, but not a concept of guilt as such. Medieval law had a theory of self-defense down to the last details, but not a concept of illegal behavior in general; it included the various manifestations of complicity, but not the concept of complicity itself. This gap was closed only after humanists began to influence the development of criminal law. Yet it is probably true to say that humanist influence was not equally great in all departments of the law; it was evidently stronger in criminal law than elsewhere. Right up to our own days it has remained significant that the discipline of criminal law was not developed until after that of civil law—in other words, not until humanism appeared on the scene and set to work on it. This is one of the reasons why problems of classification have assumed such significance, usually at the expense of important practical questions. Furthermore, humanism is of importance as regards the awakening of historical consciousness and the first attempts at a critical approach to the sources. Humanism cultivated a sense of distance from the historical sources not to be found among the Italians. For example, the municipal law of Freiburg of 1520, influenced by Zasius, shows the reception of the foreign law, not as the acceptance of a blindly revered authority, but a deliberate, clear-sighted, and critical adoption of the foreign sources, compatible with the deliberate preservation of such elements of indigenous law as had proved their worth. A jurist in the medieval tradition, like Benedikt Carpzow [1595–1666; assessor on Leipzig *Schöppenstuhl* and prolific writer on law], seemed to be utterly immersed in the Italian efforts to harmonize the authorities, interpreting the *Carolina* in terms of legal practices in use in contemporary Saxony, and trying to bring the *Carolina* itself into harmony with Roman law. But the legal writings of a later time, opinions given by legal faculties for example, made a deliberate appeal to customary law, the *usus fori*, against the *Carolina* and Roman law; which means that they were fully aware of the gap between the *Carolina* and the contemporary world. In addition to historical relativism, however, the humanist-influenced jurists also showed signs of a philosophical relativism. They thought of punishment not in metaphysical terms, but rather as an expedient method of crime prevention, deterrence, and correction—though this idea had not been unknown in scholastic times either. On the other hand, the humanists, in their attempt to base law on man's innate ideas and perceptions—on human *ratio*—rather than on authorities, built a direct bridge to natural law, which, like humanism itself, was a mixture of absolute and relativist legal ideas, and reconciled the belief in absolutely binding innate norms with a feeling for pragmatic aims and the concrete realities of life.

Thus, Roman law underwent two modifications: first through Italian jurisprudence before its appearance in Germany, and then through humanism after its adoption. And in both forms it determined the method and style of judicial thinking in Germany. It is precisely here, in the realm of methodology, that the essential element lies. At this point, however, it must be asked whether the reception constituted a revolutionary change, or whether German law had made some move in that direction on its own account. I have made an attempt to show how the German judicial organization was in a state of dissolution before the occurrence of the reception, and how the newly emerging legal order had favored the adoption of the foreign law. Were things really so very different as far as method was concerned? Is it not true that German law was advancing in this realm as well, and that even before the reception it had undergone a transformation which narrowed the gap between the old law and the new? There would seem to be a good deal to support this view.

There has already been a good deal of discussion as to whether, and to what extent, the reception can be accounted for by economic conditions. It has been suggested that the main causes of the reception are to be sought in the requirements of commerce and the emerging monetary economy, and in the inability of German law to satisfy these needs. Recently, however, there has been an increasing tendency to abandon this view; indeed there are some overwhelming arguments against it. For one thing, the economic heyday of the German cities came well before the reception. Then again, the reception seems to have stopped short of the very fields of law which touched most closely on economic life, such as the law of association and commercial law, and also to some extent the law relating to debt. Further, leading commercial cities—Lübeck, Hamburg, Bremen, Cologne, Augsburg—either rejected the reception or at least approached it very warily. And finally there is English law, which remained virtually untouched by Roman law and bore only a small trace of canon law in its law of equity; yet, developing from an ultimately Germanic root, it was able to adapt itself to modern conditions and establish itself over large areas of the globe during the nineteenth century. All this goes to suggest that German law at the time of the reception was already to a considerable extent modernized and rationalized, and it becomes perfectly clear why the Italian style of scientific and conceptual thought was not longer felt to be something totally alien. *Roman law was not adopted because German law was outdated. On the contrary, German law had for some time been approaching Italian law. For this reason the reception was not felt so strongly to be an alien intrusion.*

Looked at in this light, Coing's description of the law operative in Frankfurt before the reception becomes especially instructive. The most striking thing to be noticed is the far-reaching rationalization of law and procedures. The irrational means of giving proof contained in the old law—trial by ordeal, duel, oath helpers and so on—had disappeared (except for a few insignificant relics) and had been replaced by rational means of proof: written documents and witnesses. The old forms of the German law of contract were evidently moribund. Traditional laws relating to family property were largely undermined by wills and marriage contracts. Distraint and seizure met the requirements of modern commerce. In all branches of law a decisive role began to be played by written formulae: statute law, steps of procedure, extensive documentation. There were similar developments in other departments. One of the notable achievements of the new Roman and canonical law in criminal procedure was the suppression of arraignment in favor of inquisition, a procedure initiated by an official *inquisitio* designed to discover the truth with the aid of torture and the calling of witnesses. Recent studies, particularly those of Eberhard Schmidt into the relationship between the reception and inquisitorial procedures,[7] have shown that even the transition from arraignment to inquisition had begun in Germany long before the reception. This development, therefore, did not have to wait until the arrival of the new law; it ran parallel to the same development in Italy. This becomes more understandable in the light of the historical background. Arraignment, as understood under Germanic and later German law, was essentially a sort of judicial feud, fought with the aid of oath, duel, or ordeal. Obviously a procedure of this sort was acceptable only under restricted and clearly defined conditions, as part of an aristocratic social order in which a crime committed by a noble was a rare occurrence. Crimes by ordinary men were of course published by other means than those prescribed by the public criminal law. There followed profound changes in social conditions brought about by an increase in population, the emergence of a proletarian criminal class which could not be dealt with by any form of judicial feud, and the decline of close-knit associations and clans which had, in the past, met their own obligations, but now increasingly transferred these to the state.

With these changes, arraignment lost its meaning. In an age when German juridical procedure itself was being altered there was no longer room for judicial feud or, in consequence, for arraignment. The personal "enemy" encountered in the old procedures turned into the "criminal," or "enemy of the state," whose crime constituted an offense against an authoritarian system. As had happened earlier in Italy, so now in Germany personal and irrational elements began slowly to disappear from life and law. The emerging authority of the state approached its tasks and responsibilities with rational means. Expiation gave way to a public penal law applying to all men alike. In addition to the penal law there appeared a number of purely pragmatic measures of a preventive nature directed against harmful elements, both in Germany (for example, preventive detention as stipulated in the *Carolina*) and in Italy. Other processes pointed in the same direction: the decline of traditional forms and symbols, the increasing inability to give symbolic expression to matters of legal substance, the decay of legal terminology, the suppression of traditional forms of oral procedure in favor of the written word, and the increasing distinction made between the facts of the case and the legal principles involved. None of this had anything to do with the reception, and if it had, then only indirectly;

similar developments in Italy had likewise had no direct connection with the reappearance of Roman law. All this was, instead, the outcome of a comprehensive process of rationalization which had been going on before the reception, and which in fact had prepared the ground for it.

Thus, German law, having been rationalized long before the reception, was approaching of its own accord Roman law as practised in Italy. On its own initiative it had reached a point where it, too, would have to be transformed into a conceptual law. It is characteristic of the development of human thought that spontaneous intuition, symbolism, and—in the case of jurisprudence—personal experience of law must gradually give way to abstract concepts. The history of law is one of progressive rationalization. One may regret this development as an impoverishment of life; one may reflect that what the jurist gains in precision and clarity is offset by what the law itself loses in spiritual depth and moral force. Indeed, it is only right, even in times of progressive rationalization and civilization, to preserve as much of the substance of the law as is possible. On the other hand, we dare not doubt that such rationalizing trends are both necessary and inevitable. Around the turn of the fifteenth and sixteenth centuries German law attained a halfway stage between intuitive symbolism and scientific rationalism. Its whole fabric had been violently convulsed, but rational thought had not advanced far enough for jurists to bring conceptual precision, system, and analysis to the old German law in its multitude of local variations, to be able to reduce it to simplicity and unity. Wherever efforts were made along these lines—as during the second half of the sixteenth century in Württemberg, where jurists attempted to refashion local laws and customs into a uniform territorial code—they invariably ended in failure and in the reception of Roman law. The time was ripe for a transition to conceptual thought, but the capacity for applying scientific method to the traditional law was not yet developed. At that moment Roman law appeared on the scene, and the temptation to carry through the process of legal reform at a single bound proved well-nigh irresistible.

III

But it was not simply that a new method of juristic thought had been adopted; a substantively foreign law had been introduced into German society as well. The extent of this alien penetration varied considerably in the individual cities and territories, and also in the individual departments of the law. It was generally greater in procedural law and in the law relating to debt, property, and inheritance than in personal and criminal law. All the same, Roman law established itself even in those legal spheres that closely affected personal life, though this happened most often as a result of codifications. In Frankfurt, for example, the resistance of the indigenous law in matters relating to guardianship, marital property and inheritance, and even to some extent to debt and material law, was only overcome by the Reformation of 1509. Especially tenacious was the law of inheritance pertaining to married partners against collateral relations; also the law of joint property. Even indigenous regulations concerning landed property did not succumb immediately to Roman law. Another sphere in which the traditional law successfully defended itself was criminal law. In the *Carolina* German and Italian law were fused into a meaningful unity. It is true that the *Carolina* adopted Italian procedures and Italian criminal law. Where Roman law did not provide for the death penalty, the *Carolina* did not do so either. It was intended that Roman law should be used to fill gaps left by the indigenous law, and clients were frequently advised to seek counsel, a practice which also favored the application of Roman law. Nonetheless, the *Carolina* preserved a fairly large proportion of the indigenous law, not only in the particularist proviso of the "saving clause" but also in the use of German law for drawing up evidence in numerous types of cases (homicide, particular forms of theft, treason, etc.), and even in its terminology, which went far to Germanize a materially alien law.

Above all, it should not be forgotten that even in Italy itself Roman law had become intimately bound up with German law. We always speak of a "Romanization" of German law, but there is also such a thing as a "Germanization" of Italian law. The gloss had been preceded by the *Lombarda*, and the University of Bologna by the school of law at Pavia. Italian jurisprudence may have been at pains to see that the application of local and customary law was kept within the narrowest possible limits; but it was precisely the Italians who incorporated a large number of Germanic legal ideas into Roman law. For example, the Roman concept of liability was brought closer to the criminal law of the Germanic idea of contingent success (*Erfolgshaftung*) by means of an extension of the concept of *dolus* and the inclusion of the concept of negligence. German formulations of the law relating to landed property won recognition in the garb of common law, as in the matter of leasing inheritable property (*Erbleihe*), which was unknown in Roman law; the effect was to grant a *dominium directum* to the lender and a *dominium utile* to the borrower, and thereby to recognize a division of property, which corresponded to the German land regulations then also prevalent in Italy. Again, from the joint property of spouses, which was also to be found in Italy, there developed a doctrine of joint acquisitions on the lines of German law. Criminal law, too, offers numerous examples of this phenomenon. The Roman concept of *iniuria* came to be interpreted in terms of the totally different German concept of defamation. Under the influence of the German law, which differentiated homicide as between clandestine killing and overt killing, Italian lawyers drew distinctions between *homicidium tractatum*, *deliberatum*, *appensate commissum* and homicide committed *rixa*, *impetu*, *calore iracundiae*. This distinction in turn reappeared in Article 137 of the *Carolina*, which threatened deliberate, wanton homicide with the wheel, and homicide committed in the heat of anger with the sword, thus adopting a division of homicide which persisted as late as the penal code of 1871—murder as premeditated killing, homicide as unpremeditated killing. Another well-known example is the doctrine relating to associations and corporate bodies, which was transformed under the influence of Germanic and canon law. This meant, for instance, that a *universitas* could be liable to prosecution, even though this contradicted the principle of liability as found in Roman law. Examples might be multiplied indefinitely, but the ones given here will suffice. The essential point has been brought out: even though the situation of law and judicial organization in Germany before the reception made it conducive to the adoption of the foreign law, it is also conversely true that medieval Italian law had long before this reception made its own approach to German law.

The influence of the reception on German legal life must therefore not be overestimated. Even before the reception German law had managed to effect an entry into the foreign law; furthermore it was able to re-establish itself in the shape of the *usus fori* in judicial practice after the reception. What is more, German law was preserved to some extent in its original form and character. This is not to say that the influence of the reception must be underestimated. Law is not a sort of garment which can be draped over an object without substantially changing the object. Even where the indigenous law maintained itself in alien forms it was transformed—some would say distorted—in the process. If a woman's portion is called *dos* and the husband's property *donatio ad nuptias* this is obviously not the end of the joint property; but if, in addition, the husband's right of use in this regard, as well as the property of surviving kin, are described as *usus fructus*, if the German concept of defamation is made subject to the laws of *iniuria*, if the German *Munt* comes under the heading of *tutela* and *cura*—then law as a whole has undergone a basic alteration. Ties of personal loyalty, communal life in its innumerable expressions, and the general abundance and variety of different forms of existence provided for in German law could never be forced into the categories of Roman law, which was based on the principle of extreme formal economy, and which, moreover, tended to turn communal relations into a set of obligations between individuals. But even where German law managed to maintain itself, the Italian doctrine of legal sources proved fatal to it. It was true that Roman law, in accordance with prevailing views and also with the sources, was taken to possess a subsidiary status. Where statutory and customary law obtained these would continue to have precedence over Roman law. But this view ran into two obstacles.

First, there prevailed a widespread view among jurists that indigenous law required special proof before it could be employed; secondly, according to the Italian doctrine, local laws were to be construed in such a way as to bring them as closely as possible into harmony with the common law. Thus, where the indigenous law corresponded to Roman law—and in doubtful cases this was always presumed—it was to be interpreted in accordance with the common law. This, of course, inevitably altered it substantially, in fact subjected it to the alien law. Wherever it contradicted the common law it was to be interpreted in the narrowest and most literal sense, meaning that it might not be applied analogously to cases not expressly provided for. In this way the indigenous law, even where it survived externally, became part of a new frame of reference. Its organic unity was destroyed; it became—to use an Italianate term—sterilized.

IV

An attempt has been made here to show that German law and Roman-Italian law had been converging upon each other even before they finally met at the time of the reception. In Germany the judicial organization had begun to undergo changes long before the reception and had worked out an authoritarian order which made it easier for the alien law to be adopted. Furthermore, in the period between the Germanic codifications and the reception there had evidently taken place a radical process of rationalization which considerably reduced the differences between German and Italian legal methods. On the other hand, even in medieval Italy, Roman law had combined with Germanic, and especially Lombardic, law to form a fusion containing important elements of Germanic legal thought. These facts seem to me to provide our best explanation of the reception. True enough, the reception of Roman law in Germany, as also the revival of Roman law in Italy, was a historical phenomenon taking its natural course; like so much else in history, it must be taken for what it is, defying ultimate analysis. For this reason the widespread tendency to try to render an exhaustive account of the reception on the basis of a synopsis of isolated causes will never yield convincing results. If a process such as the reception can be explained in rational terms at all, then the interlocking events described on these pages are surely decisive. They may also be said to bring out more clearly the effects of the reception on all aspects of German law. It is an oversimplification to claim that the adoption of the foreign law destroyed, or even permanently damaged, public law and life in Germany. In particular, the destruction and confusion from which national life suffered in the nineteenth and twentieth centuries should not be blamed on the reception. German laws relating to landed property, for instance, remained essentially intact; the old system was not destroyed until the nineteenth century, as a result of the emancipation of the peasants, the mobilization of land, etc.—measures which contained no constructive substitutes. Old ties of family life and national morality were not dissolved until the nineteenth and twentieth centuries under the influence of rationalism and the Enlightenment. It was the second phase of humanism in Germany which introduced exaggerated systematic and abstract thought, separated theory from practice and law from life, and pushed the individualistic features of Roman law to the point of imperiling public order. The original function of the reception on the other hand, was one of historical progress: to reform the German judicial organization in accordance with contemporary needs, to introduce a penal code and a modern commercial law, and to impose a certain measure of unity upon the German legal scene.

The really important question, however, is to what extent the adoption of an alien system of law was responsible for destroying general legal consciousness in Germany and for driving a wedge between people's law and jurist's law. This has been a frequent subject for discussion. While some suggest that the reception was imposed from above and asserted itself only against the opposition of the German legal consciousness, others point out that it was precisely the litigating parties themselves who tended to sidestep the competence of the *Schöffengericht* and turn to magistrate, chancellery, councillor, or court of arbitration—in other words,

to professional jurists. When the practical considerations underlying all decisions to favor professional lawyers are considered—
the prospect of having a case dealt with more speedily and less
expensively, the advantage of immediate appeal to higher courts
in whose hands the ultimate decision lay—one will not lightly
conclude that such a practice represents a turning away from the
indigenous law. At the time, in fact, people were not generally
aware that an alien law was making its appearance at all. Grievances voiced by knights and peasants against lawyers and doctors
show signs of motives that have very little to do with the adoption of an alien law. The knightly class feared that professional
lawyers might enter the higher administrative and judicial posts
and thus intrude upon their own preserve. Peasants did not wish
to fall under the administration of territorial sovereigns and were
concerned for their right to administer their own affairs for themselves. Both knights and peasants were averse to any extension of
the territorial sovereign's authority, and to any intrusion by
"outsiders," which meant not so much non-Germans as people
from outside their own respective territories. On the other hand,
one also heard complaints that the old law was being thrown into
confusion and disarray; or, as in a complaint of the peasants of
Württemberg, the "doctors have caused much disturbance in old
usages and customs in our towns and villages." But this should
not be seen as a deliberate protest on behalf of the national law.
Where Estates were not exactly friendly toward the reception,
as in Jülich, Württemberg, and elswhere, or where they actively
opposed the intrusion of the alien law as in Tyrol and Hesse they
were defending not national, but local law. There were no signs
here that people were conscious of an alien intrusion; they were,
however, acutely sensitive to the dissolution and ruin of their own
indigenous, local laws and to the crisis in German legal life. This
development did, as I have tried to show, spring from a deeper
necessity. The division between popular, indigenous law and
lawyer's law is part of a larger historical pattern, a part of the
transition to a rational legal culture in general. Modern civilization has led to increasing specialization in all spheres of life.

Everywhere law became detached from custom and morality, and the ties of religion and tradition were gradually being destroyed. The more law turns into a scientific and rational technique (an inevitable historical process), the less relevance it can have to the conscience and the experience of the ordinary person. The reception did not start this process, but it doubtless encouraged and hastened it, thus preventing the old law from developing naturally and organically into new and more suitable forms. At the time, men were only very dimly aware of this. The new law was put forward as the emperor's law—a fact, incidentally, which also served to smooth the way for the reception in Germany. It was represented as "the good old law of the empire," transmitted to the German emperors by their predecessors, the Roman emperors. All that was needed was a "reformation" of the law, to remove local abuses and accretions. This, of course, was mere ideology. In actual fact, the reception destroyed once and for all the idea of the "good old law." Since it involved the adoption of what was, despite all prior approaches, an alien system, it put an end to the old idea of law as a divinely appointed, absolute and holy order embracing religion and custom, justice, right, and positive law. The ordinary man and the nation as a whole lost the sense that the law belonged to them. Wherever the reception triumphed it put an end to the law as the community's possession. It extinguished all immediate sense of touch with law as an order of society rooted in man's conscience. Law became an object of indifference to the individual, a matter for the state and for the state's lawyers to worry about.

NOTES TO CHAPTER 8

1. Helmut Coing, *Die Rezeption des römischen Rechts in Frankfurt am Main: Ein Beitrag zur Rezeptionsgeschichte* (Frankfurt am Main, 1939); Adolf Stölzel, *Die Entwicklung des gelehrten Richtertums in deutschen Territorien: eine rechtsgeschichtliche Untersuchung* . . . (Stuttgart, 1875); Adolf Stölzel, *Studierende der Jahre 1368 bis 1600 aus dem Gebiete des späteren Kurfürstentums Hessen* (Kassel, 1875); Adolf Stölzel, *Fünfzehn Vorträge aus der Brandenburgisch-Preussischen Rechts- und Staatsgeschichte* (Berlin, 1889); Georg von Below, *Das Bergische Rechtsbuch und die landständische Verfassung in Berg* . . .

(Marburg, 1886); Georg von Below, *Die Ursachen der Rezeption des römischen Rechts in Deutschland* (Munich and Berlin, 1905); Wolfgang Kunkel, Hans Thieme, and Franz Beyerle, *Quellen zur neueren Privatrechtsgeschichte Deutschlands* (Weimar, 1936).

2. To say this is obviously something of an exaggeration, but it serves to underline the main point at issue. Variations of this sort are ineluctably determined by the particular character and history of individual nations. It would be a rationalist error to believe that they can be removed overnight by transforming, say, the process of legal training. A German judge cannot be made into an English judge.

3. Max Kaser, *Roman Private Law*, tr. Rolf Dannenbring (Durban, 1965); Max Kaser, *Römische Rechtsgeschichte* (Göttingen, 1950); Max Kaser, *Das altrömische ius: Studien zur Rechtsvorstellung und Rechtsgeschichte der Römer* (Göttingen, 1949); Franz Wieacker, *Recht und Gesellschaft in der Spätantike* (Stuttgart, 1964).

4. Cf. Arthur Engelmann, *Der Civilprozess: Geschichte und System* (Breslau, 1889–1901); tr. in part by R. W. Millar, *A History of Continental Civil Procedure* (Boston, 1927).

5. Roderich von Stintzing, *Geschichte der deutschen Rechtswissenschaft* (Munich and Leipzig, 1880–1910); Erich Genzmer, *Mittelalterliches Rechtsdenken* (*Schriftenreihe zur europäischen Integration*, 1961); Wilhelm Dilthey, *Der Aufbau der geschichtlichen Welt in den Geisteswissenschaften* (Berlin, 1910).

6. Cf. Friedrich Schaffstein, *Die allgemeinen Lehren vom Verbrechen in ihrer Entwicklung durch die Wissenschaft des gemeinen Strafrechts* (Berlin, 1930); Friedrich Schaffstein, *Die europäische Strafrechtswissenschaft im Zeitalter des Humanismus* (Göttingen, 1954).

7. Eberhard Schmidt, *Einführung in die Geschichte der deutschen Strafrechtspflege* (Göttingen, 3rd ed., 1965); Eberhard Schmidt, *Die Maximilianischen Halsgerichtsordnungen für Tirol (1499) und Radolfzell (1506) als Zeugnisse mittelalterlicher Strafrechtspflege* (Bleckede an der Elbe, 1949).

9 The Fourteenth and Fifteenth Centuries in Social and Economic History

FRIEDRICH LÜTGE

Born in 1901, Friedrich Lütge has taught at the Universities of Jena, Leipzig, and Munich. He is the author of a number of important studies on agrarian, economic, and social history of a synoptic work, *Deutsche Sozial- und Wirtschaftsge-schichte: Ein Überblick* (2nd ed., 1960).

Preliminary Remarks

It is probably no exaggeration to say that approximately the hundred years from the middle of the fourteenth century to about the middle of the fifteenth remain even today one of the most obscure periods of German history, as of European history in general. Reading descriptive histories of this period one often senses a certain embarrassment on the part of historians, and one gains the impression that most of them, having noted the downfall of the late medieval empire and the cultural life of the high Gothic age, are only too happy to reach the safe shores of Renaissance and Reformation where they feel solid ground beneath their feet once more. The same embarrassment seems to grip economic historians, or at least historians with economic interests, who try to gain this solid ground by investigating the rise of "early capitalism;" every success in this direction is accompanied by a feeling of relief, for history is now seen to follow a more or less clear line of development up to the present day.

This, I think, can be said without much exaggeration to be the general historical situation with respect to the fourteenth and

A slightly revised version of this article is included in a collection of Lütge's essays: *Studien zur Sozial- und Wirtschaftsgeschichte: Gesammelte Abhandlungen* (Stuttgart, 1953), 281–335. Cf. p. 281 for a list of relevant titles appearing after the publication of the original essay.

fifteenth centuries, and it is not necessary here to provide a host of quotations from the major historical works—though, in fact, this would not be particularly difficult to do.[1] The attitude expressed in these works can be described simply and fairly as a tendency to treat the years in question purely as a period of transition, the essential structure of which, at least as far as social and economic developments are concerned, cannot be adequately grasped. The period is considered either as the outgoing, dying phase of the Middle Ages that had preceded it, in which case it is called the late Middle Ages, or else as a preliminary stage to the intellectual and cultural tendencies and economic phenomena coming to fruition in the sixteenth century, in which case the period becomes the "prelude" or "upbeat" to the modern era. In both cases the period is seen as a "transition."[2] The schematic—and really senseless—classification of our history into a "Middle Ages" and a "modern era" is no doubt largely responsible for the failure to recognize the independent inherent character of this so-called "transitional" period.

It hardly needs to be said that every age is "transitional" insofar as it is situated between what went before and what is yet to come. At any given time the past lingers on and the future sets itself in preparation. But in the case of the late Middle Ages, something different is evidently at issue: the notion that this period has no character, no value of its own but exists only in terms of another age, whether as a period of decadence following a prior, better one, or as the prelude to a new historical epoch, or as both at once.

Now, what all the accounts of this so-called transitional period emphasize is the fact that there were great tensions both in the spiritual and intellectual sphere (the rise of new religious sensibilities, "heresy," inquisition, fanaticism, new forms of relations between the sexes, etc.)[3] and in social and economic life (guild conflicts, city leagues, decline of the territorial nobility, predominance of the middle classes, etc.). Historians are generally in agreement when they describe these facts. But when it comes to interpreting them confusion sets in.

Schmeidler's famous remark is probably the most expressive of the views generally prevailing even today: "It must have seemed quite impossible to the contemporary observer (he writes) to discern any clear line of development, any comprehensible meaning in the midst of so many confused and confusing events, and even now in retrospect it is one of the hardest tasks for the historian to bring out the most important elements from the mass of details and make them form a coherent and clear-cut picture."[4] Indeed, these years will remain obscure and will go on being classified as merely "transitional" if some attempt is not actually made to extract this "comprehensible meaning" from the apparent confusion; in other words, to bring out those facts which were of central significance and on this basis to arrange the myriad individual features in a meaningful pattern. It will be necessary, in particular, to break the habit of looking at the century and a half between c. 1350 and c. 1500 as a homogeneous epoch and to realize that these fifteen decades embraced a great variety of different things: a virtually catastrophic collapse out of which arose a welter of new developments.

Now, it is true that some attempts have been made to approach the extraordinarily complicated social and economic phenomena of this period from a specific point of interpretation. Lamprecht, for instance, has pointed out that as a result of population increase land was scarce—became, in fact, a monopoly article—and that it was the peasant, at least to start with, who benefited from this situation, since ground rents fell mainly to their share while the manorial lords grew impoverished.[5] Lamprecht's view can now be counted to some extent among the established facts of social history, although, as we shall see later, it does not account for everything, and does not point to the fundamental and decisive causes.

Henri Pirenne—who saw much more clearly than most other economic historians the significance of the enormous economic disruption of the fourteenth century—advanced the thesis that the tensions, especially the social tensions, which set the fourteenth century so clearly apart from the thirteenth must be sought in the economic system itself. "Men had come to a point (he writes) when the system no longer functioned properly, and the result was that general uneasiness prevailed in city and country alike."[6] I may object to Pirenne's formulation that it was not the economic *system* so much as the economic *conditions* which caused this "general uneasiness," and consequently attention must be drawn first and foremost to these conditions, that is to say, to the actual state of the economic facts of life. But there is a valid point here— and further investigations should show its validity—namely, that much decisive information about the internal motivations of our period can be obtained from the facts of its economic life.

These facts cannot, however, be grasped in isolation; they must be seen within a meaningful context. To find this context we shall have to establish a point of departure that will enable us to fit all the individual facts into a systematic pattern. And there can be absolutely no question of considering economics as an autonomous realm in its own right. Economic affairs and relations must, rather, be seen as an integral part of life in general. Economic facts and the facts of general conditions of life affected one another reciprocally.

Our best starting point is probably to be found in the relationship between the human being and economics, and this under two aspects: one, the ideas and attitudes of men toward economic affairs—I call this the qualitative factor—and, two, their relationship as masses of men to the available economic resources— the quantitative factor.

The fruitfulness of such an approach, particularly for the period under consideration here, has been shown by the investigations of Wilhelm Abel,[7] though these are concerned primarily with what has just been described as the "quantitative factor." Abel proceeded along the lines laid down by Alfred Grund and Karl Lamprecht; he made profitable use of the abundant literature on population trends and in this way explored the development of the quantitative relationship between people and land and the effects of this relationship on agricultural economics in general. The effects occupying Abel's attention are especially those designated as the "agricultural crisis," and it has become quite clear that this crisis was brought on by population changes and to that extent was not due in the first place to market conditions.

It is this fact which will provide the point of departure for the present study. Our question concerns itself in particular with the effects produced by something which has occasionally been referred to in literature but has otherwise never been properly assessed: the collapse of the population growth of Europe, and specifically of Germany, which set in so abruptly in the middle of the fourteenth century and was to have repercussions not only on the relations of men to the world of commodities but also on their attitudes to economics in general. This question is forced upon us by the conviction that this collapse must have been one of the most decisive events in the whole of European, and specifically of German, history, not merely in economic history. The consequences resulting from this event were enormously complex and they extended to all the conditions and circumstances of life. It is for this reason that social and economic historians may be able to make definite contributions to our knowledge of this period, because they are in a better position than political and legal historians to discern the many and highly varied lines of development. All the structural changes in social and political life as a whole were in fact preceded in this case by a number of basic economic revolutions. There are, of course, examples enough in history of spiritual and intellectual factors, including the formulation of religious faiths, which have transformed economic life.[8] But in the second half of the fourteenth century it was a natural event that first affected economic relationships and then went on to produce repercussions in the most distant quarters. It is no use trying to explain history in either "idealistic" or "materialistic" terms alone; one cannot, in other words, lay exclusive emphasis on only one of the many factors which "make" history by arranging and rearranging the elements of human life, and then proceed on this basis to work out causes and effects. The shortcomings of this method show up very clearly indeed in the present case.

Let us now make a short survey of the initial facts and then observe their consequences.

Initial Facts

The first and absolutely central event of concern to us is the population collapse around the middle of the fourteenth century,[9] brought about largely by the Black Death of 1347–51 and the great epidemics which followed in its wake. For our purposes it is not of vital importance to know the exact percentage of deaths resulting from the first outbreak, whether it was one-half, or "only" a third, of the population of Germany and western and central Europe that succumbed to the plague. The decisive point is that the plague devastated almost the whole of Europe, including Germany, at the time, and though it varied locally and regionally in intensity it persisted so long that it could not fail to leave its impression on subsequent developments in social and economic life. This is obviously true considering the fact that the plague broke out repeatedly in the next few decades and seized almost the whole of Germany again in 1357–62, 1370–76 and once again in 1380–83, each time with much the same results. And it should be remembered that in addition to these major outbreaks there occurred many limited epidemics, some of which had appeared on a smaller scale even before the Great Dying; these continued to flare up until after the middle of the fifteenth century. All this is familiar to historians.[10] Georg von Below's assertion (advanced against the —quantitatively inadequate—ideas of W. Sombart and G. Schmoller concerning the population losses of the time) that "no decrease in the population set in after the thirteenth century, and in the fourteenth century the German people showed such vitality that even the plagues could not have any lasting effects on them"[11] obviously cannot stand. An examination of the material which has since been published on the subject will show how wrong Below was on this point.

It might, however, be asked how this large-scale mortality around the middle of the fourteenth century could have had such fundamental and far-reaching significance, since it would appear to have differed from earlier and later instances only in its magnitude and perhaps also in its greater shock effect (with all the psychological and even psychopathological consequences of this). After all, had such mass mortality not often occurred before? One need only think of the great famines of the first half of the fourteenth century, in particular the years of harvest failure and inflation from 1309 to 1318, which had set in throughout the whole of western Europe and during which the distress had become so great in many places that, according to the account given by Spangenberg's Mansfeld Chronicle, people in despair looked for carcasses of animals to eat, and ultimately the distress became so great "that one man would slaughter another and eat him."[12] In the train of these famines came pestilences which increased the numbers of deaths, and thousands and tens of thousands were swept away, though contemporary chroniclers were probably exaggerating when they claimed that a third of the population perished in many parts of western Europe, including western Germany. Another cause of extensive population losses must be seen in the frequent wars of the time, especially the Hundred Years' War,[13] which devastated France again and again and exacted countless lives. Similar events can be adduced for Germany also. If, then, demographical setbacks on the large scale were to some extent permanent phenomena in European history, is it possible to assert that a single such setback, or a contiguous series of setbacks (such as the plague epidemics), could be so decisive as to form a genuine turning point? The answer to this question will provide us with our point of departure.

For an economic historian the essential feature of any great population decrease is the dislocation of the ratio of man to the other factors in the productive process. Man (seen from the economic viewpoint) represents labor as a factor of production; the other factors comprise natural resources (land) and man-made economic resources (here "capital").[14] These considerations establish our link with the "general law of productivity" formulated by political economists, a law concerned with the consequences of such ratio changes.[15] Theoretically the following possibilities arise:

(a) *The equal diminution of all three productive processes.* This presupposes that the population decreases are accompanied by a corresponding destruction of produced commodities, as would be the case wherever the population decrease is equaled by destruction of human products by means of fire or plundering and by the reduction of the available agricultural land (the nature factor) through devastation, flood, reversion to marsh, and so on.

Where all three contributory factors are equally diminished the result is not a structural shift within economic life, but an absolute diminution of total volume. Obviously there is a possibility that an absolute diminution of all factors may also lead to changes in the character of the economy as a whole—such as an unequal distribution of labor in the various sectors. But this is of no great importance here.

(b) *A proportional shift in the ratio among the individual factors.* Here the balance of the complementary factors is rearranged, and this involves structural alterations which show themselves not only in a dislocation of productivity (which is what immediately occurs to the political economist) but also implies effects on the social and economic relationships among the individual social groups. Therefore this second possibility would be bound to have far-reaching repercussions on the national life as a whole.

Many different possible variations of these processes may occur. Two major ones can be identified schematically as follows:

1. The destruction of man-made economic resources is greater than the population decrease. This would mean that a proportionately greater number of people find themselves vis-à-vis the same natural factors as before, but with a proportionately smaller quantity of man-made economic resources. The inevitable result of this change is an intensification of the productive process—unless the population content themselves with a lower standard of living, or the comparative "overpopulation" is adjusted by means of emigration or a high mortality rate and low birth rate.

2. The population decrease (resulting in a loss of labor power) exceeds the diminution of other factors, especially of manufactured productive resources. In consequence there will be

proportionately fewer people for the same amount of commodities, and thus an expansion of the economic process, and especially of the productive process will occur. This effect can, at least temporarily be increased when individual productivity declines and a greater number of people begin to live off their wealth, that is, revert their resources from production (here "capital") to consumption. Conversely the tendency would be decreased if there were to be an augmentation of individual productivity.[16]

If we start our observations with population numbers, it is clear that every historical catastrophe resulting from wars, epidemics, and so on, must lead to questions about quantitative distribution as compared with the foregoing period. It will be equally important to establish with some precision whether changes have not also been brought about in the average productivity of the survivors.

However, the economy of a modern nation—and the economies of the western and central European peoples in the fourteenth and fifteenth centuries had already come very close to being genuine national economies in the modern theoretical sense—is in fact segmented into different sectors, each developing on a very different pattern. The most important economic division to be made in our case, in view of the conditions in the fourteenth and fifteenth centuries, is that between the agricultural and the craft sector, and it is important to remember that in agriculture the natural factor (land) is of paramount importance, while in a handicraft economy manufactured productive resources ("capital") predominate.

Furthermore: these individual sectors receive *income* in the form of the prices obtained for their products, and with this income a corresponding share in the total social product. Not the least among the effects resulting from the state of affairs outlined above would be an alteration in the price structure—specifically the market price for finished products as well as the price represented in the manufacturing costs—for the individual categories of commodities, leading not only to changes in the economic positions of these occupational groups, but also to changes in their social status.

Thus—to return to our historical subject—*what distinguishes the great plagues of the fourteenth century (particularly the Black Death of 1348–50 and subsequent epidemics) is that, though they took millions of human lives*, in many districts even halving the population in a very few years, and they accomplished this through a number of visitations that followed rapidly on one another, *they did not diminish either the natural factor (land) or the population's material possessions and resources.* The previous quantitative ratio of men to goods plus available land was decisively altered by the disproportionate reduction of the population (and the labor power this represented). Much the same thing had happened during the hunger epidemics of the preceding decades. But this time the disproportion occurred on a significantly larger scale; not least among the reasons for which is the fact that whereas times of famine are characterized by a radical shortage of foodstuffs, one vital branch of consumer goods thus being in extremely short supply, the Black Death left survivors with full warehouses and granaries, therefore creating conditions normally associated with a surplus of this type of consumer goods.

A reduction of the situation to these fundamental terms helps to show how mass mortality of this kind differs from, for instance, the devastations caused by war. Wars wipe out not only men, but also economic resources (implements, etc.) and consumer goods (houses, clothing, food, etc.) through fire and despoliation, though certainly in varying ratios in individual cases. As a rule they also destroy agricultural land or allow it to go to waste. In such an event the previous ratios between men, goods, and land are changed either not at all, or at most only to a relatively small extent.

To understand the radical unheaval in development which set in during the second half of the fourteenth century it is of fundamental importance to have a clear idea of the very specific consequences of human mass destruction caused by the plague, and the differences between this and earlier catastrophes. The change in the basic structure of the national economy sparked off by mid-fourteenth-century population destructions provides us with the necessary facts on which to build our subsequent discussion.[17]

The historical view still prevailing today (and not merely at the popular level) is that the great and decisive turning point in German demographic and economic history was the Thirty Years' War. The conclusion which will be reached here, on the other hand, is that the events particularly of the second half of the fourteenth century were of much more decisive significance. It may well be that during the Thirty Years' War the population in the specially hard-hit areas decreased by 50 per cent or more, though probably as a consequence of various types of epidemics rather than of direct military action;[18] all the same, the brutal methods of warfare prevailing at that time led to extensive destruction of producer and consumer goods, and caused so much agricultural land to go to waste or revert to wilderness that we must also reckon with a diminution of the natural factor.[19] It is of course impossible to state with absolute certainty if these losses and devastations altered the previous balance of the ratio between men, goods, and land. In this regard regional variations must have been considerable. Taking everything together, then, all that can be said is that after the great war the natural factor came quantitatively to the fore. The difference as compared with the catastrophic strokes of the fourteenth and fifteenth centuries is clear: the Thirty Years' War brought on an extensive destruction of man-made goods.

One this is realized, we may proceed to correct the still widespread impression that the growth of population continued by and large without interruption from the Carolingian era to the Thirty Years' War. Right up to our one time this view has been championed by authoritative economic historians who, though they do not overlook the Black Death altogether, rate it only as one of many short-term and structurally unimportant setbacks in an otherwise straight line of development. A good example of this view is Theodor Mayer, who considers that the economic stability of the Middle Ages must have been, and actually was, due to the stability of population growth, particularly in the medieval cities (up to the Thirty Years' War). In one or two places Mayer states this explicitly: "Familiarity with the figures of city populations goes to confirm the impression that, apart from a few upward and downward fluctuations of varying extents, population figures remained constant from the thirteenth–fourteenth centuries on; at all events, they did not follow an unbroken upward trend."[20] The truth of the matter is somewhat different. Apart from occasional interruptions through war and harvest failure, there was on the whole a steady rise up to the middle of the fourteenth century, followed by a considerable setback which (as we shall examine in some detail) was structurally of decisive importance. Not until the fifteenth century did the figures begin to climb again. Another view, couched in different terms but equally untenable, is that of Rudolf Kötzschke, who puts the population density of the whole of Germany in the thirteenth and fourteenth centuries at twenty to thirty per square kilometer, and in the middle of the fifteenth century at thirty to forty per square kilometer.[21] There can be no doubt that this is wrong. Kötzschke assumes a steady upward trend of population figures, an assumption we may well be forced to abandon. What is more, the sources offer abundant proof that the population, and the city population at that, suffered a setback in this period. A series of such proofs has been put together by Kulischer,[22] among others. A development of this kind may also be assumed where no exact and reliable population statistics are available, as is naturally the case for most of the cities of that time. If city walls were generally no longer pushed outward during the fourteenth century (exceptions, of course, apart), it was not because "the land hitherto enclosed by them was sufficient for a still expanding population,"[23] but because there had been a population check which by and large was not to be corrected, let alone overcome, until the old fortifications had in any case lost their practical value as a result of the new technology of artillery.[24]

The Consequences

What were the results of these facts? It has been pointed out that the events just outlined could not possibly fail to lead to considerable alterations in the structure of contemporary German and European national economies. How did these alterations work out in detail?

1. The first consequence was one which intensified all the other initial facts and must therefore be put at the head of our discussion. I refer to the falling off of the number of births, a phenomenon we are now able to substantiate. On the basis of a rough estimate, Wilhelm Abel has come to the following figures: From the eleventh century to the thirteenth the birth rate was 4·2 per cent and the mortality rate 3·6 per cent, yielding a surplus of births of 0·6 per cent. In the fourteenth and fifteenth centuries, however, the picture changes: the birth rate now was 3·9 per cent and the mortality rate 4·1 per cent, yielding a surplus of deaths of 0·2 per cent.[25] If anything, this represents an underestimate rather than an overestimate of the mortality rate. The historian will not be surprised by this, because he is aware that periods of decline frequently interrupt the general upward movement over the course of demographic history, and that such declines are not necessarily caused by violent, external factors such as war, distress, or epidemics, but often by internal causes such as fluctuations in the rates of birth and mortality. One need only think of the population declines toward the end of antiquity, about the end of the second century A.D.;[26] or, equally inexplicable in terms of external causes, the falling off of the population in France[27] from the middle of the seventeenth century to the close of the eighteenth, which, as is well known, F. Quesnay estimated as a drop from 24 to 16 million, while Mirabeau put the population at "only" 18 million.[28] It might well be pointed out that there are periods when, for reasons difficult to explain in detail, people tend to take less pleasure in children and family life. In such an event the birth rate drops and an absolute loss of population results. Even matrimonial habits, such as an abnormal age difference between husband and wife, can work in the same direction and actually did so in the fifteenth century.[29]

2. Of course, the development of numbers of births and numbers of deaths did not follow an identical pattern in town and country. In general it can be taken that the birth rate in the towns

was lower than in the country (and it is generally agreed that the small towns—and the greatest number of towns were very small— can be reckoned to all intents and purposes as "country"); but proportionately greater still was the difference in the numbers of children, that is to say, the numbers of children reaching at least the threshold of adolescence. Seldom were there more than two children to a family,[30] and not infrequently the death rate exceeded the birth rate[31] (though exact evidence for this is available only for later centuries). This was a definite and persistent tendency, at least since the emergence of the larger cities. The Rorach family of Frankfurt, for instance, recorded from the end of the four- teenth to the end of the sixteenth century sixty-five live births, but only eighteen of these children survived their fathers and only twelve married.[32] This certainly does not constitute a norm, but it is by no means an untypical example. The greater mortality of males, and the consequent surplus of women (which was further aggravated by the considerable number of clerics and members of regular orders bound to celibacy) meant that many women had to remain unmarried; this condition, again, was more pronounced in the cities than in the country, and it is another explanation of the relatively greater number of deaths in urban centers. Another factor not to be ignored in the towns was the inadequacy of hygienic and sanitary arrangements, which was responsible for many deaths all round, that is to say, it affected all age groups, though especially infants and young children. Conditions in the country were no different in principle, but their effects were not so devastating. Even today it is true that towns require completely different hygienic and sanitary measures from the country if the same conditions of health are to prevail. Ordure in the streets, manure behind the houses, cattle in the yards and so on,[33] amount to something rather different in an urban settlement with a high density of population than in a village or an individual homestead. Other contributory factors were the lack of drains and sewers and the dependence on fountains and open wells. The birth rate in the countryside was definitely higher, at all events as far as the number of children was concerned, and mortality was lower, as a result of relatively better sanitary conditions. For example, in the city of Freiburg in Switzerland in the middle of the fifteenth century children formed 39 per cent of the total population, but in the neighboring villages and hamlets they made up 49·4 per cent. In the country an established marriage had an average of 2·56 children, but in the city the long-settled population had 1·74, while newcomers from the countryside had 2·97.[34] Cities and larger towns have never, thoughout history, been able to maintain their populations on their own, let alone achieve growth. Cities have always been dependent on immigration from the countryside and often, as can be demonstrated, on immigration from small towns.[35] On the basis of the relevant statistical material from a number of large German cities during the fourteenth and fifteenth centuries it can even be demonstrated that city populations could take only about 50 per cent of their descendants from among the resident population, that is to say, for the other 50 per cent they depended on immigration.[36]

All this is well known to scholars and is not disputed in essentials. The point to be made in the present context is that, on the whole, the great mass epidemics from the middle of the fourteenth to the middle of the fifteenth century struck the cities more heavily[37] than the country. The survival of the cities depended entirely on whether rural areas would be able and willing, at least in the immediate future, and despite their own heavy losses, not only to provide the "normal reinforcements," but also to make good in a fairly short time the gaps which had so violently and suddenly been torn in their populations. For otherwise the cities would necessarily, and in the foreseeable future, become stunted. But the countryside could not provide the required numbers from its own current surplus of births, at least not during the decades when the Black Death recurred again and again. The rural population was itself considerably reduced; therefore a sort of "extra effort" was required, meaning that the replenishment of the rural population would have to be held back in favor of a proportionately greater movement into the towns. This did, in fact, happen, as is well known (and more will have to be said in detail about it later). The vital question which immediately arises concerns the motives which led people to move to the towns even though there was sufficient room on the land. After all, the decision to migrate to the towns was taken by individuals, based on individual considerations; apart from a few exceptions there was no compulsory, regulated resettlement. The decisive factors, then, must have been those which made migration to the cities seem attractive to individuals, and these factors will have to be worked out. But such migrations to the towns, added to the natural loss of large numbers of the country people, must have made the population shortage in rural areas all the more acute. This raises the question as to whether there were now too few people to fill the existing rural settlements, and this, in turn, touches upon another matter which, until very recently, has been sorely in need of examination.

3. I refer to a process known as the *development of wastelands*, a process that can only be clarified in connection with the facts as they have just been discussed. Scholars have long since discounted the old idea that the numerous wastelands which spread over the whole of Germany (as well as other parts of Europe) must be traced back to the Thirty Years' War—though this seems to be still a widespread view, taught to history classes in our schools. Credit for this long overdue change in interpretation is due to the geographer Alfred Grund;[38] he seems to have been the first to reject the so-called "war theory" (or "catastrophe theory"), that is to say, the view, previously taken for granted, that the wastelands resulted from wars, and in particular from the Thirty Years' War. "The tendency to ascribe these wastelands purely and simply to the ravages of the Thirty Years' War is now being successfully opposed," as Georg von Below was able to write shortly after Grund,[39] even though he himself did not delve more deeply into the matter. Rudolf Kötzschke,[40] following Beschoner,[41] and others, supported the so-called "theory of abortive settlements" (though not to the exclusion of other factors): "The settlements which died out (he wrote) were mainly those which were situated on unfavorable soils or were vulnerable to destructive

climatic actions." Theodor Mayer adopted this view also; in his opinion a substantial reason for the dereliction was "that colonization was frequently carried forward in areas which were unsuitable for permanent cultivation."[42] But he then proceeded, somewhat surprisingly, to argue that the wastelands were first and foremost "a consequence of general economic progress,"[43] a progress which he understood as consisting in urban growth and the heavy migration of villagers to the cities; indeed, an occasional migration of whole village communities to the nearest town. Lappe and Fröhlich[44] have varied this contention in a slightly different direction. They consider both the "abortive settlement theory" and the "war theory" as inadequate. According to them the most important motive cause of the wastelands was the need for security and protection felt by a certain number of smaller settlements which then combined to form a larger community, often urban in scale, either on their own initiative or under the direction of a manorial lord. This view might, perhaps, be described as a "security theory." A variation of it can occasionally be found in the argument that manorial lords supported or even enforced this tendency to amalgamation in order to put themselves in a better position to control the collection of dues in kind; Backhaus, for one, has seen this as the decisive factor.[45] This conjecture—for it is nothing more than that—is unsubstantiated and probably mistaken, though occasional exceptions may be granted. Completely different conclusions were reached by Wilhelm Abel, who investigated the problem of wastelands with meticulous care, and came to reject Meyer's thesis as "utterly misguided."[46] Abel also made a thorough analysis of the "war theory" and the "abortive settlement theory" and went on to form an "agricultural crisis theory." He did not go so far as to deny all validity to the other theories; following up a possible line suggested by Grund[47] he showed instead that the decisive cause of the development of wastelands was the great agricultural crisis which had by then been afflicting German agriculture for some generations. It does seem evident that it really was this agricultural crisis that contributed primarily to the formation of wastelands, though certainly partial explanations are also provided by the theories of war, abortive settlements, and security. It may also be that during the late Middle Ages small settlements were occasionally combined to form a larger village community or even a small country town for purely administrative purposes, for the sake of making a better show, or for similar reasons, thus leaving behind on the rural maps indications of a corresponding number of wastelands.[48-49] One must always start out from the fact that at the beginning of the fourteenth century most regions in Europe (I mean central and western Europe) had exhausted their capacity to support population, given contemporary techniques of cultivation, and that shortages of land had doubtless led in many cases to the creation of clearances, that is to say, sites of settlements, which may subsequently have turned out to be impracticable. But however well established this argument may seem to be, it is quite certain that such explanations are insufficient to account for the enormous extent of the wasteland areas. The only way to understand the matter—I must emphasize this again— is to grasp the structural alterations in the economic and social framework of the time, the outcome of which, in the agricultural sphere, took the form of a long-term agricultural crisis. It is undoubtedly the special merit of Wilhelm Abel that he concentrated on this fact and complemented the three other theories with his own "theory of an agricultural crisis."[50]

It is also possible to agree with Abel that the cause of this general decline setting in at the middle of the fourteenth century—which has been confirmed by other historians—is not to be sought, as Grund claimed, in the growing scarcity of precious metals, that is, in the monetary sphere (as was to a very large extent the case in the agricultural crisis following the Napoleonic Wars)[51] but instead in *population trends*, in the decline of population; in other words, in an alteration in demand.[52] The agricultural crisis expressed itself in a sharp fall in agricultural prices and in a shift in the prices for agricultural products as compared with the prices of manufactured products. There were, admittedly, differences in the way individual agricultural prices worked out; the prices for cereals sank further than those for meat and animal products. On the whole, however, the downward tendency in the agricultural sector was not balanced out but only mitigated. It was probably increased meat consumption that led to the more favorable trend in meat prices.

This radical structural alteration is recognized in modern scholarship, but the important thing now is to interpret it correctly.

Best known of all, perhaps, is Lamprecht's interpretation which, in substance, holds that the "direct causes" were, on the one hand, overproduction and, on the other, the improvement of foreign trade with its leveling and price-depressing tendency.[53] This interpretation is certainly valid insofar as trade at that time did have an effect of this kind, and also insofar as there was quite evidently an imbalance between supply and demand. The trouble would seem to be with the expression "overproduction," because the causes of the crisis did not lie in changes on the production side, but in changes in demand. One might say there was "overproduction" in the sense of a surplus of agricultural products; but this was due to a shrinkage in the number of consumers and not to an excessive expansion of production. Many people had died; on the other hand, the amount of land had remained unchanged; the underlying reason for the agricultural crisis of this period must therefore lie in the disproportion which suddenly made itself felt.[54]

We must now follow up two series of developments if we are to appreciate the critical consequences of the mass mortality of the fourteenth century. The first concerns developments in the agricultural sector, the second developments in the cities.

4. The fall in prices of agricultural products need not be gone into thoroughly here, as there is no shortage of detailed studies on the subject.[55] In order to grasp the situation it is important to start out, not from the nominal prices then obtaining, but from the real purchasing power of the monetary units. Coinage was frequently debased at that time, owing both to the falling off in the production of precious metals and to the outflow of precious metals to the Orient (to pay for the extensive imports of luxury

goods), which meant that any possible growth in real purchasing power tended to be wiped out. If this is not borne in mind it becomes all too easy to adopt Pirenne's view of a rise of prices following upon the Black Death, the effects of which "it is scarcely possible any longer to estimate."[56] In general it can be stated with certainty that cereal prices in France, if we set the prices from 1351 to 1375 at 100, dropped to 33 between 1451 and 1475 and by the beginning of the sixteenth century had risen again only to 40. The trend in Alsace and England, though somewhat mitigated, was similar.[57]

It can thus be taken that cereal prices fell, and not just occasionally as a result of good harvests or population losses, but quite generally and extending over many generations; this, taken by and large, was a completely new phenomenon, since earlier centuries had seen a consistent rise in agricultural prices, so that it was precisely the peasant whose economic and social position had steadily risen.[58] The manorial lord had shared in this upward development only to a lesser extent. Insofar as he was dependent on nominally fixed money rents he would necessarily have sustained losses, because the purchasing power of the monetary unit was constantly sinking. But insofar as he himself was engaged in cultivation on his own land and received tribute in kind from his peasants, he did share in the upward development. On the whole, therefore, the peasant had benefited more, because both factors combined to work to his advantage, while the lord of the manor benefited only insofar as he himself engaged in agriculture or received dues in kind. On the other hand, manorial lords, especially lords belonging to the territorial nobility, had always been able to draw enough in rents to lay the foundation for a richly developing cultural life. This was true at least for the wealthier nobility and for the wealthier monasteries; the lesser knights never recovered from their impoverishment, which was why they tended to turn into robber barons.

But now this upward trend was over and would remain so for generations to come. The crisis hit the peasants badly and territorial lords worse still. Previously, agriculture in Germany and other countries had been able to produce sufficient food for the growing population only under favorable weather conditions, which meant that every inclement turn of the weather led to famines. But now, unless there were definite harvest failures, more was usually produced than was required, and so prices fell. It is true that the number of producers had gone down substantially, as had agricultural production considered in absolute terms. But looking at market conditions as a whole, current production (including available reserves) had become too high, and the result was a price collapse of crisis dimensions. To such a crisis the peasant found it difficult to make the necessary adjustment. In part this failure to adjust was certainly due to the traditional conservatism of agricultural people, but there was the additional fact that peasants (or any type of farmer) generally took only part of their crops to market and kept the other (and probably greater) part for home consumption. When the crisis struck, they would therefore be tempted to wish to compensate for the reduced prices by sending a greater proportion of their products to market.

At this point a question arises which it would be well to deal with at once. How, despite these critical collapses in prices, was it possible for the agricultural economy not only to subsist but even to secure a reasonable, if diminished, standard of living?[59] An answer may be attempted, based on the principles discussed above. Land, it must be remembered, had not been destroyed by the catastrophe, and the amount of it available for further agricultural production had not changed in principle. At the same time the number of people had diminished, including the number of those engaged in agriculture (here representing labor power as a productive factor). This means, however, that agriculture was now no longer governed so strictly by the law of diminishing returns and was thus able to exist on lower prices. In other words, the situation now came to approximate an optimal combination of the factors of production. To say it in still another way: there occurred now a reversal of the development characteristic of earlier centuries, when the tendency had been to move away from the optimal situation because the amount of available land had been becoming relatively less sufficient, and this state of affairs had been able to continue because rising agricultural prices had made it economically feasible to produce at increasing prices per unit of production. As we have seen, this situation was now changed. Hence agriculture could exist on lower prices. To be sure, it must not be overlooked that prices had sunk at a quite disproportionate rate, resulting inevitably in an appreciable reduction of income, or net profit, for peasants and farmers. Still, we must remember that, since an optimal combination of the contributory factors had been reached in the form of a reduction of labor power (a tendency reinforced by the widespread impossibility of paying day laborers and farmhands), production costs were to a large extent reduced, which made it easier to accept the sharp drop in agricultural prices.

The effects of this shift in the economic situation on social relations will be observed later. The important thing at the moment is that, though taken all in all the economic development in the agricultural sector must be termed critical, a careful consideration of the structural alterations reveals that the complex connections just described did provide a certain correction, and it is necessary to keep an eye not only on the prices of products but also on the conditions, or costs, of production.

5. The development in the cities. Obviously, prices originate only in a market where something is exchanged for money; consequently attention must be directed to those circles that establish market contact with the peasants. These are first and foremost the city dwellers, or those who belong to walks of life unconnected with agriculture. Such people represent market demand.

It was precisely in this section of the total population that the greatest losses of life had been sustained. In cramped cities, with their defective hygiene, death had exacted an even higher toll than in the country. But the economic situation here was entirely different. It comprised the following factors: i. increased wealth among those sections of the urban population that had been spared; ii. higher prices for manufactured products; iii. a rise in wages; iv. influx from the country into the town; v. lower incomes from ground rents for owners of rural land; and vi. changes in both the agricultural and the general political constitution. Something must now be said about each of these factors.

The increased consumer power of the urban population resulted from the simple fact—never to be forgotten—that the plagues killed human beings but did not destroy property values. This led to a shift in the ratio of men to commodities. A relatively small number of people took possession of the goods of what before had been a very much larger number. But who were the inheritors? Partly, of course, the descendants, that is to say, the legitimate heirs. But in many cases whole families died out, leaving no one entitled to inherit. The frequent result of this situation was that complete outsiders appropriated the estates of the dead. "Goods and inheritances were many, and no one to take possession," says the Chronicle of Vienna.[60] "How many estates have remained without heirs," wrote Boccaccio, the author of the *Decameron*.[61] The same was true to much the same extent all over Europe. The important point here is that an often arbitrary occupation of ownerless property seems to have taken place on a large scale at this time, a fact that cannot fail to be of much greater sociological significance than a mere concentration of fortunes in the hands of the children of deceased parents. The same applies equally to the countryside. Here it was not only the ownerless fields, etc., that were taken over, but also grain and other reserves, and even clothes and similar articles of use. But the phenomenon was much more marked in the cities, where a considerably greater quantity of such goods was to be found and where the numbers of dead were especially high.

This transference of estates, specifically concentration of fortunes and property in the hands of a relatively small number of survivors, was to have extraordinarily far-reaching consequences. Indeed, one can hardly go far wrong in thinking that this shift contributed decisively to the structural alterations of this period.

Two facts, evidenced time and again in contemporary accounts, immediately force themselves on our attention: an almost orgiastic craving for the pleasures of life, largely taking the form of stupendous gluttony, and, together with this, a decline in individual productivity. "As soon as the plague had died out the people rejoiced and began to give themselves to gorging and drinking and to deck themselves out in sumptuous clothing." According to both the Limburg Chronicle and the Chronicle of Berne,[62] and it was the same everywhere. This means that there occurred an unusually large consumption of commodities out of all keeping with the amount produced. It will never be possible to calculate accurately how far the relation between the curves of production and consumption shifted. We cannot tell, for instance, whether these fluctuations were so pronounced that consumption occasionally exceeded production, though this seems quite likely. One thing, however, is certain: the old order prevailing in the economic structure had undergone a substantial change in this direction. The result, quite plainly, was a tendency for prices to rise, hence the decisive difference in the price structure for agricultural products and manufactured products, including luxury goods imported from abroad. The latter clearly show the upward trend which might be expected, while prices for domestic agricultural products fell in the way referred to above because, despite the increased consumption, production was relatively in excess. In the cities the only commodities not affected by rising prices were real estate and houses, since there now was a surplus of these.[63] The consequence was a disproportion between prime costs and selling prices, caused, clearly, but the fact that agricultural production had not fallen off to the same extent as the number of consumers. And the increased consumption among the survivors, to which I have just been referring, could only mitigate this downward trend, not halt it. On the other hand, prices for manufactured products rose, and their upward trend was conditioned not only by increasing demand resulting from expanding consumption, but also by a relative falling off in production due to decreased productivity,[64] and an increase in production costs in consequence of the general rise in wages (of which more later).

It would, however, be a mistake to end the roster of effects at this point. We must remember that there were also consequences in the monetary sphere and that these necessarily provoked a reaction in the sphere of production. Among the estates now accumulated in the hands of survivors there were often hoards of money and precious metals. In the words of the chronicler,[65] "The monasteries were emptied, the dead lay unburied, their houses stood open, and every man might, without hindrance, take to himself all the money and precious things which had been left behind." It had long been the practice, especially among the higher nobility and in patrician families, to lay up hoards of money as a provision for the future; a great amount of detailed scholarly investigation would be needed to find out whether this practice was either being abandoned or much reduced. Everything we know seems to indicate that the release of these hoarded resources was a very important factor indeed. In other words, a great deal of money poured back into circulation, or—to speak in terms of the functional theory—*became* money once again. Moreover, the money thus put into circulation began to change hands much more rapidly, with the inevitable result that prices rose (with all allowance for individual fluctuations). Once this is understood, new light is shed on two facts: one, the national economy as a whole became increasingly a monetary economy and not only as regards the "urban" trades but also in the sphere of agriculture), and, two, there was an increase in nominal prices during this period, especially for manufactured products and imported goods. It also helps us understand the thesis for which Sombart collected evidence so painstakingly, that a distinguishing feature of this epoch was a falling off in the production of precious metals, combined with a considerable reduction in the minting of coins.[66] Sombart's thesis is beyond dispute as far as it goes, but it ought to be somewhat differently formulated. The hoarded money now pouring into circulation and changing hands more rapidly was, to a large (if not accurately ascertainable) extent, the cause of the rise in prices; on the other hand it rendered the minting of new coins superfluous and also made it more difficult to go on working the existing mines, because sharp wage rises (to be dealt with later) had already brought the mining industry to the point where it ceased to show any profits. Had the relative increase of money in circulation not been so characteristic of the new situation, the falling off in the issue of coins would not have been able to effect a rise in prices but would inevitably have brought about a deflationary trend, and falling prices. Deterioration in the conditions for mining, which Sombart sees as decisive, was certainly not without importance, but the other facts are at least equally important, if not more so. If, beginning with the middle of the fifteenth century, mining took on a new lease of life, the reason was certainly not only, as Sombart claims, that good luck joined hands with great improvements in mining techniques[67] but that conditions of prices and wages had undergone a radical change, thus eliminating the factors referred to above. In other words, mining became profitable once more.

Another consideration of importance in connection with these decisive structural changes—actually both an effect and a cause of them—was that in many cases shifts in the ownership of fortunes resulted in changes in their use. Thus it was not just a matter of property passing into the hands of different individuals, nor even simply of hoarded possessions being concentrated in relatively few hands and becoming mobile. The shifts were often qualitative: moneys heretofore used only for consumption turned into moneys employed for investment, and vice versa. Although it is not possible to provide detailed and specific evidence (at least in the present state of research), we are probably justified in suspecting that a result of these changes, functionally speaking, was a general increase in the amount of available capital, though naturally this may in many cases have happened only after a fortune of money or property had changed hands several times. The excellent prospects of profit in manufacture and commerce—which were very soon to become clearly apparent—must have made such employment of resources seem most attractive. The same is true of the long-term investment of money at interest, mainly in the form of purchasing stocks or annuities. Italian practices must have served as examples for the development of these monetary and financial speculations, but the fact that their appearance in

Germany occurred mainly in the second half of the fourteenth century was probably due to the consequences of the events just described. Larger fortunes were converted into ready money, thus becoming available for use, and money was no longer laid aside as "treasure" but, instead, invested as "capital."

Not the least among the effects of all this was a radical psychological change in men's attitudes. The folk of the fourteenth to fifteenth centuries were spiritually and intellectually very different from the men and women of the previous generation. One need only think of the unleashing of demonic forces and of the many forms in which these expressed themselves: flagellation, belief in devils and witchcraft, the Inquisition, fanaticism, the appalling ferocity and cruelty of the so-called popular wars of the time—I mean the peasants' risings in France, Flanders and England,[68] the Hussite Wars, later on, but also the administration of justice, etc. All were characteristics of the age. It would seem obvious that the emotions evidenced in these movements had repercussions on men's behavior in the economic sphere. "Life was so strident, so confused that the smell of blood and roses came in at every breath. Men veered from excess to excess, from cruelty and harshness to tears and compassion, like a giant with a child's head. Life was lived in extremes, between absolute renunciation of all earthly joy and the frantic craving for riches and pleasure, between dark hatred and happy good nature."[69] Old ideas of *ordo* receded. The prospect of occupying ownerless property on a large scale, possibly several times over in quick succession, could hardly fail to have far-reaching consequences on human behavior. The whole style of life, and more specifically of economic activity, was virtually turned upside down. Generally speaking, it was the most resolute (or, if one prefers, the most unscrupulous) who grabbed most unhesitatingly, and then proceeded freely to spend. Very few were as innocent and harmless as that East Prussian goose girl who, sole survivor of the plague, went up to the big house, found the clothes and jewelry of her dead lady and, in the fullest sense of the word, "played" the *grande dame* in the deserted rooms.[70] Many people probably exploited the situation more shrewdly and laid the foundations for their own and their descendants' prosperity, which meant that they built up working capital and employed it to their own economic advantage. The idea of the "nutritive principle," quite inadequate in explaining earlier conditions, becomes problematic in the new circumstances.[71] What we are faced with is a combination of more or less unscrupulous appropriation of dead persons' estates, shrewd methods of acquisition, and a far stronger and far less inhibited desire for possessions than ever under the old *ordo*. The outcome was a technique for using working capital which, while not as yet coolly rational, was at least systematic compared with what had gone before. Sombart, and also Sée and Pirenne,[72] have emphasized that it was precisely the "new men" who emerged as entrepreneurs, while their sons or grandsons often receded into the background. They became collectors of annuities, as long as the families did not die out after a few generations and make room for others, as often happened.[73]

These considerations are of considerable significance for assessing the controversy about the origin of what is usually called modern "capitalism." It is neither possible nor necessary to go into, or even to summarize, the whole scholarly discussion on Sombart's theses concerning the origin of the great fortunes, as carried on by Georg von Below, Franz Oppenheimer, Jakob Strieder, and others up to our own time. The view prevailing at present is that Sombart's thesis of ground rents and (on much the same lines) Oppenheimer's about the *Bodensperre*, however instructive they may be,[74] are of no more than limited validity. Commercial and mining profits, especially speculative profits, income from monopolies, traffic in money and banking—these are now generally seen as playing a decisive part in the formation of large fortunes. This is no doubt true. Yet the considerations which have been set forth in these pages show that one important factor has not so far been accounted for: the occupation of ownerless property must have been a prevalent form of property concentration at the time. No doubt the riches gained in this way were very often quickly dissipated again; but there were many cases where the foundation was laid for a fortune which could be used as capital. Moreover, given the rise in prices for manufactured products, high profits quickly materialized for the entrepreneur who knew how to exploit the situation—especially for one who understood how profit possibilities might be increased by means of trusts, the formation of monopolies and the like. Looked at in this light, the problem of the origin of "early capitalism" will have to be answered differently, not only by placing the beginnings into the second half of the fourteenth century but also by giving the matter a new twist and recognizing that a decisive factor was the concentration of estates in the hands of survivors, often in the form of ruthless occupation of property become ownerless. This realization will throw light on the much disputed question of whether and to what extent it was possible for artisans (including artisans marketing their own products) to come by any sizable fortune. Again it was Sombart who set about analyzing this problem, and his conclusion was that it was possible only in exceptional cases, such as when a monopoly situation had been created, when good luck was a factor, or when the artisan engaged in speculative or monetary trade on the side.[75] But Sombart's view, that "the normal master-craftsman in the Middle Ages was nothing more than a simple craft-worker, hardly distinguishable from his journeymen," is untenable. For one thing it is too sweeping a generalization.[76] Secondly, one needs to know and say much more about the position of journeymen before making any such comparison. It is true enough that, during many periods of the Middle Ages, and particularly in the many small towns of the time, only a special turn of good fortune could bring anyone a sizable hoard of money. But this overlooks the fact that the structural alteration during the second half of the fourteenth century heralded the dawn of a golden age for the cities and for the municipal artisans. Reconsidering the discussion on the position of artisans in the Middle Ages one gets the impression that the various participants in the debate have their eyes on different periods. It is useless to try to grasp the character of larger periods in this oversimplified and schematic way. If one is determined to say that the extensive concentrations resulting from mass mortality were a "stroke of luck" for the beneficiaries, then Sombart is quite right, though the reservation must be made that the changes brought about by these elemental events were on a massive scale, and that the stroke of luck was *collective* rather than individual.[77]

While Sombart is at least partly right in the question just considered, another theory of his must definitely be rejected, even though he attaches "the greatest importance"[78] to it. It is the thesis that virtually the only buyers of the more expensive goods were tax receivers and those who drew ground rents.[79] This is not so. There are four other categories of buyers also to be taken into account: first, the occupiers of ownerless property plus heirs who turned fortunes into mere consumption funds; secondly, persons who drew profits from enterprises of various kinds; thirdly, independent artisan-producers, now in a position to purchase these more expensive goods as a result of the high prices paid them; and finally wage earners (especially in the trades, but also those in agriculture) who were now able to indulge increasingly in luxury goods. Although Sombart lays such emphasis upon this point, it would be truer to say that the beneficiaries of ground rents at this time were actually losing their purchasing power to a large extent and would have been unable to spend very much on purchases. At the back of Sombart's mind is evidently that inadequate idea of an "urban economy" according to which the only interchange of goods occurred between town and country. But this overlooks the fact that those engaged in the various urban trades did a great deal of exchanging among themselves, and not only within their own city walls but over large areas—insofar, at least, as they had a part in the rapidly expanding long-distance trade. In a way, this period suggests subsequent developments from the nineteenth century onward, though not, of course, on the same level. Commerce between industrial countries was becoming both intensive and profitable, and trade was no longer confined to relations between industrial centers and agricultural regions.

Frequent reference has already been made to the relative rise in prices for craft products, the result of which, considering the falling agricultural prices, must inevitably have been a disproportion between production costs and selling prices. Kötzschke expresses a fact generally acknowledged among scholars[80] when he says that the prices for agricultural products toward the end of the Middle Ages were low "and remained behind the prices for goods in wholesale distribution as well as behind those for the products of the urban trades."[81] Later on, in the fifteenth century, there was to be a downward trend[82] for at least some craft products, which may, to some extent, have mitigated the situation. In general, however, the situation remained much the same not only in the case of definite price rises but even in cases when prices either remained much the same or fell slightly.

The manifestations of this golden age of the urban bourgeoisie are well known: splendid town houses were built, old churches were enlarged and embellished, new churches were erected. Fortifications were renewed and strengthened, and city walls pushed out to include what had previously been suburbs.[83] A flowering occurred in handicrafts, for increased purchasing power had led to a growing demand for luxury articles. Although some of the results as regards sumptuousness in clothing, food, and drink were none too attractive, the general trend, even from a cultural point of view, was to the good. "The middle of this century was, in general, a time when new life was stirring everywhere in Germany," writes Walter Goetz, thinking here especially of the burgeoning of the arts and letters[84] though he does not give an account of the background to this development. There also occurred a revival of political activity; as is well known, the cities were deliberately setting out to safeguard their economic heyday. We see the struggle against rural artisans, the establishment of local jurisdictional powers, the acquisition (often by means of purchase) of privileges, etc. This was partly a process of attachment to the empire (the century saw many elevations to the status of Imperial city), partly to territorial princes who, ever since the time of Frederick II, had shown themselves accommodating toward the towns. Partly, however, the process was accomplished through their own power increased by means of federative alliances among fellow cities.

These matters are all familiar and nothing more needs to be said here in detail. But hitherto there has been no adequate account of the *underlying factors* which gave rise to this whole range of development. These factors are, by no means least of all, to be sought in the structural change resulting both from the new quantitative ratio of population to goods and from the divergence of development in the urban and agricultural sectors, together with their effects such as concentration of fortunes, the new economic style, the adoption of "realist" attitudes, etc., as described above. The fact that cities and territorial princes now found themselves obliged to issue a whole series of clothing regulations and sumptuary laws, will call for our attention in another connection.

This whole development gives us, in passing, an opportunity to test Oppenheimer's contention that "whoever creates peasants creates cities,"[85] which he interprets as meaning that the burgeoning of towns is governed by an increase of prosperity among the peasantry, and conversely that any fall in prosperity among the peasantry must needs bring about a decline in the cities.[86] If, however, the period of European history under consideration here is examined critically it will appear that this is by no means invariably or necessarily the case. What was happening now was a burgeoning of the towns *despite* a decline in the prosperity of the peasantry. Oppenheimer's view makes sense only if one accepts the thesis that ground rents alone led to concentrations of fortune. But this thesis does not always fit the facts. It certainly does not fit them in our period.

6. The position of wage laborers. In addition to the "burghers," (artisans and merchants) there existed another group of people who may be considered as beneficiaries of these changes. These were the laborers, that is, the wage workers, including both the workers employed by artisans (journeymen, servants, menials, occasional workers, etc.) and agricultural laborers (day laborers,

farmhands, etc.). There is unanimous agreement that the economic position of this group now underwent a striking improvement,[87] an improvement which is a distinctive feature of the fifteenth century. It would be difficult to give reasonably exact estimates of the trend followed by real wages as opposed to nominal wages, and Kelter's objection to Abel, that it is dangerous to calculate real wages simply on the basis of grain prices,[88] can certainly not be dismissed out of hand. For if there is a relatively sharp drop in cereal prices any calculation of real wages on the basis of these alone will inevitably give a distorted picture (make them seem higher than they really were). And there is always the question as to what sort of wages are being used as the basis of calculations—fixed wages or free wages. Another factor that should always be taken into consideration is that—to some extent—money wages were often supplemented by various payments in kind. But even though any such estimates raise virtually insoluble problems as far as details are concerned, there is no escaping the fact that wages did rise extraordinarily. Lujo Brentano, in referring to England, stated that before the Black Death the lot of yeoman peasants was highly desirable compared with that of the agricultural workers, but that afterward the situation was reversed.[89] This is more or less true for other parts of the depopulated Europe of the time. To give a further example, in Bavaria, during the fifteenth century, when taxes were being discussed at the territorial diet, the view was expressed that domestic servants were in a better position to support taxation than were the peasants.[90]

Now, there is nothing surprising in all this. To adapt Adam Smith's well-known phrase, two masters were running after one journeyman, which must necessarily have leveled out their respective social and economic situations. For there was now a shortage of men, in particular a shortage of "workers" in the narrower sense of the word, because it was among the lower-income groups living in unhygienic conditions in cities that the plague had taken such a high percentage of lives.[91] But the means of production for craftwork existed in plenty, and there was land in abundance. No former agricultural worker who had survived the disaster was forced to go on as before: abandoned hides were to be found everywhere either at low rent or (for a time at least) for nothing. Territorial lords were faced with the great problem of finding hands to till their fields. Wages must have risen high enough to make the job of the agricultural worker seem desirable. Looked at quite rationally, they must in principle have been higher than the net profits that peasants could draw from their hides. And in the cities things did not look much different. How easy it was to step into the shoes of a dead master; and this was true even for domestic servants. The disproportion between population and the available goods, particularly the factors of production, becomes exceedingly conspicuous. For the workers, too, a golden age was dawning. This was helped on by the fact that the well-to-do bourgeoisie, and the cities themselves, were now a source of rising demand for particular categories of workers and were in a position to pay well. Work to be done would have included (as mentioned above) the construction or expansion of ecclesiastical and secular buildings on a large and splendid scale, the strengthening of fortifications, improvement of roads, etc. There can be very little doubt that wages, which were tending to rise anyway, would thus have been pushed up further than ever.

The consequences were far-reaching indeed. The first effect was a general one: territorial sovereigns attempted to counter pay increases with regulatory laws to control wages. Maximum wage policies were generally introduced. This phenomenon was almost universal in Europe; in some cases work was even made compulsory, as in England,[92] and the same is related of France.[93] Edicts of much the same bearing were also known in German territories. We may cite Ludwig von Wittelsbach as of special interest among the German territorial sovereigns. Ruler of Upper Bavaria and the Tyrol, Ludwig issued, in 1352, separate mandates for each of his territories in an attempt to cope with the difficulties that had arisen as a result of the Black Death and the grievous shortage of workers. The Bavarian mandate laid down maximum wages and backed these up with penalties.[94] The reason expressly given was "that we have seen the weakness and the harm which have been brought about in our land of Upper Bavaria by farm-hands and workers, that every man seeks the highest wage he can secure and will undertake no cultivation, in consequence of which our land lies uncultivated." In a similar ordinance for Tyrol, Ludwig laid down that domestic servants, day laborers, etc., must remain with their employers at the old wage. On penalty of losing all their movable goods they were forbidden to migrate to another community; thus, in order to uphold the regulations governing work and wages, freedom of movement was suspended as well as freedom to give notice. The reason given is almost identical with that for Upper Bavaria.[95]

The supply of manpower became so short that it constituted a definite emergency. The result was the development, by the territorial sovereigns in association with the Estates, of a series of laws on preferential employment and compulsory service.[96] It would be doing less than justice to dismiss these measures summarily as "oppression of the peasants" and the like. It is important to recognize their background: the shortage of manpower, perhaps also a certain unwillingness to work, were being deliberately countered by attempts on the part of the territorial sovereign to increase productivity. In some cases the restrictions on freedom of movement applied also to the peasants renting from the lord (as we have already seen from the Tyrol example) in order to keep them from migrating.[97] This is not the place to examine the individual measures in detail or even to form a critical estimate of them. But there is one thing which might well be pointed out: these measures were intended, right or wrong, as expedients at a time of extreme emergency, and with their aid the state was wielding the weapon of economic intervention; not for the first time, perhaps, but in a much more decisive way than ever before. The state not only set out to maintain "order—this had been the old justification, as also the reason behind the economic policies of city governments[98]—but deliberately attempted to raise productivity by means of political measures. From now on there would be no letting up in the flow of such economico-political measures on the part of territorial sovereigns, who were becoming

increasingly powerful, in Germany, as everywhere else.[99] Thus,
there is every reason to trace the beginnings of mercantilism
(or cameralism) back as far as this period.[100] Looked at from
another point of view, the way was being paved for a characteristic and fundamental change in the teleological direction of the
economy (considered as a total complex of means). While the
relation of means to ends was being preserved, the metaphysically
conceived supreme end of life, which included all economic
activity and was called by Thomas Aquinas the *ordinatio ad finem*,
was now being replaced by a *political* end. This was to be the
essence of cameralism, a system originating in emergency measures such as the ones described, and proceeding from victory to
victory after the distress left behind by the Thirty Years' War
and in consequence of the growing development of the state as an
instrument of political power. The distinguishing feature of
mercantilism, as regards its practical realization, was its concern
(mainly for political reasons) with the increase of economic
potential. If the clothing regulations and sumptuary laws mentioned above were at first governed, simply by considerations of
"order," specifically the maintenance of social differentiations,
these soon gave way to economico-political considerations. On
the other hand, measures regulating wages and employment were
governed from the beginning by such considerations. For this
reason they are a prominent feature in the whole train of events
during this period, and it is necessary to emphasize them.

This policy of wage control was in general an attempt to
stabilize wages below the market level. This inevitably resulted in
countermeasures on the part of those affected. The fact that
journeymen now banded together in special associations within
the guilds, forming pressure groups to represent their particular
interests, may be considered as such a countermeasure. Brodnitz
is doubtless right in concluding that the transition from wage work
to piecework in England must be considered as another such
countermeasure against fixed wages,[101] and this would also apply
to other parts of Europe. In Silesia in 1361, Brunswick in 1377,
and Munich in 1414, fixed wages were imposed on tailors or

tailoring work, in Lübeck on coopers in 1440 and on pouch makers in 1495.[102] The original intention of these measures must have been the placing of a ceiling on payments for these forms of wage work, and the easiest way of evading such controls would have been to drop wage work altogether and move over to piecework.

7. The effects of the catastrophe tended to be even more far-reaching in the country than in the cities, though individual consequences followed much less of a pattern. Certainly the most important fact, referred to several times already, was that grain prices fell and with them the net profits left to the peasant himself; in other words what Wilhelm Abel has called the "peasant's wage."[103] This was the general trend, but alongside it, or even within it, there existed a number of unique phenomena.

Let us say first of all that there now began a time of extraordinary fluctuations.[104] The peasant, as well as the domestic servant and the day laborer, was aware of his scarcity value. He was easily swayed to leave his old surroundings if another master offered him more favorable conditions, and he used this situation to secure concessions in return for his promise to stay put (as the obstacles later placed in the way of freedom of movement indicate very clearly). But when even the most favorable conditions did not prove sufficiently attractive he moved off to the town, with the result, as was said earlier, that the devitalized cities gained an infusion of new blood from an already hard-hit countryside. The transition to an urban trade, especially to some kind of craft, was not particularly difficult, because the peasants at that time were still much more familiar with the techniques of craft production, particularly in textiles, than was to be the case later; there was therefore no need for them to earn their living as "unskilled laborers." It was relatively easy for them to settle down as townspeople. It is of almost symbolical significance that Hans Fugger, the founding father of what was later to be the great commercial house, moved to Augsburg at this time (1367) in order to specialize in weaving, an occupation he had previously pursued in rural surroundings.[105]

From the economic aspect, these extensive immigrations into the cities had a desirable effect in that they mitigated the disproportion both between town and country and between production costs and selling prices. But there are two other sets of facts to place against this. First, it must be asked whether this migration to the towns might not have been on an unhealthily large scale, at least in the large cities of the time. There can be no doubt that it was. Before long an urban "proletariat" had been formed, and the guilds began to close their doors to newcomers.[106] Secondly, it must be asked whether the population gains in the large towns were not procured at the expense of the countryside, that is, by draining off the best and ablest of men. This is a question arising whenever we are confronted with such a large-scale migration from countryside to towns.

However, this consideration also enables us to take note of another feature in the development of the period. It would be an oversimplification—and would also fall short of the truth—to say merely that the peasantry "declined" in the course of the great agricultural crisis. The effects of the great disasters on the peasantry did not all follow the same pattern. However depressed their situation may have been, they were in many cases able actually to improve their position, to gain reductions in their tributes, take possession of more land, etc. The most noticeable examples of improvement came from the ranks of those belonging to the lower strata of the peasantry: serfs, for example. Serfdom now entered a period of formal dissolution. For a considerable time serfs had been enjoying certain rights, although their social status was still looked upon as inferior. They had long been dwindling in numbers, either by rising to the status of ministeriales or knights, or by merging with the free peasantry or the townspeople. But a remnant of serfs existed still in various parts of Europe and Germany, with considerable local variations as to number and real significance. This remnant disappeared very largely during this period, apart from some quite insignificant relics, which were not completely swept away until the peasant emancipation.[107] At any rate—and this is the point here—these depressed strata of the peasantry were already definitely moving upward during the fifteenth century. On the other hand, it should not be overlooked that the policy of the territorial nobility, aimed to some extent at a leveling of differences, that is to say, of pushing down the groups that had risen particularly high, such as the owners of freeholds, copyholders, etc. This must inevitably have worked out as a further "relative" improvement, since there was now less of a gap between the higher and lower peasant groups.

A further opportunity of advancement for all groups of peasants was the possibility, now become available, of owning more land. One result of the fall in net profits was that a peasant's operations would have to be conducted on a larger scale if the previous standard of living was to be maintained; and occasions for such expansion were there for the taking, either by increasing the old property or by moving elsewhere. The same result could be achieved through a reduction of dues, particularly of tributes rendered to the territorial lord. Thus, whereas the earlier, relative overpopulation had led to widespread divisions of the hides, the increased size of farming units was to be a characteristic feature of development during the fourteenth century; together with this went a loosening of ties and a reduction of dues, a process which was especially marked at this time in many parts of Europe, as in England, France, the Rhineland, and northwest and central Germany. It must always be kept in mind that developments in grain prices and in the prices for agricultural produce in general were not, in themselves, an entirely accurate criterion for judging the position of the peasants. After all, peasants did not need all that much money. They were still largely able to supply all needed consumer goods for themselves, and to that extent they were independent of prices and could use their scarcity value to their own advantage.

All the same, it must not be forgotten that a completely contrary development set in toward the end of the fourteenth century, namely, an increase in the number of small peasants or even sub-peasants. This was especially marked in regions where *gavelkind* was the rule, and from this time onward these regions were to become sharply differentiated from those with developed customs of primogeniture.[108] The dividing up of property, the presence or absence of efficiency and farsightedness among the peasants, the lingering effects of old folk customs, measures taken by landlords or territorial sovereigns to influence customs relating to inheritance, etc.—all these became contributory factors in highly varying degrees, so that it is often scarcely possible to isolate any of them.[109]

One very interesting question which it is probably even today impossible to answer with finality, but which may well appear in a new light as a result of the approach made here, is whether the pronounced fluctuations in population, the loosening of old ties, the breaking of long-established traditions, the radical change in the psychological situation, and perhaps also the process of re-settlement in the train of the increase of wastelands may not all have combined to weaken the intensity of communal bonds, even those based on oath associations. This weakening, often pointed out, was one of the phenomena marking off the "modern world" from the "Middle Ages." Theodor von Inama-Sternegg, noting the fact that the profitability of agriculture in the second half of the fourteenth century suffered from the chronic fall in prices, went on to say: "Co-operative associations, which before had been the surest prop of individual husbandry among the peasants, now began to collapse."[110] But this is simply a statement of fact, not an explanation, since the falling off in profitability can hardly be interpreted as the original cause. However, a glimpse of this cause may well be afforded by the facts outlined above, which, taken as a whole, must be traced back to the catastrophic crisis that forms the subject of this study.

By and large, then, the position of the peasants during this period varied considerably. It is true that agriculture as a whole suffered from the crisis, but many peasants were able individually to escape its effects. This, however, brings out all the more clearly the situation of those persons who were dependent on money rents, and this involved primarily the seigneurial class.

8. The position of the landlords. It is hardly surprising that these changes also affected the landed nobility and altered its social and economic status vis-à-vis both the urban middle class and the peasants. The position of nobles as compared with the peasantry was especially crucial, because the landed nobility lived primarily on the tributes and services rendered to them by their peasants, while their own farming activities took second place. This in turn meant that, as a result of the structural alterations of the period, what happened to the lords had to have an effect on the peasants as well; the relationship between them was, after all, reciprocal. "The lord's distress was the peasant's chance."[111]

There is agreement in essentials about the vicissitudes of the nobility's status during this period. Willy Andreas writes: "The significance of the nobility was being reduced, and the causes of this are well known. The military, economic, and political basis for the continued existence of its dominant role was gradually disappearing."[112] T. von Inama-Sternegg had also noted the decline of those members of this class "who saw the value of their rents fall, who were forced to release their serfs from service and villeinage and tried to maintain their social position artificially by steadily diminishing the size of their estates—and yet had no share in the new resources which enabled the territorial princes to strengthen their hold over their subjects."[113] The decline of the nobility stood in sharp contrast to the rise of the bourgeoisie, especially of the entrepreneurial class. For the duration of about two centuries there was to be a definite "age of the bourgeoisie," which can be traced back largely, though obviously not solely, to the shift in the relative situations of the towns and the landlords.

There is, in fact, no need to give any detailed proofs of the decline of the nobility in the present context. This development finally deprived the courtly civilization of the high Middle Ages of its economic basis. And the reason for this development was that the income of the nobility, like that of the landlord class in general, was falling precipitously. To account for this in terms of decreasing ground rents, etc., is an unsatisfactory oversimplification. A closer examination reveals that four decisive factors coincided here:

(a) First of all came the diminished purchasing power of money rents nominally fixed at an earlier period, often as early as the Carolingian era.[114] Their nominal value remained constant, while the real value declined with every fall in the purchasing power of the monetary unit resulting from debasements of the coinage and alterations in the price structure. The shortage of money felt by all the seigneurs following the collapse in the second half of the fourteenth century, tempted many of them to compound the tributes due them into a single money payment; and peasants, as we have seen, were often able to secure this for themselves because of the "scarcity value" they had acquired. But any such relief was shortlived and was bought at the price of reduced income for the future.

(b) This trend was now to be accentuated by the fall in agricultural prices which I have dealt with earlier. Its effects here were upon the tributes in kind, which to a certain extent had maintained their old level. For these were, of course, sent to market by the landlords.[115] Landlords had, after all, to have ready money to cover requirements other than those of ensuring their food supply.[116] Their dues in kind, however, consisted for the most part of grain, and it was precisely grain prices which were then dropping so sharply. This in itself inevitably diminished the income of the nobility. Those especially affected were the receivers of tithes, such as ecclesiastical endowments, bishops, etc., because tithes had been largely preserved in their original form of payment in kind.

(c) A third reason for the decline of the landed nobility may be seen in the fact that many hides and other farming units were no longer occupied and were not likely to be reoccupied for some time to come. Where reoccupation did occur, it happened at the price of a reduction of the peasants' obligations. The result was a sort of competition among landlords to find peasants, and only those who made the best offers had any prospect of finding them. The speed with which the gaps were filled varied, of course, from case to case, but the important thing is that there was generally a perceptible loss of rents and tributes in kind, because so many hides went unoccupied. It is obvious that the effect of this upon landlords was a correspondingly sharp reduction of income. On the other hand, once the gaps in the rural population had begun to close again in the second half of the fifteenth century, increased opportunities for an automatic rise in seigneurial income existed, and with these prospects a corresponding economic recovery among the nobility.

(d) Finally, further setbacks were inevitable in the case of landlords who cultivated their own land and were dependent on the work of farmhands and/or free day laborers. Such work would obviously have to be paid for, not merely in kind but also in money. In all such cases sharply rising wages, which even the strictest regulations could not peg down to the prescribed level, made it necessary to find money, and this need cut the net profits from the lord's agriculture and also required a gradual transition to more extensive agricultural methods.

The end result of these combined factors was the sharp decline, mentioned at the beginning, in the economic and social status of the landowning nobility in general.[117] Many landlords, indeed, lost their land from beneath their very feet. It was a sign of the times when one of the most important noble groups—and for a long time the richest—the handsomely endowed Teutonic Order, was finally driven into bankruptcy.[118]

It might be asked how those who received seigneurial dues managed to adjust themselves to the new situation. Here a distinction must be drawn between minor land owners (those one thinks of first when one refers to the landowning nobility) and princes and other territorial rulers who owned manors "on the side," as their incomes consisted largely of various types of ground rent.

We will look first at landlords in the proper, more restricted sense. It must be realized that there were many degrees within this group and that the effects of the crisis could be extremely varied. There were small and very small seigneurs whose living suddenly melted away; and there were other, more substantial lords who, while having to retrench considerably, were still able to maintain their old way of life within the new limits. And between them there existed any number of gradations. Since the situation varied so much in individual cases, it is hardly surprising that individual reactions also varied considerably. One way out of the problem was by borrowing, and moneylenders in the towns, mostly immigrant Jews, were eager to oblige. Methods employed included interest at anything from 100 to 200 per cent and statements of liabilities in which two or three times the sum of the loan had to be formally acknowledged as the amount of the debt. This helps to explain the rapid disappearance of what little prosperity had remained to the knights. It also explains the further growth of available capital in the cities.[119] The distress among the knights (as also among far wider circles) reached such proportions that in 1390 King Wenceslas saw himself obliged to draw up a universal *Judenschuldenerlass* whereby all debts to Jewish moneylenders incurred by knights were annulled in an attempt to save the whole of this class.[120] This did help in many cases, but often enough it was too late; naturally it could do nothing to reverse the general economic situation which had forced the lords of manors into this hopeless position in the first place. Other attempts were made to save the situation. Some attempted to help themselves by turning to highway robbery. Others merged with the middle class or reverted to the peasantry, often indirectly by marrying peasants' daughters or by giving their own daughters in marriage to peasants.[121] Others again, notably in west and south Germany, sought employment in often very modest court positions, or in the territorial administration, or even in military service, either of princes or of cities. The only cases in which the position of the seigneurial class underwent any improvement was where a lord succeeded in securing extensive powers of compulsion over his peasants, usually by means of first gaining legal rights over them. He might obtain compulsory service at the legally prescribed rates, or he might impose extensive statute labor upon them. It was, in fact, at this time that the later squirearchy east of the Elbe began to develop; due to the weakness of the territorial rulers there, conditions tended to favor the landed nobility. It is incorrect to say that the east German squirearchy did not come into existence until late in the fifteenth–sixteenth century, though this is the generally accepted view, based on the assumption that the profits which could be made out of grain exports had led landed knights to switch from a military life to agriculture.[122-123] What happened, surely, was that, as a result of the plagues, many hides became vacant and fell to the landlord;[124] but the landlord was, in the first place, unable to farm them himself and generally did not wish to, and for this reason tried, usually in vain, to find new tenants, since he had neither the necessary agricultural workers nor sufficient money to engage day laborers and purchase equipment. The citizens of Metz, when approached by the curia on whether they would consider taking over vacated land, replied that they would not accept it even as a gift, because of the excessive costs of cultivation, especially of agricultural wages.[125] Much the same applied throughout Germany and even throughout central Europe. Manorial lands probably increased in size at this time (often enough against the will of the owner), but it would be wrong to assume that if an estate became somewhat larger its economic situation was thereby improved. Grain prices being as low as they were, a really substantial increase in acreage would have been required to maintain previous standards of living. And the acquisition of that much more land depended on whether and to what extent it was possible to find workers, not free day laborers whose wage demands could rarely be met, but compulsory peasant labor which, if it was to be employed profitably, would have, for the most part or even entirely, to be wrung from feeble territorial princes who found themselves in equally great financial distress. Not until this was achieved was it possible to take advantage of favorable price conditions on the West European grain markets and then proceed to exploit the possibilities of enlarged Estates. Only in this sense can it be said that "the most significant impetus to the development of the large-scale agricultural economy of the east was provided by the food situation in western Europe."[126]

A small farming property to start with, followed by acquisition of a stronger position as squire (assuming a social and political function) along with the cheap labor needed to exploit the opportunities of a profitable export market, finally the consolidation of substantial properties devoted to large-scale market produce—this was the typical course of development among the landed nobility in east Germany, leading to the growth of a squirearchy and, ultimately, large-scale agricultural operations. But there was one distinctive feature common to both landlords and agricultural squires from this time until their dissolution during the emancipation of the peasants: they gradually became part of the *administration of the territorial state*. The extent and timing of this process varied. But the principle was the same everywhere. Thus a substantial relic of the medieval state, which had been based on personal rule rather than on territorial dominion (*dominium terrae*), survived into the new era. It is probably true that the seigneurial government of the high Middle Ages had been "semistatelike in character," as Lamprecht puts it.[127] Such a governmental system had formed the basis of the reciprocal personal relations typical of the feudal state. Now, however, given the rise of the territorial principality with its Estate-dominated political system, the squirearchy came to be absorbed into the political structure, where it served two functions: it became the most powerful group in the territorial Estates who shared the government with the prince (and in this connection it hardly mattered whether seigneurial land was held allodially or in feudal tenure), and it assumed an intrinsic role in territorial administration.[128] What further distinguished the east German landed nobility was that the districts they governed were turned into administrative units enjoying equal status with districts under the immediate authority of the sovereign. In western Germany, seigneurial landowners were always subordinate to princely officials.

The extent to which the territorial sovereigns and their officials intervened in the everyday affairs of rural life in districts not governed by squires—I am referring now to the seigneurial districts of west and south Germany—varied considerably. In southwestern and central Germany the position of the peasants became so established as to be practically autonomous, which meant that it was virtually impossible for the territorial sovereign to meddle in their legal or economic affairs. In other territories, however, in Old Bavaria for example, power and importance gradually accrued to princely and also to seigneurial officials, so that one is tempted to speak of a "bureaucracy." This is not the place for a detailed examination of the highly differentiated developments in the system of seigneurial government, but in this respect, too, scholars ought to pay some attention to the consequences of the great crisis setting in at the middle of the fourteenth century.

In general, then, not until the second half of the fifteenth century, by which time the agricultural crisis had been overcome, did the landlords regain their economic power and their social status sufficiently for city patricians to consider it an honor to be raised to the status of nobility.[129]

So much for developments among the landed nobility. What, now, was the position for the territorial sovereigns?

9. Effects upon territorial sovereigns. Territorial sovereigns were first of all dependent on income from manorial lords, and to that extent they suffered in much the same way as landlords. But they had other means of coping with the difficulties. It should be emphasized that we do not know whether and to what extent territorial princes came into possession of heirless estates after the mass deaths occurring in the second half of the fourteenth century. It can be assumed that this did happen to some extent, even though there are indications that ownerless lands went mainly to the landlords. But since the sovereigns were themselves landlords, it would come to much the same thing. Detailed studies on this point would be highly desirable.

But the completion of the intruments of territorial authority, in combination with the new tendency to consider economic questions as aspects of politics—in other words, cameralism— meant that the condition of "subjecthood" came to extend ever more rigidly even to the peasant sector of society, while the maintenance of differentiations among the several estates came to mean less and less.[130] What was important now was that everyone paid taxes and assumed an increased share in other public burdens. As a result the peasantry experienced a certain leveling of the different strata which had previously been distinct occupational groups (serfs, free men, yeomen, etc.), a leveling which was inevitable and was accepted as such. It reinforced the trend toward an economic equalization of peasant groups, which has already been discussed here.

But unlike the landlords, territorial sovereigns were able to avail themselves of new, non-manorial sources of income, the basic condition for all of which was their newly augmented territorial authority on the one hand, and their population's status as "subjects" on the other. Thus territorial systems of taxation came to experience a phase of development comparable in extent to the wage, price, and employment policies already discussed.[131]

But as this new source of income was irregular, and occasionally dried up altogether, sovereigns often resorted to granting seigneurial rights against money payments (an exchange greatly to the advantage of the landlords). Or they incurred large debts to cities or to wealthy individual citizens, and occasionally also to ecclesiastical institutions—a procedure which was to be characteristic of public finance until the end of the sixteenth century.

A precondition, and at the same time a consequence, of all this was an alteration of the political structure of the whole state. Obviously it cannot be claimed that this was the first time that the body politic had showed signs of turning into a territory administered by bureaucrats. Trends pointing in this direction can be detected as early as the beginning of the fourteenth century, as can be seen from a specialist on these problems, Heinrich Mitteis, who writes: "Looking back we can see around 1300 a new concept of the state asserting itself everywhere. The feudal state, with its personal ties, was beginning to be transformed into a system of impersonal, functional regulations. Feudal rights ceased to form the organizational principle of the state, and vassals were replaced by dependent, salaried officials."[132] All the same, the very fact that this newly emerging state found itself confronted at this early stage of its development with so many, often grievous, economic problems was of considerable importance for the future growth of its political ideology. The factors and consequences outlined in the preceding pages all had their impact on this development. Economic policy must inevitably have taken a very important place among the tasks of government, and this must have determined many specific features typical of the "mercantilist" state not implicitly contained in its original idea.

The hundred years from the middle of the fourteenth to the middle of the fifteenth century offer many examples of burghers acting as important counsellors to princes, a development which clearly characterizes the rise, the golden age, of this class and conversely the decline of the landed nobility. Not until after 1500 did the balance of power shift again. In the intervening years the nobles had made their peace with the territorial principality. Either they now served the sovereign as officials, or, as members of the landed squirearchy they allowed themselves to be incorporated into the newly created state as an Estate in the constitutional sense.

Concluding Remarks

An attempt has been made here to account briefly for the salient characteristics of the fourteenth and fifteenth centuries, a period which may well be called the most obscure in our history. This period was no more an outgoing phase of the preceding era and a preparation for the next than any other. Still, it is true that it witnessed a sudden collapse, or—better—radical transformation which brought the epoch of the high Middle Ages to an end. The decisive impetus came from external causes: the great plague epidemics and their effects on social and economic life as a whole. By and large the preceding era had achieved a certain measure of balance between population and available land. Any occasional overpopulation was successfully met by an increase in the area of cultivation or by emigration to the east.

But now eastern colonization came to a sudden halt, to be revived only about a century later, though in a different style. The debate on the reasons for this sudden termination of the eastward movement would be set on a more relevant footing if the

effects of the Black Death were given more emphasis.[133] How
was the suddenly depopulated mother country (including the
newly settled regions beyond the Elbe and Saale, which had also
been hit by the plague) to provide the necessary people to carry
on the work, seeing that it was short of settlers itself?

It is, of course, always difficult to say what would have happened had this disaster—brought on by external factors and therefore a kind of historical "accident"—not occurred. One thing,
however, is fairly certain—the colonization of the east would
have continued at a steady rate.

Furthermore: since, after a certain time, this eastward movement would necessarily have come to an end, given the inevitable
political and national countercurrents and the exhaustion of available space, agricultural and craft production would then have had
to be greatly intensified if Europe's population capacity were to be
extended—unless, of course, people had resigned themselves to
fate and let starvation kill off those for whom, as Malthus put it,
nature had not laid the table. But the epidemics changed the whole
ratio of population growth to food margins at one blow. In
1350 the general situation was much the same as in 1800: available
economic techniques and forms of organization put a halt to any
further population increase. But fate decreed that the population
catastrophe of the mid-century relieved Europe of the need to
find a solution to the problem of guaranteeing the necessary
sustenance for a growing population. It can, however, be safely
assumed that the energetic peoples of Europe, and especially of
central Europe, would have found the same course as was taken
later in the eighteenth and nineteenth centuries and also, to a
lesser extent, in the sixteenth. It is true that the law of diminishing
returns would have made itself felt in the form of rising prices for
agricultural produce, but the general increase in prosperity, due
not least of all to an intensification of craft production, would
have been well able to absorb higher agricultural prices.

Instead, the population catastrophe cut short all possible
developments in this direction, and replaced the trend toward
expansion with one of contraction. This shift led to a radical

reshuffling of the respective positions of various social groups, so that cities and burghers enjoyed a sharp rise in prosperity, and also of social status, which was shared also by the wage earners, while peasants and even more so those who lived on ground rents had to adjust themselves to a fall in economic and social standing. I have made an attempt here to show how this rearrangement worked out in individual instances. The political position of territorial sovereigns was strengthened, since, in view of the distress all round them, they conceived it as their duty—and, to the extent that they were rulers in the true sense, could hardly fail to conceive it as their duty—to intervene by means of regulatory and practical measures. In particular, the regulation of wages and the efforts to raise individual productivity would appear in many essentials to have foreshadowed later mercantile politics.

But the disproportion which set in as a result of the population catastrophe, leading on the one hand to an agricultural crisis and on the other to a golden age for the towns was to be balanced out in another form. Latent, at first, then suddenly from the middle of the sixteenth century clearly pronounced, a number of factors began to converge to change the urban situation once more. Relatively overcrowded city occupations, chiefly overland trade and the crafts, began gradually to lose their economic basis once contact with the wider world, so vital for the fifteenth to sixteenth centuries, had been cut off, when nationalistic and mercantilist protective policies began to assert themselves, and when Germany began to be at a serious disadvantage because of her unfavorable geographical position. German cities were able to maintain their high standard of civilization only within the framework of a "world economy," with free access to a large trading area. And this was denied them by developments from the middle of the sixteenth century onward. It was now the turn of the cities to experience the contraction from which the rural areas had suffered two centuries before. This is perhaps the most satisfactory explanation of the decline of cities, certainly better than the suggestion of Oppenheimer[134] (who otherwise has a clear grasp of the factors at work here)[135] that the purchasing power of the peasants, the principal customers for manufactured products, had fallen off. This, indeed, does not fit the facts, since a comparison between price developments for grain and craft products will show that the former rose disproportionately higher than the latter in the sixteenth century.[136]

It has long been the practice to divide our history into "Middle Ages" and "modern times," and to fix the decisive break at about 1500. But if we reflect on the events of the fourteenth and fifteenth centuries and on their consequences we will be forced to the conclusion that the radical change (or perhaps disruption) following upon, and largely caused by, the Black Death was much more serious and far-reaching than anything resulting from the upheavals around 1500, however important these undoubtedly were. But if the crude division into Middle Ages and modern times must be preserved, then one will have to say that the Middle Ages came to an end around 1350. Once this is clear it becomes absolutely inadmissible to treat Middle Ages and late Middle Ages as a unity and to compile a series of dates from totally different centuries in an attempt to demonstrate unbroken lines of development. An apocalyptic catastrophe destroyed an intellectual, spiritual, social, and economic form of life which reached back in all essentials to the Carolingian era.[137] It put an end to an occasionally turbulent, but gradual and basically healthy development which had permitted no critical imbalance between the various economic sectors. From then on, developments were to be full of ups and downs, and these were partly the effect, partly the cause, of disproportionate situations in the particular economic sectors, notably in town and countryside. Such was to be the distinctive character of the next six centuries of European and German social and economic history. Economic upheavals were to have the most far-reaching effects on social and political life, and vice versa. That seething torrent which has been the modern history of our continent has its source in the middle of the fourteenth century. Lines of developments that might have led in quite other directions were cut short. On the other hand, forces were unleashed which were to transform all of intellectual, social, political, and economic life. Thus there is every reason to conclude that the Middle Ages died in the second half of the fourteenth century, and all that seems to be new in the fifteenth and sixteenth centuries was born at the same time.

NOTES TO CHAPTER 9

1. It will be sufficient here to refer to Rudolf Kötzschke, *Allgemeine Wirtschaftsgeschichte des Mittelalters* (Jena, 1924), which has remained the most representative work on the economic development of the Middle Ages. One chapter, characteristically entitled "The Close of the Medieval Economy" (p. 498 ff.) describes the contacts between East and West brought about by the Crusades, the state of rural and urban economy, the voyages of discovery, etc., but no further consideration is given to the questions which will be raised here. In Heinrich Sieveking's *Wirtschaftsgeschichte* (Berlin, 1935), the section on the Middle Ages is followed immediately by the age of mercantilism. Theodor Mayer, *Deutsche Wirtschaftsgeschichte des Mittelalters* (Leipzig, 1928), speaks of an age of urban economy stretching from the thirteenth to the seventeenth century, without seeing any break in development. Heinrich Cunow, *Allgemeine Wirtschaftsgeschichte*, Vol. III (Berlin, 1929), while referring here and there to population losses caused by the Black Death, does not deal with the problems to which this gave rise. An exception in many respects is provided by Franz Oppenheimer in his still very little known book, *Grossgrundeigentum und soziale Frage* (Jena, 2nd ed., 1922), esp. p. 391 ff. A critical analysis of this book would require an extensive study of its own; side by side with a number of completely false deductions from his premises Oppenheimer advances arguments and observations which throw valuable light on the age.

2. Much the same line of thought is to be found in Heinrich Bechtel, *Wirtschaftsstil des deutschen Spätmittelalters* (Munich and Leipzig, 1930). The merits of this book are not to be denied, and it adduces an abundance of facts and interpretations for the economics of the period from 1350 to 1500; yet the decisive break which occurs during this period is not made clear. This century and a half does not form a uniform entity.

3. The most vivid account is perhaps still that of J. Huizinga, *Herbst des Mittelalters* (Stuttgart, 5th ed., 1939), chapter 1. [English translation: *The Waning of the Middle Ages*, several editions. Also discussed in chapters 2 and 4 of this book.]

4. Bernhard Schmeidler, *Das spätere Mittelalter* (Leipzig and Vienna, 1937).

5. Karl Lamprecht, *Deutsches Wirtschaftsleben im Mittelalter*, Vol. I, 2 (Leipzig, 1886), pp. 862 ff., 1506 ff., etc.

6. Henri Pirenne, *Sozial- und Wirtschaftsgeschichte Europas im Mittelalter* (Berne, n.d.), p. 186. The original appeared under the title, *Histoire du moyen age*

du XIe au milieu du XVe siècle. Cf. my review of this book in *Jahrbücher für Nationalökonomie und Statistik,* Vol. 162 (1950), Heft 2, p. 142 ff. [English translation: *Economic and Social History of Medieval Europe* (London, 1936).]

7. Wilhelm Abel, *Agrarkrisen und Agrarkonjunktur in Mitteleuropa vom 13. bis zum 19. Jahrhundert* (Berlin, 1935); *idem,* "Wachstumsschwankungen mitteleuropäischer Völker seit dem Mittelalter," *Jahrbücher für Nationalökonomie und Statistik,* Vol. 142 (1935), p. 670 ff.; *idem, "Die Wüstungen des ausgehenden Mittelalters. Ein Beitrag zur Siedlungs- und Agrargeschichte Deutschlands* (Jena, 1943), for which, cf. the review by R. Kötzschke in *Jahrbücher für Nationalökonomie und Statistik,* Vol. 161 (1949), p. 467 ff.

8. In addition to Max Weber's well-known studies in religious sociology, cf. the recent contributions of Alfred Müller-Armack, in particular his book, *Das Jahrhundert ohne Gott* (Münster, 1948).

9. I cannot here give references to the essential sources and literature, let alone analyze them. But in addition to the two important books of Wilhelm Abel referred to above, mention should be made of Maxime Kowalewsky, *Die ökonomische Entwicklung Europas bis zum Beginn der kapitalistischen Wirtschaftsform,* Vol. v (Berlin, 1911). He devotes 220 pages to the Black Death and its economic consequences, though Germany definitely receives rather short treatment compared with the rest of Europe. All the important literature is given in both Abel and Kowalewsky.

10. Hence no attempt will be made to recapitulate the facts or to refer to any but the most important literature, particularly since the two works mentioned in the preceding note give all the necessary information.

11. G. von Below, *Probleme der Wirtschaftsgeschichte* (Tübingen, 2nd ed., 1926), p. 454. In contrast, Georg Brodnitz, *Englische Wirtschaftsgeschichte* (Jena, 1918), p. 73 ff., has given perhaps a more thorough account than anyone else of the losses due to the plague and the consequences of the catastrophe.

12. Quoted in W. Abel, *Die Wüstungen des ausgehenden Mittelalters,* p. 57.

13. Henri Sée, *Französische Wirtschaftsgeschichte,* Vol. 1, (Jena, 1930), p. 35 ff.

14. Changes in population distribution resulting from an imbalance in age groups and the ratio of the sexes need not be accounted for here in any detail, quite apart from the fact that it would probably be very difficult to form an accurate picture.

15. I need refer only to O. von Zwiedineck-Südenhorst, *Allgemeine Volkswirtschaftslehre* (Berlin, Göttingen and Heidelberg, 2nd ed., 1948), p. 131 ff.; and Walter Weddigen, *Theoretische Volkswirtschaftslehre* (Meisenheim am Glan, 1948), esp. pp. 53 ff. and 130 f.

16. There is, logically, a third possibility, i.e., that the loss of land (natural factor) might exceed that of population and means of production; but there is no need to include this possibility, since it has no practical relevance.

17. Franz Oppenheimer, *op. cit.,* p. 391 ff., *passim,* repeatedly emphasized that the decisive break came around 1370. This is perfectly acceptable, as the present account will show. All the same, he has missed a large number of decisive facts, such as the population development stressed here, which he

370   PRE-REFORMATION GERMANY

only refers to occasionally in passing. His omission of this fact and its consequences is doubtless the reason for so many of his mistaken judgments.

18. This is also pointed out by Günther Franz in his *Der Dreissigjährige Krieg und das deutsche Volk* (Jena, 2nd ed., 1943), p. 12, *passim*, a book full of material which can probably at present rank as a standard work. (See also Robert Ergang, *The Myth of the All-Destructive Fury of the Thirty Years' War* [Pocono Pines, Pa., 1956].) The long article, "Bevölkerungswesen (Geschichte der Bevölkerungsbewegung)," in *Handwörterbuch der Staatswissenschaften*, Vol. 2 (Jena, 4th ed., 1924), p. 670 ff., by T. von Inama-Sternegg and Häpke is unfortunately of no help for this period. Many individual items of information, however, have been collated in Erich Keyser, *Bevölkerungsgeschichte Deutschlands* (Leipzig, 3rd ed., 1943), p. 337 ff.

19. Much the same applies to the Hundred Years' War in France and for many other wars and feuds.

20. Mayer, *op. cit.*, p. 106. Cf. also the quotation from Georg von Below, given above.

21. These figures (unfortunately without the source) can be found in Erich Keyser, *op. cit.*, p. 36.

22. Josef Kulischer, *Allgemeine Wirtschaftsgeschichte des Mittelalters und der Neuzeit*, Vol. 1 (Munich and Berlin, 1928), p. 170.

23. Thus verbatim in Georg Steinhausen, *Geschichte der deutschen Kultur* (Leipzig, 3rd ed., 1929), p. 229.

24. This, of course, is not to exclude the possibility that occasionally a growing population, as for instance in the sixteenth century, was accommodated by means of increasing the density of the built-up area or that the suburbs sometimes became of greater importance. Cf., for example, R. Eberstadt, *Handbuch des Wohnungswesens* (Jena, 4th ed., 1920), p. 35; Friedrich Lütge, *Wohnungswirtschaft* (Stuttgart, 2nd ed., 1949), p. 6.

25. Wilhelm Abel, *Die Wüstungen des ausgehenden Mittelalters*, p. 69.

26. A recent account based on earlier preliminary studies can be found in Michael Rostovzeff, *Geschichte der alten Welt* (Leipzig, 1942), and *Gesellschaft und Wirtschaft im römischen Kaiserreich* (Leipzig, 1931); [English translations: *A History of the Ancient World* (London, 1945); *The Social and Economic History of the Roman Empire* (Oxford, 1957)]; in Fritz M. Heichelheim, *Wirtschaftsgeschichte des Altertums* (Leiden, 1938), demographic discussions are given conspicuously little place.

27. According to P. Boissonade, *Le socialisme d'État, l'industrie et les classes industrielles en France* . . . (Paris, 1927), p. 157, the devastating religious wars of the seventeenth century, with all the desolation they caused, cost France "only" about 1 million lives and 184,000 buildings. Such a loss of life, however heavy it may have been, and the dwindling of population, cannot therefore be ascribed solely to the fury of war. As far as I can see from the literature there is a shortage of adequate studies of this chapter of French social and economic history.

28. W. Abel, who also adduces these two estimates, considers the second more correct ("Wachstumsschwankungen europäischer Völker seit dem

Mittelalter," *op. cit.*, p. 683); Henri Sée, *Französische Wirtschaftsgeschichte*, gives a bare exposition of these questions; the same is true of Émile Levasseur, *La population française* (Paris, 1889).

29. Cf. Wilhelm Abel, *Die Wüstungen des ausgehenden Mittelalters*, p. 67 f. Friedrich Zöpfl, *Deutsche Kulturgeschichte*, Vol. 1 (Freiburg, 2nd ed., 1931), p. 417 ff., examines in somewhat greater detail the surplus of women at this time as well as the marriage practices, and particularly the abnormal differences in the ages of marriage partners.

30. Typical examples have been collated in Kulischer, *op. cit.*, p. 170. Figures for the sixteenth and seventeenth centuries have been assembled from detailed studies in Keyser, *op. cit.*, p. 420 f.

31. *Ibid.*, p. 421 f. Cf. also Abel, *op. cit.*, p. 70, as also the book quoted there, Hans Apel, *Jenas Einwohner aus der Zeit von 1250–1600* (Görlitz, 1937), which states that, of the 1,406 recorded families, only 25 per cent were still in existence a century later.

32. Cf. Fritz Rörig, "Die europäische Stadt," *Propyläen-Weltgeschichte*, Vol. IV (1932), p. 346.

33. It is scarcely comprehensible today that the medieval towns had no privies and that people would use the courtyard, and even vessels, to be emptied into the streets or, at best, into the garden. There are some drastic examples in Kulischer, *op. cit.*, Vol. II, p. 12 f.; Cunow, *op. cit.*, p. 73 ff.; Georg von Below, *Das ältere deutsche Städtewesen und Bürgertum* (Bielefeld and Leipzig, 1898), p. 88 ff.

34. F. Baumberger, "Bevölkerungs- und Vermögensstatistik in der Stadt und Landschaft Freiburg (im Uechtland) um die Mitte des 15. Jahrhunderts," in *Zeitschrift für Schweizerische Statistik*, 36 (1900), p. 205 f.; Wilhelm Abel, *Die Wüstungen*, p. 70.

35. Evidence collected in Kulischer, *op. cit.*, p. 170.

36. Erich Keyser, *Bevölkerungsgeschichte Deutschlands*, p. 298.

37. In Florence the first onslaught of the plague in 1348 swept away two-thirds of the population, and in 1350 in Bremen three-quarters of the city council died (F. Rörig, *op. cit.*, p. 345 f.). It is reported that in Osnabrück only seven marriages remained intact (W. Abel, *Die Wüstungen*, p. 59 where numerous other pieces of information from the literature can be found).

38. Alfred Grund, "Veränderungen der Topographie im Wiener Wald und Wiener Becken," *Geographische Abhandlungen*, XIII, 1 (1901).

39. Georg von Below, *Probleme*, p. 73, note 1.

40. Rudolf Kötzschke, *Allgemeine Wirtschaftsgeschichte des Mittelalters*, p. 560.

41. Hans Bschorner, "Wüstungsverzeichnisse," in *Deutsche Geschichtsblätter* (1904).

42. Theodor Mayer, *Deutsche Wirtschaftsgeschichte des Mittelalters*, p. 113.

43. *Ibid.*, p. 116.

44. Josef Lappe, "Die Wüstungen der Provinz Westfalen." Introduction: "Die Rechtsgeschichte der wüsten Marken," *Veröffentlichungen der Historischen Kommission für die Provinz Westfalen*, XV. For a searching analysis of this see Karl Frölich, "Städte und Wüstungen," in *Vierteljahrschrift für Sozial- und Wirtschaftsgeschichte*, Vol. XV (1919–20), p. 546 ff.

45. Alexander Backhaus, *Entwicklung der Landwirtschaft auf den Gräflich Stolberg-Wernigerodischen Domänen* (Jena, 1888), p. 24.

46. Wilhelm Abel, *Die Wüstungen*, p. 4.

47. *Ibid.*, esp. p. 71 ff.

48. R. Kötzschke, *op. cit.*, p. 560; Theodor Mayer, *op. cit.*, p. 112.

49. More information will probably be needed to settle the argument as to how far a decisive climatic shift, similar to that in the Iron Age, might have threatened the existence of settlements situated along the climatic borderline. Special studies have been made of this question in Scandinavian works. Facts and figures in W. Abel, *Die Wüstungen*, p. 76 f. Even assuming that a climatic shift could definitely be demonstrated to have occurred at this time, this would not be unique; one has only to think of the climatic deterioration during the transition from the Bronze to the Iron Age.

50. See in particular Abel's book, *Agrarkrisen*. Cf. the favorable review of this by C. von Dietze in *Jahrbücher für Nationalökonomie und Statistik*, Vol. 147 (1938), p. 103 ff.; Ernst Kelter and Siegfried von Ciriacy-Wantrup, in their review of this book, *Schmollers Jahrbuch*, 60 (1936), p. 465 ff., have expressed a number of misgivings as to both the method and the assessment of material, but I cannot consider these here in detail.

51. Cf. the fundamental study of Siegfried von Ciriacy-Wantrup, *Agrarkrisen und Stockungsspannen* (Berlin, 1936).

52. W. Abel, *op. cit.*, p. 45 ff. This vantage point also provides grounds for criticizing the view put forward by Werner Sombart in his *Der moderne Kapitalismus*, Vol. 1, p. 515 ff., according to which the total development of the economy is to be explained simply in terms of the production of precious metals. In view of the fact that the production of these metals assumes comparatively little significance in other chapters of the book this is surely a misguided attempt.

53. Karl Lamprecht, *Deutsches Wirtschaftsleben im Mittelalter*, Vol. 1, p. 623.

54. That this was a general European phenomenon is a well substantiated fact. Cf., for instance, Kulischer, *op. cit.*, p. 129 f. Kowalewsky, *op. cit.*, Vol. v, p. 277 ff., assembles a large body of information coming from all over Europe, as does Abel, *op. cit.*, p. 27, note 4. For England, see G. M. Trevelyan, *History of England* (London and New York, 1926), which shows that during the Black Death the population decreased from 4 to 2½ million in sixteen months. Brodnitz, *op. cit.*, p. 426, notes that the population in England after the plague remained stationary at about 2½ million. For France, cf. E. Levasseur, *La population française*, Vol. 1, p. 39 ff.

55. Material on prices has been painstakingly assembled by Abel, *op. cit.*, p. 277 ff. Cf. also M. J. Elsas, *Umriss einer Geschichte der Preise und Löhne in Deutschland*, Vol. 1 (Leiden, 1936). Elsas, however, yields little for us, not only because few of the price details go back to the period of interest to us here, but also because the abundant material assembled has not been worked out in any meaningful pattern. A great deal of statistical material for the development in France, in Henri Hauser, *Recherches et Documents sur l'Histoire des Prix en France de 1500 à 1800* (Paris, 1936). Hauser's

statistics begin only from 1501, but they do bring out the upward development in the agricultural sector, at first very slow, then suddenly rapid, during the first decades of the sixteenth century. There are a number of wrong ideas in Cunow, *op. cit.*, p. 48 f.

56. Henri Pirenne, *Sozial- und Wirtschaftsgeschichte Europas im Mittelalter*, p. 186. Obviously, Pirenne does not mean to exclude the possibility of genuine temporary price rises either locally or over a larger area resulting, say, from harvest failures. Our concern here is to establish the general trend.

57. Cf. the figures given in Abel, *op. cit.*, p. 34. These three countries are put forward as examples because they afford the best statistical material.

58. Heinrich Cunow, *Allgemeine Wirtschaftsgeschichte*, Vol. III (Berlin, 1929) must be contradicted when he asserts that the agricultural boom had no real effect on the situation of the peasants (p. 17 f.).

59. Insofar as it was possible to avoid using wage workers. See my remarks on this point, below.

60. Quoted in Abel, *Die Wüstungen*, p. 59.

61. Quoted in Kowalewsky, *op. cit.*, Vol. V, p. 293.

62. *Ibid.*, p. 271. Instead of the many other citations that might easily be assembled, see the facts given by the same author on p. 277 ff. Cf. also Georg Steinhausen, *Geschichte der Deutschen Kultur*, p. 227 ff., esp. p. 271 ff.; Friedrich Zöpfl, *Deutsche Kulturgeschichte*, Vol. I, p. 406 ff.

63. Cf., for instance, the evidence from the sources in Kowalewsky, *op. cit.*, p. 272.

64. Such a thoroughgoing distaste for work could occasionally even lead to local and shortlived rises in grain prices.

65. Kowalewsky, *op. cit.*, p. 233.

66. Sombart, *Der moderne Kapitalismus*, Vol. I, 2, p. 523, gives figures for the issue of English coins. According to these the stamping of silver went down from an annual average of £8,906 (present value) between 1272 and 1377 to one of £1,157 between 1377 and 1461. Although other figures are not available he is probably right in assuming this to be symptomatic for the whole of western and central Europe.

67. *Ibid.*, p. 524. This is not to deny all validity to Sombart's two reasons, but only to set them in proper perspective.

68. Pirenne, *op. cit.*, p. 191, observes that the rebellions among the rural population in the fourteenth century were distinguished by the peasants' brutality, which was later to be their undoing. There were "fits of rage without consequences."

69. Huizinga, *op. cit.*, p. 30 f.

70. Thus Abel, *Die Wüstungen*, p. 60.

71. Cf. my article, "Die Preispolitik in München im hohen Mittelalter. Ein Beitrag zum Streit über das Problem 'Nahrungsprinzip' und 'Erwerbsstreben,'" *Jahrbücher für Nationalökonomie und Statistik*, Vol. 153 (1941), pp. 162 ff. Also important in this connection is Udo Froese, *Der Wirtschaftswille im deutschen Hochmittelalter* (Würzburg, 1937), even though it contains a number of errors or at least exaggerations.

72. See, for instance Henri Sée, *Die Ursprünge des modernen Kapitalismus,* p. 33 f.
73. Cf. Huizinga, *op. cit.,* p. 33: "There was now much greater scope for gratifying unbridled appetites and for accumulating stocks of money. And these stocks had as yet none of that ghostly intangibility which the modern credit system has given to capital; it was still the yellow gold itself which took hold of people's imagination. And the use of riches did not yet partake of the automatic, mechanical quality attaching to regular investment of money: gratification was still a matter of violent extremes, greed or extravagance."
74. This is emphasized also by Carl Brinkmann, *Wirtschafts- und Sozialgeschichte* (Munich and Berlin, 1927), p. 73 f.
75. W. Sombart, *Der moderne Kapitalismus,* Vol. 1, 2, p. 610 ff. Cf. the very critical remarks by Georg von Below in *Probleme der Wirtschaftsgeschichte,* p. 445 ff.
76. Kulischer, *Allgemeine Wirtschaftsgeschichte,* Vol. 1, p. 177, also points out that "considerable differences in resources" could be found among craft workers and guilds. Similarly, Kötzschke, *Grundzüge der deutschen Wirtschaftsgeschichte* (Leipzig and Berlin, 2nd ed., 1921), p. 129, and Heinrich Sieveking, *Wirtschaftsgeschichte,* p. 77. An informative set of figures is given in Horst Jecht, "Studien zur gesellschaftlichen Struktur der mittelalterlichen Städte," *Vierteljahrschrift für Sozial- und Wirtschaftsgeschichte,* Vol. xix (1926), p. 48 ff., esp. p. 72 ff.
77. The fact that political economists, as a matter of principle, do not—and indeed cannot—include luck among the data on which they found their theories, but restrict themselves to rational economic processes, should not blind economic historians to the fact that good fortune of this sort does occasionally have some part to play in history.
78. Sombart, *op. cit.,* p. 619.
79. *Ibid.,* p. 616.
80. R. Kötzschke, *Allgemeine,* p. 561.
81. Cf. the remarks in Abel, *Agrarkrisen,* p. 33 f., where series of prices for building materials, textiles, and iron products from England are given (based on investigations by Rogers). Of importance even today is J. Falke, "Geschichte der Statistik der Preise im Königreich Sachsen," *Jahrbücher für Nationalökonomie und Statistik,* Vol. xiii (1869).
82. Cf. T. von Inama-Sternegg, *Deutsche Wirtschaftsgeschichte,* Vol. iii, 2, p. 464.
83. There is still a lack of well-founded investigations into the relatively high expenditure on the defensive installations of towns and cities. Only a few individual facts give any indication of how high this was. In the city budget of Cologne for 1397, about 79 per cent of all expenditure went directly or indirectly to defense, especially fortifications, and also to soldiers' pay, etc. (Cf. Rörig, *op. cit.,* p. 377).
84. Walter Goetz, "Deutschland vom 13.–16. Jahrhundert," *Propyläen-Weltgeschichte,* Vol. 4 (Berlin, 1932), p. 431. It is perhaps almost symbolical that the first German university (Prague) was set up in 1348.

85. Franz Oppenheimer, *System der Soziologie*, Vol. IV, 2 (Jena, 1933), p. viii. The same author's *Grossgrundeigentum und soziale Frage*, (Jena, 1922), centers on this problem. "When agricultural income grows, so will that of the towns; when agricultural income is fixed, that of the towns is unable to expand." This is one of the key sentences of the book (p. 357).
86. F. Oppenheimer, *System*, Vol. IV, p. ix.
87. Wilhelm Abel, in his *Agrarkrisen*, gives the relevant section the title: "The 'Golden Age' of the Wage Earner" (p. 35). Cf. also Kulischer, *op. cit.*, p. 130 f., where a great deal of evidence can be found. There is a complete misunderstanding of this phenomenon in Oppenheimer, *Grossgrundeigentum*, p. 350, where, on the basis of a number of facts taken uncritically from Lamprecht, he reaches the conclusion that day wages rose during most of the fifteenth century and then fell off again. The luxurious clothing habits of the time, and the wage legislation of territorial princes are advanced as proof of this contention.
88. Ernst Kelter, in *Schmollers Jahrbuch*, 60 (1936), p. 66 f.
89. Lujo Brentano, *Eine Geschichte der wirtschaftlichen Entwicklung Englands*, Vol. I (Jena, 1927), p. 331.
90. Hanns Platzer, "Geschichte der ländlichen Arbeitsverhältnisse in Bayern," *Altbayerische Forschungen*, II/III (Munich, 1904), p. 53.
91. Rörig, *op. cit.*, p. 345.
92. For England, cf. G. Brodnitz, *op. cit.*, p. 77 ff. As early as 1349—immediately after the first plague epidemic—a royal ordinance was issued (later ratified and expanded by Parliament as the "Statute of Laborers"), which contained provisions for compulsory labor and fixed wages. Cf. also Lujo Brentano, *op. cit.*, p. 331 f. For Germany, see the extensive material in Ernst Kelter, *Geschichte der Obrigkeitlichen Preisregelung* (Jena, 1935), p. 91 f. Important also is Otto Könnecke, *Rechtsgeschichte des Gesindes in West- und Süddeutschland* (Marburg, 1912), in particular p. 609 ff. Cf. also Kötzschke, *op. cit.*, p. 557 ff.
93. For France, cf. Émile Levasseur, *Histoire des classes ouvrières* (Paris, 2nd ed., 1901), Vol. I, p. 676 ff.; H. Sée, *Französiche Wirtschaftsgeschichte*, Vol. I, p. 47 f. In France the general distress was increased all the more by the miseries caused by the Hundred Years' War.
94. Hanns Platzer, *op. cit.*, p. 65. He adds: "This provision was in all respects typical for similar edicts that were to be issued in subsequent centuries" (p. 66).
95. "On account of the great dangers that have beset us and many others in all territories as a result of the dying which has been in the territory and especially among peasants, artisans, and laborers." Quoted in T. von Inama-Sternegg, *Deutsche Wirtschaftsgeschichte*, Vol. III, p. 304; von Inama-Sternegg is quite right when he adds that "the depopulation of the land setting in as a result of the serious plagues of the last few years was the specific cause of these conditions." Cf. also Otto Könnecke, *op. cit.*, p. 613. These measures have been more closely examined recently by Otto Stolz, *Rechtsgeschichte des Bauernstandes und der Landwirtschaft in Tirol und Vorarlberg* (Bozen, 1949), pp. 119 f., 153 f. On p. 119 he rightly refutes (though

perhaps not sharply enough) the view of A. Jäger, who had been of the opinion that this reason was nothing more than a pretext.

96. Compulsory labor measures of this sort were frequently and repeatedly promulgated after this period. In the age of mercantilism they belonged, so to speak, to the reserve stock in the arsenal of economic policy. Times of special emergency occasionally demand special measures. Thus, to take an example from a later period, after the ravages of the Seven Years' War in the kingdom of Saxony, four years' obligatory land work was prescribed for all country-born children of subjects. Cf. Friedrich Lütge, *Die Mitteldeutsche Grundherrschaft* (Jena, 1934), p. 197. For more general reading, see especially W. Kähler, *Gesindewesen und Gesinderecht in Deutschland* (Jena, 1896); Robert Wuttke, *Gesindeordnungen und Gesindezwangsdienst in Sachsen* (Leipzig, 1893).

97. Otto Stolz, *op. cit.*, p. 119.

98. One need only look at the older ordinances concerning farm workers to see this: the important points in these cases were regulations governing the commencement and termination of service, the nature of payment, the employer's liability for damages caused by his workers, clothing regulations, etc. Wage stipulations are found only occasionally and built into the other settlements. Striking examples of city policies for ensuring supplies can be found in Hans-Gerd von Rundstedt, "Die Regelung des Getreidehandels in den Städten Südwestdeutschlands und der deutschen Schweiz," Supplement 19 to *Vierteljahrschrift für Sozial- und Wirtschaftsgeschichte* (Stuttgart, 1930). Also Ernst Kelter, *Geschichte der Obrigkeitlichen Preisregelung*, Vol. 1.

99. To give a few examples: There were corresponding provisions in Waldeck (1386), the Prussian territory of the Teutonic Order (1406), Nassau (1424), etc. (Könnecke, *op. cit.*, p. 613 f.).

100. It is usual to try to find the roots of these early developments in the discoveries and other transformations at the beginning of so-called modern times. Cf. Kurt Zielenziger, *Die alten deutschen Kameralisten* (Jena, 1914), p. 59.

101. Brodnitz, p. 176.

102. Könnecke, p. 610.

103. Wilhelm Abel, *Die Wüstungen*, esp. p. 43 ff. Abel devotes an especially detailed study to this particular question.

104. Kulischer, *op. cit.*, p. 133 ff.

105. Götz von Pölnitz, *Jakob Fugger* (Tübingen, 1949), p. 5.

106. Franz Oppenheimer, *Grossgrundeigentum*, p. 397 ff., has many useful observations on this problem. He collates evidence from the literature on the migration from small towns and the rural areas (cf. p. 443 ff.).

107. Cf., for example, R. Kötzschke, *Allgemeine Wirtschaftsgeschichte des Mittelalters*, p. 549 ff. For northwest Germany, cf. Werner Wittich, *Die Grundherrschaft in Nordwestdeutschland* (Leipzig, 1896), a classical work in which very few points have proved in need of revision. In my own *Mitteldeutsche Grundherrschaft* (Jena, 1934), p. 8 ff., I was able to confirm the disappearance, almost without trace, of all earlier bondage in central

Germany. For the situation in Bavaria, see also my book, *Die Bayerische Grundherrschaft* (Stuttgart, 1949), p. 69. A recent account of the Tyrol is provided by Otto Stolz, *op. cit.*, pp. 70, 93 f., 127 ff. For England, cf. G. M. Trevelyan, *op. cit.*

108. This is probably the conclusion to be drawn from Kötzschke's article, "Bauer, Bauerngut und Bauernstand," *Handwörterbuch der Staatswissenschaften*, Vol. II (Jena, 4th ed., 1924), p. 374.

109. On this far-reaching problem, see Barthel Huppertz, *Räume und Schichten bäuerlicher Kulturformen in Deutschland* (Bonn, 1939), p. 25 ff.; and also my own *Die Bayerische Grundherrschaft*, p. 94 ff. It is impossible to go any further into this problem here. There is a lamentable shortage of special studies on the fourteenth and fifteenth centuries.

110. T. von Inama-Sternegg, *Deutsche Wirtschaftsgeschichte*, Vol. III, 1, p. 314.

111. Cf. Trevelyan, *op. cit.*

112. Willy Andreas, *Deutschland vor der Reformation* (Stuttgart and Berlin, 1932), p. 276; Friedrich Zöpfl, *op. cit.*, 368. *Deutsche Kulturgeschichte*, Vol. I (2nd ed., Freiburg im Breisgau, 1931), p. 368

113. T. von Inama-Sternegg, *Deutsche Wirtschaftsgeschichte*, Vol. III, 1, p. 168.

114. Cf. Lamprecht, *Deutsches Wirtschaftsleben im Mittelalter*, Vol. I, 2, p. 862 ff. When Werner Stark, *Ursprung und Aufstieg des landwirtschaftlichen Grossbetriebs in den böhmischen Ländern* (Brünn, 1934), p. 21, contends that inflation was the "arch-enemy" of all those who lived on rents he is quite right, though it is surely wrong to infer from this, as he does, that it was the decisive factor in the transition from the seigneurial system to squirearchy.

115. Cf. Abel, *Die Wüstungen*, p. 110 ff. On p. 103 ff., he furnishes some interesting details, painstakingly assembled, on the payments made by peasants to both lords and church.

116. This has been pointed in particular by Alfons Dopsch, *Herrschaft und Bauer in der deutschen Kaiserzeit* (Jena, 1939), p. 173 f. (to some extent advanced as a criticism of the untenable views of T. von Inama-Sternegg). Dopsch's arguments, though principally based on sources from Austria and southwest Germany, also apply to other parts of Germany, including East Prussia. According to Lothar Weber, *Preussen vor 500 Jahren* (Danzig, 1878), p. 572, the Teutonic Order (probably the largest holder of seigneurial property at that time) had about 30,000 tons of grain stored up in its strongholds in *c.* 1400; only the smaller part of this was destined for consumption, the rest was to be marketed. Cf. also Abel, *op. cit.*, p. 112 f.

117. Wilhelm Abel is thus quite right to reject the sumptuary theory, at least in its exaggerated form, i.e., that it was primarily the increase in luxurious living which brought on the economic ruin of the lords of the manor (*op. cit.*, p. 133 f.).

118. For dates see *ibid.*, p. 119 ff.

119. Cf. Karl Bücher, *Die Bevölkerung von Frankfurt am Main im 14. und 15. Jahrhundert* (Tübingen, 1886), a comprehensive book packed with material.

120. Cunow, *Allgemeine Wirtschaftsgeschichte*, Vol. III (Berlin, 1929), p. 46.

121. Cf., for example, Zöpfl, *op. cit.*, p. 368.

122. It is obviously impossible here to go any further into this wide and complex set of questions. It will be sufficient to refer to Werner Wittich, "Epochen der deutschen Agrargeschichte," in *Grundriss der Sozialökonomik*, VII (Tübingen, 1914), p. 16; also, though differing in some respects, "Der Osten und der Westen Deutschlands. Der Ursprung der Gutsherrschaft," the first of a collection of monographs by Georg von Below printed in *Territorium und Stadt* (Munich and Leipzig, 1900). Georg Friedrich Knapp, *Die Bauernbefreiung*, Vol. I (Munich and Leipzig, 2nd ed., 1927), p. 38, while recognizing that the Black Death had left many peasant holdings vacant, thus thrusting them into the lap of the landlords, sees the most important factor in the profits to be made in grain export. It seems to me that the drawback of all these studies is their inadequate notion of squirearchy, which is simply equated with large-scale agriculture. On this point, see what I myself have said in my *Die mitteldeutsche Grundherrschaft*, p. 195 ff.; and *Die Bayerische Grundherrschaft*, p. 180.

123. It might be well, just in passing. to make the following observation. Georg von Below, *Vom Mittelalter zur Neuzeit* (Leipzig, 1924), p. 91, polemicized against E. von Frisch, *Der Übergang vom Lehndienst zum Solddienst in Österreich* (Vienna, 1916), by asserting that Frisch was mistaken in placing this transition during the second half of the fourteenth century: "This is really rather too early." Frisch is probably right. His line of argument, however, is deficient, since its general purport is that the decisive factor in this development is to be sought in the many wars and feuds of this age, and in particular in the shortage of retainers brought about by the decline of feudalism. Closer consideration should be given to the following line of thought: the shortage of retainers was decisively conditioned by the Black Death; the nobles were in no position to offer the pay necessary for winning new followers, and they were soon unable for their own part to raise the money for armaments. Only cities and princes were able to pay mercenaries, and these they recruited from among the impoverished and rootless country people. This brief indication is all that is possible here.

124. It might be pointed out here that the same process was to repeat itself, for exactly the same reasons, after the ravages of the Thirty Years' War. For a summary of this, see Günther Franz, *Der Dreissigjährige Krieg und das deutsche Volk* (Jena, 2nd ed., 1943), p. 112 ff.

125. Taken from Abel, *Die Wüstungen*, p. 129.

126. Barthel Huppertz, *op. cit.*, p. 80, relying on G. Aubin, *Zur Geschichte des gutsherrlich-bäuerlichen Verhältnisses in Ostpreussen* (Leipzig, 1910).

127. Lamprecht, *op. cit.*, p. 991 ff.

128. More details in my *Bayerische Grundherrschaft*, p. 4 f.

129. Rörig, *op. cit.*, p. 352 f.

130. Stolz (*op. cit.*, p. 102 *passim*) approaches the question from a different angle and comes to the same conclusion on the basis of abundant archival material.

131. The following details concerning the income of the territorial ruler of Tyrol may be taken as typical: his revenue from manorial property came to about 8,000 florins in 1300 (about a tenth of his total revenues), and to

about 29,000 florins in 1750 (only about a twenty-fifth). Stolz, *op. cit.*, p. 276 f.

132. Heinrich Mitteis, *Der Staat des hohen Mittelalters* (Weimar, 2nd ed., 1944), p. 490.

133. Hermann Aubin, "Das Gesamtbild der mittelalterlichen deutschen Ostsiedlung," in *Deutsche Ostforschung*, Vol. 1 (Leipzig, 1942), p. 351. At this point, referring to the sudden cessation of colonization in the east and the reasons for it, Aubin says that "we still have a long way to go before a satisfactory explanation is found." In my opinion, the considerations put forward in this article do go at least a part of the way.

134. This is the thesis put forward especially by Oppenheimer, *op. cit.*, p. 401 ff. It seems to me quite mistaken to call the flowering of the German towns up to the middle of the sixteenth century a "false flowering," as he does. Oppenheimer, *op. cit.*, p. 404.

135. *Ibid.*, p. 405.

136. Abel, *Agrarkrisen*, p. 60.

137. Cf. also Will-Erich Peuckert, *Die grosse Wende* (Hamburg, 1948), a provocative book, full of ideas. [Also discussed at length in Chapter 2 of this book.]

10 Willibald Pirckheimer: A Study of His Personality as a Scholar

HANS RUPPRICH

Born in 1898, Hans Rupprich has taught at the University of Vienna since 1929; since 1951 he has been Professor of German Language and Literature. He has published numerous works on German humanism and its significant representatives, including books and articles on Nicholas of Cusa, Pirckheimer, Celtis, Dürer, and Reuchlin.

THE finest portrait of Pirckheimer is Dürer's well-known copper engraving of 1524. It is a likeness that has retained all its original authenticity; even today the beholder seems to see before his eyes the personality of the man not only as he appeared to others but as he really was. It is a pictorial representation springing from intimate familiarity with the subject, both his appearance and his character; and no verbal description given by contemporary scholars or poets has come anywhere near it for sheer expressiveness—not even Pirckheimer's own autobiographical fragment. The picture does not speak with words or concepts; it makes a direct visual impact on posterity, though—needless to say—allowances must always be made for the aesthetic ideals and the prevailing style of its own age.

An attempt to translate a pictorial impression into intellectual terms calls for careful analysis and sympathetic interpretation, though any characterization produced in this way will be liable to the same subjectivity as a verbal description, since all applications of intellect and language will inevitably bear the marks of the individual thinker. This is the criterion by which we must judge the efforts of scholars to offer a literary portrait of that great German humanist, Willibald Pirckheimer.

The first scholarly attempts to grasp the essentials of Pirckheimer's personality were not made until a hundred years after Dürer's death. Pirckheimer's descendant, Hans Imhoff (1562–1629), published a selection of his great-uncle's German writings in his *Theatrum Virtutis et Honoris, oder Tugend Büchlein* (Nuremberg, 1606). He also commissioned Konrad Rittershausen and Melchior Goldast to begin work on an edition of Pirckheimer's Latin *Opera* (Frankfurt am Main, 1610). Each of these books was prefaced with a lengthy biography. An attempt to edit Pirckheimer's correspondence was undertaken by the jurist Johann Heumann: *Documenta literaria* (Altdorf, 1758). Three volumes were planned, but only the first appeared.

More recent endeavors to understand and present Pirckheimer's personality started among local historians in Nuremberg.[1] Karl Hagen set out to produce a comprehensive biography by showing Pirckheimer to be the central figure of his age and its events.[2] Hagen was followed by David Friedrich Strauss, whose biography of Ulrich von Hutten (1871) contained a brilliantly written characterization of Pirckheimer, and then by Moriz Thausing's biography of Dürer (1st ed. 1875; 2nd 1884), which contained an assessment of Pirckheimer's place in Dürer's artistic career. Friedrich Roth's *Willibald Pirckheimer, ein Lebensbild aus dem Zeitalter des Humanismus und der Reformation* (Halle, 1887), and Ludwig Geiger's article in the *Allgemeine Deutsche Biographie*, Vol. 26 (1888), marked the end of this second stage of Pirckheimer scholarship.

A new and decisive phase in the attempts to do justice to Pirckheimer's personality began with the early studies of Arnold Reimann (1870–1938), who examined Pirckheimer's papers and library while doing research for a dissertation at the University of Berlin. Part of Reimann's thesis was printed as *Pirckheimer Studien, I und II* (Berlin, 1900). Another part was published by me after Reimann's death, *Die älteren Pirckheimer* (Leipzig, 1944). These studies indicate that Reimann would have been the man to produce a significant scholarly study of Pirckheimer. Reimann also intended to collaborate with Emil Reicke, who had been working since 1891 on an edition of Pirckheimer's correspondence.

The first two volumes of this correspondence did, in fact, appear (1940 and 1956);[3] but Reimann's attempts at a biography and a family history remained at the research stage, and were finally cut short by his untimely death.[4]

So far it had been left largely to historians and theologians to occupy themselves with Pirckheimer. The reasons for this are obvious. Pirckheimer was active in diplomacy; he was himself a historian; and he intervened in many of the controversies of the Reformation. However, by far the greater part of his intellectual and literary activities lay in other spheres: in philology—strictly speaking, in translating from Greek into Latin and German—in editing, theology and, last but not least, in his avid thirst for learning and his contributions to it. Inasmuch as the portrait of Pirckheimer has hitherto remained rather one-sided, I shall make an attempt in these pages to assess his true intellectual significance by going more closely into these latter aspects of his life and work.

While still a student, Arnold Reimann realized that Pirckheimer's personality could not be studied in isolation from the family to which his life was so firmly tied both by blood and by intellectual tradition. This family had been established ever since the fourteenth century in Nuremberg, a city with a very special character. The political and social history of Nuremberg in the late Middle Ages was governed, not by guilds and artisans, but by its old patrician families. These patricians were a conservative, shrewd lot, equipped with an acute sense of propriety, and disapproving, or at least wary, in their attitudes toward everything new and unfamiliar. The city had close commercial and cultural links with the south. Throughout the fifteenth century young Nurembergers attended Italian universities. Groups of scholars and merchants, small in number at first but increasing, became familiar with the innovations in scholarship, jurisprudence, art, and literature that had been taking place in the south and began gradually to assimilate them. The Pirckheimer family, as no other family in Germany, allows us to observe the process which, in the space of three generations, brought the new elements of humanist and Renaissance culture into the rapidly changing world of the late Middle Ages.[5] The Pirckheimers who determined this process were clerics, jurists, and diplomats by calling.

At the beginning of the new era stood Thomas Pirckheimer (c. 1410–73), Willibald's great-uncle, jurist and statesman in the service of the church, associate of Nicholas of Cusa and, for a time, of Enea Silvio Piccolomini. During his protracted residence in Italy like many of his contemporaries, he became familiar with the new learning in the course of his legal studies. His main interests can be glimpsed from a collection of letters and orations of contemporary Italian humanists (contained in Cod. Arund. 138 of the British Museum), in all 181 treatises, invectives, orations, and letters of Petrarch, Filelfo, Beccadelli, Poggio, Guarino, Bruni, Aretino and others.[6] This collection surpasses by far the *Margarita poetica* of Albrecht von Eyb and puts its owner in the top rank of the early German humanists. In the course of his life and activities Thomas Pirckheimer had frequent encounters, friendly and hostile, with Gregor Heimburg, Martin Mair, Leubing, Tröster, Hinderbach, Roth, Blumenau, and Eyb. He was associated with Gossenbrot and with Hartmann Schedel, and he belonged to the circle of men gathered round Bishop Johann of Eichstätt. Thomas's sister Katharina was the "highly learned great-aunt" of whom Willibald spoke occasionally.

Another man to assimilate the elements of the new learning at this early date was Thomas's brother and Willibald's grandfather Hans Pirckheimer (c. 1415–92). After attending a number of German universities he became a merchant, but following the death of his young wife in 1447 he returned to scholarly pursuits and engaged in humanistic and juristic studies in Perugia, Bologna, and Padua. Back in Nuremberg, he took his place on the city council, serving mainly in a diplomatic capacity. When introduced to humanism by his friend and teacher Giovanni Lamola in Bologna, he compiled there a collection of humanist treatises, model orations, and epistles of Lamola, Guarino, Poggio, Filelfo, Beccadelli, Bruni, Aretino, Traversari, and others, copying them all out in his own hand. (The volume has come down to us on

Cod. Arund. 70.) Even as a councillor of Nuremberg Hans Pirckheimer continued to pursue his humanist studies. He made an anthology, again similar to Eyb's *Margarita*, entitled *Liber de practica sive morali scientia* (Cod. Arund. 262, completed 1462). The arrangement of the material is still old-fashioned, but the questions asked, and the authorities quoted for answers, are distinctly humanist. Deep down, Pirckheimer still adhered to the scholastic attitude to life. But for the new problems that forced themselves upon him he took counsel from antiquity. In his anthology all the favorite humanist themes turned up in due order: the benefits and delights of friendship, respective advantages of youth and old age, love in general and love of one's country in particular, posthumous fame and contempt for death, the problem of *fortuna*, the merits of learning, art and science, the value of eloquence, of liberty, of memory, of self-knowledge, and so forth. An extensive library was necessary for such studies, and Hans Pirckheimer began to lay the foundation for one.

It may be imagined that a man with such interests as these would introduce his son to the world of learning. The son was Johann Pirckheimer (*c.* 1440–1501), Willibald's father. In keeping with family custom, Johann traveled to Italy in his twentieth year, obtaining his doctorate in both laws in Padua in 1465. Among his university friends in Italy were the Nurembergers Georg Prinzing, Konrad Schütz, Hartmann Schedel, and his future brother-in-law Johann Löffelholz. All these young men fell under the influence of Peter Luder, who was then living in Italy. In this circle there was performed a brief, witty students' comedy in Latin, the chief actor and author of which was Johann Pirckheimer.[7]

Following his return, Johann married Barbara Löffelholz in Nuremberg, in 1466. Then he went off to serve at the court of Bishop William II of Reichenau in Eichstätt, later as legal consultant of his native city. From 1475 onward he was active in Munich in the service of Duke Albert IV of Bavaria, and in Innsbruck of Duke Sigismund. Everywhere he established relations with intellectual circles. Upon his wife's death in March 1488 he sought retirement in Nuremberg, devoting himself to the administration of family property, serving the city as legal consultant, and pursuing his studies. In 1496, with the cooperation of his son Willibald, he was active in setting up a poets' school in the spirit of Italian humanism.[8] His library was rich in juridical and humanist volumes, which he used to compile what amounted to a complete encyclopedia of Roman and canon law.[9] At the same time he was one of the first Greek scholars north of the Alps. Like his father he collected letters and treatises of famous humanists, and his bent toward systematic arrangement led him to draw up a lexicon of heroic myths and an encyclopedia of rhetoric. The titles of his library manifest an enduring interest in antiquity and its revival, in poets, historians, and cosmographers. But despite his intimate and lively contact with all things new—or perhaps because of it— he turned in his advancing years increasingly to the satisfaction of religious needs and a taste for philosophical meditations. It was Marsiglio Ficino and the Neoplatonism of Ficino's Florentine circle which made the deepest impression upon him and drew him away from nearly everything else. Neoplatonist inclinations, melancholy, anxiety for the salvation of his soul, and the longing for divine grace led him in the end to withdraw altogether from public life, to enter the Franciscan monastery in Nuremberg, and to take priestly orders. Thus the cunning jurist, the sophisticated diplomat, the humanist scholar finally sought rest and peace in the ascetic life of a mendicant order and in the spirit of Fransiscan theology.

The third generation of this gifted family is represented by Willibald Pirckheimer (1470–1530). Willibald was born, not in Nuremberg, but in Eichstätt, where his father was councillor to the bishop. In a brief family chronicle, written on a leaf attached to a manuscript of the *Rhetorica ad Herennium* (Cod. Arund. 449), Willibald's father recorded his son's birth. The boy grew up away from his family's native city and received his early education from his father. Willibald notes in his autobiography that his father removed him from the company of his many sisters the

moment he was old enough to sit in the saddle. He took him along
on his many ambassadorial journeys, instructing him while they
rode. Willibald soon got to know not only Bavaria but also Tyrol,
Switzerland, the Low Countries and, in all probability, Italy. At
the age of sixteen he went to Eichstätt, where he began his training in the arts of knightly culture, learning courtly manners and
bearing at the residence of his godfather, the bishop. The youth
soon became so adept at his knightly exercises that he could out-
strip all his companions in wrestling, pitching, and running. It
was said that he could leap effortlessly over the tallest horse. In
several minor campaigns he learned to face danger and proved
himself a skilled and disciplined soldier.

As his son approached his twentieth year Pirckheimer senior
decided to send him to Italy so that he could resume his interrupted studies. The young man would have preferred to continue
with his military career—he wished to participate in the campaigns of the imminent war between France and the Emperor Maximilian—but when his father set before him the
respective advantages and disadvantages of a military life and
the life of the scholar, he allowed himself to be persuaded, and
obeyed.

It was, in all probability, in the autumn of 1488 that Pirckheimer left for Padua. The university there had two divisions, a
juristic faculty staffed by legists and canonists, and a faculty of
theology, philosphy and medicine. Pirckheimer's father seems to
have had considerable control over his son's university studies, as
may be seen from the rules of conduct he laid down for his work
at Padua.[10] The sheet of paper, dutifully preserved by Willibald,
on which these rules were written, confirms in general the facts
set down in Willibald's autobiography.[11] Pirckheimer senior
wanted his son to be educated in both law and the humanities;
priority was to be given to law, next the *studia humanitatis*,
including instruction in poetic composition. If possible the son
was to find accommodation with a certain Master Heinricus (so
far not identified) or at least in a household recommended by
this man.

A testimony to Pirckheimer's legal studies at Padua has come down to us: a carefully kept notebook for the lectures of Johannes Zacharias Campegius (1448–1511) on the Pandects. He began to take notes on the lectures in 1490 and finished them toward the end of 1491. As for general intellectual background, the young student at Padua found himself surrounded at first by influences ranging from late scholasticism to the new philosophy of religion. As regards the former, his father would seem to have impelled him toward the lectures of the Scotists, whose metaphysics were being expounded at Padua by the Franciscan Antonius Trombetta, "*Scotistarum aetatis suae princeps*" (1437 c. 1518). Scotism carried on the Augustinian tradition of the Franciscan school, the character of which was less Aristotelian than Platonic. In its fundamental doctrines it drew a distinction between two types of reason, the speculative (or intellectual) and the practical (or active). Philosophy availed itself of the former, religion of the latter. Theology was divided by Scotus and his followers into a *theologia naturalis* (the part that can be proved by reason) and a *theologia revelata* (which depends on revelation).

At Padua Pirckheimer seems also to have become familiar with Averroist Aristotelianism, championed at the university since 1488 by Pietro Pomponazzi, an independent, self-willed thinker and a man of passionate temperament. Although Pomponazzi founded his thought on Alexander of Aphrodisias, his aim was to develop Aristotle's doctrines on the original principles of Aristotelianism. In matters of ethics he inclined toward Stoicism. He regarded nature as a unity and man as an ethical being. He denied the immortality of the soul (in a certain sense) and advocated the principle of two truths, according to which a thing could be philosophically true but theologically false, or vice versa. Like the Scotists he apportioned philosophy to speculative reason and religion to practical reason. Elements of these and other views of Pomponazzi were to reappear occasionally in Pirckheimer's later writings.[12]

Plato's philosophy was expounded at Padua by Johann de Rosellis and Gabriel Zerbus. Like the Paduan philosophers and the Florentine Neoplatonists, Pirckheimer was later to combine

Aristotelian and Platonic teachings and to explain their assimilation to Christianity.

Even at this early date Pirckheimer showed great interest in the natural sciences: astronomy, mathematics, geography, and medicine. But his greatest enthusiasm was given to Greek studies. His teacher in Greek was the learned Laurentius Camers (d. 1503 or 1505), whose introductory courses in Greek language and literature drew large numbers of students to Padua. In a very short time Pirckheimer made such progress that even his teacher was astonished. Besides Camers, Pirckheimer also enjoyed the instruction of Johannes Calphurnius, who from 1478 to 1502 gave lectures in grammar and rhetoric at Padua. Under Calphurnius' direction he read Cicero and Horace.

A glimpse into Pirckheimer's intellectual interests at this time is afforded by Codex 12466 of the *Nationalbibliothek* in Vienna. Written in Italy, though later much elaborated, the codex contains a treatise on cheiromancy, a prescription against gout, a letter to Marsiglio Ficino dated 1472, and Ficino's Latin commentary on Platos' *Symposium*. Of the letters he wrote from Padua to his father, one, dated May 4, 1491, was concerned with money matters and with certain books he had been commissioned to obtain for his father—an "opus Marsilii Ficini" (perhaps the *De vita triplici*) and a number of classics. The other letter, dated July 12, 1491, reveals that Willibald had come into some sort of conflict with the rector.[13]

Friction with university authorities, and his father's constant insistence that he should spend less time on humane and philosophical subjects and more on practical jurisprudence, led to his departure from Padua during the second half of 1491. He moved to Pavia, where he remained four years. Pavia was the university of the dukes of Milan, with whose court Pirckheimer senior had long had connections. During his earlier diplomatic travels he had introduced his son to society there. Pirckheimer names his law teachers at Pavia as Jason Mainus (1435–1519) and Lancelotus Decius (d. 1500 or 1503). From his later correspondence we learn that he made the acquaintance also of another teacher of law,

Prothasius Bozuluz, and struck up a friendship with him. Further, his consuming interest in Greek studies caused him to seek association with Demetrius Chalkondylas (d. 1511), who was teaching in Milan at the time.

Much more decisive, however, than his juristic studies in Pavia and Milan was the social and cultural life he observed and participated in there. Duke Ludovico Maria Sforza had gathered to his court a distinguished group of scholars, humanists, poets, engineers, and artists. It is not known to what extent young Pirckheimer came into contact with them. But there is some evidence that he had two princely friends at the Sforza court: Galeazzo Visconti, the leader of the Milanese Ghibellines, and Giovanni Galeazzo di San Severino (who was to fall in the battle of Pavia in 1525),[14] the son-in-law and favorite of the duke and patron of Leonardo da Vinci.

Of the two surviving letters from Pavia, that of September 23, 1494, is addressed to his father and gives an account of the political developments in Italy resulting from the intrigues of Ludovico Moro and the invasion of Italy by Charles VIII of France. The other letter was written on November 14, 1495, by Bernardina, his mistress in Pavia, who gave it to Gian Galeazzo di San Severino to take to Nuremberg. We also have a number of Latin poems dating from Pirckheimer's years in Padua and Pavia. The most noteworthy of these are a poem of thanks to one Georg Nuremberger, a cleric, and some verses addressed to his grandfather and to Emperor Maximilian I. All were composed in Padua in 1491. In Pavia he wrote a poem to Stephan von Gundelfingen, apparently a student friend, as well as epitaphs on Andreas von Wallenrodt and Wilhelm von Bulzingsleben, fellow students most likely. It may also have been during these years that he made the Latin translations of two epigrams from the Greek anthology, on marriage and on the choice of a profession. Pirckheimer also interested himself in the poetic efforts of other men, and copied them down —as, for instance, the verses of Engelhard Funk, who was then living in Rome. It is not known how he got hold of these, though it may well be that he paid a visit to Rome.

During his student years in Italy Pirckheimer's attention was drawn to the significance of ancient inscriptions. The impetus to this may have come from Lorenz Beheim, a Nuremberger who occupied an important position at the court of Pope Alexander VI.[15] Pirckheimer's manuscript collection of inscriptions can be found in the Egerton Ms 1926 at the British Museum.[16]

The last year of Pirckheimer's residence in Italy (1494–95) may well have been the beginning of his friendship with Albrecht Dürer, an event of the most profound importance for his later life. This is suggested by the fact that an illustration in one of the books he acquired at this time may be by Dürer. While still in Italy, probably very shortly after its publication, Pirckheimer obtained the Greek edition of the *Anthologia Graeca Planudea*, published by John Lascaris, and from this, as has been mentioned above, he translated the two epigrams into Latin. His copy—to be found today in the Koenig Collection in Haarlem—bears on the lower margin of fol. 2 the Pirckheimer arms in body colors and gold relief. The miniature must have been painted very shortly after the appearance of the book, probably 1494–95, while he was still in Italy. At all events it was done before his marriage in October 1495, since the books he obtained after then (and until 1504, the year of his wife's death) bore the arms of the Rieters as well as of the Pirckheimers. Rosenthal,[17] who rediscovered this volume, has ascribed the painting to Dürer, supporting his statement with reference to the Italian art of book production.[18]

Pirckheimer's residence as a student in Italy, lasting, as it did, nearly seven years, could hardly have failed to play a considerable part in the development of his scholarly, religious, and philosophical attitudes, as well as in his personal life and conduct. The greater part of his subsequent activities as editor and translator would have been unthinkable without the extensive knowledge of Greek which he had gained in Italy. In both university cities Pirckheimer associated closely with Italians, including, as Bernardina's letter shows, members of aristocratic and elevated society, the *civilitas* and *eruditio* of the Italians attracted him more than the *ludus*, the *comissationes*, the *potus ac immodestus sumptus* of his German compatriots. And the Italians, for their part, considered him to be *humanitate praeditum*. Most of all, however, they seem to have admired his musical abilities.[19] No wonder, then, that Pirckheimer's culture, learning, and style of life should even later remain distinguished by a broad combination of the German and the Italian intellectual heritages.

As late as the summer of 1495 Willibald Pirckheimer intended to conclude his studies with a doctorate in civil and canon law and then enter the service of Emperor Maximilian. But suddenly his father called him home. His wife and father having died, the elder Pirckheimer saw himself obliged to take possession of his inheritance and administer the family property. He dissuaded his son from a career in the imperial service, advising him instead to marry and become a city councillor in Nuremberg. It was only with very great difficulty that Willibald could bring himself to part from the Italian way of life and the intellectual and artistic atmosphere of Milan and Pavia. His marriage to Crescentia Rieter on October 13, 1495, was an act of submission to his father's will. The marriage produced several daughters and a stillborn son, in giving birth to whom the mother died.

Pirckheimer devoted the years following his marriage to a variety of concerns. He administered his father's property and fortune, he made himself useful to his family's city as councillor, soldier, diplomat, and adviser in legal matters, he was active in education, publishing, and the institution of libraries. In October 1496 he was elected to the city's Governing Council and belonged to this body, with occasional interruptions, until 1523. His judicial knowledge and his oratorical skill served him in good stead. He possessed the social graces, a distinguished bearing, quick perception, an unusual power of discernment, and a splendid memory. As a respected and statesmanlike negotiator, he was often entrusted with ambassadorial journeys in the foreign affairs of the imperial city. In 1505 he went with Anton Tetzel to the Diet of Cologne, where, in the presence of emperor and princes, he successfully asserted Nuremberg's claims to several towns in Bavaria and the

Palatinate which had been acquired as a result of the Bavarian War of Succession (1504). He represented his city with equal zeal in its dispute with the Margrave of Brandenburg, who was pressing his claims to sovereign jurisdiction almost to the very doors of Nuremberg. He was active at the Diet of Cologne in 1512, standing up for the policies of the Nuremberg city council toward the Franconian landed gentry. In 1514 he went with Kaspar Nützel to the emperor's court at Linz and Innsbruck,[20] and in 1519 with Dürer and Martin Tucher to Switzerland in order to persuade the Swiss to enter into an alliance with Nuremberg. It is also known from various sources that Pirckheimer was occasionally active as legal adviser, which means that he engaged in private legal practice—either "for the sake of God" (that is, out of compassion) or because he was interested in a particular case.[21]

Anyone interested in forming a mental picture of Pirckheimer's external appearance during the first period of his residence in Nuremberg could well supplement all these facts with a portrait that can be traced to Dürer.[22] It is a small but very unusual woodcut, an illustration for the *Trilogium animae* (Nuremberg, 1498: Hain* 10315) of the fifteenth-century Franciscan Louis of Prussia (or Pruthenius) where the illustration on sheet E^r has been fitted into the second column as *caput physicum*.[23] We see a minutely detailed study of a head, covered with a cap, at the side of which the letters B, C, D, E and F demonstrate the seat of the various faculties. Pirckheimer was the model for this head. He has a fleshy face, large eyes, a well-shaped ear, a squashed nose, an eloquent mouth, and a double chin. Since the print is dated March 6, 1498, Dürer's preliminary drawing for the woodcut must have been made some time earlier, either toward the end of 1497 or at the beginning of 1498.

In the war of 1499 between Maximilian and the Swiss Confederation, Nuremberg had to support the emperor, and Pirckheimer, in virtue of his knightly training and military experience, was made captain of the city's contingent of troops. Much later, toward the end of his life, some time between 1526 and 1530, he set about writing a literary description of this campaign.[24]

Pirckheimer again rendered military service to his city in a conflict with the Margrave of Brandenburg in 1502.

In the midst of these multifarious concerns of the world he found time for his scholarly interests, and especially for his theological concerns. These latter show that Pirckheimer was far more deeply rooted in the religious tradition of the late Middle Ages than has generally been supposed. A piece of early evidence for this is the fragmentary draft of a letter to a person unnamed, dating from his early days as a member of the city council (perhaps 1496).[25] During the course of a convivial meal, Pirckheimer had referred to the contradiction in the biblical account of the creation between the making of light on the first day and the making of the sun on the fourth. One of those present—an older man, perhaps a cleric—described this as a schoolboy's question. Offended at this remark, Pirckheimer addressed a letter to his critic containing a detailed investigation of the entire matter. What he wrote shows a thoroughgoing acquaintance with theological literature, both patristic and scholastic: Augustine, Peter Lombard, Thomas Aquinas, and probably the Greek fathers as well: Basil, Gregory of Nyssa, John Chrysostom, and John of Damascus.

Another example of his familiarity with religious literature, and here in particular of his interest in destiny and the next world, is the description of a dream he said he had on August 25, 1501 (Cod. Arund. 175, fol. 90 f.), entitled *Colloquium de animae post mortem statu.*[26] In this dialogue he relates how there had appeared to him his brother-in-law, Johannes Rieter, who died in January 1501. From the ensuing colloquy of the two men it transpires that Rieter is still in purgatory. Pirckheimer asks where and what sort of place purgatory is, and what its torments are. Rieter supplies the information. Prickheimer asks: Are good works and the giving of alms of any assistance to the suffering souls? Rieter does not reply, but his gesture suggests that he would appreciate suffrages of this sort. Pirckheimer goes on to inquire whether souls in purgatory have any knowledge of their relatives on earth.[27] Rieter says they do, and tells of a universal Book of Life in which the souls can read the predestined fate of anyone still living. Pirckheimer asks what is in store for him, but Rieter defers the answer until a later time. Pirckheimer then wants to know whether souls in the next world can visit the living whenever they like. This, so the reply, is up to God, but he very rarely permits it. To the question as to whether it is right that men should be damned for minor trespasses, Rieter says that it is. Pirckheimer asks about the fate of his father. Rieter: He is in heaven. Pirckheimer asks whether there is such a thing as ineluctable destiny (*fati necessitatem*),[28] but Rieter remains silent. When Pirckheimer repeats his question about the Book of Life and Pirckheimer's own fate, Rieter replies: "It has been appointed by fate that you will become a very great and powerful man; but this power will cause great hatred to fall upon you, even insidious attempts on your life will be made. Despite this, you will come to no harm. But follow my advice and govern with clemency when such power is bestowed upon you. Fear God, by weighing up the punishment for the wicked and the appointed rewards for the good; and if you reflect on your last hours you will not sin in all eternity."

The work is a dream vision, a conventional piece with the appearance of the soul of a close relative who had recently died. Conversation turns on themes that might well arise from a traditional medieval spirituality, though there are obviously connections with Pirckheimer's theological and philosophical studies in Padua.

But this religious side of Pirckheimer's nature was far from being the dominant factor in his personality. One need only compare the religious views just cited with two Dürer portraits of him, done in 1503, and it will be seen at once that much more earthly elements prevailed. The first portrait, a silverpoint drawing (Winkler 268),[29] is rather like a momentary impression, not intended for publication. It is a profile of the festive Pirckheimer, the *bon vivant*: fat neck and double chin, mouth half open in speech, squashed nose, eye and ear expressively draw, a netlike hood pushed back somewhat on the head. All in all, a powerful head. Along the upper edge the subject himself inscribed a coarse phrase referring to Paidon Eros, probably a quotation.

The second portrait, a charcoal drawing (Winkler 270), would appear to be a revised version of this study from life. It forms a pendant to a similar portrait of his wife (Winkler 269) and is considerably stylized: the eye flashing and significant, the ear modeled rather more plastically, the upper lip longer. The mouth, here fresh and full, is somewhat nobler, and the chin juts out boldly. The majestic head, crowned with a tall cap, has the heaviness of a face that has not yet attained a fully developed shape, or has early lost it. There is a gravity, a resigned indolence. The head can only be thought of as belonging to a thickset body which has already gone to flesh.[30] The silverpoint drawing, which was not intended for the public, obviously offers a much less veiled insight into his personality than the stylized charcoal portrait.[31] But both impressions show a highly temperamental personality, intelligent, disputatious, self-willed, and self-indulgent.

Following the early death of his wife in 1504 Pirckheimer could not bring himself to remarry, preferring not to sacrifice the freedom which seemed to him so indispensable. There is evidence—among it some letters of Lorenz Beheim and Albrecht Dürer—that for a long time he enjoyed the good things of life with few inhibitions and with scarcely any fear of the great metaphysical forces that haunted the late medieval world.

Pirckheimer's life in Nuremberg was in every way an exception to the rule, a life according to his own conventions and principles. Between the city and himself there was a constant tension often leading to conflicts. After the death of the Losunger [treasurer; the highest political official of Nuremberg] Gabriel Nützel, he fell out with his successor, Paul Volckhammer, and in 1502 left the city council. In 1505 he joined it again, but a few years later he was being spitefully persecuted by Anton Tetzel. In 1507 he struck a citizen of Donauwörth in the face for having abused him, whereupon the council sentenced him to two days' imprisonment in the tower in addition to the usual fines.[32] In 1511 he came into conflict with the council and had to justify himself. And in 1514 Hans Schütz circulated a libelous publication containing various accusations against him.[33] Pirckheimer vindicated himself in a written defense, whereupon the council accorded him a full apology. After Tetzel's fall from office the squabble went on, this time with Konrad Imhoff; and finally he fell out altogether with Lazarus Spengler, who had been his friend for many years.[34] As late as 1522, a certain "Bärble, Grätz's girl" bore him an illegitimate son called Sebastian, a gifted and handsome child.

But behind all this external turmoil Pirckheimer created for himself a private life of very different character. He extended the library he had inherited from his father and grandfather, he practised generous hospitality, he corresponded widely, and acted as patron of the arts. The "European conversation" in his house never came to a stop. It included princes and scholars, Italians and Germans, cranks and enthusiasts, revolutionaries and reactionaries, men of the old faith and of the new. The emperor considered him to be "the most learned doctor in the empire." And hardly a day went past without his seeing Dürer.

Another of his special friends was Lorenz Beheim (c. 1475–1521),[35] who had returned from Rome late in 1503 or early in 1504 to assume his benefice at St. Stephan's in Bamberg. Beheim was a member of a Nuremberg burgher family, the brother of Georg Beheim, the prior of St. Lorenz. Their sister, Anna, was married to Nikolas Porst, and as a widow continued to belong to Pirckheimer's circle. After studying at the universities of Ingolstadt and Leipzig, where he had taken his master's degree in 1478, Lorenz Beheim had gone to Italy and there become *doctor decretorum*. In the early 1480's he was employed in Rome as majordomo to Cardinal Rodrigo Borgia, and after the latter's elevation to the papacy as Alexander VI in 1492 he served at his court. From 1492 on he seems also to have been active as military engineer or master of ordnance. The pope himself named Beheim his *familiaris* in 1494, and his *continuus commensalis* in 1501. Among the other men in the immediate vicinity of the pope were Giovanni Francesco Poggio (d. 1522), the son of Poggio Bracciolini, and the historian Sigismondo de' Conti.

During his twenty years or so of service Beheim shared in the life and activities of the Borgia court, and was on the best of terms with the cardinal's children, Lucrezia, Juan, and Cesare. When Cesare Borgia died in 1507, Beheim wrote to Pirckheimer giving the duke a memorial filled with deeply felt admiration.

Beheim was the possessor not only of numerous ecclesiastical benefices but also of extraordinarily wide learning, especially in the natural and occult sciences of those days—astrology, alchemy, and medicine. He was an ardent caster of horoscopes, and of all the German humanists he had had the most experience of life, having shared for years in the life of the Italian high Renaissance— and this at a time when its representatives and its achievements were entering a period of moral decline.

Pirckheimer formed a close friendship, both personal and intellectual, with this man, who seems to have spurred him into concentrating his attention on astrology. The draft of a letter written in about 1507[36] shows that Beheim was able to lay at rest the misgivings Pirckheimer had felt on the subject from his reading of Pico's *In Astrologiam libri XII* and Giovanni Francesco Pico's *De rerum praenotatione libri IX* of 1506.

Most of Pirckheimer's literary activity consisted of translations from Greek into Latin or from these two languages into German, as well as of editions of the classics of Greek and Latin literature. These philological labors have remained to this day unstudied and unassessed; in fact, there is not yet even a systematic catalogue of them. True enough, many of these editions and translations were rendered not long after their appearance superfluous by the spreading knowledge of Greek, or were replaced by better editions. But to conclude from this without any more ado that they were of no importance is to take a very unhistorical view. Quite apart from the fact that they were Pirckheimer's work and, as such, the expression of his intellect, they also exercised a definite and by no means small influence upon his age.

This is not the place to give an account of the reception of Greek literature and ideas in the fifteenth and sixteenth centuries. Suffice it to bring out the following points. Some of the most important teachers of the Greek language and literature were Byzantine philologists such as Manual Chrysoloras, Gemisthos Pleton, and Basilius Bessarion. In the course of the activities of these men a Neoplatonism developed, appearing in Germany with Nicholas of Cusa, and with Ficino and Pico della Mirandola at the Florentine academy in Italy. The decisive fact here was that Nicholas of Cusa was also a mathematician and a natural scientist, and Johannes Regiomontanus possessed such a mastery of Greek that he was able to evaluate the usefulness of the relevant Greek literature for his own mathematical and astrological studies. Rudolf Agricola, Celtis, Pirckheimer, Reuchlin, and others then went on to bring about a flowering of Greek studies in Germany. The significance of this revival of the Greek intellectual world lay first in the special educative value of the language itself, and secondly in the circumstance that it allowed the literature, philosophy, and science of ancient Greece once more to exert its influence directly upon the cultural life of Europe.

The sheer linguistic ability, the gift of sympathetic insight, and the sure sense of style and form which Pirckheimer needed for his work as translator had been acquired during his residence at Italian universities. His interests—encyclopedic in the Greek sense of the word—extended from literature to philosophy, to theology, history, and the natural sciences.

To the best of my knowledge, the first evidence of Pirckheimer's systematic activity as a translator is a letter to Anton Kress at Pavia dated December 19, 1501, in which Pirckheimer, after discussing a number of matters concerning books, writes: "*Cuperem etiam, ut inquireres, si aliquis pauper graeculus Papiae esset, qui convenienti precio transferret mihi de verbo ad verbum aliquas comoedias Aristophanis*".[37] Nothing is said about the language into which the "poor little Greek" was to translate. The phrase, however, affords us a glimpse of Pirckheimer's early interests in Greek comedy; and it shows that, in the beginning at least, he was not above asking for expert assistance.

At Padua, and perhaps even earlier through his father, Pirckheimer's attention had been drawn to Platonic and pseudo-Platonic literature. But it is impossible to say exactly when he began translating with a view to publication. At all events, it must have been very soon after 1500.

A third sphere of Pirckheimer's interest was the work of Lucian. On March 10, 1503, he wrote to Konrad Celtis to the effect that he had translated many of Lucian's dialogues.[38] His fondness for Lucian put Pirckheimer in a distinct line of tradition which had commenced in Italy with Aurispa and Filelfo and continued with Guarini, Rinucci, Poggio, Lapo, and others. Elsewhere in Europe the representatives of this tradition were Rudolf Agricola, Erasmus, Thomas More, Petrus Moselanus, Othmar Luscinius, and Melanchthon. Lucian, the rhetorician and satirist, directed his shafts against superstition, deceit, arrogance, sanctimoniousness, sterile moral theology, and the like. His Epicurean and sceptical inclinations may well have appealed to Pirckheimer.[39]

Another author whom Pirckheimer made accessible to a wider public of Latin readers was Plutarch. Pirckheimer's main interest was in Plutarch's moral treatises, with their concern for the general questions of ethics and morality in everyday life; but he also took an interest in treatises on religious and philosophical subjects.

A considerable part of Pirckheimer's philological activity was devoted to making Latin translations of the Greek Fathers, as well as to editions of Nilus, Fulgentius, and particularly of Gregory of Nazianzus. We do not know what attracted Pirckheimer to this, his favorite author. Presumably it was Gregory's mastery of rhetoric and philosophy, which moved very much along the paths of Platonism—though, in the ethical sphere, it also showed the influence of Greek cynicism, to which Pirckheimer became increasingly drawn. As early as 1503, as may be seen from a letter to Celtis dated September 17, Pirckheimer had translated the oration to Demonicus—ascribed to Isocrates—into Latin, intending it to be printed.[40] Around 1506 Pirckheimer wrote to Sebastian Sprenz, saying that he had translated Xenophon's *Hellenica* from Greek into Latin.[41]

Although Pirckheimer wrote most of his own works in Latin and usually translated into that language, he maintained that

German could stand comparison with Latin, and he championed the view that the German tongue was adequately equipped to reproduce the classical idiom. Translation, he maintained, must render the sense of the original, not the precise wording. In the dedicatory letter to his German translation of Plutarch's treatise, *How one may draw profit from one's enemies*, addressed to his friend Johann von Schwarzenberg[42] (Augsburg, 1591), Pirckheimer described the principles he followed, for translating in general, as well as for translation into German in particular. He wrote:

> Your Grace has often heard me say that it is possible to render everything in an understandable way from one language into another. Some think it is impossible to turn Latin perfectly into German. But to my way of thinking this error arises from their lack of understanding, or from the fact that they follow too closely the letter of the Latin and expend much more effort on the invention of elegant German words than on the sense. Thus it often happens that the translator does not himself understand what he is supposed to be communicating to others, and he hides his incompetence under the claim that it is impossible to turn Latin into German. But the truth of the matter is otherwise. Anyone who sets out to translate from one language into another must look away from words and instead render the meaning, clearly and reliably, in the intended language, and in such a way that anyone who knows that language may easily understand what he has translated.[43]

Pirckheimer's views agree with those in Luther's Letter on Translating. Pirckheimer was thus well able to appreciate the quality and significance of Luther's German Bible of 1522.

It was not until rather late that Pirckheimer made up his mind to publish his translations. The series began with Plutarch's *De his qui tarde a numine corripiuntur* (Nuremberg, 1513), dedicated to his sister Charitas Pirckheimer;[44] and *De vitanda usura* (Nuremberg, 1515), dedicated to Bernhard Adelmann.[45] In the preface to Charitas he notes that, "The Stoics rightly maintain that life is a gift of God, but that a good life is a gift of philosophy. And indeed, man has been given nothing greater and more precious than philosophy: I am not speaking of that captious and quarrelsome philosophy which contributes little or nothing to a good and happy life, but of that other which (in Cicero's words) heals souls, dispels needless cares and banishes all fear."[46] He goes on to paraphrase the moral content of the work. The wicked are unable to escape God's judgment, either in life or in death; God will awaken at the end and compensate for the lateness of his judgment by the severity of his punishment. "It is not to be thought that a perjurous, lying man should have the power to sustain himself indefinitely. Even if good fortune should assist him for a while, the time will come when (as Demosthenes says) this power will vanish." Pirckheimer expresses the wish that his sister and the readers of his translation may come to realize "what the ancient Greeks—even though they gave supremacy to the flesh and not to the spirit—wrote about the slow-moving vengeance of the divinity and the long drawn-out punishment of evil men." On the last page of this edition Pirckheimer adds a concluding remark addressed to Johannes Cochlaeus, refuting the idea that Holy Scripture lacks good style, and attacking the false representatives of Christ's teaching.[47]

The fact that Pirckheimer published this particular work of Plutarch's in 1513 would seem to have a personal reason beside his general didactic objective. In his self-vindication before the council in 1514 against the accusations of Hans Schütz, he defended himself against the complaint that he had printed a small book "against pious people." He said: "My little book portrays the reasons why evil, mischievous people are allowed to remain on earth and are not punished straightway by God for their misdeeds. to which end I, who have seen many things of this kind, have been moved to set it forth clearly. The book concludes that no mischievous, evil, lying man can come to a good end. If God has long passed over his deeds in silence, he will be punished all the more severely in the end."[48]

The publication of Plutarch's essay on the avoidance of usury also touched on a topical subject. The book was launched as a contribution to the heated debate going on at that time concerning the prohibition of interest and was directed against, among others, Johann Eck, who in the autumn of 1514 at Augsburg (and later in Bologna in July 1517) defended the charging of interest of up to 5 per cent on productive capital—in violation of the usual attitude taken on this matter by the Church. Plutarch and his translator, in common with Plato, Aristotle, Cato, and Seneca, rejected usury. Furthermore, Pirckheimer's dedication was addressed to a man who was known to be sternly opposed to the exploitation of other men's need or inexperience for the sake of financial advantage.[49]

Even these first two translations from Pirckheimer's pen show the translator using the dedicatory preface as a means of giving the text a topical twist in the service of a concrete polemical idea.[50]

A peculiar circumstance attaches to Pirckheimer's rendering of the *Hieroglyphica* of the Egyptian Horapollo.[51] This ancient work —it first appeared in the second half of the fifth century and was handed down in Greek translation—describes and explains Egyptian hieroglyphics, containing some correct information, but also much that is highly fanciful. Pirckheimer's Latin translation puts him in the company of those fifteenth- and sixteenth-century humanists who were beginning to extend the concept of Renaissance beyond the "Hellenocentric sphere" and to include Egypt and the East in their work of revival. An interest in this had been stimulated by the Florentine academy, with which both Johann and Willibald Pirckheimer had had close intellectual affinities. There Marsiglio Ficino, building on such earlier attempts as the *Hypnerotomachia* of Francesco Colona and the *Hieroglyphica* of Pierio Valeriano, had utilized so-called "enigmatic hieroglyphs" for the development of his mystical philosophy, while Pico della Mirandola had found in them a starting point for his theosophical speculations. The first Greek edition of Horapollo's *Hieroglyphica* had been published by Aldus Manutius in 1505. The difficult task of restoring the text had been carried out by the Aldine academy under the direction of Urbano Bolzanio. Pirckheimer's translation was made—in 1514—at the wish of Emperor Maximilian; at the same time Dürer was commissioned to illustrate the text. The translation bore the title: *Hori Apollinis Niliaci hieroglyphica quae ipse lingua edidit Aegyptiaca, Philippus autem in Graecum transtulit idiomo.*[52] Through this translation Pirckheimer became the purveyor of a new symbolism into Germany, which the emperor later caused to be incorporated in his two great projects of woodcuts, the "Triumphal Arch" and the "Triumphal Car."[53]

In August 1514 Emperor Maximilian approached Pirckheimer, through his counsellor and secretary Jacob Bannisius, with a request for a Latin translation of the world chronicle of the East Roman historian Johannes Zonaras, a copy of which Cuspinian had recently rediscovered in the library of the king of Hungary. Maximilian's intention may well have been to inspire his imperial successors to complete the work of reuniting the East with the empire.[54]

Following these imperial commissions Pirckheimer set to the publication of his translations of Lucian's *De ratione conscribendae historiae* (Nuremberg, 1515), dedicated to Emperor Maximilian,[55] and *Piscator seu reviviscentes* (Nuremberg, 1517), dedicated to Lorenz Beheim.[56]

In a manuscript brought from Greece just before the Turkish conquest, and sent to him by Jacob Bannisius, Pirckheimer came across an anthology of maxims compiled by St. Nilus. During the Christmas holiday of 1518 he translated the maxims into Latin and dedicated them in the new year to his sister Clara, who was mistress of novices at the convent of the Clares in Nuremberg.

Mention should finally be made of Pirckheimer's German translations. These comprise religious, moral, and didactic works, intended largely for Pirckheimer's relatives. Most of them are contained in Cod. Arund. 503 in the British Museum, a manuscript compilation made for subsequent publication and therefore neatly written out by a copyist. The following seven translations are by Pirckheimer: 1. *The Moral Maxims of the Most Holy Bishop and Martyr Saint Nilus, Rendered from Greek into German by Herr*

Willibald Pirckheimer. 2. John of Damascus' treatise, *How one may overcome the evil inclinations of the heart.* 3. *Sundry Useful and Elegant Instructions of the Renowned Orator Isocrates, which he Wrote for a Young Man named Demonicus, whose Father had been Associated with him in Friendship*; 4. *An Instruction of the Renowned Orator Isocrates Addressed to Nicocles, a King in Cyprus.* 5. Plutarch's treatise, *How one may draw profit from one's enemies,* with dedications to Johann von Schwarzenberg. 6. *The Preface of Crispus Sallustius on the book of Catiline.* 7. *The Five Virtues which God infused into Humanity and from which the Other Virtues Flow and Take their Source.* An eighth translation is not Pirckheimer's: *Discourse, or Oration, of King Agrippa which he Held before the Senate of the Jewish People in Jerusalem, with the Intention of Dissuading them from War with the Romans, translated from Latin into German by Lazarus Spengler of Nuremberg* (that is, Hegesippus, *De Bello Judaico,* Book II, Chapter 9).

The manuscript would seem to have been arranged according to content. First came the five translations from the Greek, then two from the Latin, and finally another from the Greek. The Greek pieces begin with two tracts on ascetic morality, these are followed by two educative and instructional works of Isocrates and an ethical treatise of Plutarch. In the translations from the Latin, Sallust was to be augmented by a passage from Cicero's *De officiis* on the conduct "befitting those who are in the government." Space was left for this on some empty sheets. Pirckheimer's friend Spengler, the secretary to the Nuremberg council, had been invited to contribute. The volume is rounded off by the moral maxims of the Byzantine philosopher and mystic, Maximus Confessor (*c.* 580–662). Some of the translations were clearly intended for a monastic readership, others for laymen in better circles.

Unfortunately these translations were not published in their entirety while Pirckheimer was living. All that was printed during his lifetime was Isocrates' instruction to Demonicus (Augsburg, 1519). After his death the maxims of Nilus were printed, edited probably by Hans Straub, in 1536. None of the other pieces appeared until a century later in Hans Imhoff's *Theatrum Virtutis et Honoris oder Tugend Büchlein* (Nuremberg, 1606).

While thus engaged as translator, Pirckheimer did not neglect his interest in theological questions. His "apologia" for Mary Magdalen, *Dissertatio sive ἀνασκοπὴ historica et philologica de Maria Magdalena, quod falso a quibusdam habeatur pro illa peccatrice seu πρόνη*,[57] concerns itself with the woman in Luke 8:2 and John 20:17, who was delivered by Christ from demonic possession, followed him faithfully up to his death and burial, and was the first to receive the Easter message. Invoking the authority of Greek and Roman Fathers, Pirckheimer attacked the numerous scriptural exegetes who interpreted her possession by evil spirits and sickness as evidence of grave sinfulness and equated her with the "woman of the city who was a sinner" of Luke 7:36 ff.[58] The composition of this defense came during the time of the Fifth Lateran Council (1512–17). At this council several false doctrines of the Averroists were condemned in the Bull *Apostolici regiminis*, namely the mortality of the soul, the existence of a single intellect, and the doctrine of the double truth. Pietro Pomponazzi was not mentioned by name in this condemnation, but he was doubtless included by implication.

Some of the arguments advanced by Pirckheimer in the apologia seem to be related to these events. For example he demands obedience to the Church's doctrines, but goes on to assert: "While I would not venture to say anything against the Holy Church— far be it, indeed, for me to do so—I should be the last to discourage any one from inquiring into the truth. For truth—as that good man Plato said—is the most powerful thing both with God and with man, and those who share in it are surely those who are destined for future happiness." Faith and knowledge seem therefore to have been separate for Pirckheimer. Theology was no longer identical with philosophy. This brought him very close to the Averroist position on the double truth. In the same way, Pomponazzi, despite the divergence of some of his teachings from Catholic dogmas, asseverated his readiness to submit to the Church's judgment.

To what extent ecclesiastical authority had already disintegrated, and how far satirical assaults on the late medieval intellectual system could go, may be seen from the *Letters of Obscure Men*, written in the course of the controversy between Pfefferkorn and Reuchlin. These letters do not simply contain the most biting humanist criticism of the ignorance and general conduct of a large proportion of the clergy; they also bear witness to the existence of resolute demands for intellectual and ecclesiastical reform. To give expression to this feeling, and to take a position in the controversy, Pirckheimer used the dedication to Lorenz Beheim prefacing Lucian's *Piscator* as a thoroughgoing defense of Reuchlin, thus making his own contribution to the European conflict between the new intellectual ideas and the outdated traditional ones.[59]

The Fisherman, or the Philosophers Returned to Life, is one of the wittiest and most eloquent of Lucian's dramatic compositions, packed with critique and irony. Not only these, but also the many possibilities of application to various representatives of late scholasticism, as well as the role accorded in it to true philosophy, combined to make Pirckheimer's dedicatory epistle an ideal place for an apologia for Reuchlin personally and for the principles proposed by him and his supporters. The first part of this apologia concerns itself with the opposition's moral failings, while the second sets forth some positive demands. Pirckheimer first turns against the intellectual dishonesty of certain scholastic theologians and their sophistries. "What use is it, dear brethren, if a man says he has faith but does not do works?" Pirckheimer's principal attack is directed at the dialectic of scholasticism; it contains a suggestion for reforming scholastic theology. He sketched an ideal picture of the modern theologian, at the head of whose qualifications stands the striving for moral integrity. "Theologians should be free from vices and rich in virtues;" they must know the three sacred languages and pursue true dialectic and true rhetoric; they should study natural and religious philosophy, Aristotelianism, but principally the Platonic system. They should be learned in both canon law and civil law. They should know in what points Aristotle and Plato agree and where they differ.

Does Aristotle allow the immortality of the soul or not? What reason does Plato adduce to prove it? Theologians ought to be familiar with Plato's position on the eternity of the world, on providence, destiny, free will, and so on. The highest place in this new system of knowledge should be accorded to the natural and religious philosophy of Plato; for Plato stood closest among all the pagans to the Christian religion. At the same time, however, Pirckheimer argued for a thorough grounding in the works of the major scholastic theologians. Nonetheless, the basis of all theological studies must be Holy Scripture. On his list of true theologians the names of Luther, Erasmus, Eck, Giovanni Pico della Mirandola stood peacefully side by side.[60]

The tensions that had become so clearly evident in the Reuchlin controversy reached the breaking point when Luther intervened in the indulgence controversy against Tetzel through his posting of the Ninety-five Theses in October 1517. Luther's and Karlstadt's disputation at Leipzig with Johann Eck in the summer of 1519, finally ranged the disputants on two fronts in the religious sphere as well.[61] Eck and Karlstadt disputed about grace and free will, Eck and Luther more particularly on the primacy of the pope. Formally considered, the debate was probably won by Eck, who had conducted the disputation with great theological erudition and dialectical dexterity, and had declared Luther a heretic and a defender of the Hussites. As a counterthrust designed to castigate Eck's personality and conduct, an ingenious and pungent satirist of the pro-Reuchlin, pro-Luther circle composed and released the *Eckius dedolatus* ("Eck with the corners trimmed off") in 1519 or 1520, which touched Eck on a number of sore points.[62] This biting comedy was a sequel to the *Letters of Obscure Men* and in particular to the second part, which had been composed very largely by Ulrich von Hutten. The plot depends on the academic custom of the *depositio beani* and uses elements of coarse carnival farces popular in the late Middle Ages. As far as the language goes, the writer was obviously familiar with Greek and Roman drama, at least with Aristophanes, Seneca, and Plautus. The play appeared without the author's name, but the man whose corners had been planed off took Pirckheimer to be the writer.[63] Lazarus Spengler was said to have translated the satire into German. As a consequence of these allegations Pirckheimer found himself drawn into the religious altercations from the very beginning of the struggle for and against Luther.

On the grounds of the minutes of the Leipzig disputation, taken by Eck to Rome, the Bull, *Exsurge Domine*, was issued on June 15, 1520. It was directed against Luther and his companions, and condemned forty-one of Luther's propositions concerning human frailty, faith, justification, grace, the sacraments, the hierarchy, and purgatory. It ordered Luther's works to be burned in public, and threatened him with excommunication if he would not recant within sixty days. The proclamation of the Bull was entrusted to Eck and the papal nuncio Aleander. Eck was given the power to add other names; the result was that Luther's name was joined in the Bull by those of the theologians Karlstadt, Dölsch, Wildenauer, and Bernhard Adelmann, and by the laymen Pirckheimer and Lazarus Spengler—Spengler, because he had been the author of an apologia for Luther in 1519, and Pirckheimer because Eck suspected him of being the author of *Eckius dedolatus*. Within the stipulated sixty days all seven were to apply to Eck for absolution; only the last three men, however, actually did so. Adelmann, at his own request and at the intercession of the dukes of Bavaria, was absolved *ad cautelam* in the middle of November 1520; but for the Nurembergers Eck made things a little more difficult. At first Pirckheimer and Spengler petitioned the Bishop of Bamberg in an attempt to gain a *purgatio*, or clearance. But Eck rejected this as inadequate. They then appealed to the pope. When Eck persisted in his negative answer, the two defendants, at the recommendation of Nuremberg city council, decided to submit. Pirckheimer was forced to appeal to Eck for the *absolutio simplex*, which required an acknowledgment of guilt and the abjuration of the forty-one stated errors. Only on strong pressure from Duke Wilhelm of Bavaria did Eck agree to grant the absolution. Since Eck had drawn out the affair as long as he was able to, Pirckheimer's name could not be removed from the text of the definitive Bull of Excommunication directed against Luther when it appeared on January 2, 1521. The whole matter stood in need of clarification. Pirckheimer was obliged to go to the Netherlands to present his supplication in person to the cardinal legate Aleander. In the end he gained final absolution, by means of Roman acknowledgment of Eck's absolution.[64]

This distressing business quite unjustifiably put Pirckheimer into the front line of the Reformation movement, but even as the affair was going on he set to work publishing his translations of Gregory of Nazianzus from Greek into Latin. Gregory was a master of both prose and verse, schooled at Athens, "the heathen university still radiant in the glow of evening," subsequently baptized and ordained priest and bishop. Pirckheimer first published six discourses: *D. Gregorii Nanzanzeni theologi orationes sex* (Nuremberg, 1521), with one possible exception all formal addresses. Pirckheimer dedicated the translation to his and Dürer's friend, Wenzeslaus Link (1483-1547), vicar-general of the Augustinians in Germany, and an early supporter of Luther.

Pirckheimer's publications and translations of Greek pagan writings were, for the most part, brought to a conclusion during these first years of the Protestant Reformation. Lucian was concluded with the *Fugitivi* (Hagenau, 1520), dedicated to Count Hermann von Neuenar, *Rhetorum praeceptor* (Hagenau, 1520), dedicated to Hieronymus Emser, and *Navis seu vota* (Nuremberg, 1522), dedicated to the imperial councillor, Ulrich Varnbühler.[65] He also published Plutarch's *De ira compescenda* (Nuremberg, 1522), dedicated to the Elector Frederick of Saxony, *De garrulitate* (Nuremberg, 1523), dedicated to Konrad von Thüngen, Bishop of Würzburg, *De curiositate* (Nuremberg, 1523), dedicated to Count Ulrich von Helfenstein, and, as an afterthought in 1530, *De his qui tarde a numine corripiuntur.*

From the literary remains of Johannes Trithemius (d. 1516) Pirckheimer received a manuscript containing the works of Claudius Gordianus Fulgentius (468-533) and the writings of Johannes Maxentius, the Scythian monk well known in connection with the Theopascite controversy (519). Pirckheimer immediately recognized their importance and decided to edit them. Several difficulties had to be cleared away, but the project was finally realized with the help of Johannes Cochlaeus, and the edition was published as *Opera Fulgentii Aphri . . . item Opera Maxentii Joannis* in Hagenau, 1520, dedicated to Charitas Pirckheimer.[66] Pirckheimer's interest in these works can probably be explained by their Augustinian doctrine of grace, their views on predestination, their attitude to the Greek Fathers, particularly to Gregory of Nazianzus, and their historical accounts of the Germanic tribes in North Africa.

In 1521 there followed the collective edition of translations of pseudo-Platonic dialogues and writings, comprising: *Axiochus*, *Eryxias*, *De justo*, *Num virtus doceri possit*, *Demodocus*, *Sisyphus*, *Clitophon*, and *Definitiones*—all of which Pirckheimer ascribed to Plato. It is no accident that this set of translations, also dedicated to Bernhard Adelmann, should have included a description of his life and activities at the *Neunhof*, an account particularly expressive of his feelings for life and nature.[67]

Pirckheimer's translation of Xenophon's *Graecarum rerum libri septem* was not published until after his death (Nuremberg, 1532). Other translations remained unpublished. They are: Aristophanes, *Plutus*;[68] Demosthenes, *Olynthiacus sermo I*; Lucian, *De luctu*, translated in 1512; Thucydides, *Historiarum liber I*; Aristotle, *Historia animalium I et II*;[69] Galen, *Philosophorum historia*; and Pseudo-Proclus, *Sphaera*. Pirckheimer had also begun a translation of Lucian's *Charidemus*.[70]

Pirckheimer's studies of Lucian, most especially of the facetious tragedy *Tragopodagra*, were the direct source for his single major original composition, the *Apologia seu Podagrae Laus* (Nuremberg, 1522). His own experience of illness—he suffered from gout of feet and hands—had prompted him in 1512 or 1513 to start a sort of diary of attacks and remedies; and in the end he came to have enough cheerful wisdom to give a satirical account of his afflictions. The work was dedicated to Jacob Bannisius, [71] the head of Maximilian's Latin chancellery—perhaps in gratitude for his help in procuring absolution from excommunication. The Lady

Podagra is brought to trial by the many men and women who have been subjected to her painful dominion, and she very skillfully justifies herself before the court in a structurally impeccable speech of self-defense. Everything laid at her door, she says, has been brought on by the accusers' own foolish actions. She never freely seeks anyone out; she only responds when revellers and carousers call on her. Apparently innocent sufferers may blame their parents and ancestors. In any case, gout is not all that bad: the sick man is visited by his friends, cheered and supplied with the latest news; he is treated with solicitude in society, on journeys, and even in the presence of kings and princes; at dinner parties he receives special attention. He is spared the perils of hunting, of sea voyages and war. Gout encourages a man to keep himself busy at home; he may thus gain a love of learning. Gout serves as a defense against excess and licentiousness, and turns sinners into pious, god-fearing people, and this can hardly fail to be of benefit to their eternal salvation. Pirckheimer's little work is in the form of a "Declamation," the kind of book he had frequently translated and a form that he himself mastered brilliantly. This, together with its abundant good humor and its irony turned on himself, make it a worthy companion piece to Erasmus's *Praise of Folley*. It is so utterly different from the *Eckius dedolatus* that one would be hard put to it, on closer comparison, to see how these two satirical products could have had the same author.

When Hadrian VI, a man noted for his piety and erudition, was elected pope in January 1522, Pirckheimer sent him an open letter on the underlying cause of the Reformation in Germany.[72] The letter was a defense of Reuchlin and Luther and a violent attack on Eck and the Dominicans, whom Pirckheimer blamed for the religious turmoil in Germany. It is clear that Pirckheimer expected understanding from the pope, who conceived it as his main duty to contain the religious innovations by reforming the church, and who had attempted to intervene in German affairs by sending the nuncio Francesco Chieregati to the Diet of Nuremberg in 1522–23 in order to publicize his reform plans and give assurances that complaints would be heard and remedied.

Another glimpse of Pirckheimer on the Protestant side is afforded by a fragmentary essay entitled "Concerning the Persecutors of Evangelical Truth, their Designs and Intrigues,"[73] composed in 1524 in Nuremberg, following the meeting of the diet there. But later that same year, when Erasmus, in his polemic battle with Luther on the question of free will, disputed the Reformers' idea of faith, warned of the dangers of a rigid determinism, and took his stand in support of the authority and traditions of the old church,[74] Pirckheimer found himself between two stools. His letter to Erasmus of September 1, 1524, condemned the stubborn resistance on the one side and the coercive methods on the other. In the preliminary stage of the Reformation, and also during its early years, Pirckheimer had been able to give his wholehearted assent to Luther and the movement. But as soon as it seemed to him that the excesses and misuses of the new freedom were convulsing the foundations of civilization and morality he felt obliged to defend what he had previously attacked.

But however deeply these religious matters may have engaged Pirckheimer during his last years, they were never his main intellectual occupation. This remained, as always, an intellectual and scholarly one.

Ever since the sojourn of Regiomontanus in the city, Nuremberg had been a leading center of astronomical, mathematical, and geographical studies in Germany. Regiomontanus had died in Rome in 1476. His literary remains and, most important of all, his library, had been left behind in Nuremberg, where they came into the possession of his pupil and admirer Bernhard Walther, a melancholy and taciturn man who withheld them from use and refused to let anyone so much as inspect them. Even after Walther's death in 1504 the books and instruments, which had been substantially increased in the years following Regiomontanus's departure, remained for some time in the hands of the executors.

Regiomontanus had copied out Ptolemy's *Geography* in the Latin translation of Jacopo d'Angiolo for the purpose of comparing the text and the figures with the Greek manuscripts; and he had made detailed corrections in this translation with references to the original Greek.[75] One of the few men who gained a glimpse into Regiomontanus's papers after Walther's death was the learned Johannes Werner (1468–1522). Werner found, among other things, Regiomontanus' *Trigonometry* and also notes on Ptolemy's *Geography*. In 1514 Werner published a commentary on Ptolemy, entitled *Recens interpretamentum in primum librum Geographiae C. Ptolemaei*, expounding Ptolemy's geographical theories and offering a paraphrase of his method of projection. A related treatise, entitled *Libellus de quatuor terrarum orbis in plano figurationibus* (printed in the same omnibus volume, Nuremberg, 1514), was dedicated to Pirckheimer, who had also come to be interested in Ptolemy.[76] At that very time Pirckheimer acquired the largest part of Bernhard Walther's library, and soon afterward, following Werner's death in 1522, he gained possession of further books from the library of Regiomontanus. In 1524 he attempted— apparently unsuccessfully—to find a publisher in Basel for two works of Regiomontanus which had been left in manuscript: *De triangulis* and the *Defensio Theonis contra G. Trapezuntium*.[77]

Once Regiomontanus's and Walther's books were in his possession Pirckheimer, spurred by the scholarly tradition of his city as well as by his familiarity with both Greek and mathematics, embarked on a fresh translation and commentary of Ptolemy's *Geography*. This task became his principal scholarly occupation during the last years of his life. The result was the *Geographicae enarrationis libri octo* (Strassburg, 1525) in two volumes with fifty large maps, including the large-scale map of America, and Dürer's woodcut "The Armillary Sphere." The *Geography* of Ptolemy is Pirckheimer's most substantial editorial achievement.[78] It was dedicated to Sebastian Sprenz, successor of Nicholas of Cusa in the bishopric of Brixen.[79] Pirckheimer notes in the dedicatory epistle that the available Latin translations, when compared with the original text, reveal many inadequacies. Scarcely a trace of Ptolemy's elegance and erudition had been preserved in previous renderings. Jacopo d'Angiolo had understood Greek, but had no knowledge of mathematics. Johannes Werner knew mathematics, but little Greek. He, Pirckheimer, was convinced that his own rendering was both clearer and closer to Ptolemy's original meaning, as he had followed the interpretations of the most authoritative mathematician of his age, Regiomontanus, whose *Annotationes* had served him as a model. To remove a second major inadequacy of older translations, he was adding maps to the volume, as these were required for full understanding of the text.

Despite this expenditure of philological and geographical erudition, Pirckheimer was not satisfied with his labors. What pained him even more than the misprints in the text was the fact that the publisher, Grieninger, for reasons of economy, had used the old Waldseemüller-Friesschen maps from earlier Ptolemy editions of 1513 and 1522 instead of having new ones made. Knowing, too, that even the best of translations could not do justice to the original, Pirckheimer announced to Hermann von Neuenar in the dedication to his *Germaniae explicatio* that he intended shortly to publish the first book of Ptolemy in both Greek and Latin, and that the other books would follow later, together with newly drawn maps.[80]

Pirckheimer's occupation with Ptolemy's *Geography*, especially with its cartography and tables, led him to his next work, the *Germaniae ex variis scriptoribus perbrevis explicatio* (Nuremberg, 1530). In this brief study he attempted to establish the location of places, mountains, and rivers mentioned in ancient authors (Caesar, Tacitus, Pomponius Mela, Pliny, Procopius, Solinus, Strabo, Ptolemy), and show correspondences between the ancient geographical designations and modern places and their names. These studies in critical classification comprised all the regions in which Germanic peoples, and particularly the Germans themselves, had settled. The first chapter deals with territories and towns, the second with mountain ranges and forests, and the third with the names of rivers.

Also connected with his work on Ptolemy was a treatise found among his papers, entitled *Chorographia* or *Geographia historialis Aegypti*. Pirckheimer had earlier manifested a keen interest in things Egyptian, and there may also be a connection between this work and Dürer's forty-eight constellations of the *Sphaera barbarica*, divided into two celestial charts and appended to *Cl. Ptolomaei Phaenomena stellarum MXXII fixarum* (Cologne, 1537). Dürer's charts are probably the oldest European illustrations of the Egyptian firmament.[81]

Like Konrad Peutinger, Pirckheimer realized that coins, as well as inscriptions, were important historical sources. We do not know when he began to collect systematically. Toward the end of his life (in 1528) he wrote a description of his collection, which appeared in 1533 under the title *Priscorum numismatum ad Nurembergensis monetae valorem facta aestimatio*, published by his secretary Andreas Rüttel along with a number of other minor writings.[82] Here, too, Pirckheimer attempted to establish verifiable connections between antiquity and modern Germany.

By the beginning of the 1520's Pirckheimer had reached the peak of his intellectual activity. The individual features of his life and personality had attained full maturity, and this at a time when his powers were at their height and fully concerted, with perhaps here and there even a trace of overripeness. It was this mature Pirckheimer whom Dürer caught in his copper engraving of 1524 (mentioned at the beginning of this essay) thus creating an authentic and permanently valid portrait. Subject and artist alike intended the picture for the public, as a memorial for the generations to come. Prickheimer asked Dürer to write at the bottom of the tablet the verse: "*Vivitur ingenio caetera mortis erunt.*"[83] The massive head, on a thick neck, crowns a large and powerfully built frame. Its features have undergone an improvement over the last twenty years.[84] The eyes fully dominate the face. The squashed nose no longer distracts attention from the face, whose expression has become more refined. The mouth, resigned now, but still eloquent, suggests the intellect and wit of the subject. It is not hard to detect a roguishness playing round the corners. All in all—and even if we assume that Dürer, in this portrait of his best friend, was concerned to render an ideal account—a monumental character, a significant face, full of energy, vigor, individuality, and dignity.

With the spread of the Reformation, Pirckheimer became increasingly aware of the darker aspects on each side. The leaders of the Catholic Church suppressed innovations by coercive methods; agitators and fanatics were active among the Reformers; scholarship declined—he even sensed contempt for study; the deserted monasteries, the hostility toward the monastic way of life, and the demands of the "rabble" for equal distribution of goods—all these appalled him. As soon as the reform of the church began to have cultural and social effects of this kind, Pirckheimer, the aristocratic patrician, felt himself called upon to take a stand against it in public.

Prickheimer's return to the acustomed tradition took visible shape in his defense of monastic life, in particular of the rights of the Poor Clares in Nuremberg. But he did not stop there. He entered into a controversy with Oecolampadius over the eucharist, and intervened in the dispute concerning remarriage for clerics. In the course of these altercations Pirckheimer ranged himself more and more clearly on the side of Catholic doctrine. His final pronouncement against Oecolampadius is an unmistakable rejection of the Reformation.

Pirckheimer had a host of female relatives in various convents. His sisters Charitas and Clara and his daughters Crescentia and Katharina were among the Poor Clares in Nuremberg, his sisters Felicitas, Eufenia, and Sabina and his daughter Charitas belonged to the Benedictine convent at Bergen near Neuburg on the Danube. His sister Katharina was in the Benedictine convent at Geisenfeld, and his sister Walburg in the convent of the Poor Clares in Munich. When Lutheranism had been adopted in Nuremberg and the city council took measures to dissolve the monasteries, Abbess Charitas Pirckheimer of the Clares resisted the government with force and ingenuity. She considered the attacks to be a restriction of religious liberty and felt herself obliged to protect her charges. In this predicament it was natural that the abbess and her nuns should turn for advice and assistance to their influential brother and father. Pirckheimer gave them his full support. He encouraged the nuns to persevere, called upon them to remain true to their faith and promised them his own house and home in the event of their being driven from their convent. He furthermore resolved to approach his friend Philip Melanchthon with a request for help, and did so in the well-known letter *Über die Drangsale der Nonnen*[85] (*Concerning the Afflictions of Nuns*). The letter remained unfinished, so it is not known whether it was ever sent in this form at all. It is, however, certain that Melanchthon visited the Nuremberg convent of the Clares in 1525; and once he had assured himself that the abbess and her nuns were acting in accordance with their religious convictions he brought his influence to bear upon the council, persuading its members that the nuns should be allowed to remain in their convent, though novices should no longer be admitted. In March 1525 the Reformation was officially introduced in Nuremberg. In the same year, Dürer dedicated to Pirckheimer his *Instruction in Measuring with Compass and Ruler*, in the dedicatory letter of which he protested against the hostility toward art and images which was making its presence felt in Nuremberg and elsewhere.

Dürer took an even more definite stand in 1526 in the captions to his paintings of the four apostles. Here he called upon all secular authorities in these perilous times not to allow God's word to be distorted by men, and quoted in urgent warning the words of the apostles he had depicted. Two passages counsel against following teachers of error and leaders of pernicious sects; the third and fourth passages warn against false prophets and against the scribes.[86]

It has long been known that Dürer's protest and warning were not directed against the old Catholic faith and its representatives, but against certain radical currents among the representatives of the new teachings[87] which were appearing in Nuremberg and elsewhere, and which he considered a threat not only to his existence as an artist, but to his religious and moral convictions as well. It is, therefore, hardly a coincidence that Pirckheimer should have intervened in his own way in the Reformation disputes. He did this at the end of 1525 and in the years 1526 and 1527, at the same time as Dürer, in fact, and to some extent concerning the same questions. He attacked a man whom he accused of being a radical, an iconoclast and a distorter of God's word: Johannes Oecolampadius and his interpretation of Christ's words at the Last Supper.

The two men had originally been friends. In 1517 Oecolampadius had dedicated to Pirckheimer his composition *Nemesis Theophili*, the hero of which was evidently the saint in the legend of the pact with the devil.[88] A further sign of common interests was the fact that both men had made translations of Gregory of Nazianzus and John of Damascus.[89] Oecolampadius had been living in Basel since 1522. He later sided with Zwingli. The relationship between Pirckheimer and Oecolampadius began to be clouded when, on January 21, 1525, Hans Denk was expelled from Nuremberg. Denk, rector of the school of St. Sebald in Nuremberg since 1523 had been accused of "un-Christian errors"—meaning, in this case, Anabaptism.[90] Denk had assumed his rectorship in 1523 on the recommendation of his teacher Oecolampadius and through the good offices of Pirckheimer. Always inclined to religious enthusiasm, Denk considered the Holy Spirit in the human soul as the principal source of revelation. He asserted the freedom of the human will against predestination, and believed, like Origen and Gregory of Nazianzus, in apocastasis—universal forgiveness—at the end of time. Pirckheimer, who had himself considerable leanings toward Neoplatonism, seems to have been for a time favorably disposed toward Denk, as was Dürer, too. But as Denk moved closer and closer toward Anabaptism the final break came. Pirckheimer now suspected Oecolampadius of being one of the leaders of the radical social and religious innovators.

When, on February 26, 1525, Oecolampadius wrote to Pirckheimer asking for an explanation of the circumstances of Denk's expulsion from Nuremberg, Pirckheimer would appear to have answered that both Oecolampadius and himself were being accused of secretly sympathizing with Denk. On April 25, 1525, Oecolampadius replied with a detailed account of his attitude toward Denk and explained his position as regards the eucharist. Pirckheimer did not find this defense entirely convincing. Then came news attributing to Oecolampadius sympathies to Thomas Münzer and the Anabaptists. On September 21, 1525, therefore, Pirckheimer wrote again to ask Oecolampadius to explain his connection with Münzer as well, The reply from Basel confirmed Pirckheimer in his suspicions that Oecolampadius was associated with men who openly preached sedition and were stirring the peasants to rebel against their lords.

In the meantime Oecolampadius had intervened in the eucharistic controversy with his *De genuina verborum Domini: "Hoc est corpus meum" iuxta vetustissimos authores expositione liber* (Strassburg, 1525). In this treatise he sought to refute the doctrine of the real presence of Christ in the eucharist and to demonstrate the figurative sense of the words of institution. This, in turn, prompted Pirckheimer at the end of 1525 to write *De vera Christi carne et vero eius sanguine ad Joannem Oecolampadium responsio* (Nuremberg, 1526), his first open attack on his old friend. Pirckheimer defended the bodily presence of Christ in the eucharist with all the meticulousness and the passion of a trained theologian. Though his views coincided generally with the eucharistic doctrine of the late Middle Ages, his ideas concerning the conversion of the eucharistic species agree with Luther's, who, while defending the real presence, rejected transubstantiation and proposed consubstantiation in its place.[91]

Despite this conflicting provenance of its ideas Pirckheimer's treatise was received with approval by the Luterans, indeed by Luther himself, who had never before credited the author with any particular seriousness in religious matters. From accounts given by Melanchthon, who frequently visited Pirckheimer's house in 1525 and 1526, it can be seen that Dürer was another ardent participator in the eucharistic discussions there. If the reports of Peucer and Manlius are to be believed, Dürer was often in opposition to Pirckheimer.[92] In the Catholic camp the treatise met with only limited approval. Johannes Cochlaeus immediately saw in it the heretical idea of consubstantiation; and even Erasmus expressed himself negatively. Zwingli's supporters were, of course, embittered.[93]

Oecolampadius himself replied with his *Responsio ad Bilibaldum Pyrkaimerum de re eucharistiae*, printed in Zürich in the spring of 1526. This response moved Pirckheimer to launch his second attack, entitled *De vero Christi carne et vero eius sanguine adversus convicia Joannis, qui sibi Oecolampadii nomen indidit, responsio secunda* (Nuremberg, 1527). The decisive element in this second onslaught was the unmistakable departure from Luther: "It is frivolous to fall away from the old Church," Pirckheimer wrote. The authority of the traditional teachers of the Church who had formulated Christian dogma should not be undermined. All the same, he went on, their authority must not be placed before that of Scripture.

Oecolampadius, in his turn, replied with a *Responsio posterior ad Bilibaldum Pyrkaimerum de Eucharistia* (March 1527); which, in due time, provoked Pirckheimer's passionate *De convitiis monachi illius, qui graecolatine Caecolampadius, germanice vero Ausshin nuncupatur, ad Eleutherium[94] suum epistola* (Nuremberg, 1527), containing as its motto the curse *"Corripiat te deus, Satan"*—May God punish thee, thou adversary, thou father of lies.

But while Pirckheimer found himself in this way in the very thick of the religious struggle of the day, he managed to find time and composure to publish, in 1527, his translation and edition of the *Characteres ethici* of Theophrastus of Ereso (327–287 B.C.).[95] This famous collection, of which Pirckheimer's edition contains the first fifteen chapters, offers "an account of thirty reprehensible and mostly ridiculous characters according to their modes of behavior in life." They originated in the Aristotelian and Peripatetic interest in moral characteristics. Pirckheimer's Greek text, together with its Latin translation, was the first printed version of this hitherto unknown work. The Greek manuscript of the *Characteres* had once been given to Pirckheimer as a gift by his friend Giovanni Francesco Pico della Mirandola, and Pirckheimer now inscribed the work to his friend Dürer in both Greek and Latin dedications: May he (Dürer), and all readers, realize the masterly way in which Theophrastus has depicted human appetites and propensities. Law and morality may succeed for a

long time in holding these ambitions in check, but when opportunities arise, they will break out again from the depths of the
human heart. That this is so can be seen from the present age, "in
which an excess of freedom breeds an excess of presumption,
and even though the truth is preached everywhere, its demands
are nowhere observed. As things are it would seem as though the
Kingdom of God consisted in mere words rather than in practical
action through good works." Thus Pirckheimer saw to it that
the topical importance of the Theophrastus character sketches for
the age of the Reformation was made clear. Only when this had
been done did he turn, in the dedication, to the ethical purpose of
the book. He considered it profitable, he said, to read books in
which every man could see his own particular temperament revealed as in a mirror, and in consequence begin to improve himself.

In the year of this Theophrastus edition Pirckheimer also
intervened in the controversy concerning the remarriage of
clerics. In 1525 Dominicus Schleupner, preacher at St. Sebald in
Nuremberg, had taken as his first wife Dorothea, the daughter
of one Georg Schmiedmaier. Following her death he remarried
in December 1527. This second marriage prompted Pirckheimer
to compile twenty-eight *Propositiones contra digamiam episcoporum*,
and distribute them in manuscript and anonymously.[96] Pirckheimer was prepared to allow clerics to marry once, but not
twice.

In due course, Pirckheimer's propositions came before Luther,
who in 1528 replied with 139 countertheses, printed along with
Pirckheimer's own twenty-eight propositions. The foreword of
this publication did not mention the author of the propositions
by name, but Luther intimated that he knew him. Wenzeslas
Link and Andreas Osiander had written a reply to the propositions
shortly before Luther, and Pirckheimer may well have been
justified in suspecting that it had been they who appealed to
Luther for help.

A letter of Johannes Cochlaeus of March 10, 1529[97] shows that
Pirckheimer had also sent him a manuscript on priestly celibacy
(*De votivo coelibatu*), and that Cochlaeus had sent it on to Leipzig,

where it was intended for immediate printing. The letter also shows that Pirckheimer had drawn up a further five hundred propositions against clerical remarriage and was at work on satirical orations "against the monk"—Luther.

Amidst the polemics of these final years occurred the death, on April 6, 1528, of his friend Dürer; and in his distress Pirckheimer came into his own for once as a genuine poet. His *Elegia Bilibaldi Pirckheimeri in obitum Alberti Dureri* is a deeply moving lament, unrivaled in contemporary literature. Indeed, in all literature there are few of its kind.[98]

As in the case of the edition and translation of the *Characteres ethici*, Pirckheimer gave a topical twist to the three published translations of the orations of Gregory of Nazianzus. They were the *Orationes duae Julianum Caesarem infamia notantes* (Nuremberg, 1528), dedicated to Hermann von Neuenar; the *Oratio de officio episcopi* (Nuremberg, 1529), dedicated to Ulrich Zasius; and the *Orationes XXX*, edited under the auspices of Erasmus by Hans Straub (Basel, 1531), dedicated at Pirckheimer's express wish to Duke Georg of Saxony, Luther's most vehement opponent.[99] The same presumably applies to Pirckheimer's translation of the dialogue *De incarnatione verbi* of Maximus Confessor (Nuremberg, 1530). But it is the first two of these translations which were most clearly intended as contributions to the polemical controversies of the Reformation. In the first, the present situation is compared with the age of Constantine the Great and Constantius, a period when, as today, the church was riven with endless heresies. The time is ripe, Pirckheimer notes, for another Julian the Apostate. In the preface to the oration on the episcopal office Pirckheimer expresses his concern over the new role of preachers and the effects of Luther's doctrine. He counters Luther's distinction between the priest's pastoral charismata and his personal virtues with the fiery words: "Away with all those who declare that the person counts for nothing with God in this matter." With great pathos he calls upon his opponents to see the fruits of their new sowing of the Gospel, using the words of Gregory: "I denounce you with the authority of the apostolic word: show your faith through your works, and make men see for themselves that you are good soil by the abundance of fruits that you bear."[100]

Pirckheimer's final utterances on the Reformation can be found in his "Defense of the convent of the Clares" in Nuremberg of 1529[101] and in his letter of November 1530 to Johann Tschertte in Vienna.[102]

The Defense, written in the name of the nuns of the convent of the Poor Clares and addressed to the city council, contains four main points of criticism and remonstration which seem to him fraught with the gravest significance. They are the effects of arbitrary interpretation of scripture, the abuse of religious freedom, the contradiction between faith and behavior among the innovators, and the decline of learning and morality. He writes: "A final piece of evidence for the perversion of the Gospel is the fact that no worthy fruit can be seen to sprout from this doctrine; on the contrary, everything is collapsing—languages, learning, civic and private morals, holy and beneficial institutions, peace harmony, fear of God, and all love and affection for one's neighbor." Each man interprets Scripture to his own benefit and advantage. Christian freedom, which in his opinion is purely spiritual, is turned into the freedom of the flesh, as is proved by the behavior of deserting monks and nuns, and by the insurrection of the peasantry.

In his long letter to the architect and builder Tschertte, Pirckheimer turned first of all to the rout and desertion of German *Landsknechts* during the siege of Vienna by the Turks. He explains it as a consequence of the contradiction between words and works among the supporters of Luther: "I, too, was a good Lutheran at the beginning, like our Albrecht—may he rest in peace—[their mutual friend Dürer]. For we all had the hope of setting to rights the Roman knavery, as well as the roguery of monks and priests. But, as can be plainly seen nowadays, the situation has become so intolerable that the Evangelical rogues make the Catholics seem pious by comparison." He was particularly scandalized by the behavior of certain clerics and runaway monks.[103] The Roman authorities may have duped the people with their hypocrisy and cunning; but the Lutherans are the cause of all manner of immorality due to their ideas concerning works and faith. Pirckheimer remains faithful to the Epistle of James, which teaches a Christian piety founded on works and on a faith expressed through works, as opposed to a mere fiduciary Christianity. The "works" of those who call themselves "evangelical" reveal them to be without religion and without Christian morality and learning, intent only upon the enjoyment of things of this world. Almsgiving, confession, and the sacrament of the altar have vanished, at least no one believes in them any longer. People of the lower sort think of nothing now but the coming universal distribution of property. Where marriage is concerned things are very bad; were it not for the public hangman we would soon have complete community of womenfolk.

Despite these hard words (which, incidentally, referred mainly to conditions in Nuremberg) Pirckheimer managed to preserve his old position between the two parties—though with a definite bias toward the old Church. His criticisms were aimed at both sides.

I am writing all this, not because I find myself able, or even willing, to say anything in favor of the pope and his priests and monks, for I know well that they are in many ways deserving of punishment and that their conduct needs putting to rights. . . . But it is clear to anyone who has eyes to see that the other side is no more worthy, as Luther himself now plainly admits. And many pious and learned people who adhere to the true Gospel confess with pain in their hearts that things cannot go on much longer. The papists, at least, are united among themselves; but those who call themselves evangelical are utterly disunited and divided into sects. They must go their ways like the rioting peasants, until in the end they will destroy everything.

But the Reformation did not end in the way Pirckheimer predicted, despite its internal dissentions. Even the imperial mandate for which Pirckheimer was hoping did not succeed in putting it down. Deep in his heart and soul Pirckheimer still belonged to the juridical Church of the late Middle Ages. But the morally cleansed Church, as Pirckheimer visualized it, existed neither in Nuremberg nor anywhere else. Pirckheimer was too distinct a personality, too complex a mind, and as a scholar too critical and skeptical, to be able to beat a full retreat into the past. He remained consistent in his beliefs; and—according to the report of Christoph Scheurl, who also continued to support the old Church—"died without confession or sacrament, *sine crux et lux*." The welfare of his country and the pacification of the Church remained till the very end the major concerns of this highly unusual man.[104]

Willibald Pirckheimer was the last male descendant of a Nuremberg family which had been unique in the cultural life of Germany during the late Middle Ages for its traditions, its intellectual endowments, and its achievements. One cannot account for this man in isolation from that intellectual and cultural family tradition built up over three long generations. His father, his grandfather, his uncles had long before Willibald's birth been open to the new ideas of their times, and had attempted to harmonize the inherited medieval norms with modern trends. These attempts had been external and formal at first, later internal and substantive, and in the case of Willibald's father not without spiritual and religious conflicts, brought on by the attempt to synthesize late scholasticism with the Neoplatonism of the Renaissance.

While the lives of his forefathers had centered mainly on their professional careers, Willibald devoted far more time to scholarly and intellectual pursuits than to his job as councillor and diplomat. He, too, remained at pains to join the traditional to the new. No one could ever accuse him of being lacking in pious reverence.

Contemporaries like Erasmus were right in considering Pirckheimer's major literary and intellectual achievements to be his edition of Ptolemy, his translations of the discourses of Gregory of Nazianzus, and the first publications of the works of Fulgentius and of the *Characteres* of Theophrastus. Pirckheimer was one of the most prolific translators of his time: Aristophanes, Aristotle, Demosthenes, Thucydides, Xenophon, Lucian, Plutarch, Galen, Pseudo-Proclus, Horapollo, and a number of Platonic and pseudo-Platonic dialogues—all these he turned from Greek into good Latin. His interests ranged from comedy and satire to the Greek patristic literature, from history, ethics, and philosophy to the symbolism of what were then thought to be the occult religion and philosophy of ancient Egypt. Beyond these translations intended for erudite circles he published an impressive number of translations into German, mainly on religious and moral subjects, destined either for clerics or for pious laymen of his own social class.

In nearly all these translations and editions some part or other was played by Albrecht Dürer. During thirty years or so of close, often daily, association with Pirckheimer, Dürer was intimately acquainted with his friend's scholarly and literary labors as well as with his religious views. These facts are of great importance for the interpretation of hitherto unexplained aspects of Dürer's work.

Pirckheimer's literary work also includes an account of his own experiences during the war with the Swiss and the fragment of an autobiography. The picture they give is completed by his correspondence, which throws much light upon contemporary history and culture.

Pirckheimer's last years have been considered here mainly from the religious, not to say denominational, viewpoint. Pirckheimer, like Luther, had a deep religious conscience and a powerful religious mind. But they were on a different level from Luther's. Pirckheimer had sufficient erudition and judgment to appreciate the significance of what was new in the Reformation, but he was also critical enough to reject it. His was the fate of the brilliantly gifted, highly cultivated man during a time of ceaseless upheavals. The truth about him was summed up once and for all in the words placed below the engraved portrait made of him by his friend Dürer: "Man lives through his creative spirit. The rest belongs to death."

NOTES TO CHAPTER 10

1. Johann Friedrich Heinrich Panzer, *Willibald Pirkheimer und Charitas Pirkheimerin* (Erlangen, 1802); Friedrich Campe, *Zum Andenken Willibald Pirkheimers* (Nuremberg, 1828); Julius Merz, "Willibald Pirckheimer. Ein Lebensbild aus Nürnbergs Vorzeit," *Album des literarischen Vereins zu Nürnberg* (1852); G. W. K. Lochner, "Willibald Pirkheimer," *Lebensläufe berühmter und verdienter Nürnberger* (Nuremberg, 1861).
2. *Deutschlands literatische und religiöse Verhältnisse im Reformationszeitalter. Mit besonderer Rücksicht auf W. Pirkheimer* (Erlangen, 1841 ff.; Frankfurt am Main, 2nd ed., 1868).
3. *Willibald Pirckheimers Briefwechsel*, Vol. I, ed. Arnold Reimann and Emil Reicke (Munich, 1940); Vol. II, ed. Siegfried Reicke and Wilhelm Volkert (Munich, 1956). These volumes include Pirckheimer's correspondence up to 1515.
4. While Reimann was working on his projected life of Pirckheimer, Ernst Borkowsky produced a life of Pirckheimer based on the earlier literature; this appeared in a book intended for a popular audience: *Aus der Zeit des Humanismus* (Jena, 1905). Emil Reicke's popular work, *Willibald Pirckheimer. Leben, Familie, Persönlichkeit* (Jena, 1930), written on the occasion of the fourth centenary of Pirckheimer's death, contains a large number of accurate facts, but offers no detailed examination of Pirckheimer's principal intellectual achievements. Contributions to an appreciation of his personality were made in a paper read by Carl J. Burckhardt in 1937 in Zürich. Here Pirckheimer was considered, not as a characteristic representative of the upper middle class, nor as the embodiment of a tradition culminating in a proud cultural development, but as an exceptional figure who was primarily concerned in forging a link between tradition and the new spirit—an attempt, however, which did not really succeed. Cf. Carl J. Burckhardt, *Gestalten und Mächte. Reden und Aufsätze* (Munich, 1941), p. 47 ff. [Cf. also the chapter on Pirckheimer in Lewis W. Spitz, *The Religious Renaissance of the German Humanists* (Cambridge, Mass., 1963), chapter 8.]
5. Cf. A. Reimann, *Festgabe der Gesellschaft für deutsche Literatur für Max Herrmann* (Berlin, 1935); idem, *Die älteren Pirckheimer* (Leipzig, 1944).
6. Cf. *Catalogue of Manuscripts in the British Museum N.S. (Arundel Manuscripts)* I (London, 1834), p. 32 ff.
7. Ed. by J. Bolte, *Zeitschrift für vergleichende Literaturgeschichte und Renaissance-Literatur*, NF I (1887–88), p. 77 ff.
8. Cf. G. Bauch, *Mitteilungen des Vereins für Geschichte der Stadt Nürnberg*, 14 (1901), p. 1 ff.
9. Cod. Arund. 437 and 460.
10. Reprinted from Reimann and Reicke, eds., *Willibald Pirckheimers Briefwechsel*, Vol. I, p. 29 f.
11. Ed. by K. Rück, along with Pirckheimer's "Schweizerkrieg" (Munich, 1895).

12. Thus, for instance, Pomponazzi's notion of fate in Pirckheimer's account of the dream vision in 1501; or his opinion about psychopannychia (sleep of souls, death as a sleep lasting till the final resurrection) in Pirckheimer's elegy on the death of Dürer.

13. This was the rector of the faculty of jurists, Albertus de Curia, probably an illegitimate son of Duke Albert IV of Bavaria.

14. In the autumn of 1495 he went to Nuremberg for Pirckheimer's wedding; he visited him again in 1502.

15. Beheim provided Roman inscriptions also for Hartmann Schedel. Cf. R. Stauber, *Die Schedelsche Bibliothek* (Freiburg, 1908), p. 51.

16. Cf. H. Rupprich, *W. Pirckheimer und die erste Reise Dürers nach Italien* (Vienna, 1930).

17. Cf. E. Rosenthal, "Dürers Buchmalereien für Pirckheimers Bibliothek," *Jahrbuch der Preussischen Kunstsammlungen*, 49 (1928–29), Beiheft, p. 18 ff.; E. Offenbacher, *La Bibliofilia*, 40 (1938), p. 253.

18. H. Tietze and E. Tietze-Conrat, *Kritisches Verzeichnis der Werke A. Dürers*, II, 2 (Basel, 1938), no. A 322, p. 115, have pronounced themselves against this ascription to Dürer, in my opinion wrongly.

19. Pirckheimer's musical abilities were also extolled by Johannes Cochlaeus in the dedication of his *Tetrachordum musices* (Nuremberg, 1511). Cf. *Briefwechsel*, Vol. II, p. 79 ff.

20. Cf. *Briefwechsel*, Vol. I, p. 220 ff.; Vol. II, pp. 173 ff., 464 ff.

21. Cf. *Briefwechsel*, Vol. II, esp. p. 98.

22. Brought to light and pronounced as Dürer's work by F. Dornhöffer, *Kunstgeschichtliche Anzeigen*, III (Innsbruck, 1906), p. 84; further J. Meder, *Dürer-Katalog* (Vienna, 1932), no. 254; H. Tietze and E. Tietze-Conrat, *Kritisches Verzeichnis der Werke A. Dürers*, I, no. 151.

23. The *Trilogium animae* is a sort of manual of knowledge for regular clerics. It is without originality but of interest for literary history on account of its wealth of material and its references to many medieval authors. The edition was prepared by Nikolaus Glassberger, who had been in Nuremberg since 1483. Cf. P. Minges, *Franziskanische Studien*, 1 (1914), p. 291 ff.; Lexikon für *Theologie und Kirche*, 4 (2nd ed., 1932), p. 519, and 6 (1934), p. 698.

24. Cf. E. Münch, *W. Pirkheimers Schweizerkrieg und Ehrenhandel mit seinen Feinden zu Nürnberg* (Basel, 1826); K. Rück, *W. Pirckheimers Schweizerkrieg*, an edition based on Pirckheimer's autograph and including his autobiography (Munich, 1895); idem, *Blätter für das Gymnasial-Schulwesen*, 44 (1908), p. 338 ff.; E. Reicke, *Jahrbuch für Schweizerische Geschichte*, 45 (1920), p. 131 ff.; idem, *Mein Frankenland*, 4 (1931), p. 45 ff.

25. *Opera*, p. 393 f.; *Briefwechsel*, Vol. I, p. 60 ff.

26. *Op. cit.*, Vol. I, p. 128 ff.

27. According to Aquinas souls in purgatory have no knowledge of earthly things.

28. As was maintained by the philosophic fatalism of the Stoics and of Pomponazzi (*De fato*, 1523).

29. F. Winkler, *Die Zeichnungen A. Dürers*, II (Berlin, 1937).

30. The charcoal portrait has been further analyzed by C. J. Burckhardt, *op. cit.*, p. 55: "A passionate face, as though hammered out from within, shrewd, yet with some of the obtuseness of a sensual and self-willed man. We are confronted with something forceful yet unfinished, the tentative outline of a human type never to be fully established in Germany. All that is noble about the bold chin and the youthful though already bitter mouth becomes lost in a coarse, fat, bull-like neck. This head combines many conflicting elements—good breeding with formless heaviness, seriousness with obtuseness and an almost plebeian slovenliness. The only feature that can be singled out for its special fineness is the ear. Of really perfect structure, it is the ear of a musician, with its beautiful convolutions open to every sound, even the lightest breath; set close and firm to the head, its very form suggests intelligence and sensitivity."

31. Other portraits of Pirckheimer are the following: 1. On the death portrait of his wife Crescentia (d. May 17, 1504); the likeness can probably be traced to a sketch by Dürer. 2. A portrait of 1505 in the Borghese Gallery in Rome; Schleyer, *Zeitschrift des deutschen Vereins für Kunstwissenschaft* (1934), p. 198, and Otto Benesch, *Pantheon* (October, 1934), p. 299, have ascribed it to Dürer, though Winkler (268) thinks Schäuffelin more likely. 3. On the "Martyrdom of the Ten Thousand," next to Dürer. 4. The profile of 1517 on a medallion, which may perhaps have been executed from one of Dürer's drawings; H. Tietze and E. Tietze-Conrat, *Kritisches Verzeichnis*, I, 2 (1938), no. A 442.

32. Cf. E. Mummenhoff, *Mitteilungen des Vereins für Geschichte der Stadt Nürnberg*, 26 (1926), p. 311 ff.; a consideration of the personality can also be found in E. Mummenhoff, *War W. Pirckheimer ein Verleumder?* (Nuremberg, 1928).

33. Cf. E. Reicke, *Mitteilungen des Vereins für Geschichte der Stadt Nürnberg*, 24, 1921 (1922), p. 35 ff.; *Briefwechsel*, Vol. II, p. 340 ff.

34. Cf. the pungent verses Pirckheimer directed against him and Andreas Osiander in G. E. Waldau, *Vermischte Beyträge zur Geschichte der Stadt Nürnberg*, 1 (Nuremberg, 1786), p. 250 f.

35. Cf. E. Reicke, *Forschungen zur Geschichte Bayerns*, 14 (1906), p. 1 ff.; *idem*, *Pirckheimers Briefwechsel*, Vol. II, p. 292 f.; J. Schnitzer, *Beiträge zur bayerischen Kirchengeschichte*, 19 (1912), p. 220 ff.

36. *Briefwechsel*, Vol. I, p. 460 ff.

37. *Briefwechsel*, Vol. I, p. 141. A translation by Pirckheimer of the *Plutus* (line 270 to the end) is contained in Cod. Arund. 338. Pirckheimer's copy of the Greek edition of *Aristophanes, Comoediae novem* (Venice, 1498), was decorated with a miniature by Dürer.

38. *Briefwechsel*, p. 194 ff. According to this letter Pirckheimer was apparently engaged on a translation of Homer into Latin as well.

39. Pirckheimer possessed the first Greek edition of Lucian's *Opera* (Florence, 1496); this copy, too, was decorated with a Dürer miniature. It was Pirckheimer who introduced Dürer to the many descriptions of classical paintings contained in Lucian, and Dürer adapted this material for his own purposes. The "Rape of Europa" (1494–95), based on Lucian's

dialogue of the same title, was probably drawn from an upper Italian original which may have prompted one of Poliziano's poems. Cf. E. Panofsky, *Jahrbuch für Kunstgeschichte*, 1 (1921–22), p. 47. But the drawing "Europa on the Bull," dated 1503 (Winkler 216), may very well have been due to Pirckheimer's influence. Pirckheimer certainly provided the inspiration for the drawing "Centaur's Family" (Winkler 345) and the engraving "Family of the Satyr" (Tietze 275), both of 1505, the source of which was Lucian's preface "Zeuxis or Antiochus." Another literary stimulus may well be found in Lucian's panegyric to the fly, an insect which appears in the picture of the *Rosenkranzfest* (1506) and which drew the attention of A. Weixlgärtner, *Die graphischen Künste*, 51 (1928), *Mitteilungen*, p. 20 ff.

40. *Briefwechsel* Vol. I, p. 198 ff. It is contained in two fragments among Pirckheimer's papers (147 and 230); no edition of it has ever come to light.

41. *Ibid.*, I, p. 459. The appearance of this translation was announced at the end of the translation of Lucian's essay on the art of historiography (1515).

42. Hans von Schwarzenberg (1465–1528), a humanist and the *Landhofmeister* of the bishops of Bamberg, author of the *Bambergische Halsgerichtsordnung* (1507).

43. *Theatrum Virtutis et Honoris oder Tugend Büchlein*, p. 112 f.

44. Cf. the dedication as well as the more detailed drafts for this in *Briefwechsel*, Vol. II, p. 231 ff. For the printed edition Dürer had designed a title page with the coat of arms held by two *putti* (Tietze W 8). The illustration was used again for Plutarch's *De vitanda usura*, Lucian's *De ratione conscribendae historiae* (1515) and *Piscator* (1517), and the *Maxims* of Nilus (1516). Cf. Meder, *Dürer-Katalog*, p. 283.

45. Cf. the dedication in *Briefwechsel*, Vol. II, p. 516 ff. It is possible that the publication of Plutarch's *De exilio, Angelo Barbato interprete* (Nuremberg, Peypus, 1517) was also instigated by Pirckheimer. Cf. K. Schottenloher, *Die Entwicklung der Buchdruckerkunst in Franken bis 1530* (Würzburg, 1910), p. 64.

46. Cf. Münch, *op. cit.*, p. 25.

47. *Briefwechsel*, Vol. II, p. 245 ff.

48. *Ibid*, p. 393.

49. F. X. Thurnhofer, *Bernhard Adelmann von Adelmannsfelden* (Freiburg, 1900), (Erläuterungen zu Janssen's *Geschichte des Deutschen Volkes*, II, 1, p. 53.

50. K. Schottenloher, *Die Widmungsvorrede im Buch des 16. Jahrhunderts*, *Reformationsgeschichtliche Studien und Texte*, 76/77 (Münster, 1953), does not explore this characteristic aspect.

51. G. Boas, *The Hieroglyphics of Horapollo* (New York, 1950). Translating Horapollo's work was considered in both Italy and Germany as a most difficult task.

52. The Österreichische Nationalbibliothek contains in addition to a number of original drawings copies of all Dürer's illustrations.

53. Cf. K. Giehlow, "Die Hieroglyphenkunde des Humanismus in der Allegorie der Renaissance, besonders der Ehrenpforte Kaiser Maximilians I," *Jahrbuch der Kunsthistorischen Sammlungen des Allerhöchsten Kaiserhauses*, 32 (1915), p. 170 ff., which also prints most of Pirckheimer's translation; *idem*, "Dürers Entwürfe für das Triumphrelief Kaiser Maximilians I. im Louvre," *ibid.*, 29 (1910–11).

54. Cf. *Briefwechsel*, Vol. II, p. 454 f.; P. Kalkoff, *Der Wormser Reichstag 1521* (Munich, 1922), p. 149.

55. Cf. the dedication in *Briefwechsel*, Vol. II, pp. 485 ff., 525 f.

56. While Pirckheimer resumed his work on Lucian, Dürer produced two drawings: "The Allegory of Eloquence" (Winkler 664), derived from Lucian's *The Gallic Hercules*, and "Arion" (Winkler 662), which may be traced to Lucian's *Navis seu vota* and the dialogue *Arion*. For both drawings Dürer referred to examples in the Cod. lat. Mon. 716 of Hartmann Schedel. For a full interpretation of the former, see R. Egger, *Jahreshefte des österreichischen Institutes*, 35 (1943), p. 130. It is also possible that Lucian's *Piscator* prompted Felix Frey of Zürich to commission a "Dance of the Monkeys" from Dürer. Near the end of this work there is a story of an Egyptian king who took it into his head to teach monkeys to dance. As monkeys have no difficulty in imitating human actions, they learned so well that they were soon exhibiting their accomplishments in public, clad in purple coats, wearing masks. But while they were delighting the spectators someone threw a handful of nuts into their midst. All at once the dance was forgotten; the monkeys ceased being dancers and became monkeys once more, squabbling and biting one another in their rush to get at the nuts. In a matter of seconds the masks were chipped to pieces and the clothes torn to rags. The dance of the monkeys came to an end amidst the laughter of the spectators. This, according to Lucian, summed up in a few words the story of our latter-day philosophers. The drawing (Winkler 927) which Dürer sent to Frey, however, is not an exact illustration of the passage; the only thing in common is the subject.

57. Printed in *Opera*, p. 220 ff.

58. The merging of all three Biblical figures (Mary Magdalen, the repentant sinner, and Mary of Bethany) can be found in the *Legenda aurea* (c. A.D.96) and throughout western art, where Mary Magdalen during the late Middle Ages appears almost invariably at the feet of the crucified in memory of her once having anointed his feet.

59. He had already expressed his sympathy to Reuchlin on December 1, 1513, in a letter giving him full support. Reuchlin published the letter in the *Clarorum virorum epistolae* (1514). Cf. also *Briefwechsel*, Vol. II, p. 210 ff.

60. The esteem which Pirckheimer enjoyed among the younger generation for this stand can be seen most clearly from the confidential letter written to him by Ulrich von Hutten on October 25, 1518, in which he opened his heart with passion and warmth and attempted to give a justification of his personal life and activity. This document was later to delight the young Goethe when he read it in Strassburg. Cf. Hajo Holborn, *Ulrich von Hutten* (Leipzig, 1929), p. 77 ff.

61. For Pirckheimer's attitude to the Reformation, cf. from the Protestant side R. Hagen, *Mitteilungen des Vereins für Geschichte der Stadt Nürnberg*, 4 (1882), p. 61 ff.; P. Drews, *Pirckheimers Stellung zur Reformation* (Leipzig, 1887); O. Clemen, *Die Religion in Geschichte und Gegenwart*, 4 (2nd ed., 1930), cols. 1264 f.; and from the Catholic viewpoint, M. Fassbinder, *Lexikon für Theologie und Kirche*, 8 (2nd ed., 1936), cols. 286 f. [Cf. also the chapter on Pirckheimer in Lewis Spitz, *op. cit.*]

62. Ed. by S. Szamatolski, *Lateinische Literaturdenkmäler des 15. und 16. Jahrhunderts*, 2 (Berlin, 1891); cf. also A. E. Berger, "Deutsche Literatur in Entwicklungsreihen," *Reformation*, 2 (1931).

63. The question of its authorship has still not been completely settled. That Pirckheimer was responsible is suggested by the opinion of Eck himself, the fact that the satire made its first appearance among circles close to him, and the fragment of a sequel, *De Eckio bibulo*, to be found among Pirckheimer's papers: J. Schlecht, "Pirckheimers zweite Komödie gegen Eck," *Historisches Jahrbuch*, 21 (1900), p. 402. Against this, however, must be set the work as such, that is to say, literary, linguistic and structural considerations. P. Merker, *Der Verfasser des Eccius dedolatus und anderer Reformationsdialoge* (Halle, 1923), set out to show that Nikolaus Gerbelius, a humanist from Pforzheim, was the author. In my own book, *Der Eckius dedolatus und sein Verfasser* (Vienna, 1930), I tried to offer some reasons for thinking that this satire could have been composed only by a personality whose essential talents were satirical and dramatic, and who was presumably a physician by profession, was a regular visitor in Pirckheimer's house and, most important, was in close contact with Hutten. I suggested that, although Pirckheimer may well have had something to do with the comedy, its principal author was probably Fabian Gorteler (Fabius Zonarius) from Goldberg in Silesia. However, my suggested indications have found only limited acceptance. Final clarification can be hoped for only from a further, and extremely accurate, philological analysis, or from the discovery of new documents. If it should turn out that the whole of the *Eckius dedolatus* really was Pirckheimer's work then he will be seen as a man of much wider gifts and promise. It would certainly place him at the side of the great satirists of the age, Crotus and Hutten.

64. Cf. P. Kalkoff, "Pirckheimers und Spenglers Lösung vom Banne 1521," *Jahresbericht über das städtische evangelische Gymnasium zu St. Maria-Magdalena in Breslau* (Easter 1896), p. 3 ff.; H. Westermayer, *Beiträge zur bayerischen Kirchengeschichte*, 2 (1896), p. 1 ff.; H. von Schubert, *L. Spengler und die Reformation in Nürnberg* (Leipzig, 1934), p. 201 ff.

65. It was at this time that Pirckheimer's work on Lucian brought forth fruit in Dürer's art with the sketch entitled "Verleumdung des Apelles" (Winkler 922), executed in 1521 for the decoration of the city hall in Nuremberg. The source is Lucian's "Against slander, or that we should not believe those who tell evil about others," together with the well-known description of paintings given in 1435 by Leon Battista Alberti in his treatise on painting.

66. Cf. the dedicatory epistle in *Opera*, p. 247.

67. The dedicatory epistle is printed in *Opera*, p. 232 ff., and a German version can be found in M. M. Mayer, *W. Pirckheimers Briefwechsel*, Vol. I, p. 142.

68. The translation among the Pirckheimer papers in the possession of the Nurenberg city library (146) is by Venatorius (Panzer VII, 479, No. 286). Cf. *Briefwechsel*, Vol. I, p. 142.

69. Pirckheimer possessed a Greek edition of Aristotle's complete works in five volumes (Venice, 1495–98). The third volume contains the Natural History, for which Dürer provided a marginal decoration.

70. Cf. *Briefwechsel*, Vol. II, p. 100. Pirckheimer, according to a letter written to him by Cuspinian on October 18, 1515, had also translated Plutarch's *Symposiacon*, i.e., either the *Convivium septem sapientium* or the nine books of the *Quaestiones convivales*. Cf. *Briefwechsel*, Vol. II, p. 577 f.

71. Jacopo Bannissio (1467–1532), an Italian, had been a friend of Pirckheimer's for many years. They shared an interest in classical studies.

72. *Opera*, p. 372 ff.

73. *Opera*, p. 385 f. The treatise was not published.

74. Cf. J. Huizinga, *Erasmus*.

75. Cf. E. Zinner, *Leben und Wirken des Johannes Müller von Königsberg, genannt Regiomontanus* (Munich, 1938), p. 183 ff. [On Regiomontanus in Nuremberg, cf. Gerald Strauss, *Nuremberg in the Sixteenth Century* (New York, 1966).]

76. Cf. *Briefwechsel*, Vol. II, p. 476 ff.

77. Cf. Pirckheimer to Oecolampadius, January 23, 1524, in E. Staehelin, *Briefe und Akten zum Leben Ökolampads*, I (Leipzig, 1927), p. 265 f. The ms. of the *Trigonometry* was edited, together with the writings of Nicholas of Cusa, in 1533 by Johann Schöner.

78. Cf. S. Günther, *Das Bayerland*, 4 (1893), p. 569 ff.; M. Weyrauther, *K. Peutinger und W. Pirckheimer in ihren Beziehungen zur Geographie* (Munich, 1907).

79. Sebastian Sprenz (d. 1525) of Dinkelsbühl was schoolmaster at St. Lorenz in Nuremberg in 1499, later professor at Ingolstadt, finally secretary of Matthäus Lang the imperial confidential secretary, and from 1521 bishop of Brixen.

80. *Opera*, p. 54. Nothing appears to have been preserved either of these texts or of the maps, both of which presumably came into the hands of Peter Apian.

81. Cf. E. Zinner, *Geschichte und Bibliographie der astronomischen Literatur in Deutschland zur Zeit der Renaissance* (Leipzig, 1941), pp. 67 and 191.

82. Cf. T. Hampe, *Mitteilungen des Vereins für Geschichte der Stadt Nürnberg*, 16 (1904), p. 62.

83. *Ingenium* is to be understood in the Neoplatonic sense as "creative spirit." Hans Imhoff translated the verse in his *vita* of Pirckheimer in the *Theatrum Virtutis et Honoris*, p. 89.

84. Cf. H. Wölfflin, *Die Kunst Albrecht Dürers* (Munich, 1926), p. 340.

85. *Opera*, p. 374 f.

86. 2 Peter 2:1–2; 1 John 4:1–2; 2 Timothy 3:1–7; Mark 12:38–40. Cf. my *Dürers schriftlicher Nachlass* (Berlin, 1956), Vol. I, p. 210 ff.

87. Cf. E. Heidrich, *Dürer und die Reformation* (Leipzig, 1909). [On the sectarian movements in Nuremberg and elsewhere, see now George H. Williams, *The Radical Reformation* (Philadelphia, 1962).]

88. All that remains of this Faustian composition is the prologue. Cf. E. Staehelin, *op. cit.*, p. 39 f.

89. Cf. *ibid.*, pp. 90 ff., 152 f.

90. Denk's theories can be seen from his "On true love" (1527) and his commentary on the prophet Micah (1531). Cf. T. Kolde, *Beiträge zur Bayerischen Kirchengeschichte*, 8 (1901–02), p. 1 ff.; A. Coutts, *Hans Denk 1495–1527, Humanist and Heretic* (Edinburgh, 1927); O. E. Vittali, "Die Theologie des Widertäufers H. Denk" (diss., Freiburg, 1933). On Denk see also G. H. Williams, *op. cit.*

91. For the eucharistic controversy, cf. Walther Köhler, *Zwingli und Luther*, I, *Quellen und Forschungen zur Reformationsgeschichte*, 6 (Leipzig, 1924), esp. p. 229 ff.; G. Krodel, *Zeitschrift für bayerische Kirchengeschichte*, 25 (1956), p. 40 ff.

92. *Dürers schriftlicher Nachlass*, Vol. I, pp. 306, 328.

93. In the summer of 1526 Pirckheimer found an ally in John Fisher, who had also come out against the eucharistic doctrine of Oecolampadius in his *De veritate corporis et sanguinis Christi in eucharistia* (Cologne, 1527).

94. The name Eleutherius refers neither to Luther nor to Erasmus, as is assumed by Drews, *op. cit.*, p. 106, but most probably to Pirckheimer's Swiss acquaintance Felix Frey.

95. He also helped to promote the editorial activities of younger scholars. Thus the Nuremberg council, following Pirckheimer's recommendation, financed a number of pioneering editions of Roman legal sources by Gregor Holoander: the *Pandectae* (3 vols., 1529), the *Institutiones* (1529), the *Codex Justinianus* (1531 in Greek with a Latin translation), and the *Enchiridion* of Epictetus (1529). In the case of the pandects Pirckheimer helped Holoander with editorial advice. Cf. J. F. H. Panzer, *W. Pirckheimers Verdienste um die Herausgabe der Pandecten G. Holoanders* (Nuremberg, 1805); R. Stintzing, *Geschichte der deutschen Rechtswissenschaft*, Vol. I (1880), p. 180 ff. Vincentius Obsopeus dedicated his Greek edition of letters of Basil the Great and Gregor of Nazianzus (Hagenau, 1528) to Pirckheimer in gratitude for permission to use an old manuscript which had come into Pirckheimer's possession from the library of Matthias Corvinus.

96. Cf. G. Kawerau, *Beiträge zur bayerischen Kirchengeschichte*, 10 (1903), p. 119 ff.

97. *Opera*, p. 396.

98. Cf. H. Rupprich, "Pirckheimers Elegie auf den Tod Dürers," *Anzeiger der Österreichischen Akademie der Wissenschaften*, Phil. hist. Kl. (1956), Nr. 9, p. 136 ff.

99. Gregory's discourse to his sister Gorgonia remained unpublished; likewise the translation of Athanasius, *In psalmos*.

100. *Opera*, p. 239.

101. The Latin text is in *Opera*, p. 375 ff.; the manuscript draft, differing in some details, is in the Stadtbibliothek Nuremberg, Pirckh. Nr. 364, 18. A German translation was made by K. Vetter, Ingolstadt, 1614. Cf. G. Krabbel, *Festgabe für Ludwig Schmidt-Kallenberg* (Münster, 1927), p. 122 ff.

102. Printed, with commentary, in my edition of *Dürers schriftlicher Nachlass*, Vol. 1, p. 283 ff.

103. Pirckheimer also attacked them in his German poem "Weh euch jr münch und nunnen, So aussgeloffen seyt" (Woe to you, you monks and nuns who have run away), printed in G. E. Waldau, *Vermischte Beyträge zur Geschichte der Stadt Nürnberg*, 1 (Nuremberg, 1786), p. 251 ff.

104. This is reported by Erasmus, in the dedication to the edition of Pirckheimer's translation of Gregory of Nazianzus' *Orationes XXX* (*Opera*, p. 43). Cf. also Hans Inhoff, *op. cit.*, p. 91.

General Bibliography

Andreas, Willy, *Deutschland vor der Reformation*, 6th ed. (Stuttgart, 1959).
Bachmann, Adolf, *Deutsche Reichsgeschichte im Zeitalter Friedrichs III und Maximilians I* (Leipzig, 1884–94).
Baraclough, Geoffrey, *Origins of Modern Germany* (Oxford, 1946).
Brandi, Karl, *The Emperor Charles V*, trans. C. V. Wedgwood (London, 1939).
Carsten, F. L., *Princes and Parliaments in Germany* (Oxford, 1959).
Dahlmann-Waitz, *Quellenkunde zur deutschen Geschichte*, 9th ed. (Leipzig, 1931).
Gebhardt, Bruno, *Handbuch der deutschen Geschichte*, ed. Herbert Grundmann *et al.*, 8th ed. (Stuttgart, 1954–55).
Hartung, Fritz, *Deutsche Verfassungsgeschichte*, 5th ed. (Stuttgart, 1950).
Holborn, Hajo, *A History of Modern Germany; The Reformation* (New York, 1959).
Janssen, Johannes, *History of the German People at the Close of the Middle Ages* (London, 1905 ff.)
Kaser, K., *Deutsche Geschichte zur Zeit Maximilians I* (Stuttgart, 1912).
Kraus, Victor von, and Kaser, K., *Deutsche Geschichte im Ausgange des Mittelalters, 1438–1519* (Stuttgart, 1888–1912).
Schnabel, Franz, *Deutschlands geschichtliche Quellen und Darstellungen in der Neuzeit*, vol. 1 (Leipzig and Berlin, 1931).
Schottenloher, Karl, *Bibliographie zur deutschen Geschichte im Zeitalter der Glaubensspaltung 1517–1585*, 7 vols (Stuttgart, 1955–66).
Ulmann, Heinrich, *Kaiser Maximilian I* (Stuttgart, 1884–91).

Index

Aachen, 62, 81

Abel, Wilhelm, 319, 328, 332, 333, 348, 352, 370, 372, 374, 376, 377

Ackermann aus Böhmen, 23, 174

Address to the Christian Nobility of the German Nation (Luther), 70, 210

Adelmann, Bernhard, 400, 408, 410

"Administration of Peace and Justice", 108, 113, 116, 120, 124, 152

Adolf of Nassau, 57

Agricola, Rudolf, 27; and humanism, 195–6, 213, 398, 399

agriculture, 324; crisis in, 332–7, 339, 346, 353–64; prices, 333–7, 346, 352, 354, 357, 360, 367; wages, 348–50, 352, 358

Agrippa of Nettesheim, 42

Albert (Albrecht) Achilles of Brandenburg, 51, 75, 146

Albrecht of Habsburg, 57

Albrecht of Brandenburg, Cardinal, his collection of relics, 19

Albrecht, Archduke of Bavaria, 135

Albrecht III, Duke of Saxony, 77, 89, 90, 94, 107, 228; and Leipzig partition, 229; administrative reforms, 230, 236, 237

Alexander VI, Pope, 396

Alexander of Roes, 59–60, 61, 66

Alsace: humanist group of, 180–1, 184, 194, 204; rise in prices after Black Death, 335

Altenburg: electoral court, 242, 244; judicial court, 253

Anabaptism, 418–19

Andreae, Johann Valentin, 218

Andreas, Willy, 43, 44, 139, 142, 157, 356

Angiolo, Jacopo d', 412, 413

Anhalt, 252

Anjou, 56–7

Anne, St., Silesian endowments in honor of, 16

Anthologia Graeca Planudea, 390

Apel, Hans, 371

Apologia seu Podagrae Laus (Pirckheimer), 410–11

Apostolici regiminis (papal Bull, 1517), 405

Aquinas, Thomas, 36, 212, 351, 428

Aragon, 56

Ariosto, Ludovico, 172

Aristotle, Aristotelianism, 59; humanists and, 167, 170, 171, 211, 212, 214, 215; Luther's struggle against, 208; Pirckheimer and, 387, 406–7

Arminius, 209

Arnheim, 19

Arnold, Peter, 256

arraignment, suppression of, 305–6

Ars moriendi, 68

art, religious, 23–4, 38, 67

artisan class, 48, 344, 345

Aubin, Hermann, 65, 379